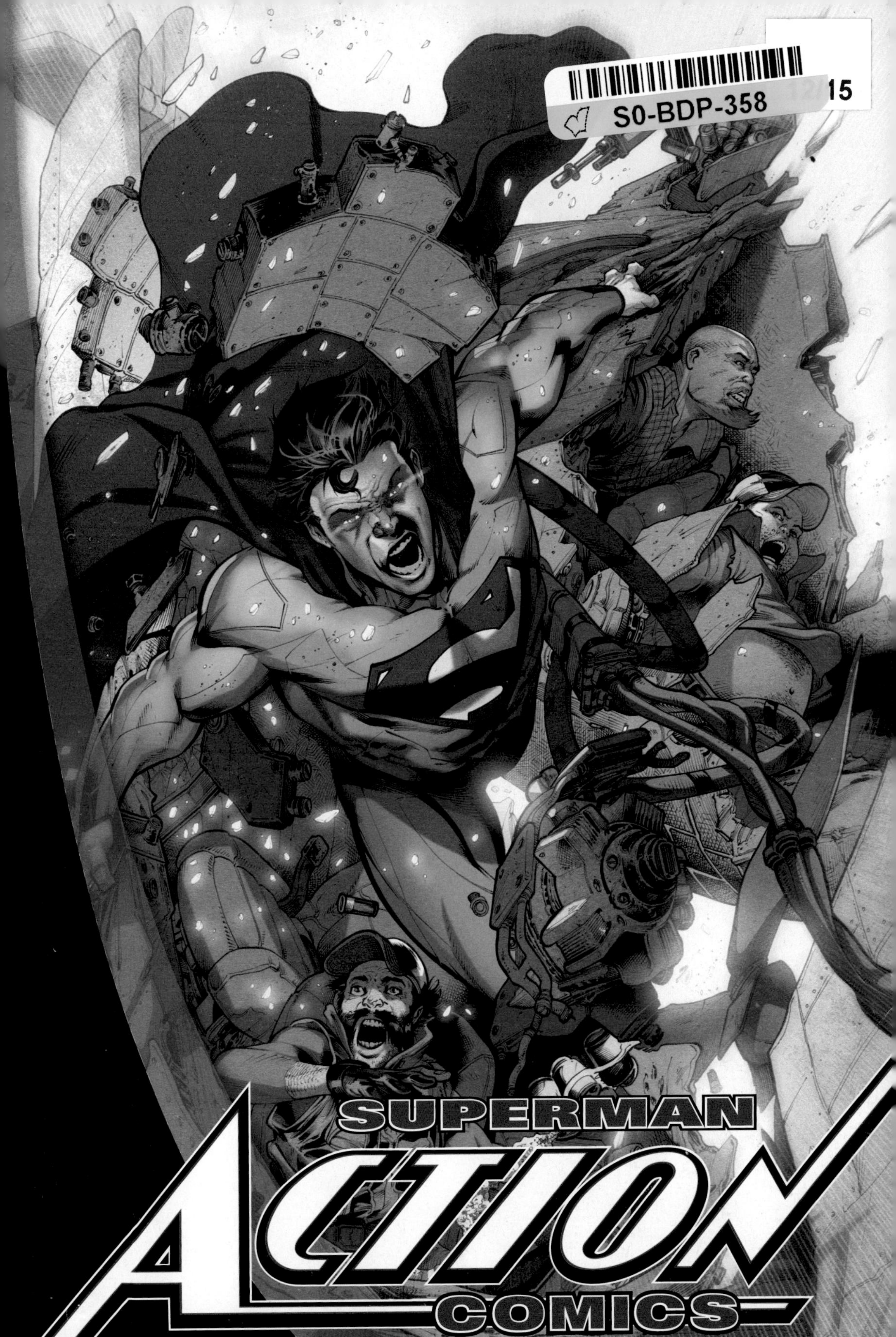

SUPERMAN ACTION COMICS

VOLUME 6 SUPERDOOM

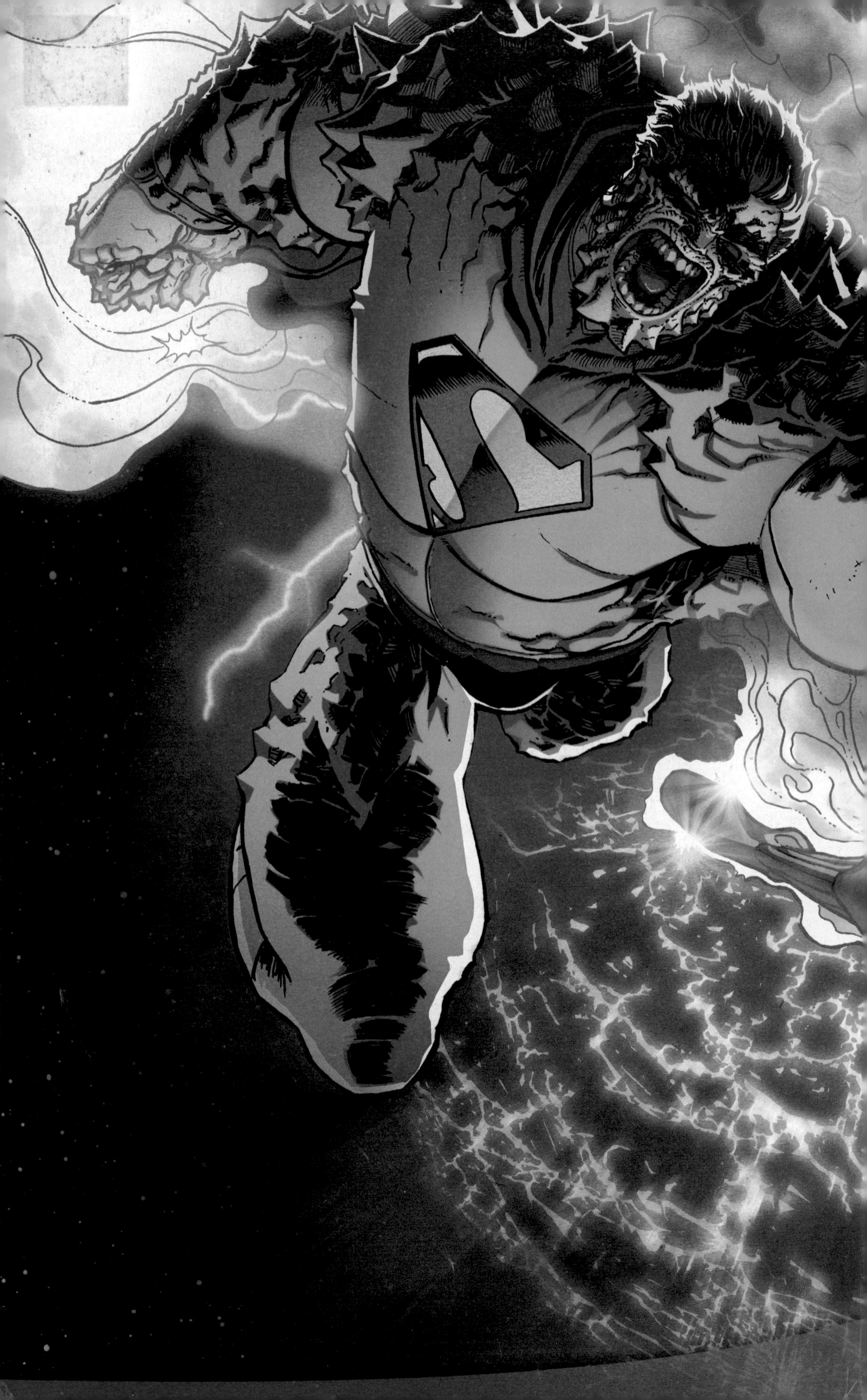

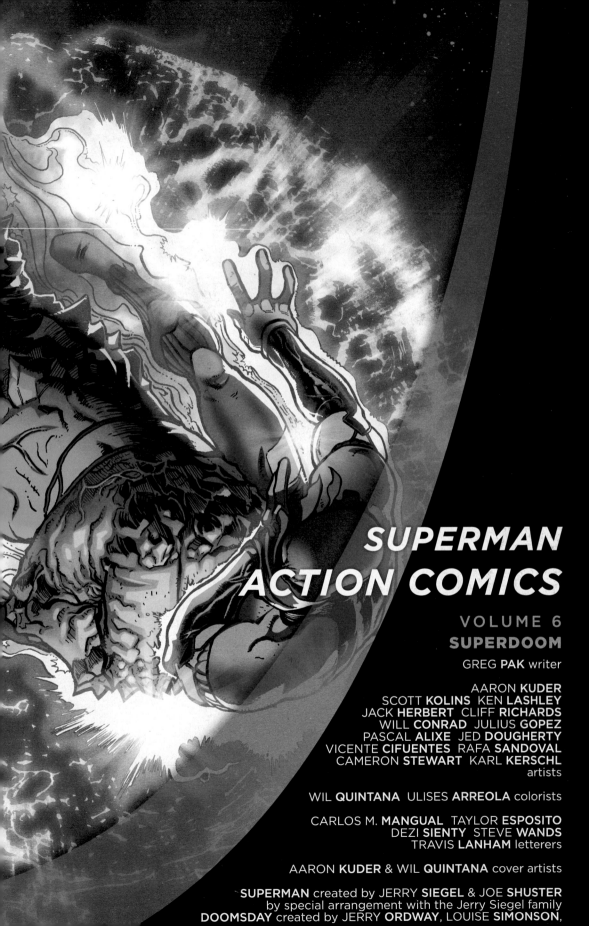

SUPERMAN
ACTION COMICS

VOLUME 6
SUPERDOOM

GREG **PAK** writer

AARON **KUDER**
SCOTT **KOLINS** KEN **LASHLEY**
JACK **HERBERT** CLIFF **RICHARDS**
WILL **CONRAD** Julius **GOPEZ**
PASCAL **ALIXE** JED **DOUGHERTY**
VICENTE **CIFUENTES** RAFA **SANDOVAL**
CAMERON **STEWART** KARL **KERSCHL**
artists

WIL **QUINTANA** ULISES **ARREOLA** colorists

CARLOS M. **MANGUAL** TAYLOR **ESPOSITO**
DEZI **SIENTY** STEVE **WANDS**
TRAVIS **LANHAM** letterers

AARON **KUDER** & WIL **QUINTANA** cover artists

SUPERMAN created by JERRY **SIEGEL** & JOE **SHUSTER**
by special arrangement with the Jerry Siegel family
DOOMSDAY created by JERRY **ORDWAY**, LOUISE **SIMONSON**,

EDDIE BERGANZA Editor – Original Series ANTHONY MARQUES Assistant Editor – Original Series
JEB WOODARD Group Editor – Collected Editions PAUL SANTOS Editor – Collected Edition
ROBBIE BIEDERMAN Publication Design

BOB HARRAS Senior VP – Editor-in-Chief, DC Comics

DIANE NELSON President DAN DIDIO and JIM LEE Co-Publishers
GEOFF JOHNS Chief Creative Officer AMIT DESAI Senior VP – Marketing & Global Franchise Management
NAIRI GARDINER Senior VP – Finance SAM ADES VP – Digital Marketing
BOBBIE CHASE VP –Talent Development MARK CHIARELLO Senior VP – Art, Design & Collected Editions
JOHN CUNNINGHAM VP – Content Strategy ANNE DEPIES VP – Strategy Planning & Reporting
DON FALLETTI VP – Manufacturing Operations LAWRENCE GANEM VP – Editorial Administration & Talent Relations
ALISON GILL Senior VP – Manufacturing & Operations HANK KANALZ Senior VP – Editorial Strategy & Administration
JAY KOGAN VP – Legal Affairs DEREK MADDALENA Senior VP – Sales & Business Development JACK MAHAN VP – Business Affairs
DAN MIRON VP – Sales Planning & Trade Development NICK NAPOLITANO VP – Manufacturing Administration
CAROL ROEDER VP – Marketing EDDIE SCANNELL VP – Mass Account & Digital Sales
COURTNEY SIMMONS Senior VP – Publicity & Communications
JIM (SKI) SOKOLOWSKI VP – Comic Book Specialty & Newsstand Sales
SANDY YI Senior VP – Global Franchise Management

SUPERMAN – ACTION COMICS VOLUME 6: SUPERDOOM

DC Comics, 2900 West Alameda Avenue, Burbank, CA 91505
Printed by RR Donnelley, Salem, VA, USA. 11/20/15. First Printing.
ISBN: 978-1-4012-5865-8
Library of Congress Cataloging-in-Publication Data

Pak, Greg, author.
Superman - Action Comics. Volume 6, Superdoom / Greg Pak, writer ; Aaron Kuder, artist.
pages cm. — (The New 52!)
ISBN 978-1-4012-5865-8
1. Graphic novels. I. Kuder, Aaron, illustrator. II. Title. III. Title: Superdoom.

PN6728.S9P35 2015
741.5'973—dc23

2014027375

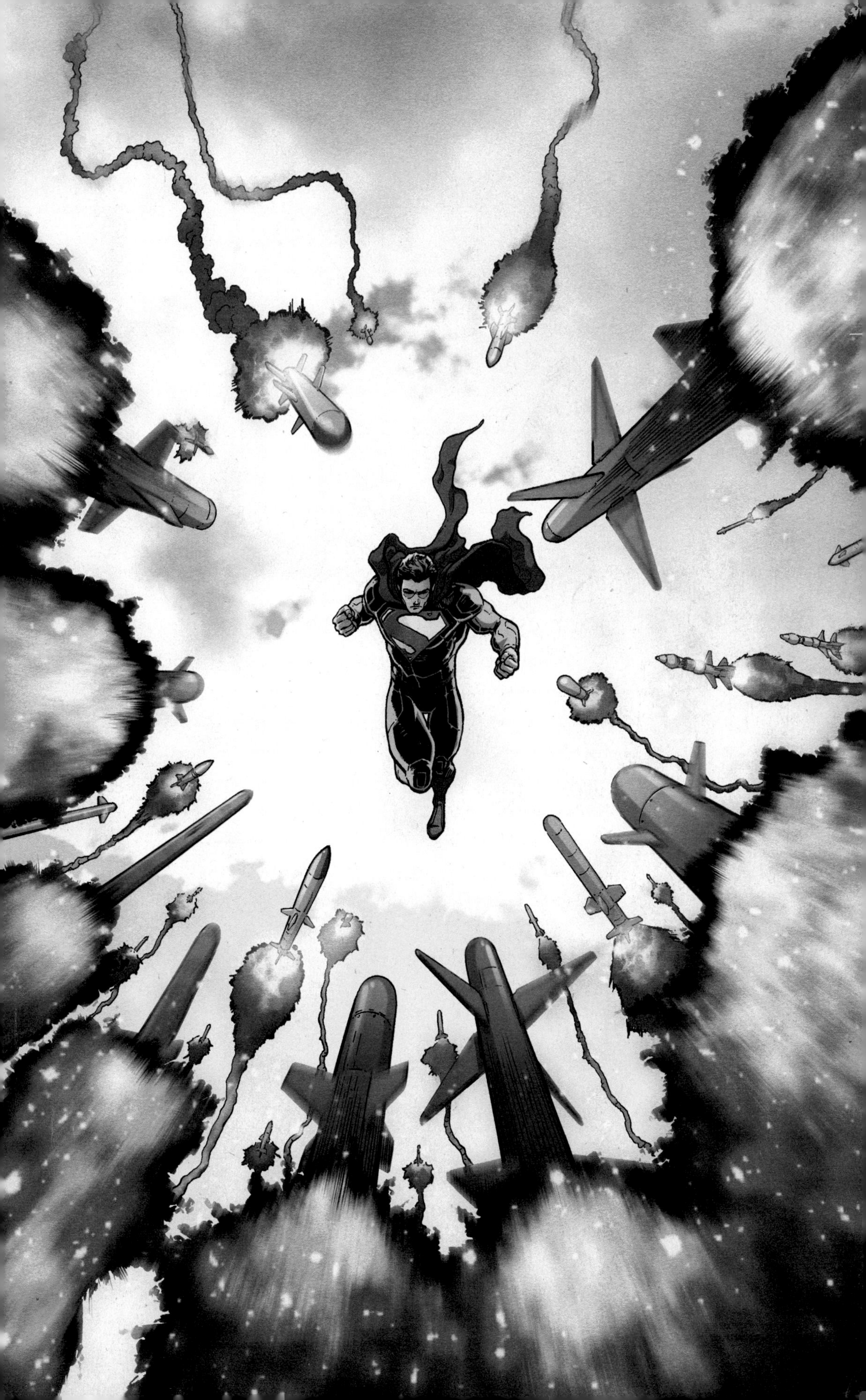

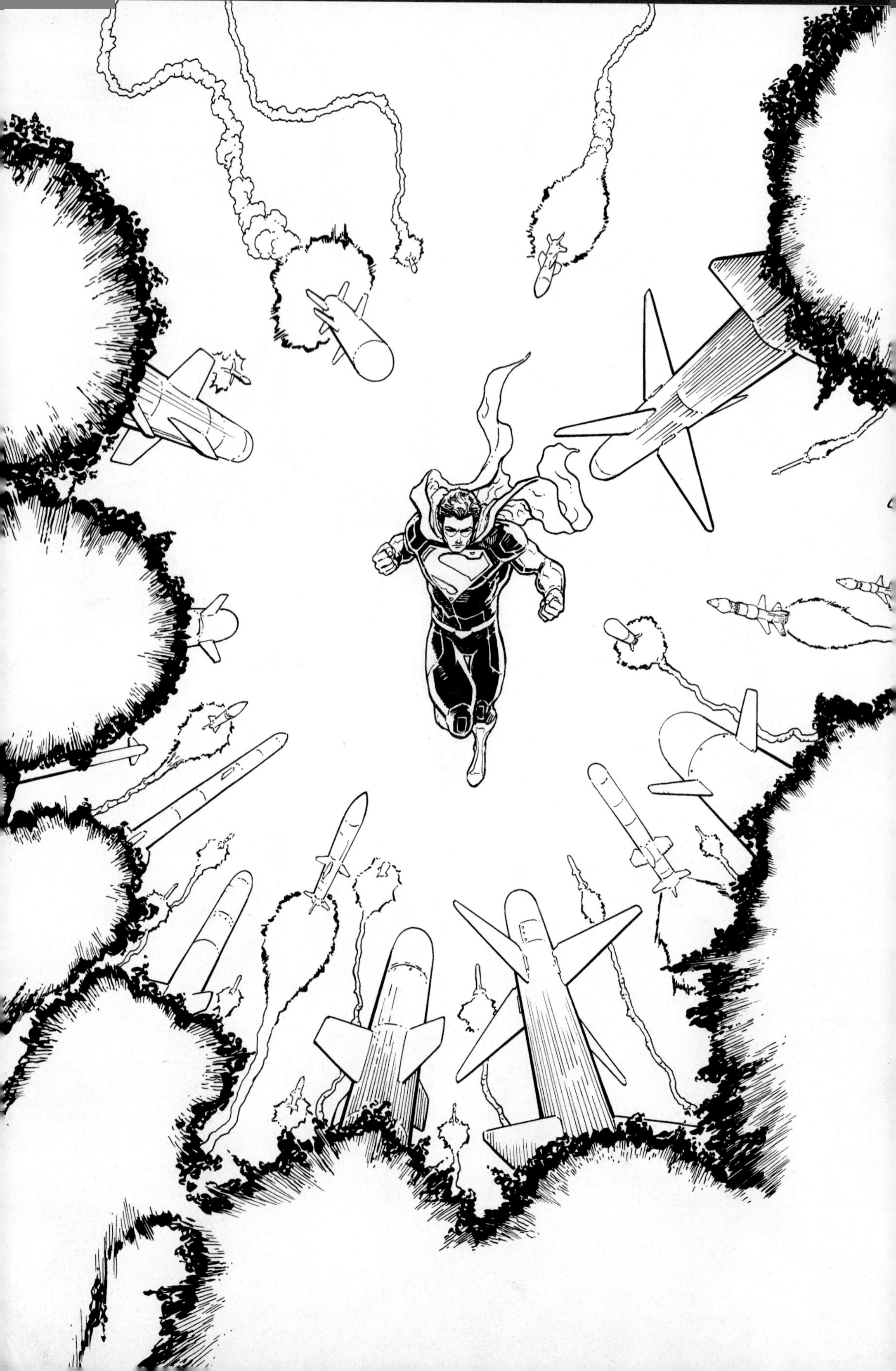

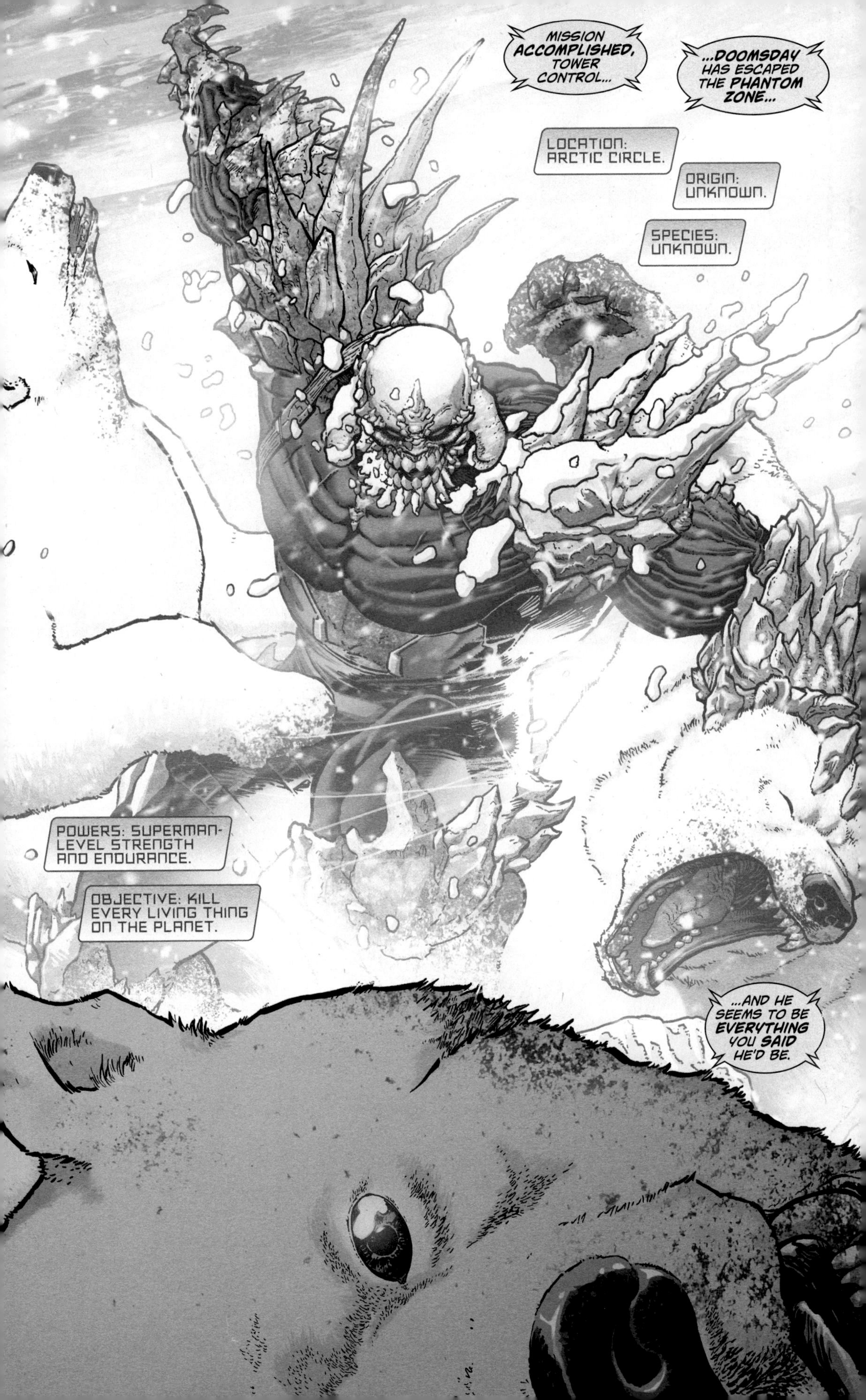
MISSION ACCOMPLISHED, TOWER CONTROL...
...DOOMSDAY HAS ESCAPED THE PHANTOM ZONE...
LOCATION: ARCTIC CIRCLE.
ORIGIN: UNKNOWN.
SPECIES: UNKNOWN.
POWERS: SUPERMAN-LEVEL STRENGTH AND ENDURANCE.
OBJECTIVE: KILL EVERY LIVING THING ON THE PLANET.
...AND HE SEEMS TO BE EVERYTHING YOU SAID HE'D BE.

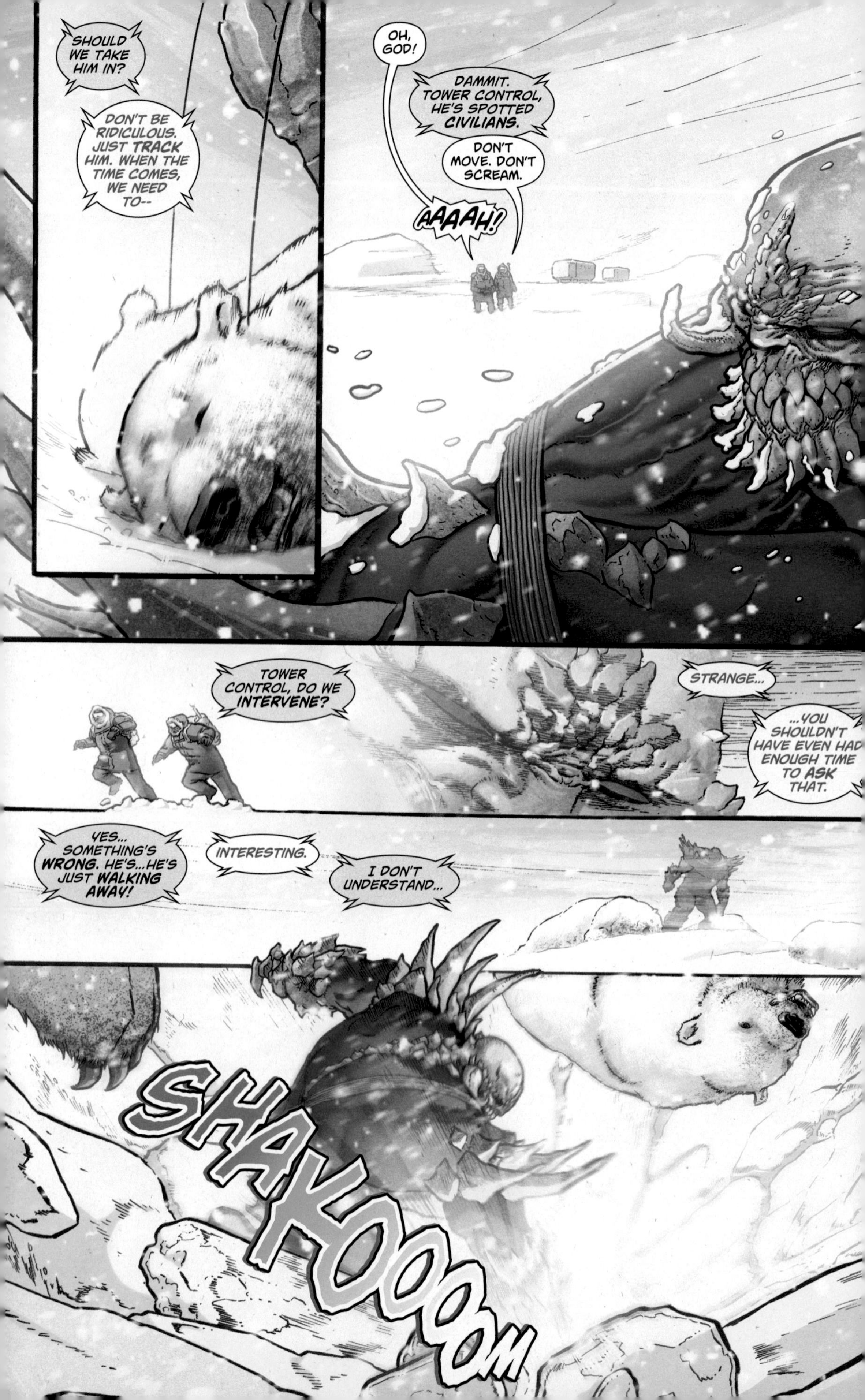
SHOULD WE TAKE HIM IN?
DON'T BE RIDICULOUS. JUST TRACK HIM. WHEN THE TIME COMES, WE NEED TO--
OH, GOD!
DAMMIT. TOWER CONTROL, HE'S SPOTTED CIVILIANS.
DON'T MOVE. DON'T SCREAM.
AAAAH!
TOWER CONTROL, DO WE INTERVENE?
STRANGE...
...YOU SHOULDN'T HAVE EVEN HAD ENOUGH TIME TO ASK THAT.
YES... SOMETHING'S WRONG. HE'S...HE'S JUST WALKING AWAY!
INTERESTING.
I DON'T UNDERSTAND...
SHAKOOOOM

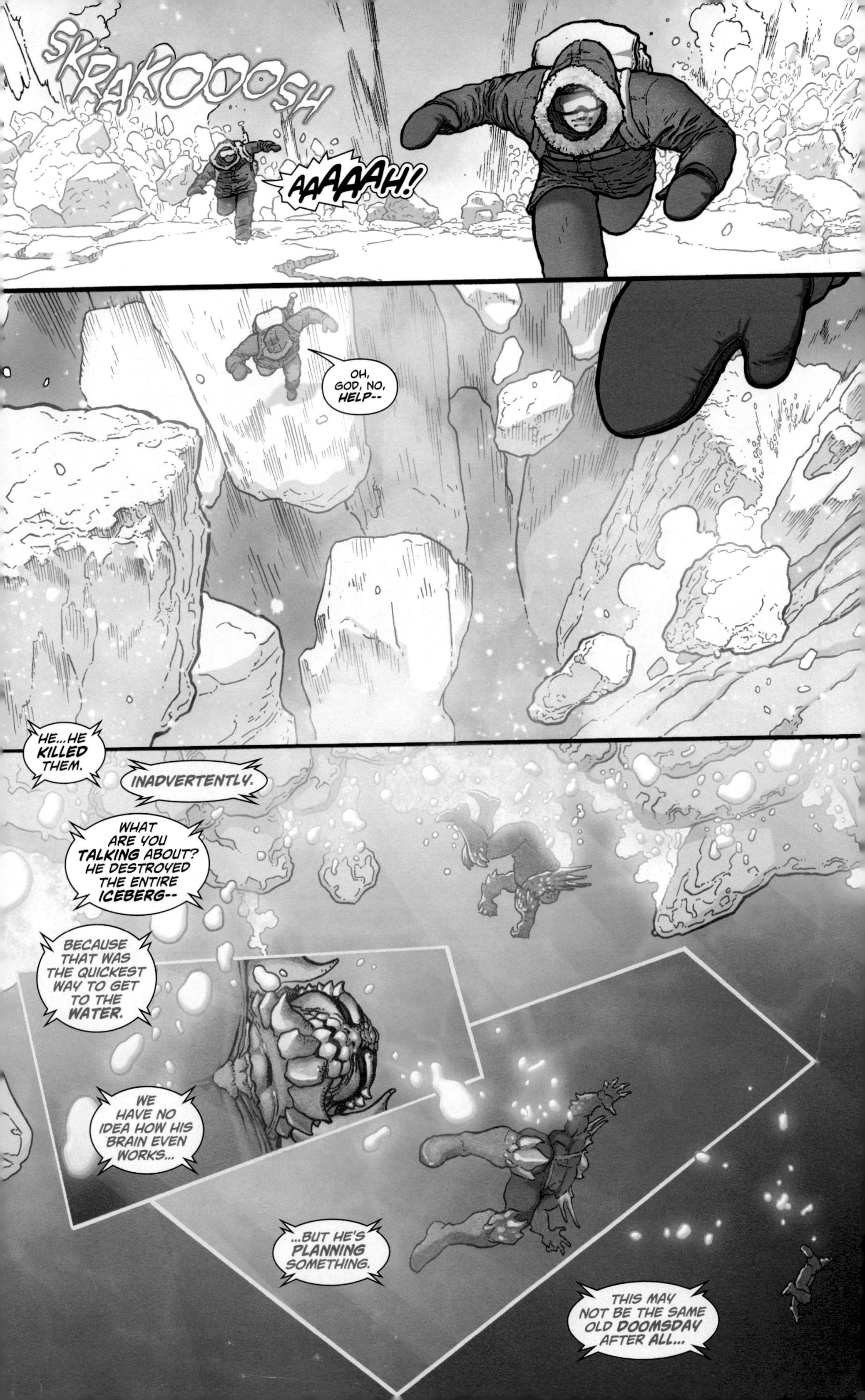
SKRAKOOOSH
AAAAAH!
OH, GOD, NO, HELP--
HE...HE KILLED THEM.
INADVERTENTLY.
WHAT ARE YOU TALKING ABOUT? HE DESTROYED THE ENTIRE ICEBERG--
BECAUSE THAT WAS THE QUICKEST WAY TO GET TO THE WATER.
WE HAVE NO IDEA HOW HIS BRAIN EVEN WORKS...
...BUT HE'S PLANNING SOMETHING.
THIS MAY NOT BE THE SAME OLD DOOMSDAY AFTER ALL...

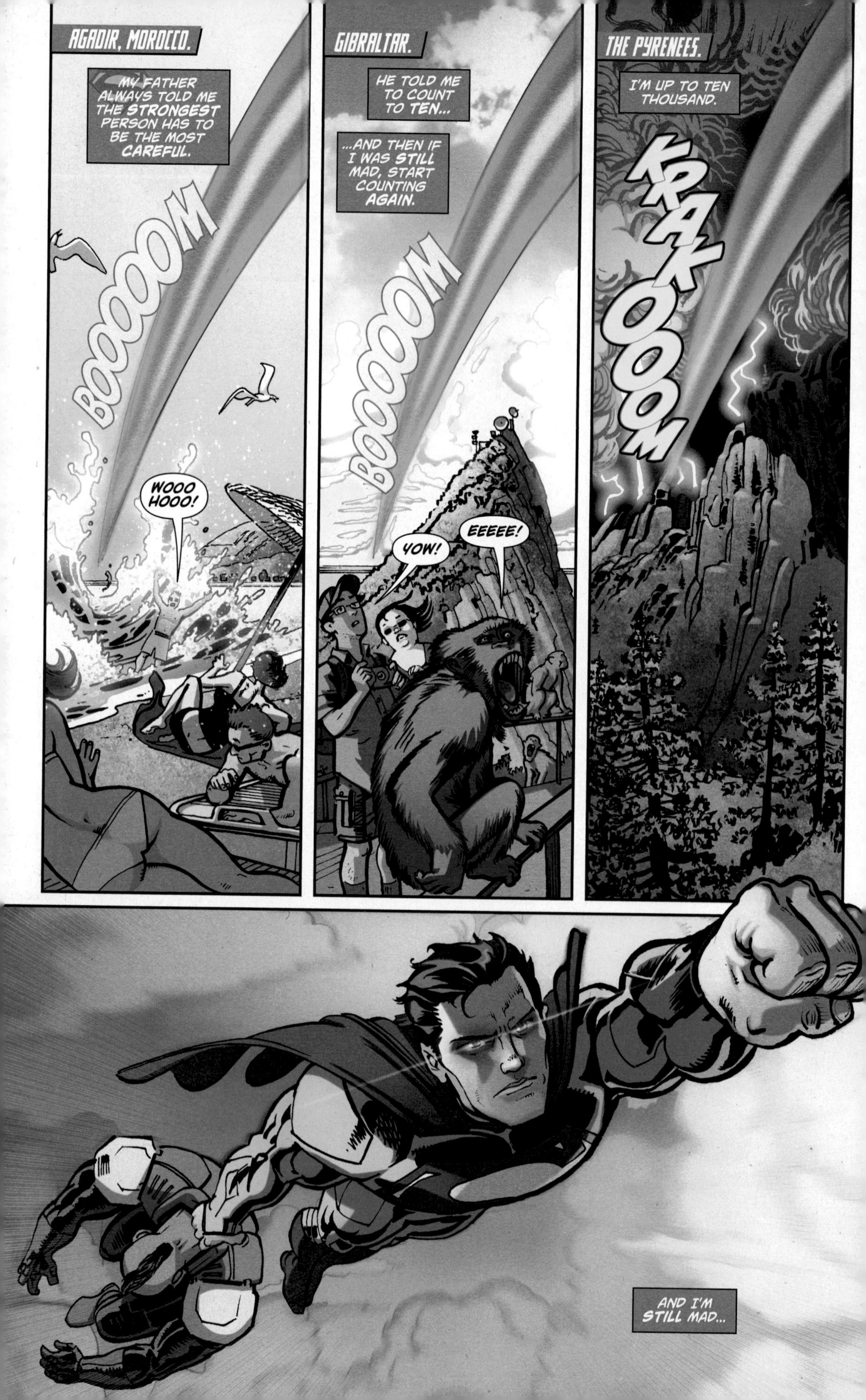
AGADIR, MOROCCO.
MY FATHER ALWAYS TOLD ME THE STRONGEST PERSON HAS TO BE THE MOST CAREFUL.
BOOOOOOM
WOOO HOOO!
GIBRALTAR.
HE TOLD ME TO COUNT TO TEN...
...AND THEN IF I WAS STILL MAD, START COUNTING AGAIN.
BOOOOOOM
YOW!
EEEEE!
THE PYRENEES.
I'M UP TO TEN THOUSAND.
KRAKOOOOM
AND I'M STILL MAD...

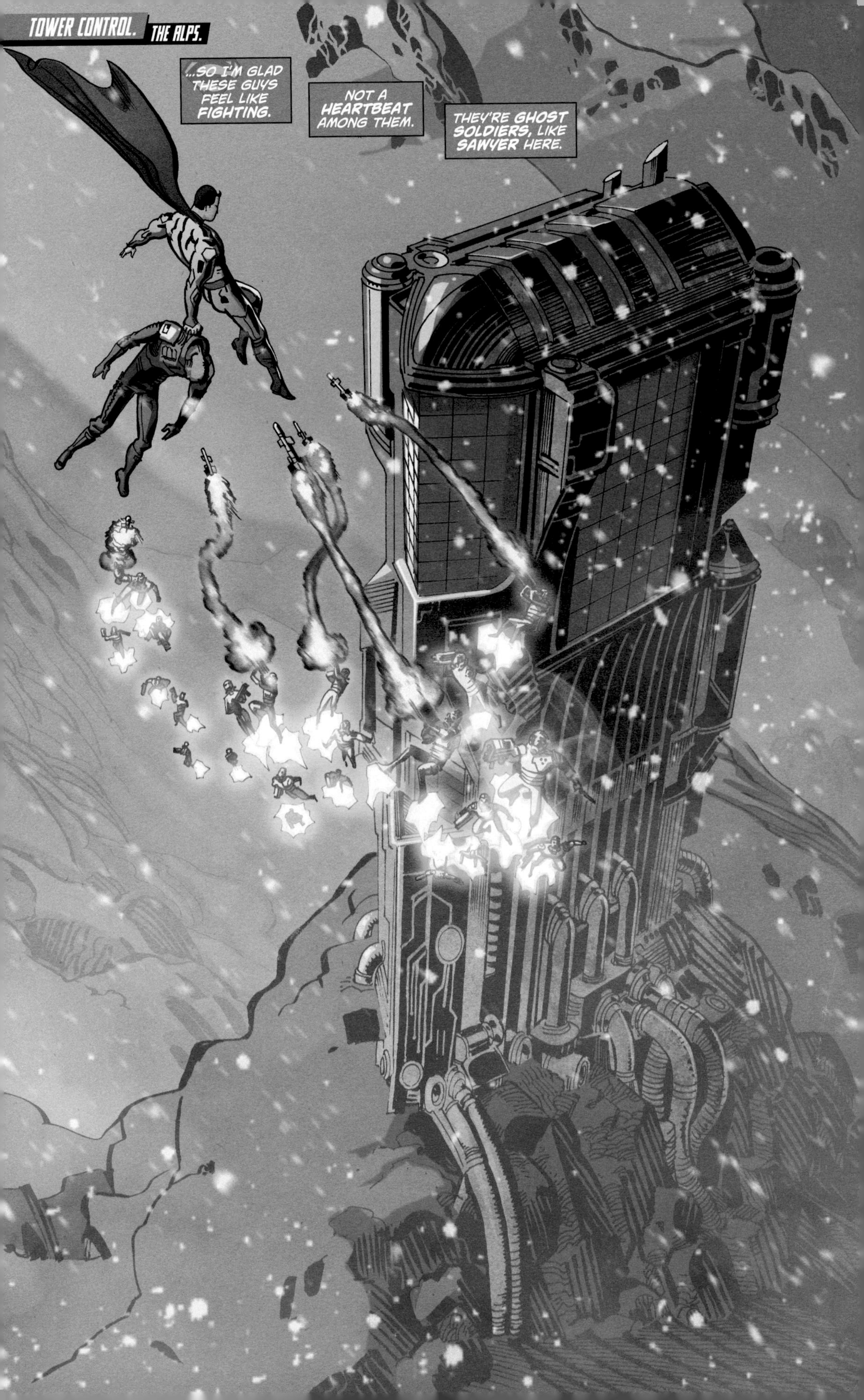
TOWER CONTROL.
THE ALPS.
...SO I'M GLAD THESE GUYS FEEL LIKE FIGHTING.
NOT A HEARTBEAT AMONG THEM.
THEY'RE GHOST SOLDIERS, LIKE SAWYER HERE.

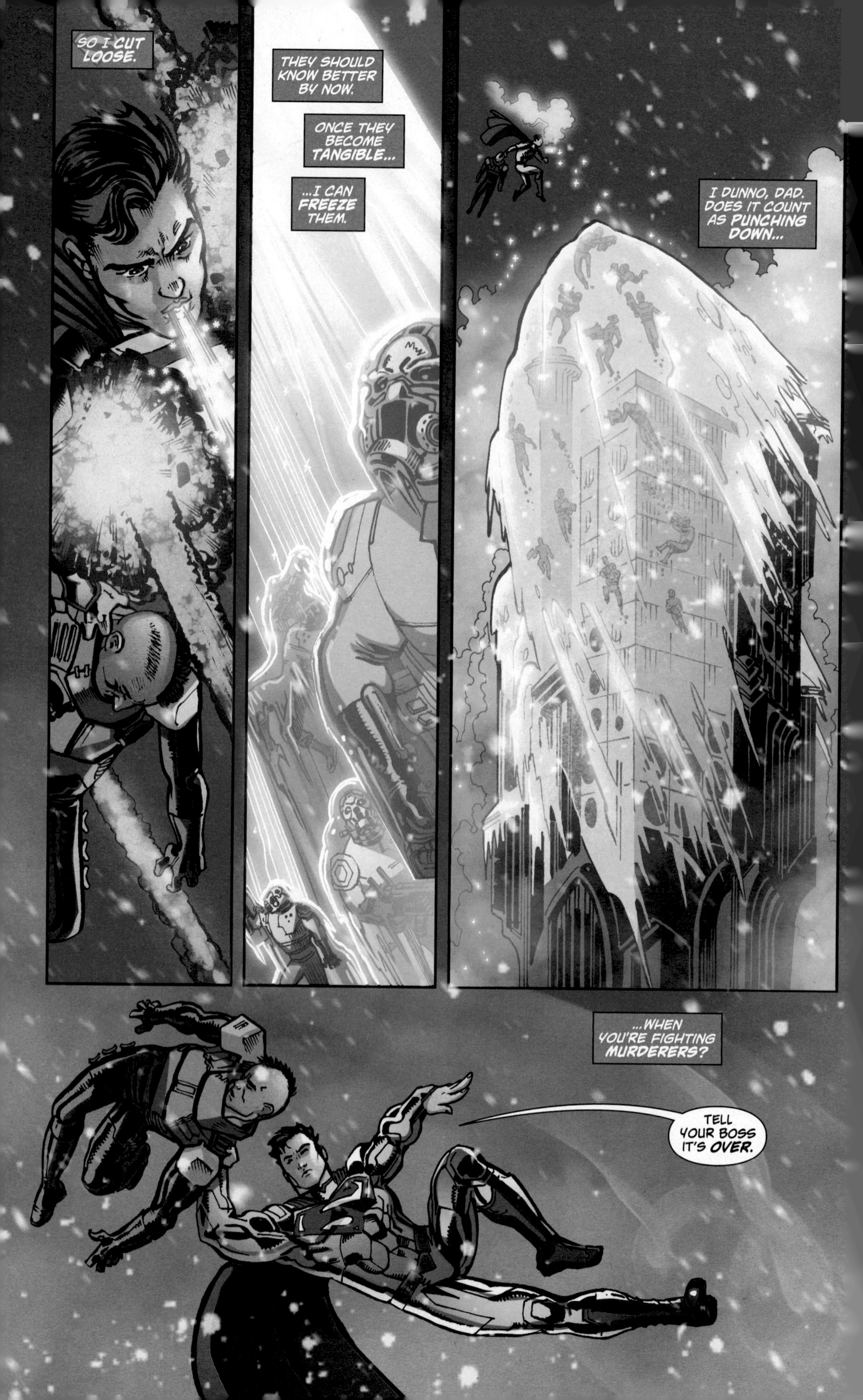
SO I CUT LOOSE.
THEY SHOULD KNOW BETTER BY NOW.
ONCE THEY BECOME TANGIBLE...
...I CAN FREEZE THEM.
I DUNNO, DAD. DOES IT COUNT AS PUNCHING DOWN...
...WHEN YOU'RE FIGHTING MURDERERS?
TELL YOUR BOSS IT'S OVER.

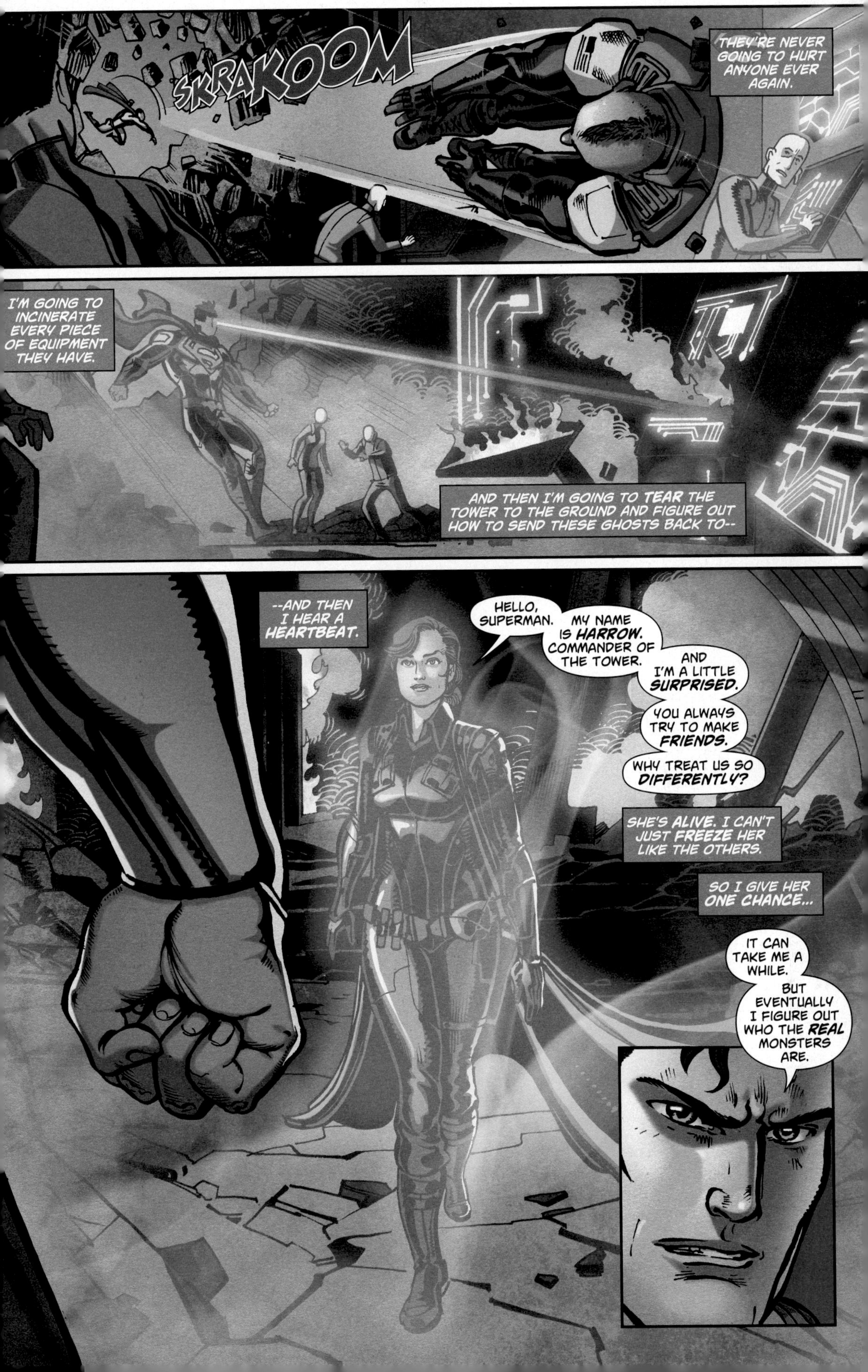
SKRAKOOM
THEY'RE NEVER GOING TO HURT ANYONE EVER AGAIN.
I'M GOING TO INCINERATE EVERY PIECE OF EQUIPMENT THEY HAVE.
AND THEN I'M GOING TO TEAR THE TOWER TO THE GROUND AND FIGURE OUT HOW TO SEND THESE GHOSTS BACK TO--
--AND THEN I HEAR A HEARTBEAT.
HELLO, SUPERMAN.
MY NAME IS HARROW. COMMANDER OF THE TOWER.
AND I'M A LITTLE SURPRISED.
YOU ALWAYS TRY TO MAKE FRIENDS.
WHY TREAT US SO DIFFERENTLY?
SHE'S ALIVE. I CAN'T JUST FREEZE HER LIKE THE OTHERS.
SO I GIVE HER ONE CHANCE...
IT CAN TAKE ME A WHILE.
BUT EVENTUALLY I FIGURE OUT WHO THE REAL MONSTERS ARE.

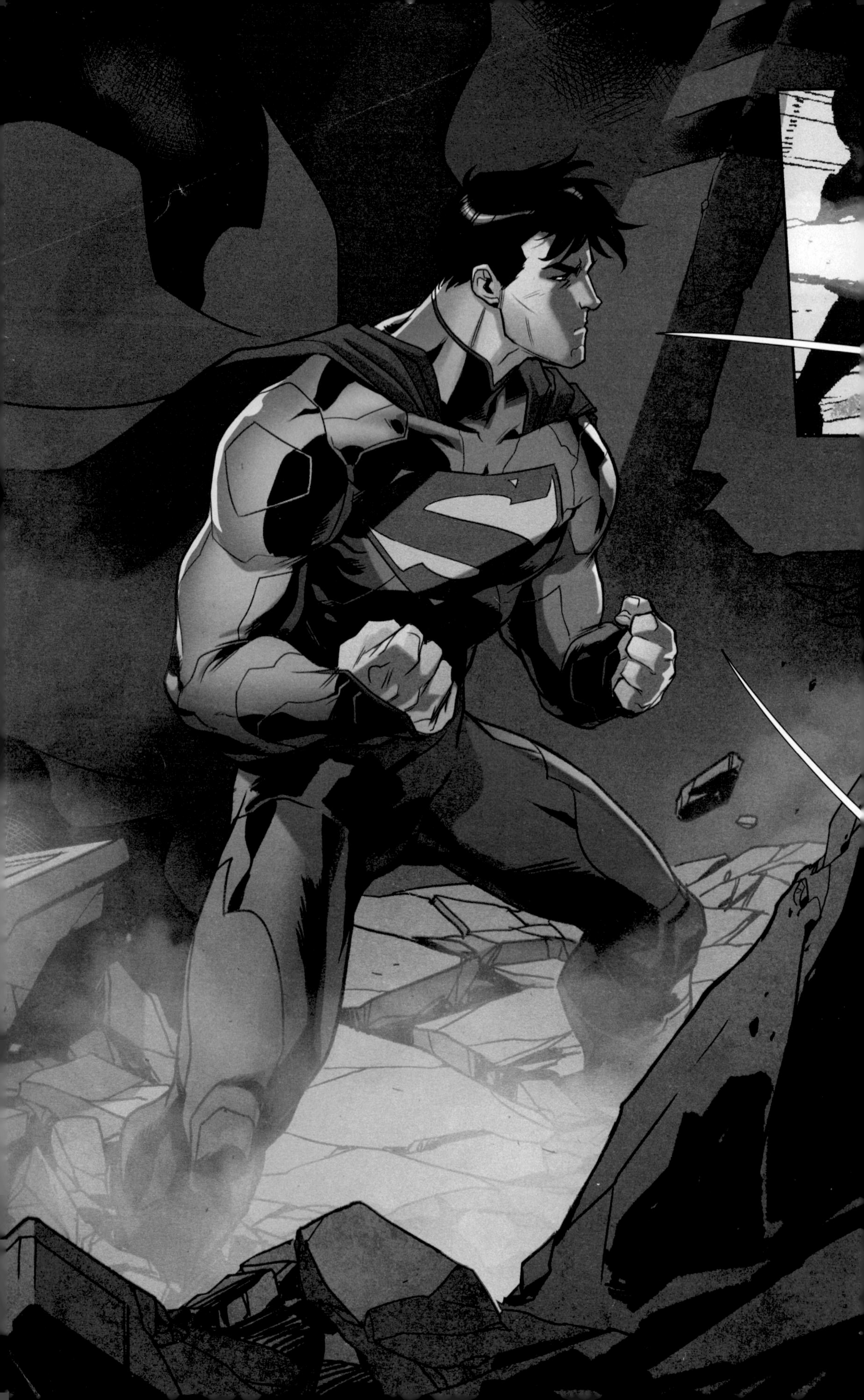

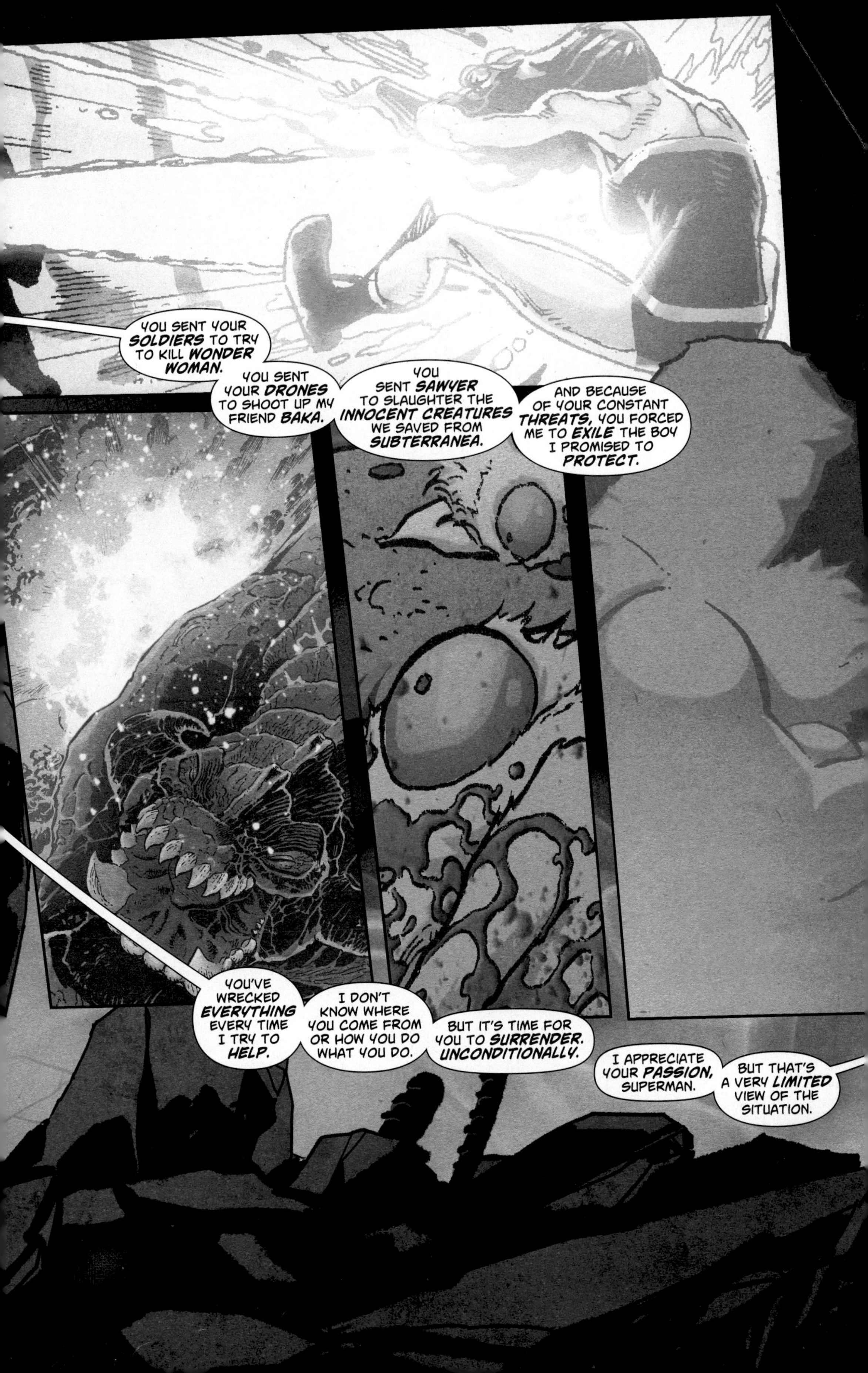

YOU SENT YOUR SOLDIERS TO TRY TO KILL WONDER WOMAN.
YOU SENT YOUR DRONES TO SHOOT UP MY FRIEND BAKA.
YOU SENT SAWYER TO SLAUGHTER THE INNOCENT CREATURES WE SAVED FROM SUBTERRANEA.
AND BECAUSE OF YOUR CONSTANT THREATS, YOU FORCED ME TO EXILE THE BOY I PROMISED TO PROTECT.
YOU'VE WRECKED EVERYTHING EVERY TIME I TRY TO HELP.
I DON'T KNOW WHERE YOU COME FROM OR HOW YOU DO WHAT YOU DO.
BUT IT'S TIME FOR YOU TO SURRENDER. UNCONDITIONALLY.
I APPRECIATE YOUR PASSION, SUPERMAN.
BUT THAT'S A VERY LIMITED VIEW OF THE SITUATION.

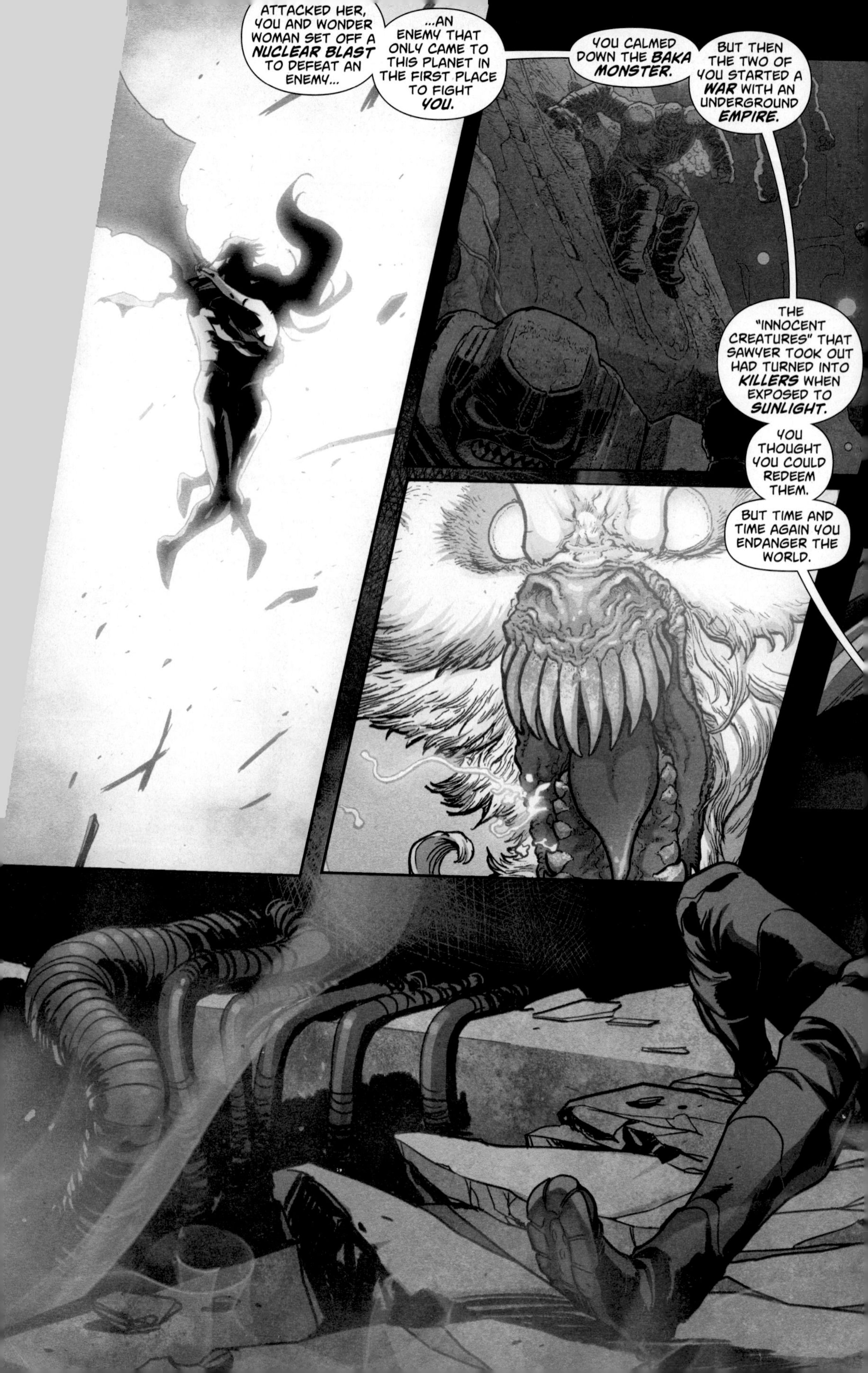
ATTACKED HER, YOU AND WONDER WOMAN SET OFF A NUCLEAR BLAST TO DEFEAT AN ENEMY...
...AN ENEMY THAT ONLY CAME TO THIS PLANET IN THE FIRST PLACE TO FIGHT YOU.
YOU CALMED DOWN THE BAKA MONSTER.
BUT THEN THE TWO OF YOU STARTED A WAR WITH AN UNDERGROUND EMPIRE.
THE "INNOCENT CREATURES" THAT SAWYER TOOK OUT HAD TURNED INTO KILLERS WHEN EXPOSED TO SUNLIGHT.
YOU THOUGHT YOU COULD REDEEM THEM.
BUT TIME AND TIME AGAIN YOU ENDANGER THE WORLD.

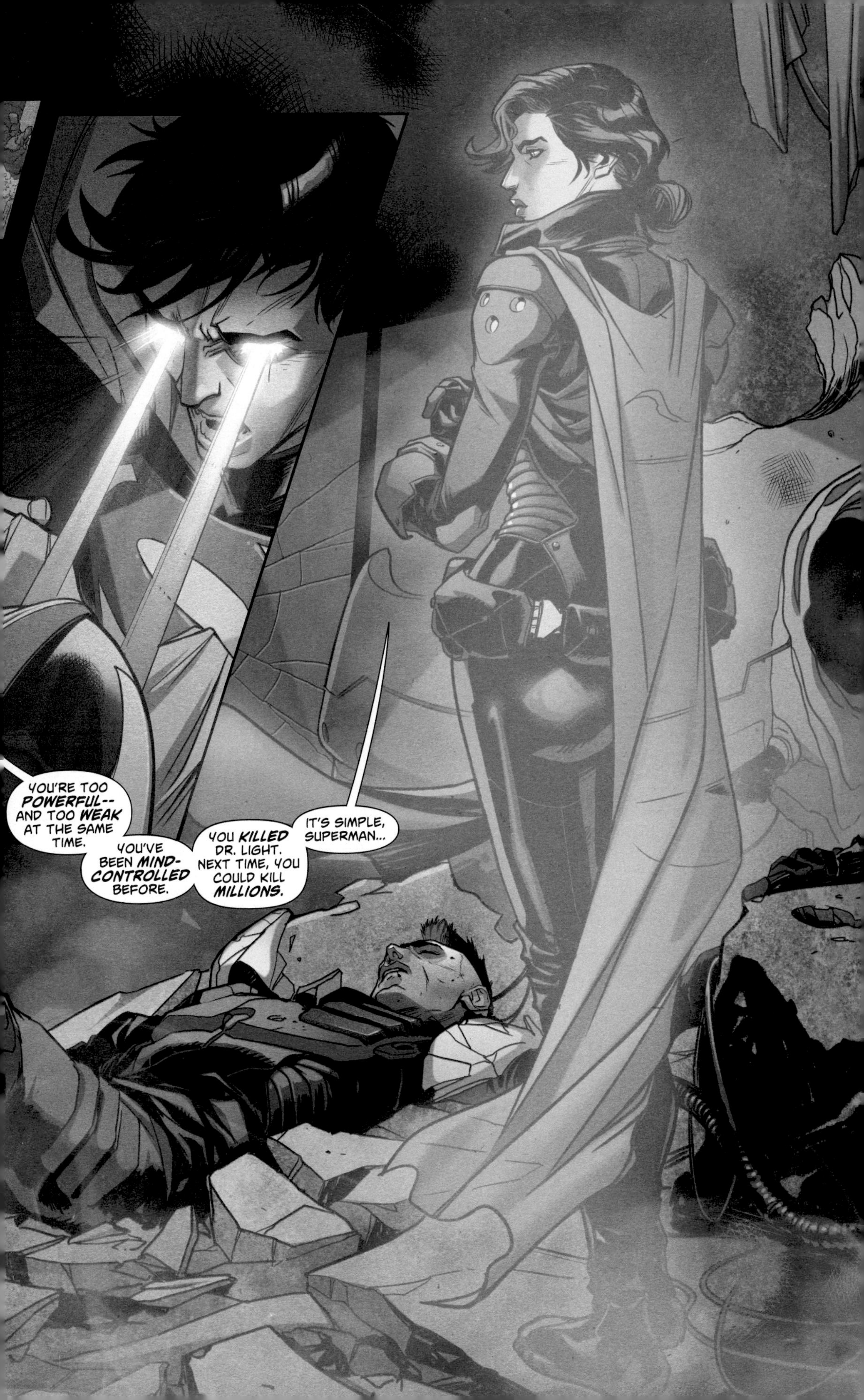
IT'S SIMPLE, SUPERMAN...
YOU KILLED DR. LIGHT. NEXT TIME, YOU COULD KILL MILLIONS.
YOU'VE BEEN MIND-CONTROLLED BEFORE.
YOU'RE TOO POWERFUL-- AND TOO WEAK AT THE SAME TIME.

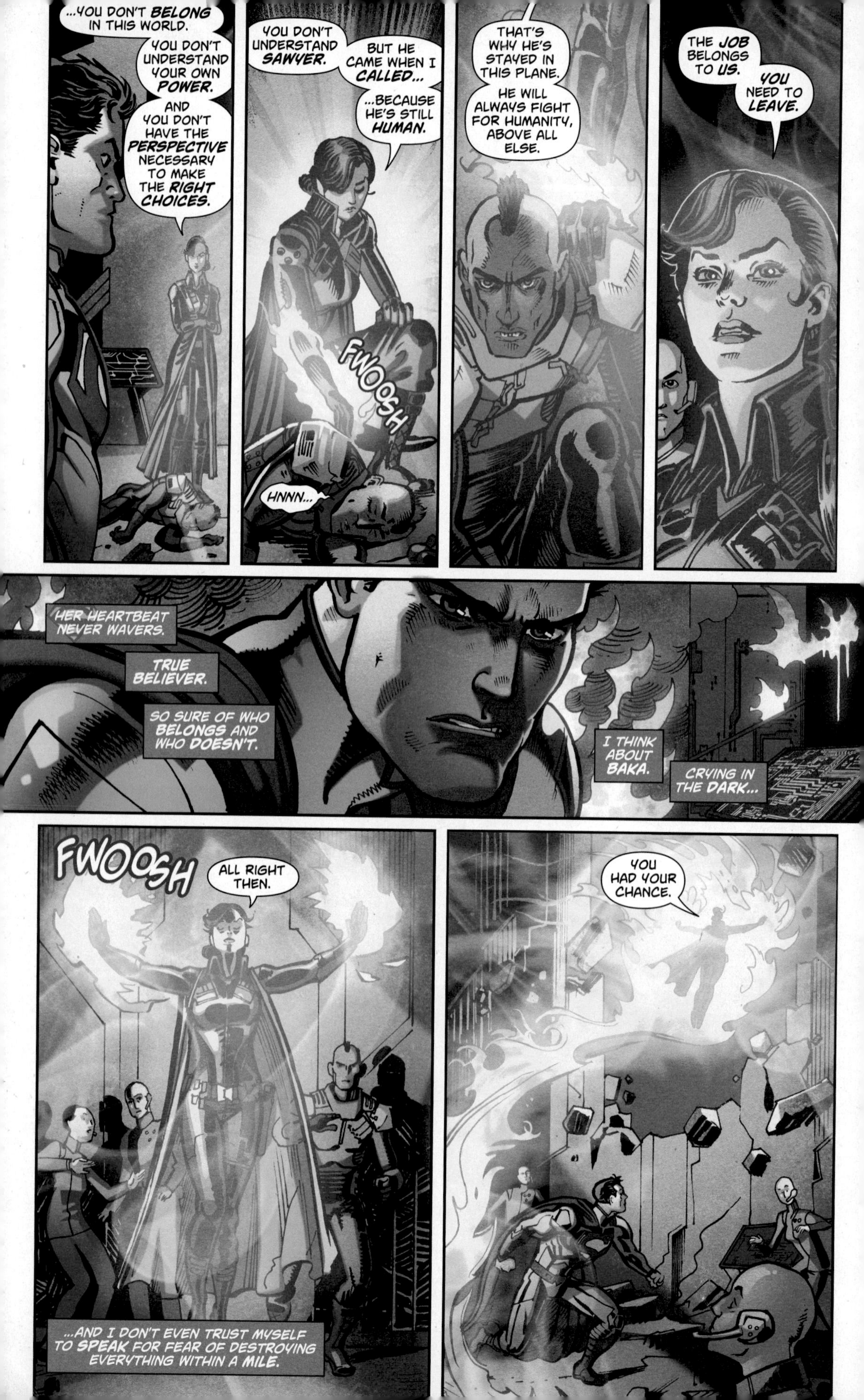
...YOU DON'T BELONG IN THIS WORLD.
YOU DON'T UNDERSTAND YOUR OWN POWER.
AND YOU DON'T HAVE THE PERSPECTIVE NECESSARY TO MAKE THE RIGHT CHOICES.
YOU DON'T UNDERSTAND SAWYER.
BUT HE CAME WHEN I CALLED...
...BECAUSE HE'S STILL HUMAN.
FWOOSH
HNNN...
THAT'S WHY HE'S STAYED IN THIS PLANE.
HE WILL ALWAYS FIGHT FOR HUMANITY, ABOVE ALL ELSE.
THE JOB BELONGS TO US.
YOU NEED TO LEAVE.
HER HEARTBEAT NEVER WAVERS.
TRUE BELIEVER.
SO SURE OF WHO BELONGS AND WHO DOESN'T.
I THINK ABOUT BAKA.
CRYING IN THE DARK...
FWOOSH
ALL RIGHT THEN.
...AND I DON'T EVEN TRUST MYSELF TO SPEAK FOR FEAR OF DESTROYING EVERYTHING WITHIN A MILE.
YOU HAD YOUR CHANCE.

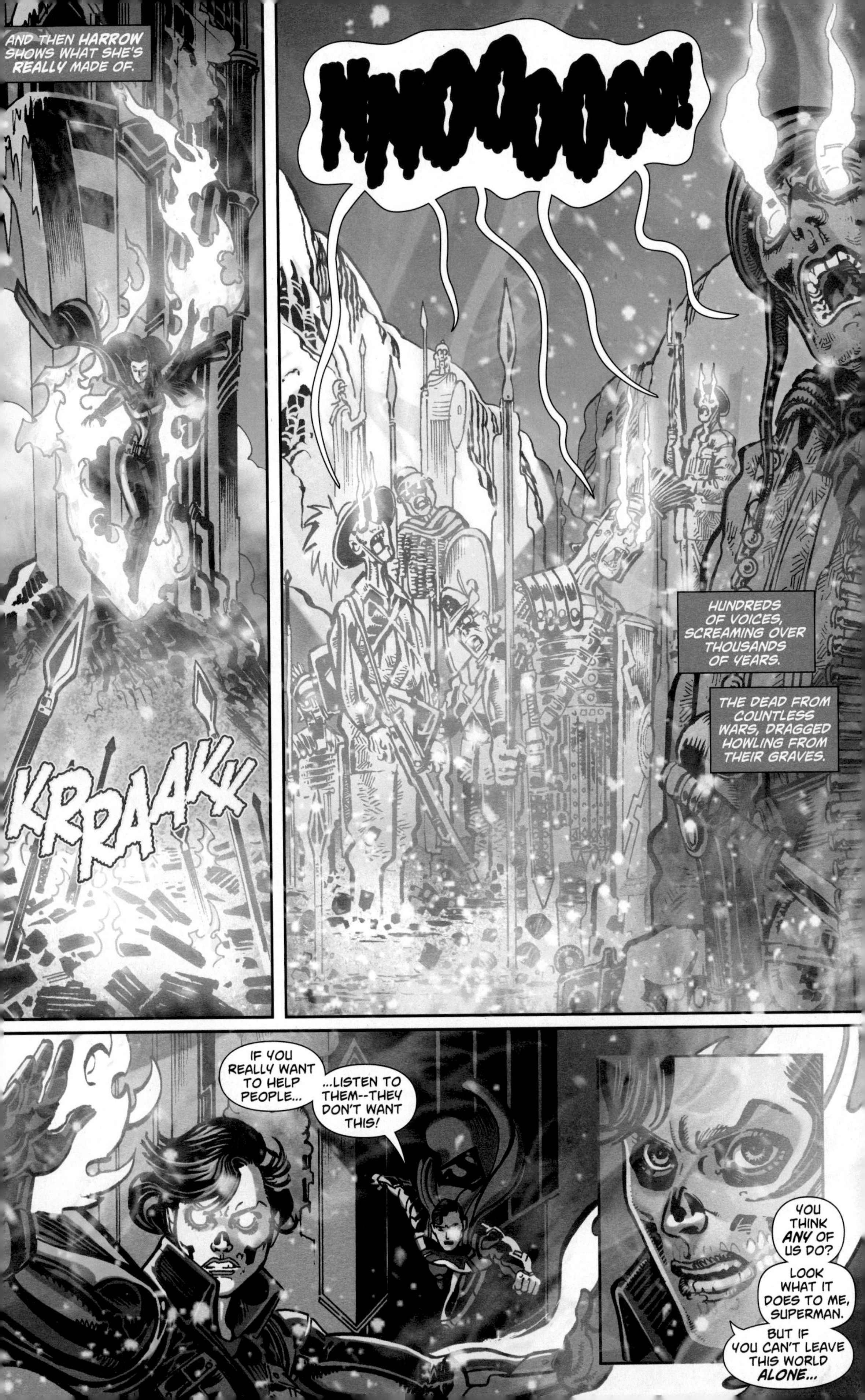
AND THEN HARROW SHOWS WHAT SHE'S REALLY MADE OF.
KRRAAKK
HNOOOOOO!
HUNDREDS OF VOICES, SCREAMING OVER THOUSANDS OF YEARS.
THE DEAD FROM COUNTLESS WARS, DRAGGED HOWLING FROM THEIR GRAVES.
IF YOU REALLY WANT TO HELP PEOPLE...
...LISTEN TO THEM--THEY DON'T WANT THIS!
YOU THINK ANY OF US DO?
LOOK WHAT IT DOES TO ME, SUPERMAN.
BUT IF YOU CAN'T LEAVE THIS WORLD ALONE...

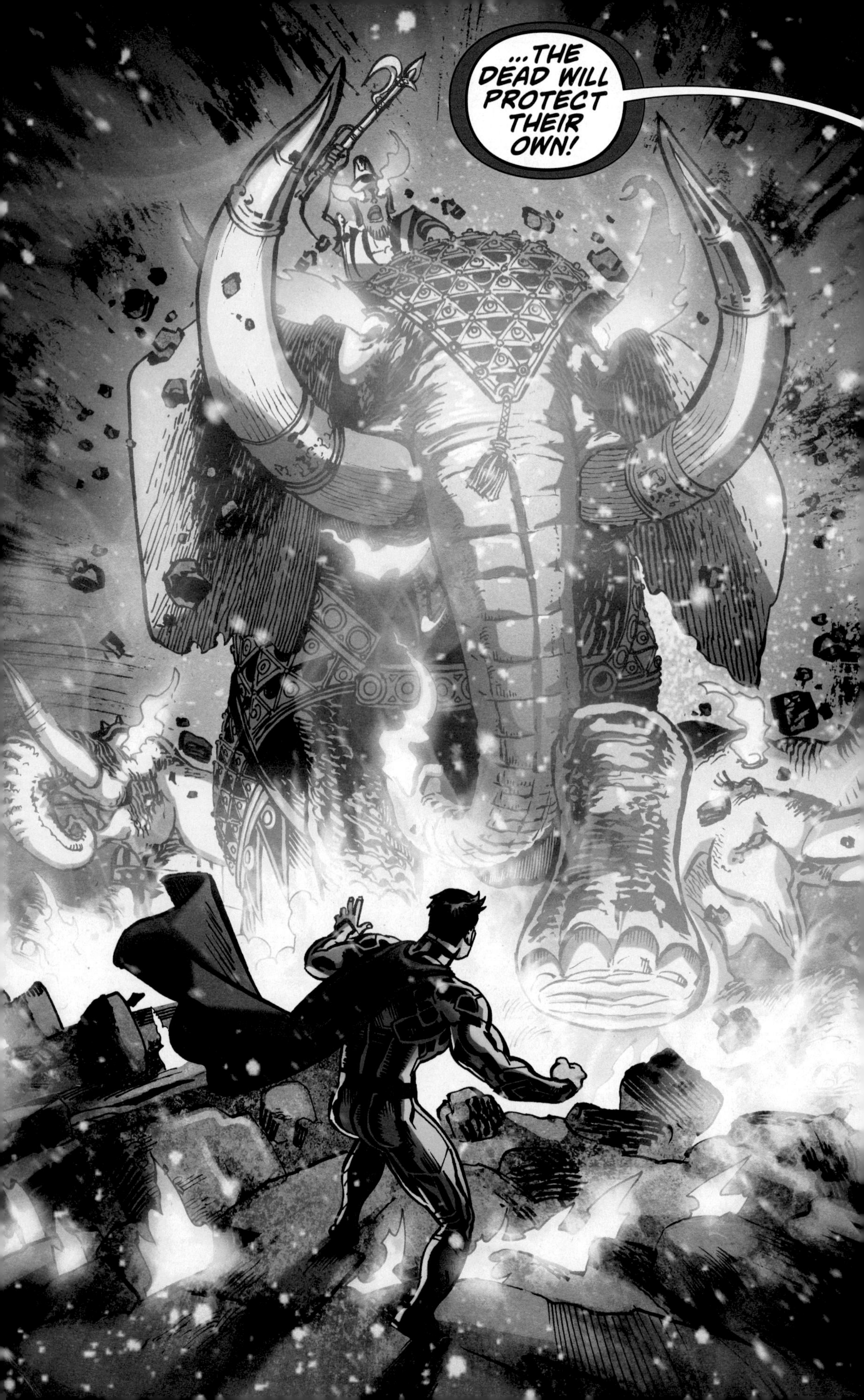
...THE DEAD WILL PROTECT THEIR OWN!

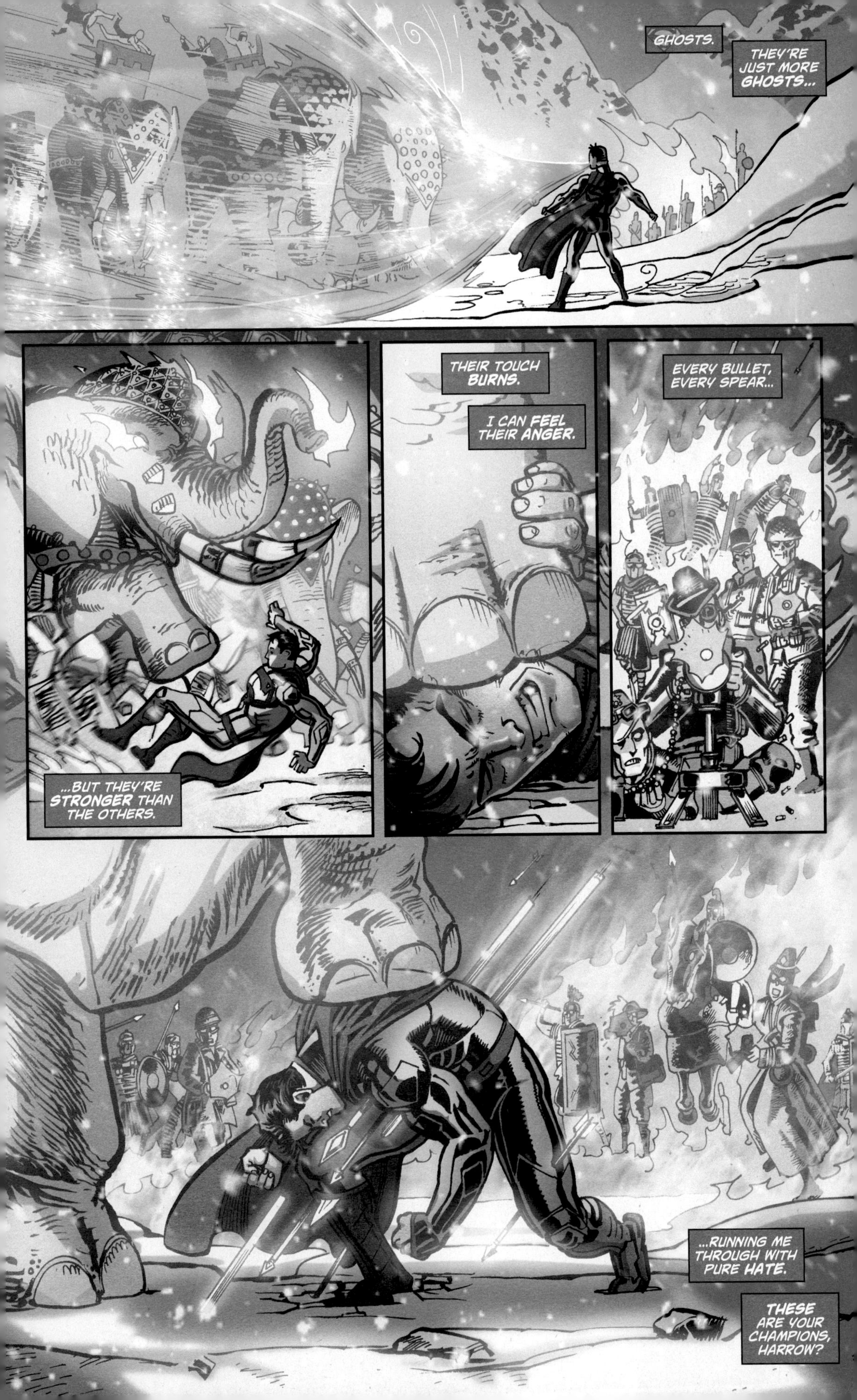
GHOSTS.
THEY'RE JUST MORE GHOSTS...
...BUT THEY'RE STRONGER THAN THE OTHERS.
THEIR TOUCH BURNS.
I CAN FEEL THEIR ANGER.
EVERY BULLET, EVERY SPEAR...
...RUNNING ME THROUGH WITH PURE HATE.
THESE ARE YOUR CHAMPIONS, HARROW?

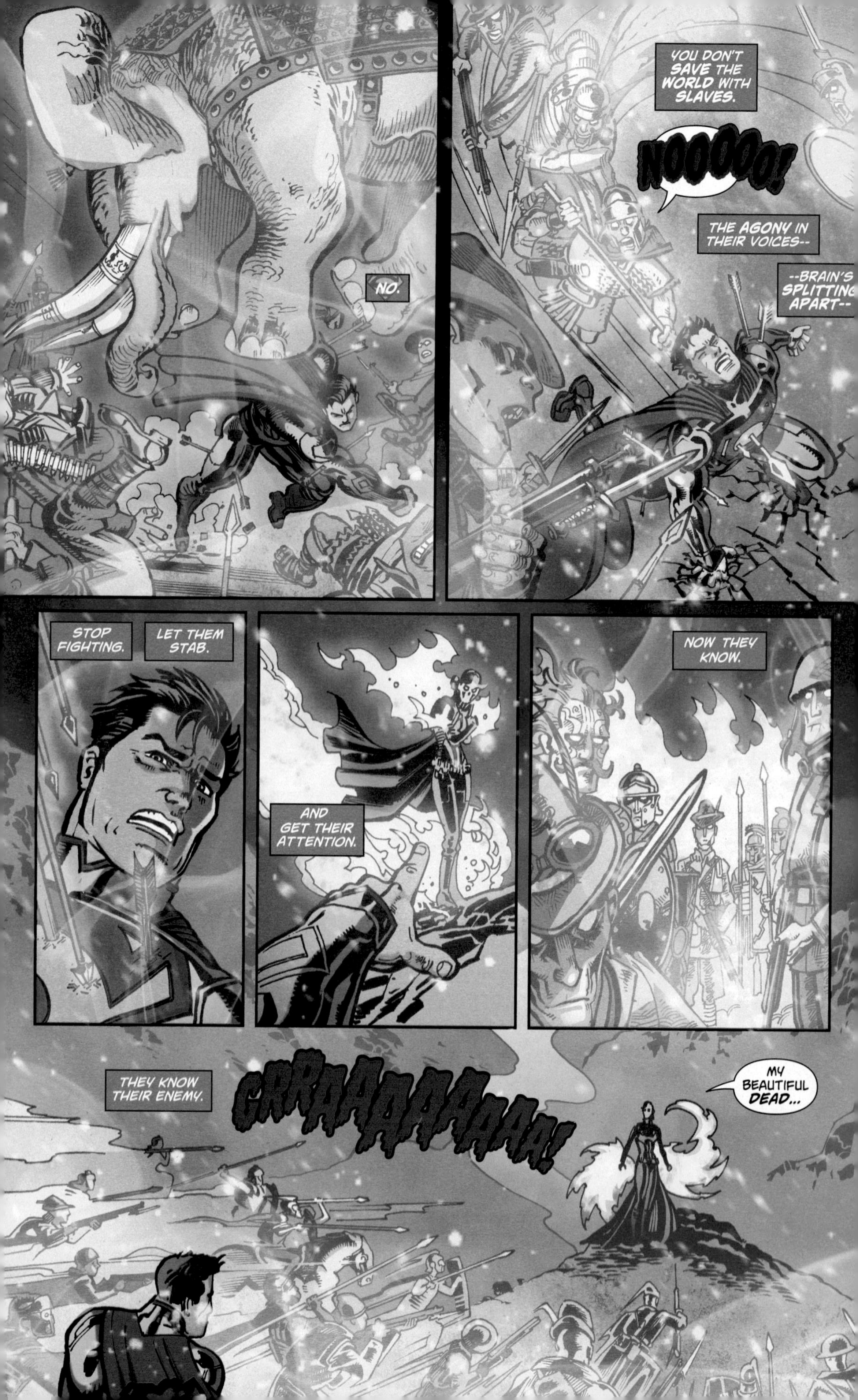
NO.
YOU DON'T SAVE THE WORLD WITH SLAVES.
NOOOOO!
THE AGONY IN THEIR VOICES--
--BRAIN'S SPLITTING APART--
STOP FIGHTING.
LET THEM STAB.
AND GET THEIR ATTENTION.
NOW THEY KNOW.
THEY KNOW THEIR ENEMY.
GRRAAAAAAAAA!
MY BEAUTIFUL DEAD...

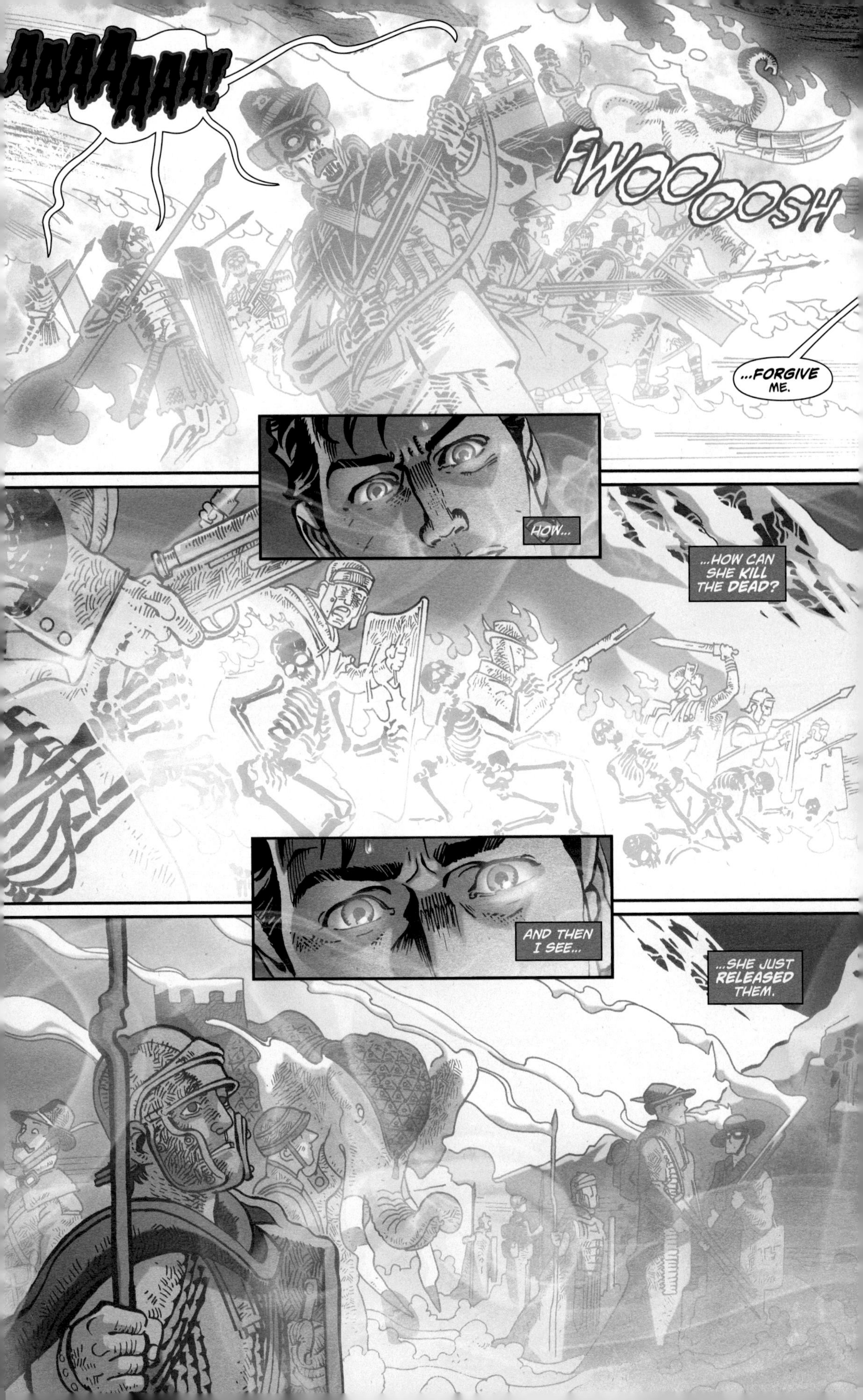
AAAAAAA!
FWOOOOOSH
...FORGIVE ME.
HOW...
...HOW CAN SHE KILL THE DEAD?
AND THEN I SEE...
...SHE JUST RELEASED THEM.

HARROW...

CONGRATULATIONS, SUPERMAN.

YOU WIN.

MOSTLY I RECRUIT THE *WILLING* DEAD.

THIS...WAS *DIFFERENT.*

TOOK ALL I HAD.

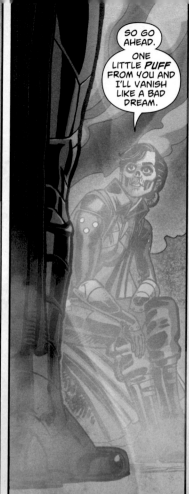

SO GO AHEAD.

ONE LITTLE *PUFF* FROM YOU AND I'LL VANISH LIKE A BAD DREAM.

COUNT TO TEN...

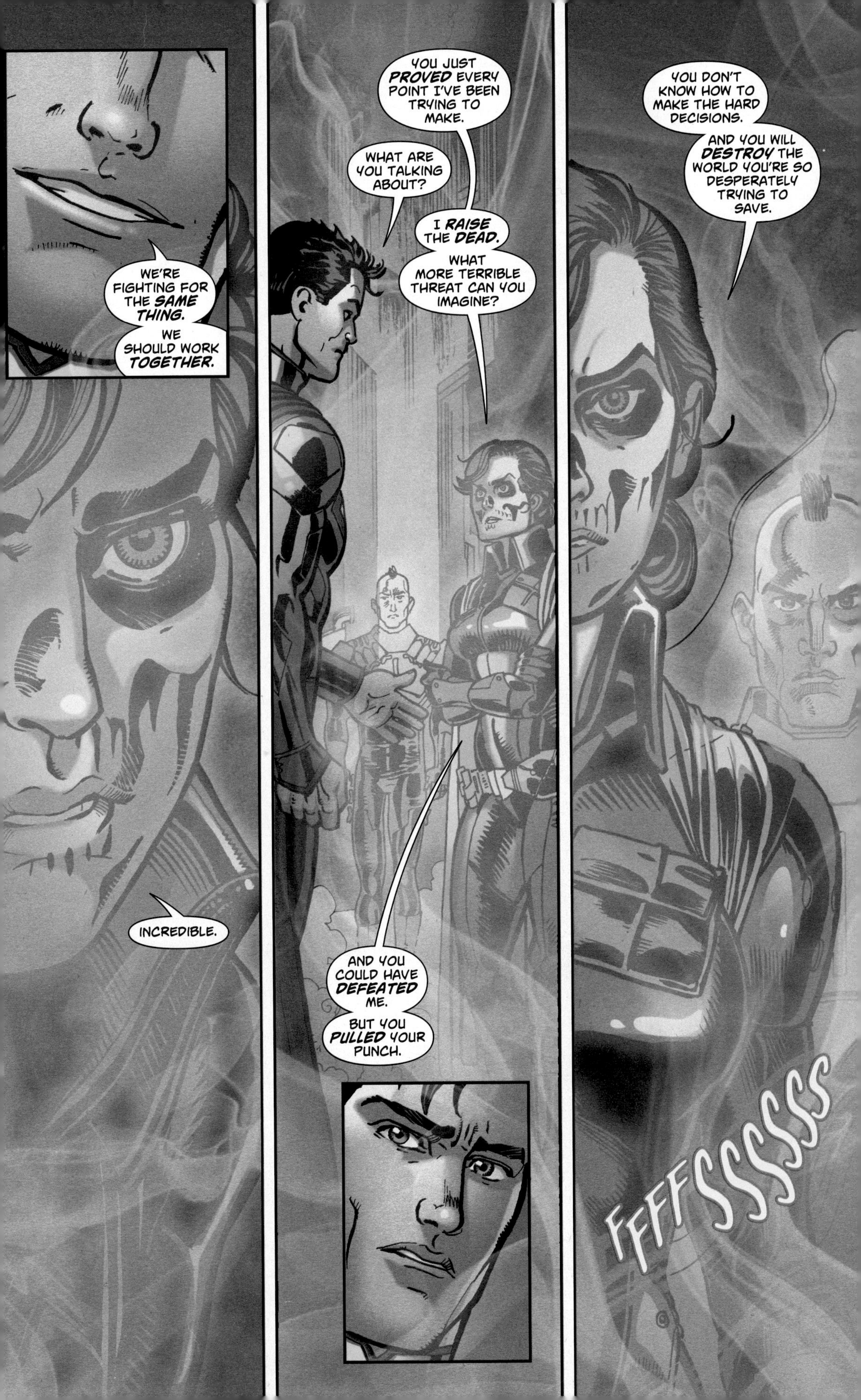
WE'RE FIGHTING FOR THE SAME THING.
WE SHOULD WORK TOGETHER.
INCREDIBLE.
YOU JUST PROVED EVERY POINT I'VE BEEN TRYING TO MAKE.
WHAT ARE YOU TALKING ABOUT?
I RAISE THE DEAD.
WHAT MORE TERRIBLE THREAT CAN YOU IMAGINE?
AND YOU COULD HAVE DEFEATED ME.
BUT YOU PULLED YOUR PUNCH.
YOU DON'T KNOW HOW TO MAKE THE HARD DECISIONS.
AND YOU WILL DESTROY THE WORLD YOU'RE SO DESPERATELY TRYING TO SAVE.
FFFSSSSSSS

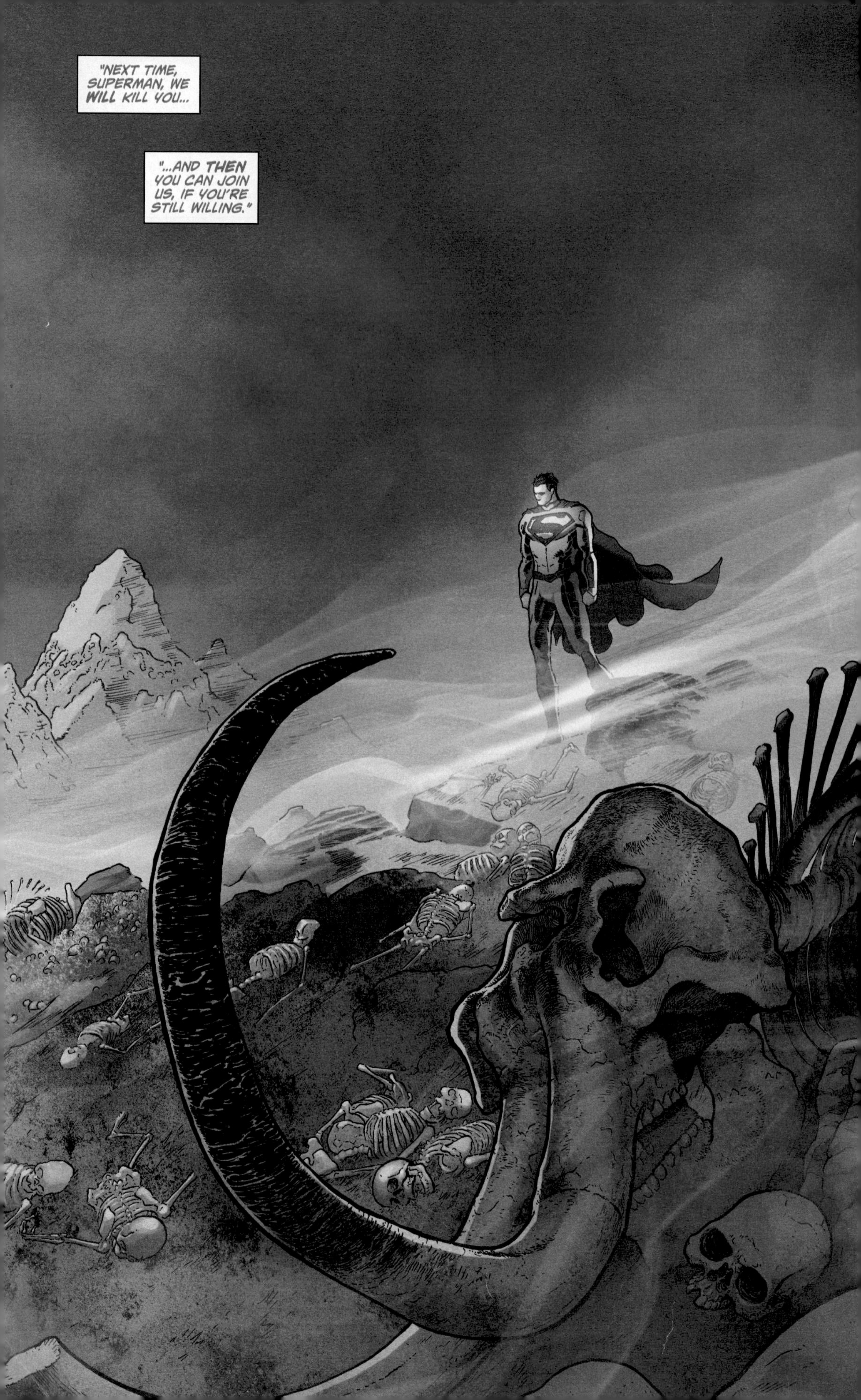
"NEXT TIME, SUPERMAN, WE WILL KILL YOU...
"...AND THEN YOU CAN JOIN US, IF YOU'RE STILL WILLING."

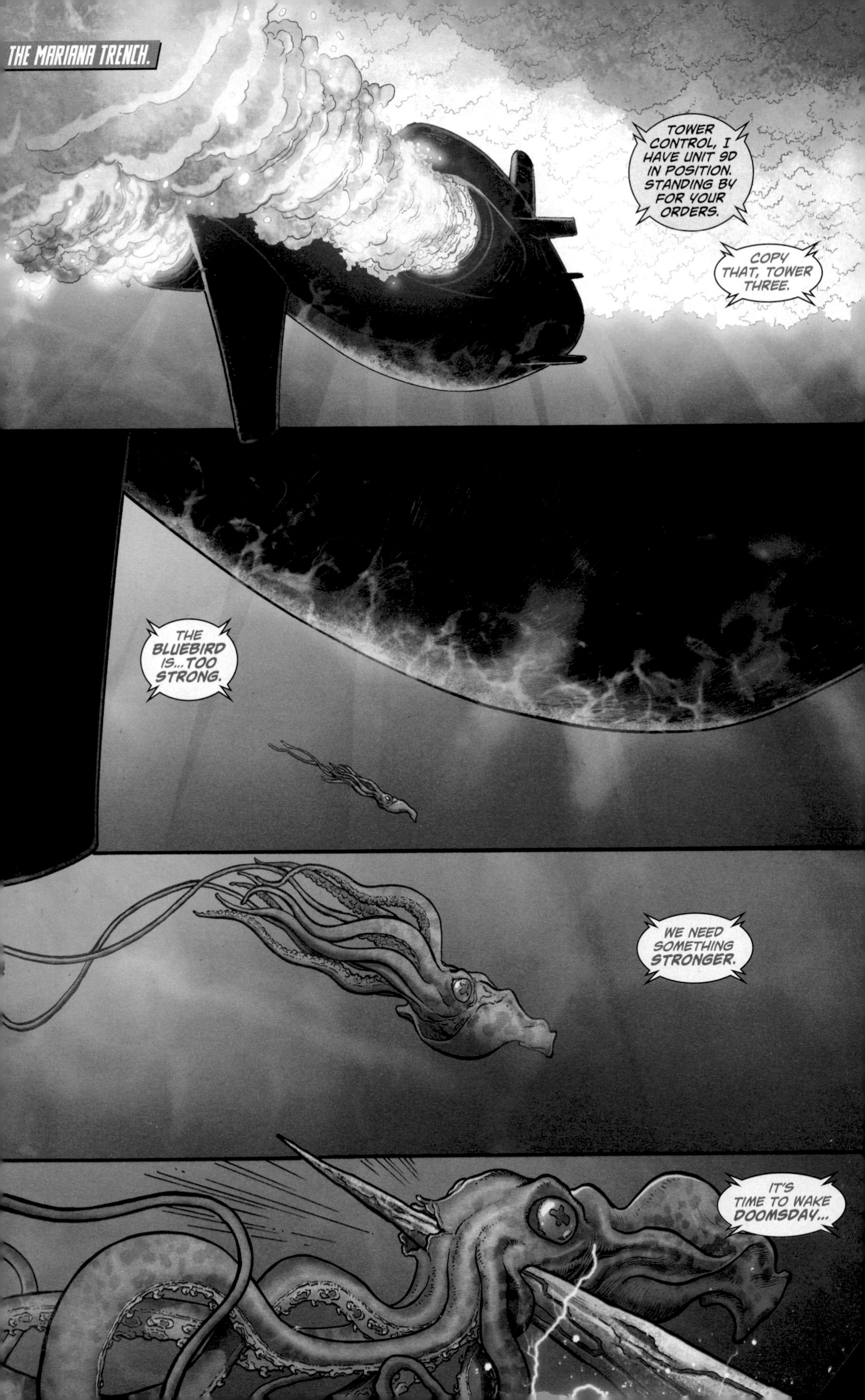
THE MARIANA TRENCH.
TOWER CONTROL, I HAVE UNIT 9D IN POSITION. STANDING BY FOR YOUR ORDERS.
COPY THAT, TOWER THREE.
THE BLUEBIRD IS...TOO STRONG.
WE NEED SOMETHING STRONGER.
IT'S TIME TO WAKE DOOMSDAY...

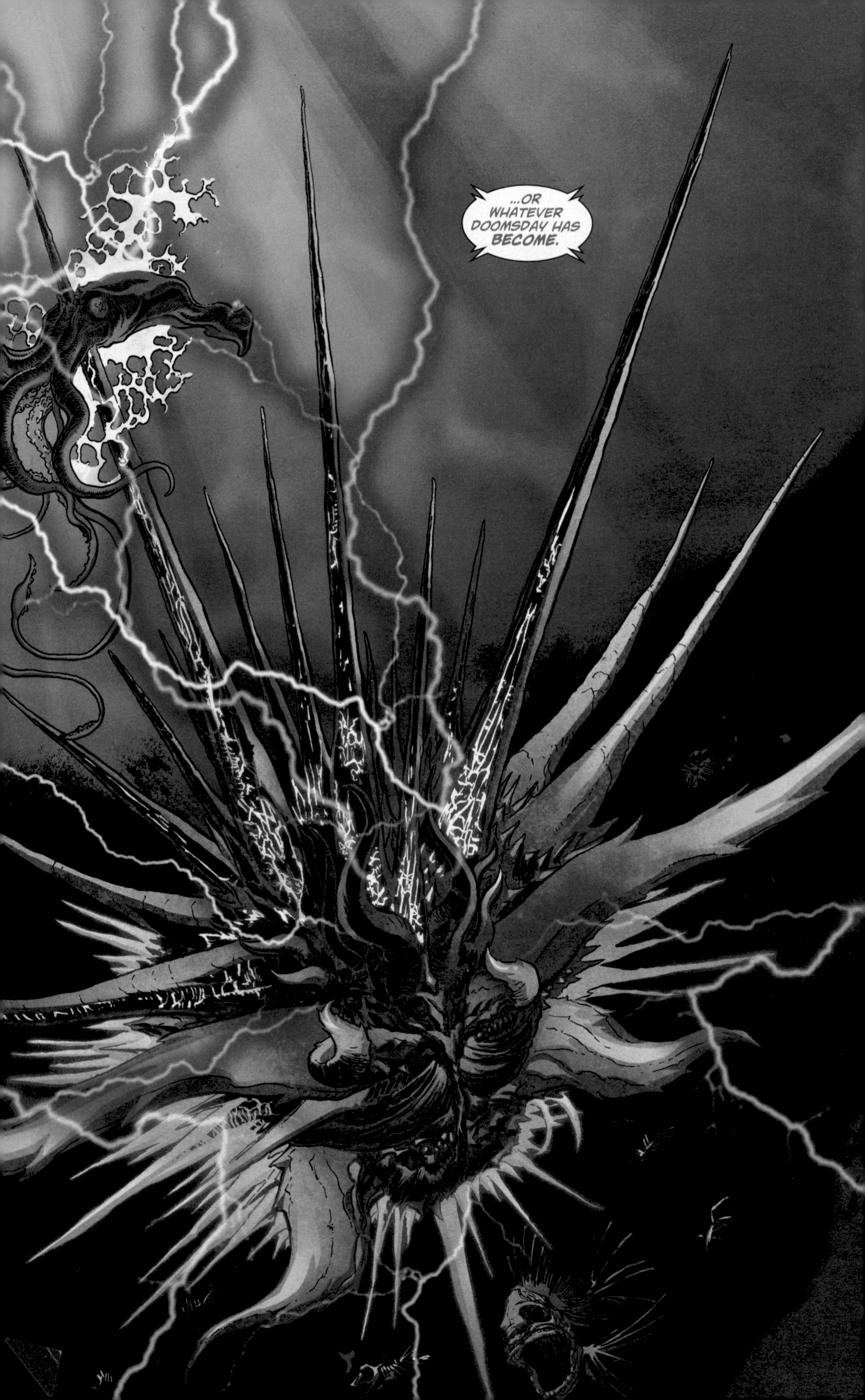
...OR WHATEVER DOOMSDAY HAS BECOME.

GREG PAK writer   AARON KUDER RAFA SANDOVAL CAMERON STEWART artists   VICENTE CIFUENTES inker   WIL QUINTANA colorist

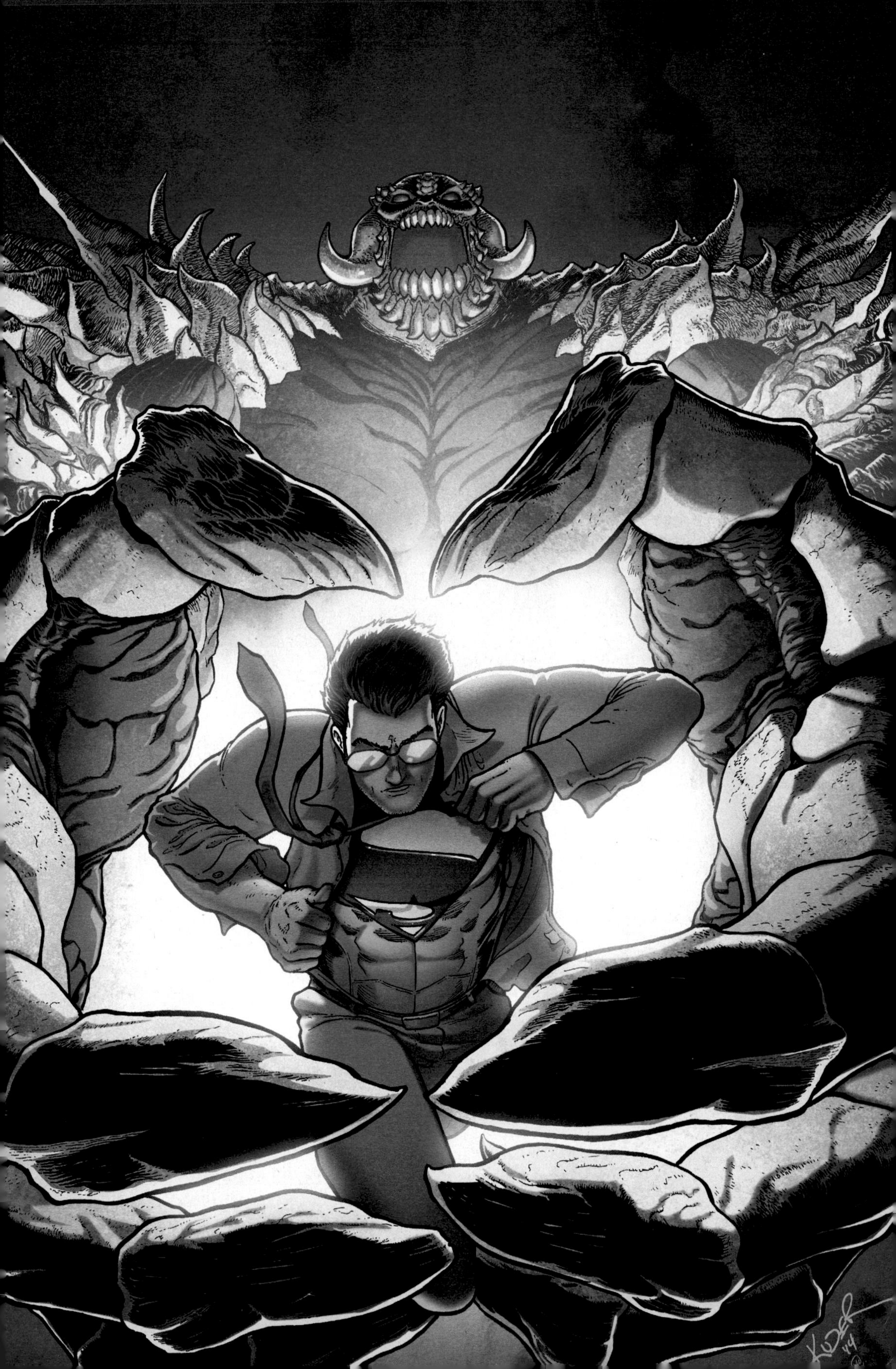

WORLD   U.S. METROPOLIS   BUSINESS   OPINION   SPORTS   ARTS   STYLE   VIDEO

Daily Planet

May 7, 201

DAILY PLANET

SUPERMAN DOOMED!

BY LOIS LANE

It was DOOMSDAY around the world, both figuratively and literally.

A massive creature of unknown origin resembling one that SUPERMAN fought once before appeared first in the Bahamas, subsequently in Botswana and then Mumbai, India, causing untold destruction.

Doctor Silas Stone, of S.T.A.R. Labs, had been tracking the creature after its initial appearance in the Bahamas.

Photo by James Olsen

Artist Rendition by Ken Lashley

"The creature was generating a corrosive force field that produced rapid biological decay in anything that came within its radius."

Efforts by world governments to stop the creature were unsuccessful.

Members of the Justice League looked to halt the rampaging monster's path of destruction by confronting it. The Man of Steel, in a display of brute force never before witnessed, eventually defeated the monster by tearing it apart.

This final battle took place in the midwestern town of Smallville, where a day before its citizens fell inexplicably into a coma. Experts theorize the event was linked to the appearance of the behemoth. However, the destruction of Doomsday has not revived them. And as Superman recovers from this epic struggle, everyone is wondering what effect this battle has had on the Last Son of Krypton himself.

Watch exclusive video footage of the destruction in the Bahamas.

"Doomsday" Origins
Recovery in the Northwestern Indies
Newly appointed Senator Sam Lane being considered at for "cleanup" in the U.S.

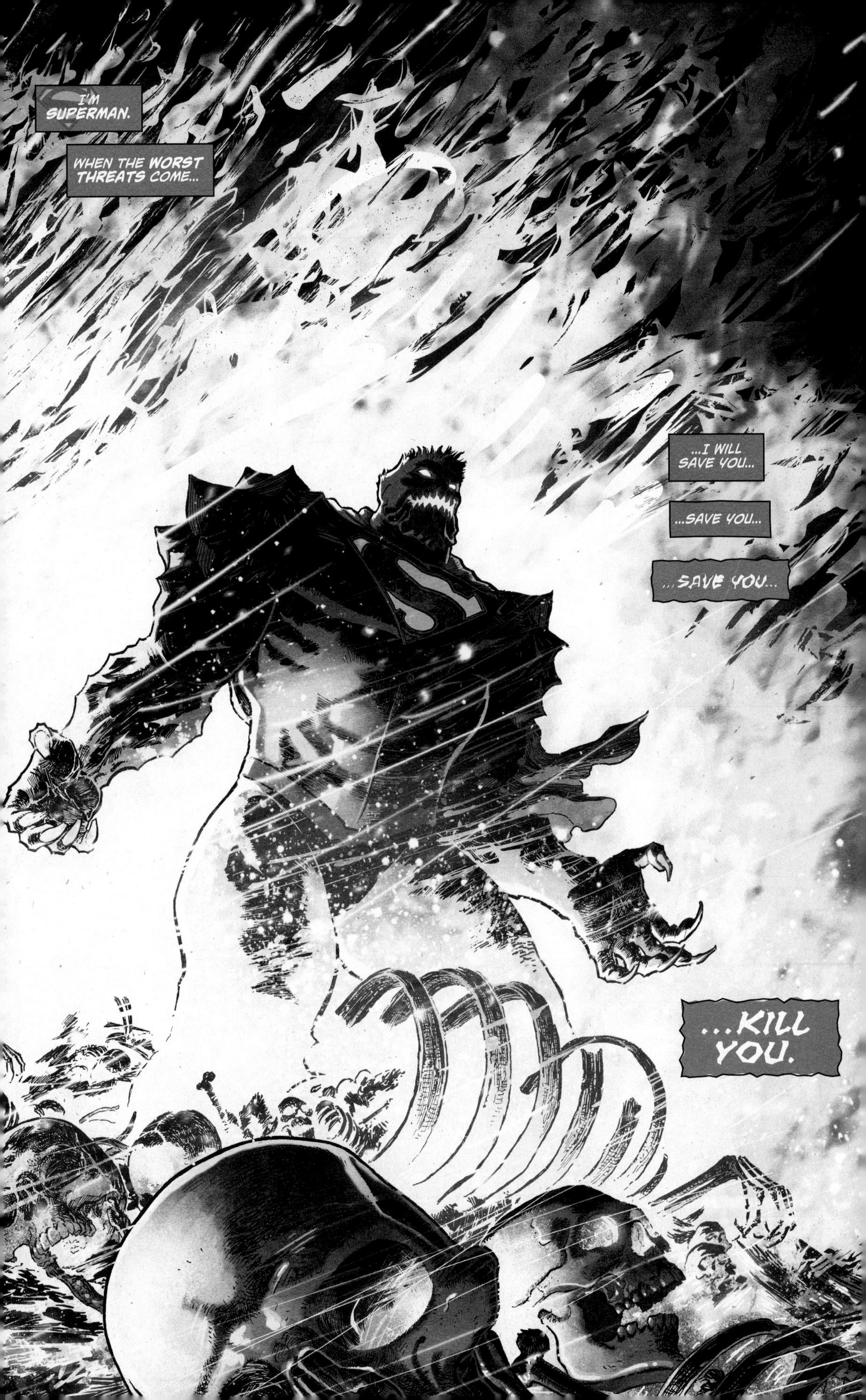
I'M SUPERMAN.
WHEN THE WORST THREATS COME...
...I WILL SAVE YOU...
...SAVE YOU...
...SAVE YOU...
...KILL YOU.

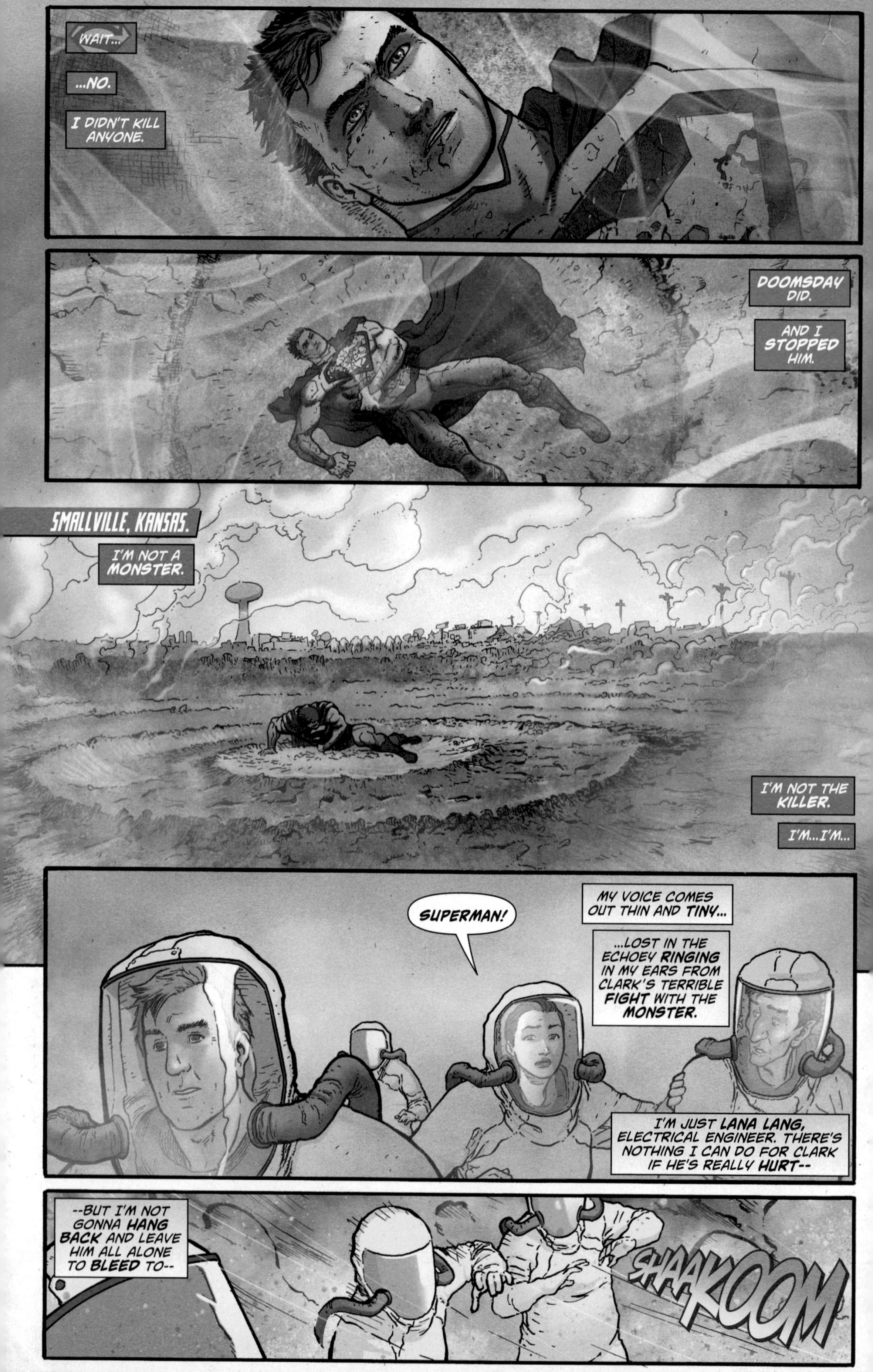
WAIT...
...NO.
I DIDN'T KILL ANYONE.
DOOMSDAY DID.
AND I STOPPED HIM.
SMALLVILLE, KANSAS.
I'M NOT A MONSTER.
I'M NOT THE KILLER.
I'M...I'M...
SUPERMAN!
MY VOICE COMES OUT THIN AND TINY...
...LOST IN THE ECHOEY RINGING IN MY EARS FROM CLARK'S TERRIBLE FIGHT WITH THE MONSTER.
I'M JUST LANA LANG, ELECTRICAL ENGINEER. THERE'S NOTHING I CAN DO FOR CLARK IF HE'S REALLY HURT--
--BUT I'M NOT GONNA HANG BACK AND LEAVE HIM ALL ALONE TO BLEED TO--
SHAAKOOM

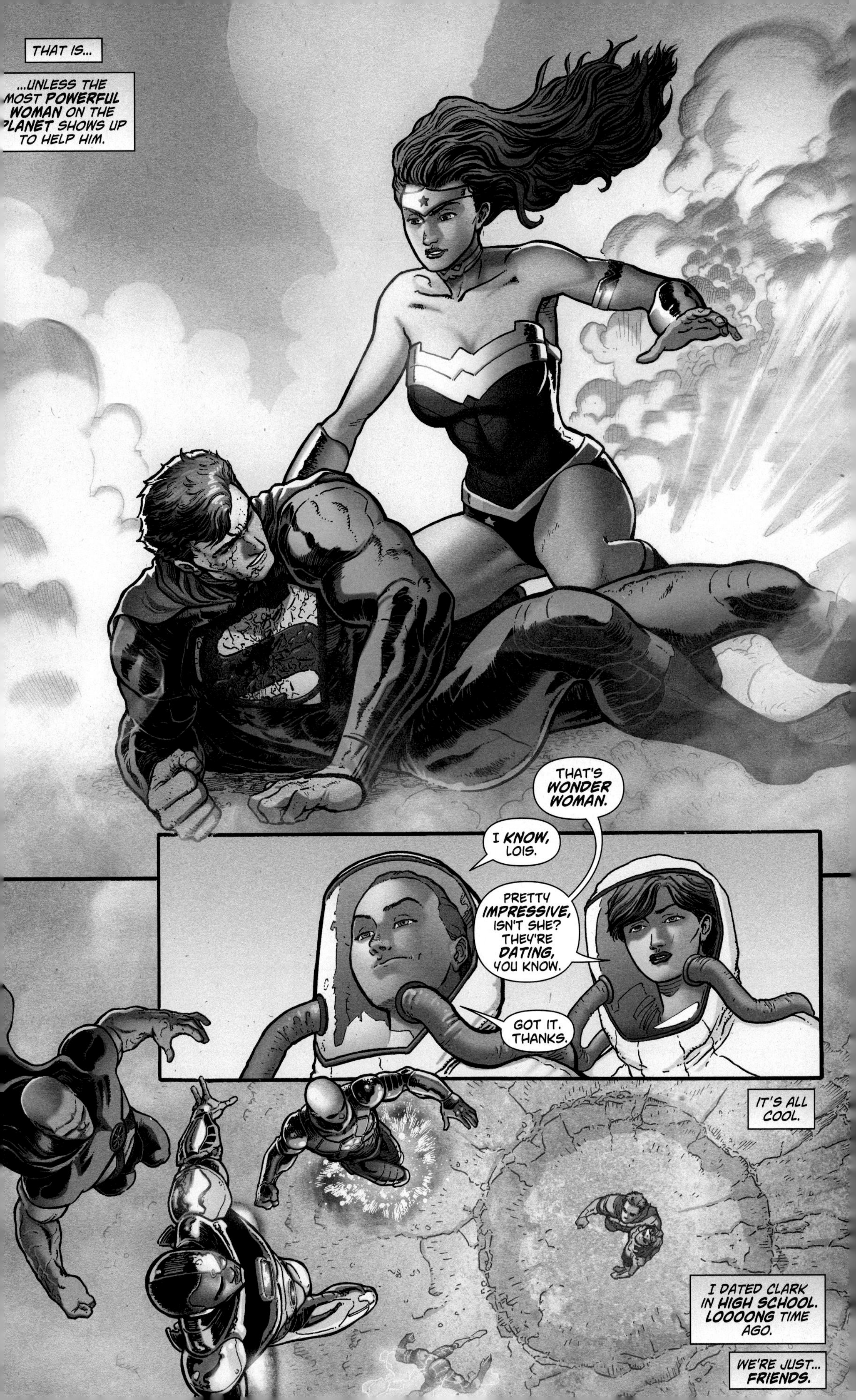

THAT IS...
...UNLESS THE MOST POWERFUL WOMAN ON THE PLANET SHOWS UP TO HELP HIM.
THAT'S WONDER WOMAN.
I KNOW, LOIS.
PRETTY IMPRESSIVE, ISN'T SHE? THEY'RE DATING, YOU KNOW.
GOT IT. THANKS.
IT'S ALL COOL.
I DATED CLARK IN HIGH SCHOOL. LOOOONG TIME AGO.
WE'RE JUST... FRIENDS.

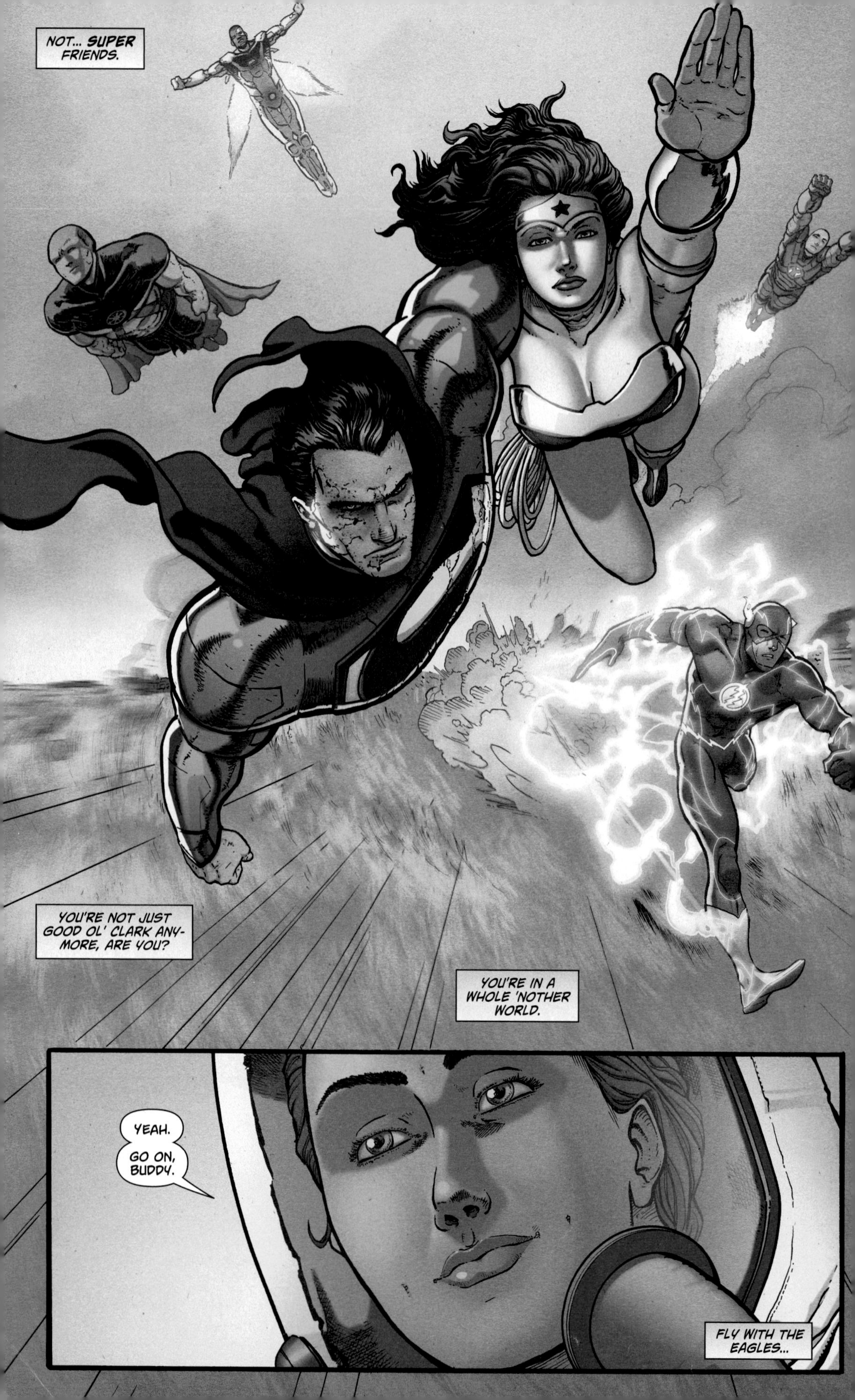
NOT... SUPER FRIENDS.
YOU'RE NOT JUST GOOD OL' CLARK ANY-MORE, ARE YOU?
YOU'RE IN A WHOLE 'NOTHER WORLD.
YEAH.
GO ON, BUDDY.
FLY WITH THE EAGLES...

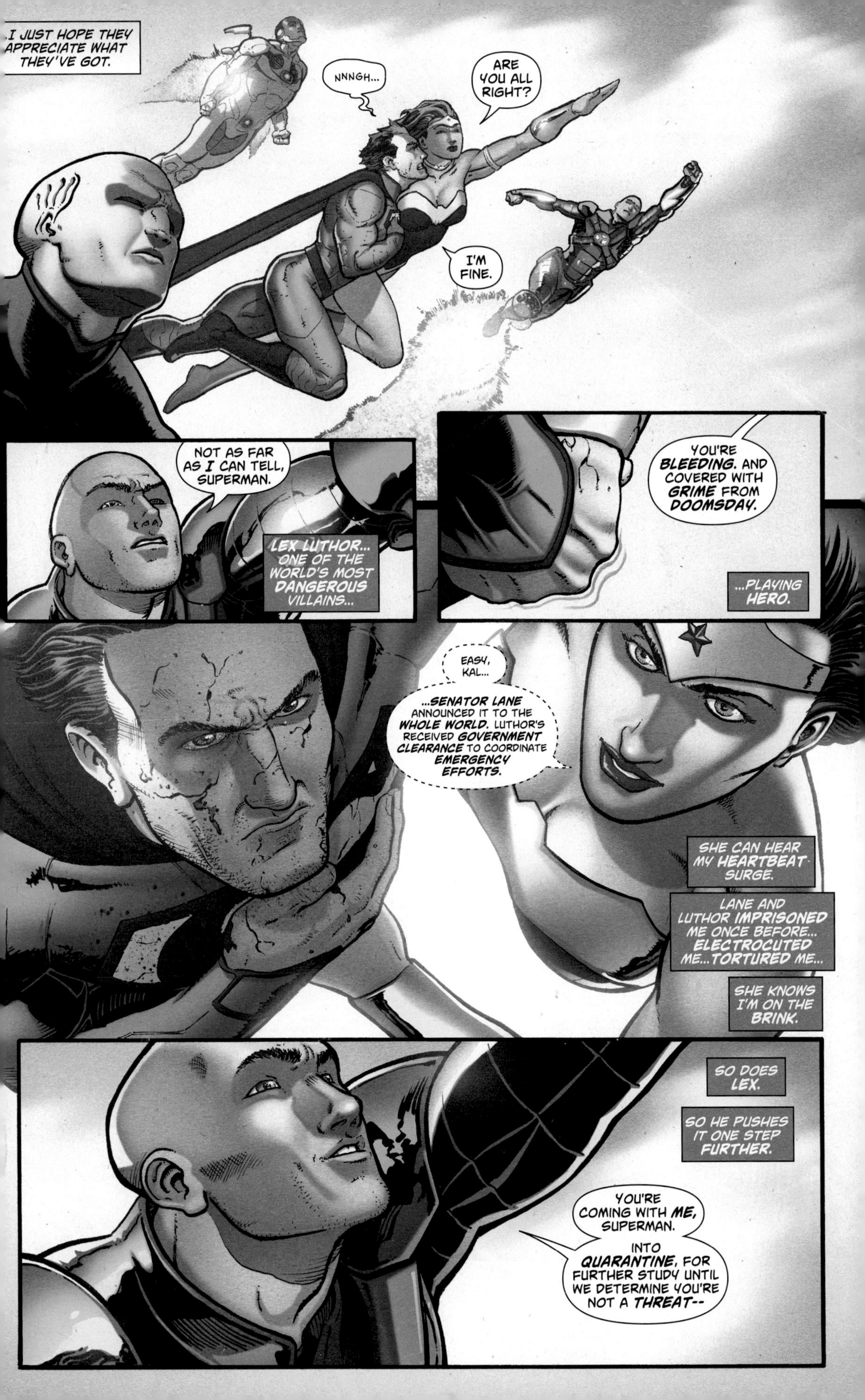

I JUST HOPE THEY APPRECIATE WHAT THEY'VE GOT.
NNNGH...
ARE YOU ALL RIGHT?
I'M FINE.
NOT AS FAR AS I CAN TELL, SUPERMAN.
LEX LUTHOR... ONE OF THE WORLD'S MOST DANGEROUS VILLAINS...
YOU'RE BLEEDING. AND COVERED WITH GRIME FROM DOOMSDAY.
...PLAYING HERO.
EASY, KAL...
...SENATOR LANE ANNOUNCED IT TO THE WHOLE WORLD. LUTHOR'S RECEIVED GOVERNMENT CLEARANCE TO COORDINATE EMERGENCY EFFORTS.
SHE CAN HEAR MY HEARTBEAT SURGE.
LANE AND LUTHOR IMPRISONED ME ONCE BEFORE... ELECTROCUTED ME...TORTURED ME...
SHE KNOWS I'M ON THE BRINK.
SO DOES LEX.
SO HE PUSHES IT ONE STEP FURTHER.
YOU'RE COMING WITH ME, SUPERMAN.
INTO QUARANTINE, FOR FURTHER STUDY UNTIL WE DETERMINE YOU'RE NOT A THREAT--

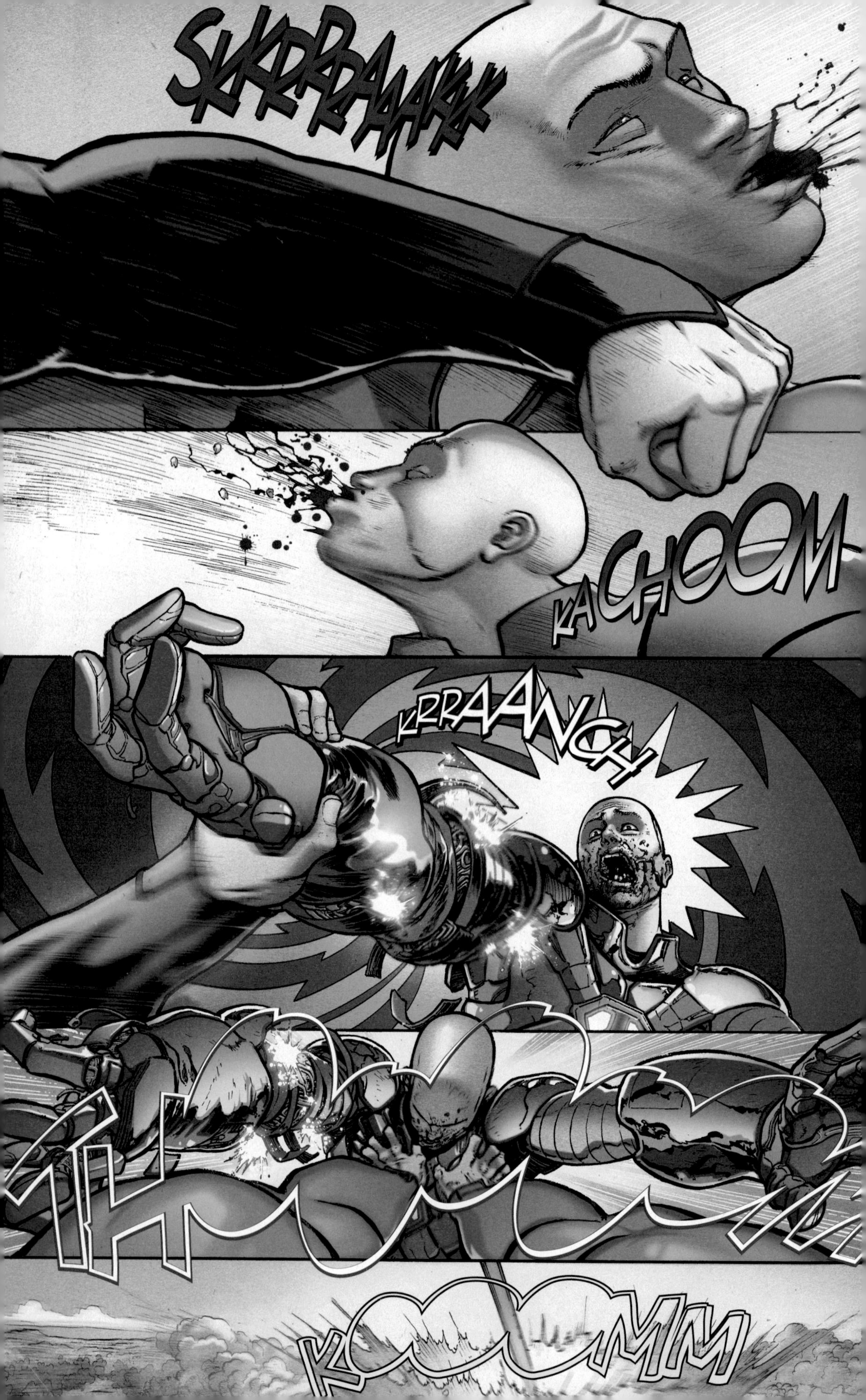
SKKRRBRAAKKK
KACHOOM
KRRAANCH
THUUUUM
KOOOMM

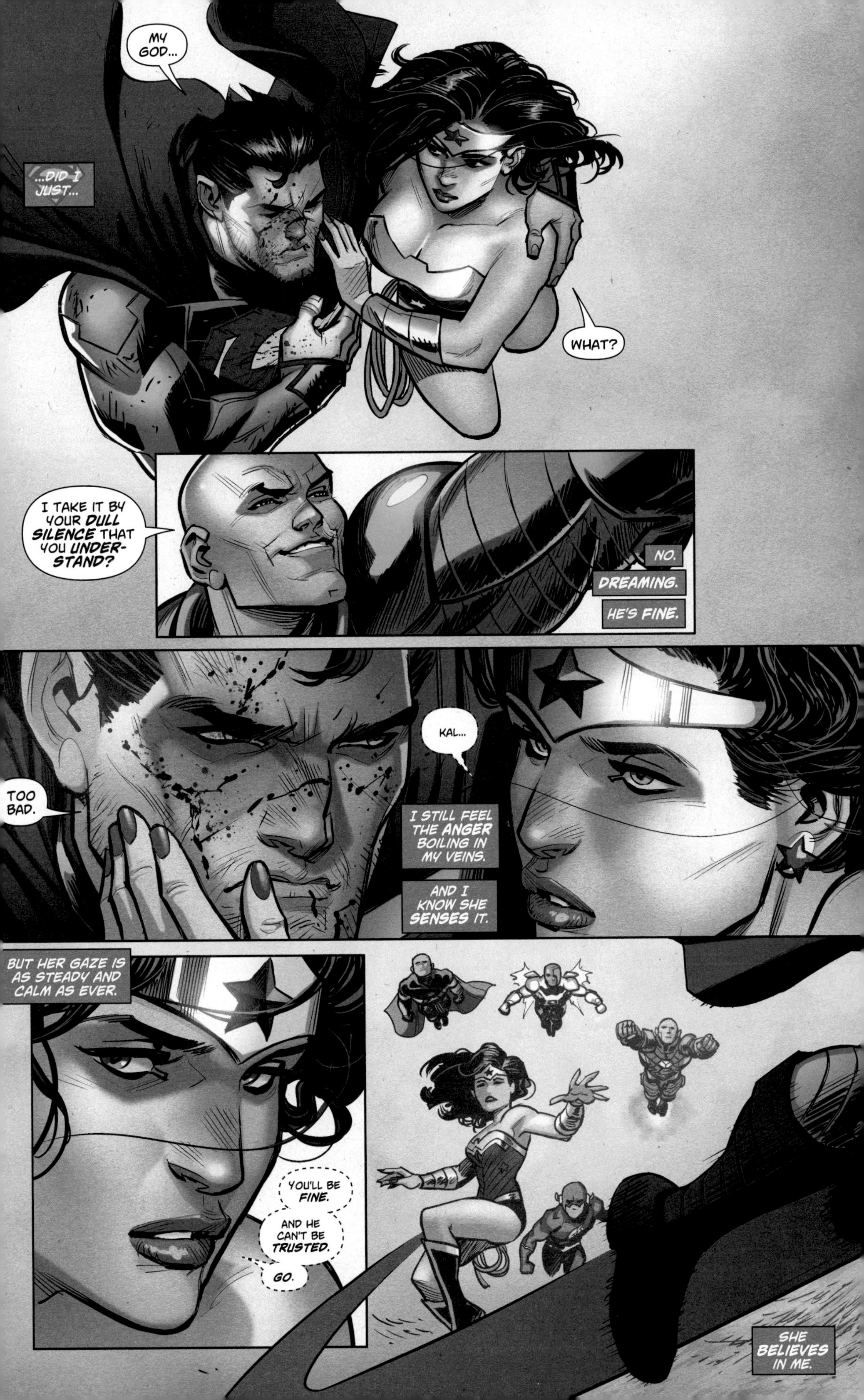
MY GOD...
...DID I JUST...
WHAT?
I TAKE IT BY YOUR DULL SILENCE THAT YOU UNDER-STAND?
NO.
DREAMING.
HE'S FINE.
KAL...
TOO BAD.
I STILL FEEL THE ANGER BOILING IN MY VEINS.
AND I KNOW SHE SENSES IT.
BUT HER GAZE IS AS STEADY AND CALM AS EVER.
YOU'LL BE FINE.
AND HE CAN'T BE TRUSTED.
GO.
SHE BELIEVES IN ME.

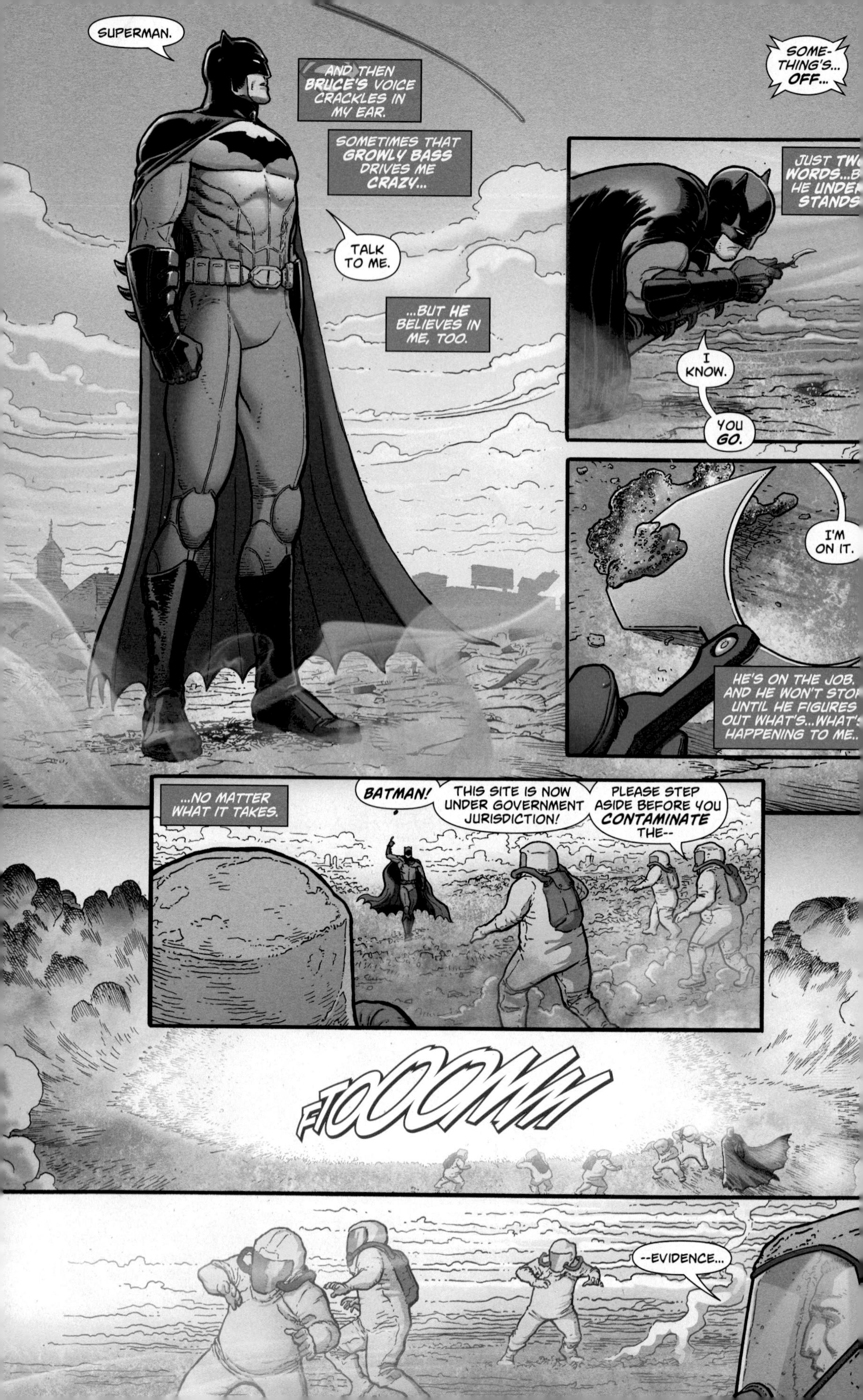

SUPERMAN.
AND THEN BRUCE'S VOICE CRACKLES IN MY EAR.
SOMETIMES THAT GROWLY BASS DRIVES ME CRAZY...
TALK TO ME.
...BUT HE BELIEVES IN ME, TOO.
SOME-THING'S... OFF...
I KNOW.
YOU GO.
I'M ON IT.
HE'S ON THE JOB. AND HE WON'T STO UNTIL HE FIGURES OUT WHAT'S...WHAT' HAPPENING TO ME..
...NO MATTER WHAT IT TAKES.
BATMAN!
THIS SITE IS NOW UNDER GOVERNMENT JURISDICTION!
PLEASE STEP ASIDE BEFORE YOU CONTAMINATE THE--
FTOOOMM
--EVIDENCE...

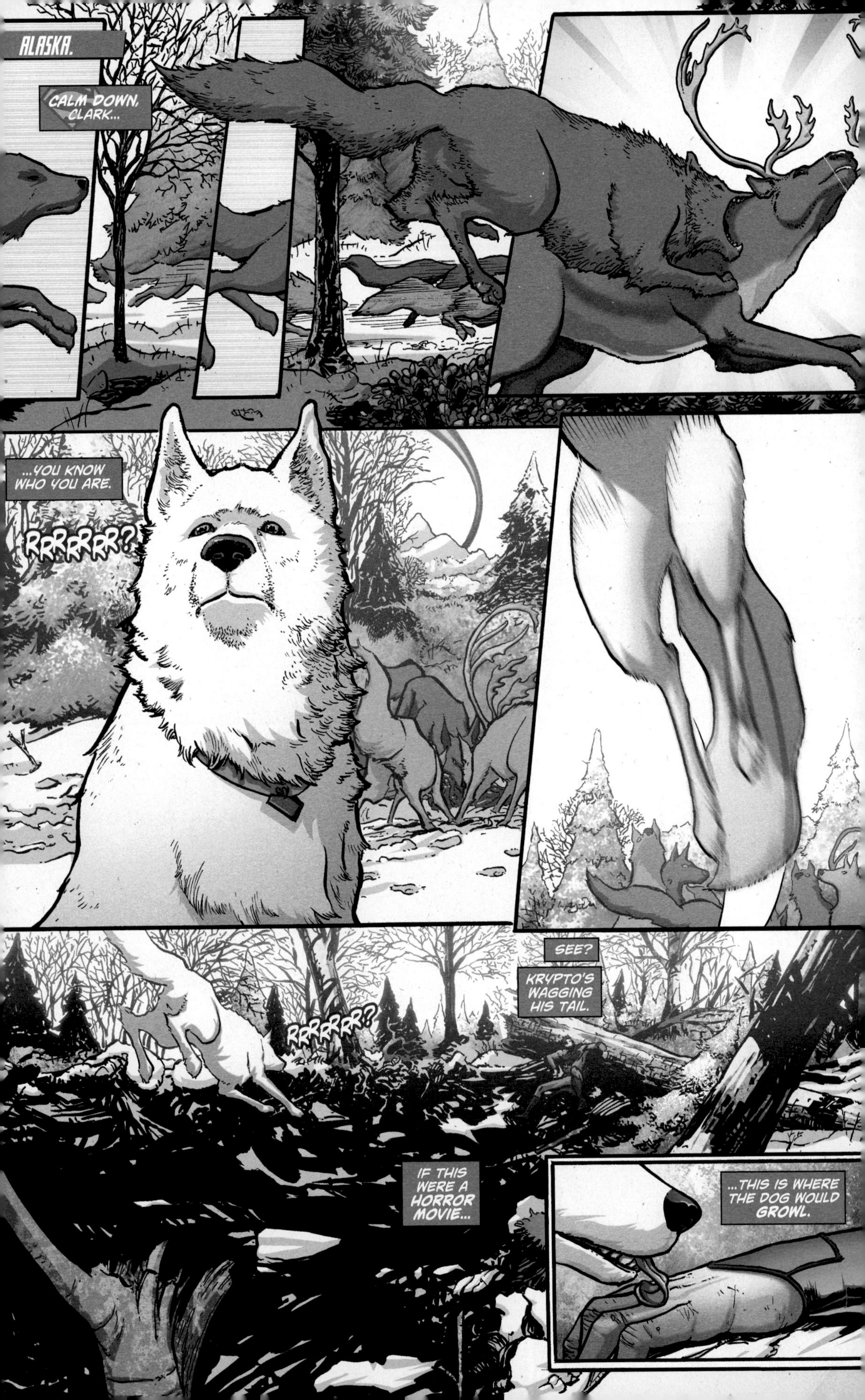
ALASKA.
CALM DOWN, CLARK...
...YOU KNOW WHO YOU ARE.
RRRRRRR?
SEE?
KRYPTO'S WAGGING HIS TAIL.
RRRRRRR?
IF THIS WERE A HORROR MOVIE...
...THIS IS WHERE THE DOG WOULD GROWL.

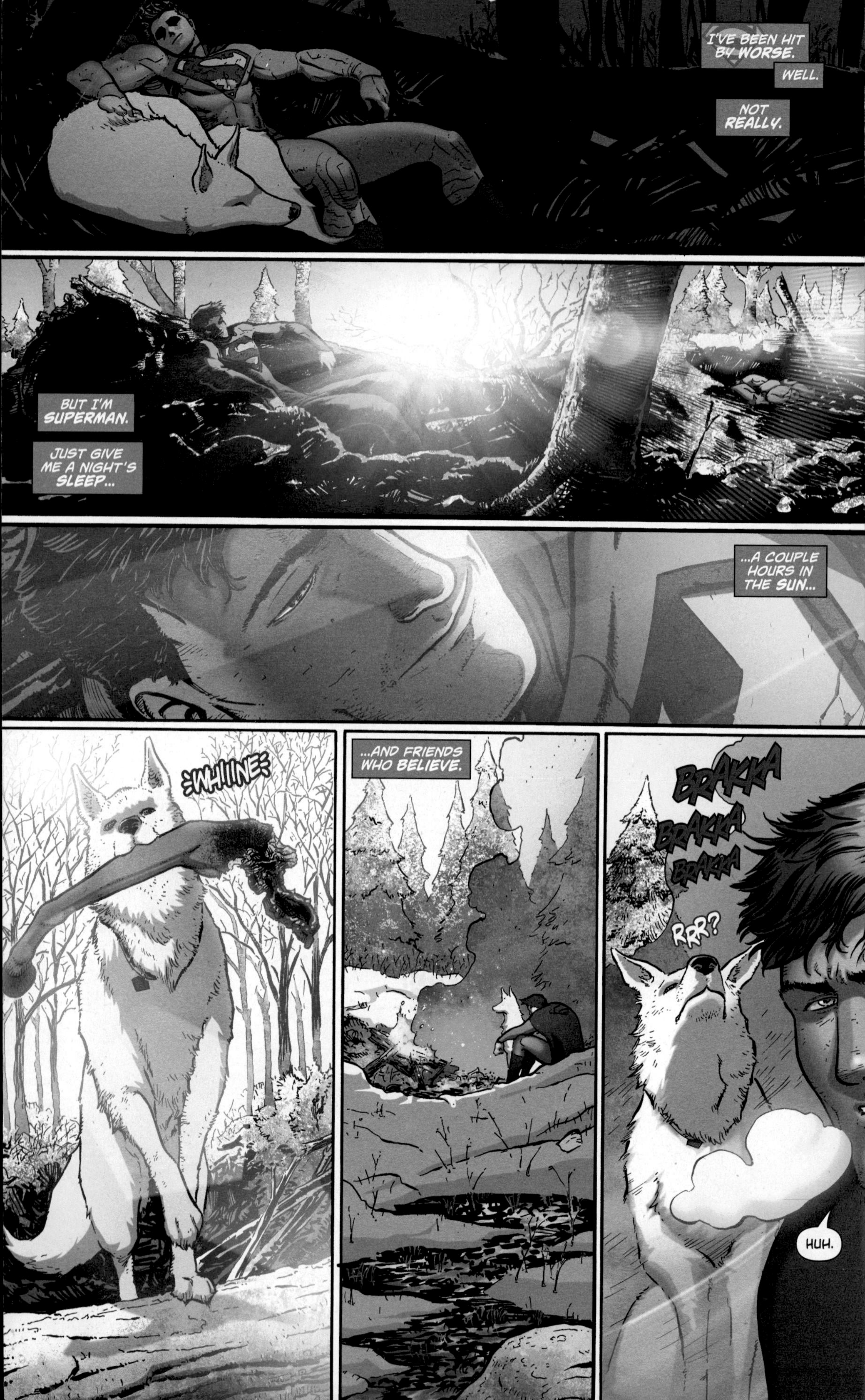
I'VE BEEN HIT BY WORSE.
WELL.
NOT REALLY.
BUT I'M SUPERMAN.
JUST GIVE ME A NIGHT'S SLEEP...
...A COUPLE HOURS IN THE SUN...
WHIIINE
...AND FRIENDS WHO BELIEVE.
BRAKKA
BRAKKA
BRAKKA
RRR?
HUH.

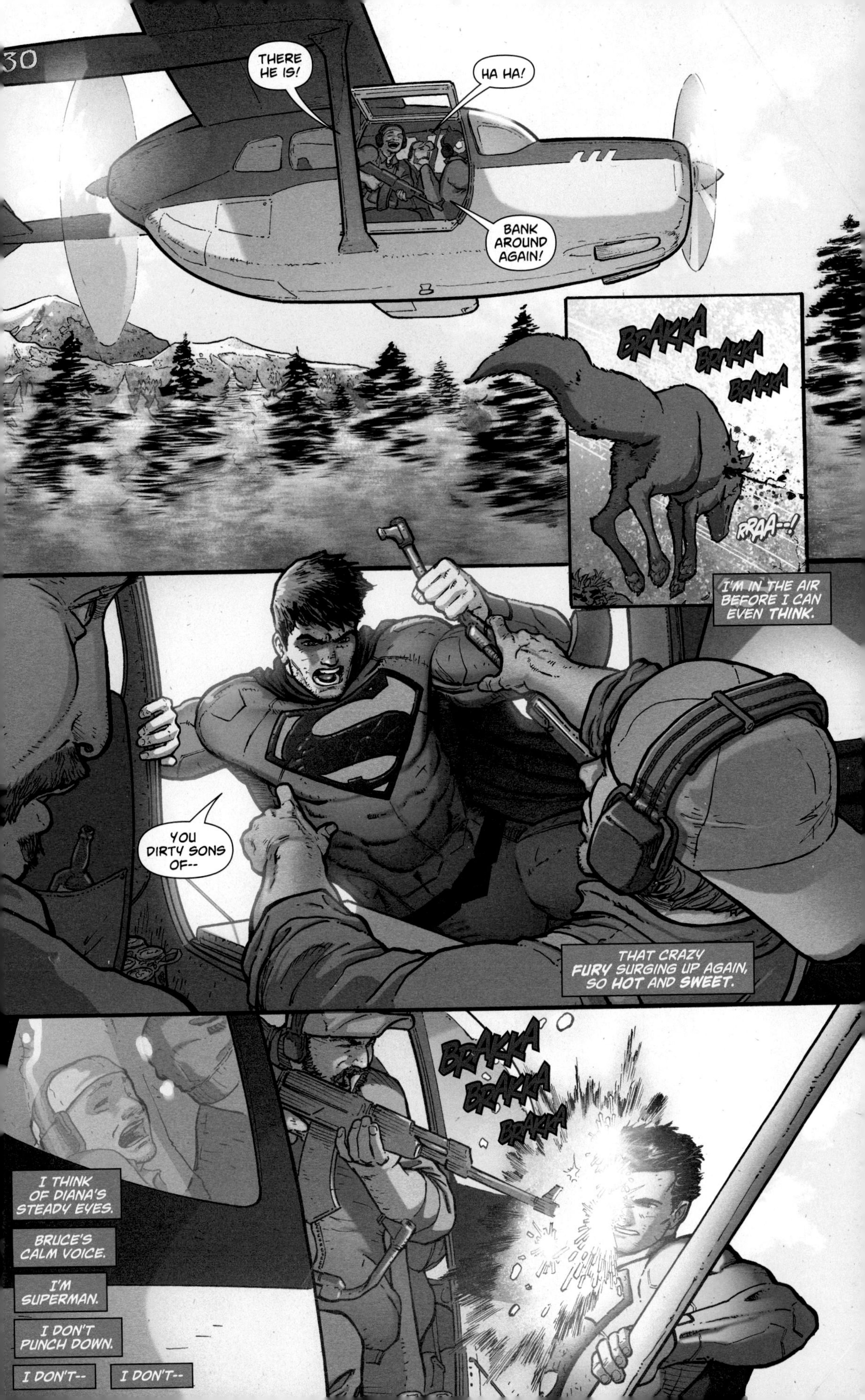
THERE HE IS!
HA HA!
BANK AROUND AGAIN!
BRAKKA BRAKKA BRAKKA
RRAA--!
I'M IN THE AIR BEFORE I CAN EVEN THINK.
YOU DIRTY SONS OF--
THAT CRAZY FURY SURGING UP AGAIN, SO HOT AND SWEET.
BRAKKA BRAKKA BRAKKA
I THINK OF DIANA'S STEADY EYES.
BRUCE'S CALM VOICE.
I'M SUPERMAN.
I DON'T PUNCH DOWN.
I DON'T--
I DON'T--

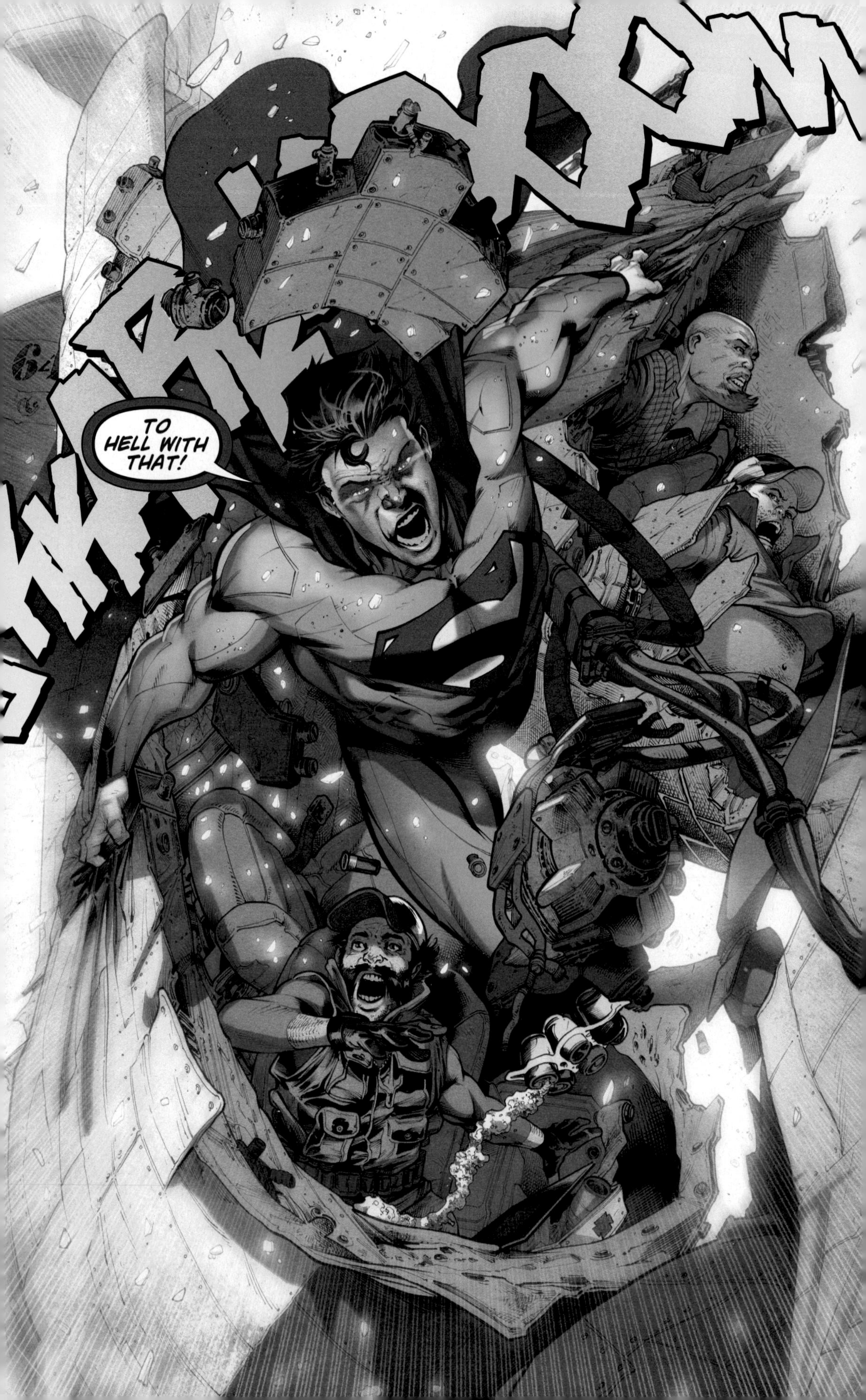
TO HELL WITH THAT!

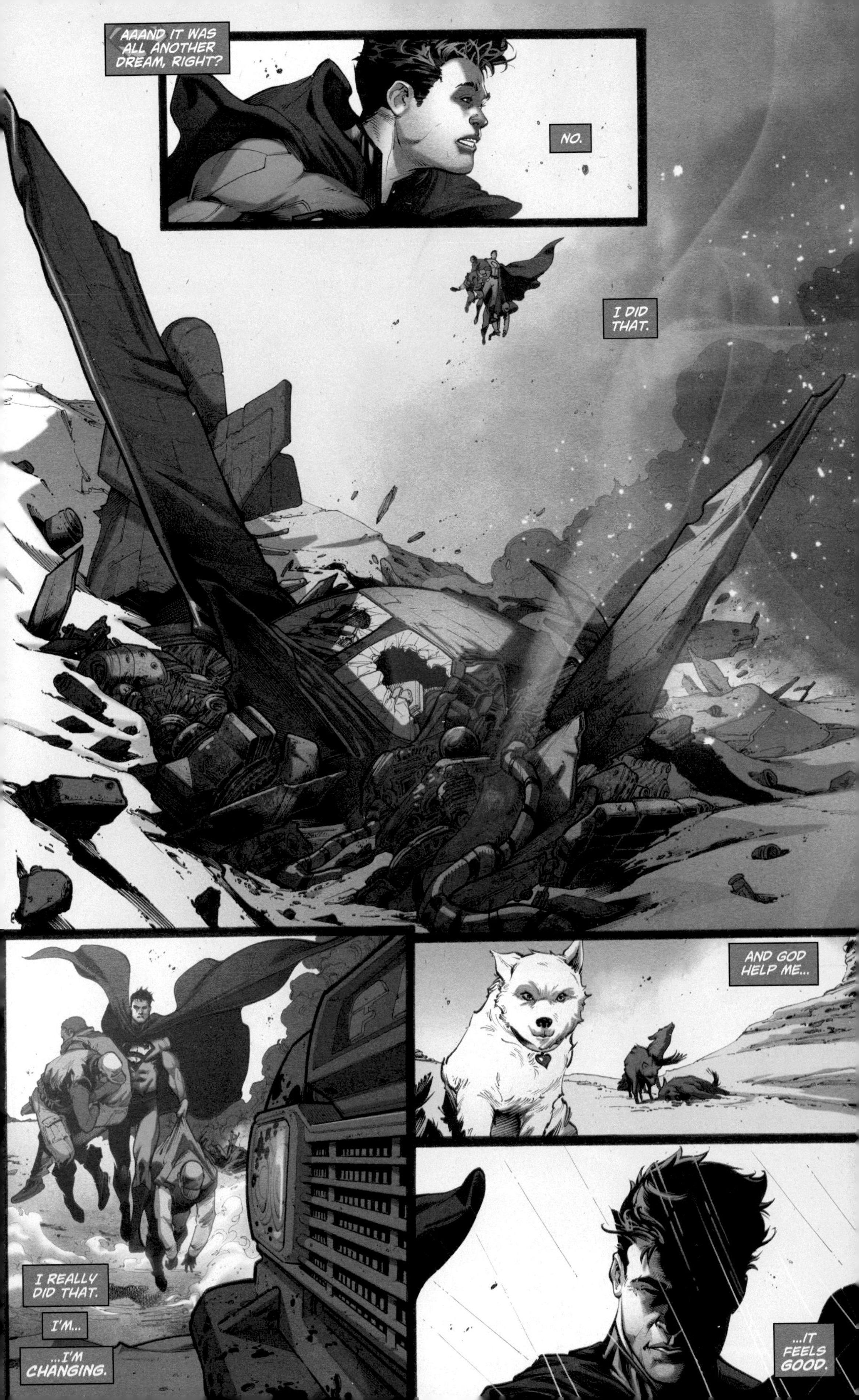
AAAND IT WAS ALL ANOTHER DREAM, RIGHT?
NO.
I DID THAT.
I REALLY DID THAT.
I'M...
...I'M CHANGING.
AND GOD HELP ME...
...IT FEELS GOOD.

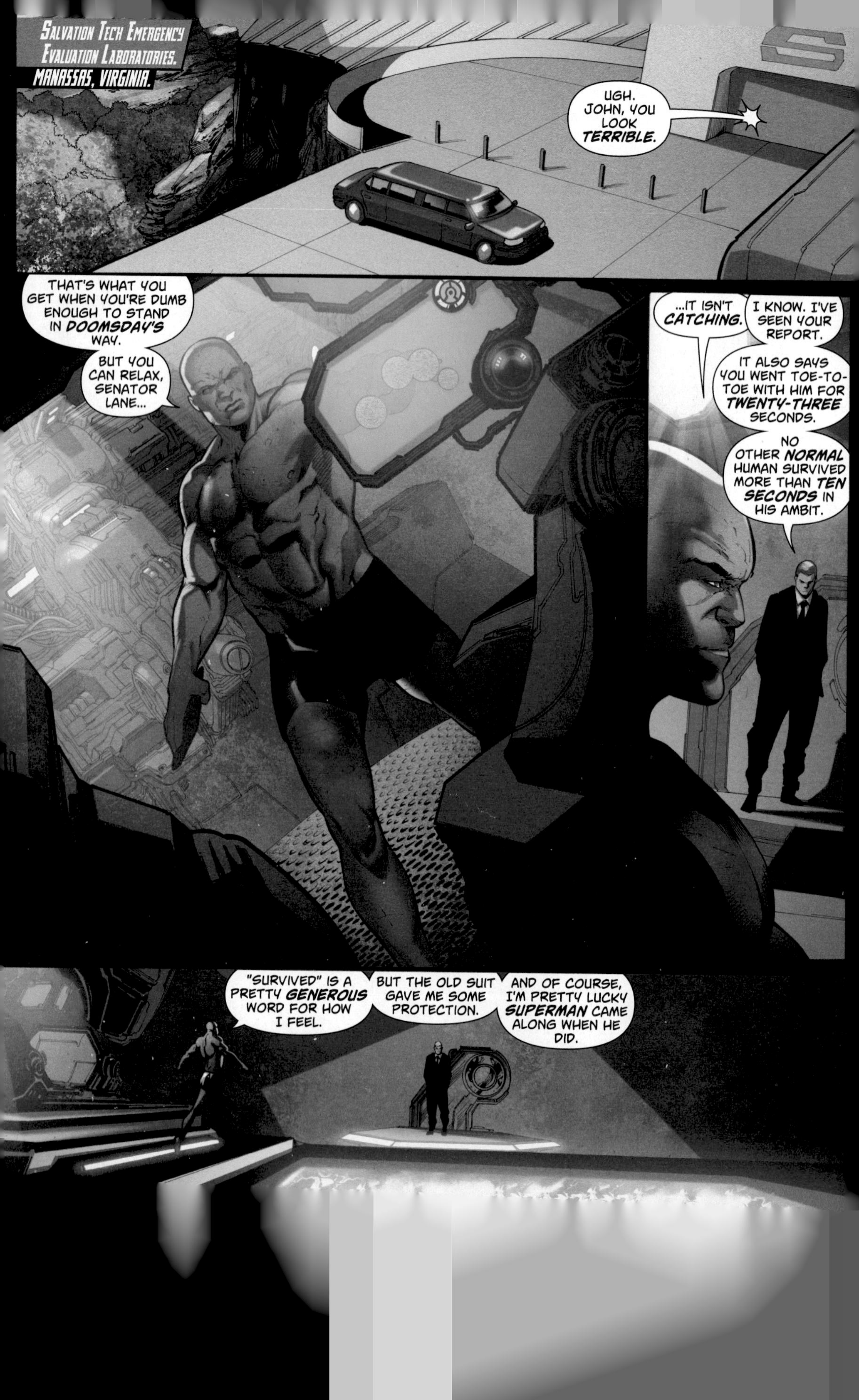
SALVATION TECH EMERGENCY EVALUATION LABORATORIES. MANASSAS, VIRGINIA.
UGH. JOHN, YOU LOOK TERRIBLE.
THAT'S WHAT YOU GET WHEN YOU'RE DUMB ENOUGH TO STAND IN DOOMSDAY'S WAY.
BUT YOU CAN RELAX, SENATOR LANE...
...IT ISN'T CATCHING.
I KNOW. I'VE SEEN YOUR REPORT.
IT ALSO SAYS YOU WENT TOE-TO-TOE WITH HIM FOR TWENTY-THREE SECONDS.
NO OTHER NORMAL HUMAN SURVIVED MORE THAN TEN SECONDS IN HIS AMBIT.
"SURVIVED" IS A PRETTY GENEROUS WORD FOR HOW I FEEL.
BUT THE OLD SUIT GAVE ME SOME PROTECTION.
AND OF COURSE, I'M PRETTY LUCKY SUPERMAN CAME ALONG WHEN HE DID.

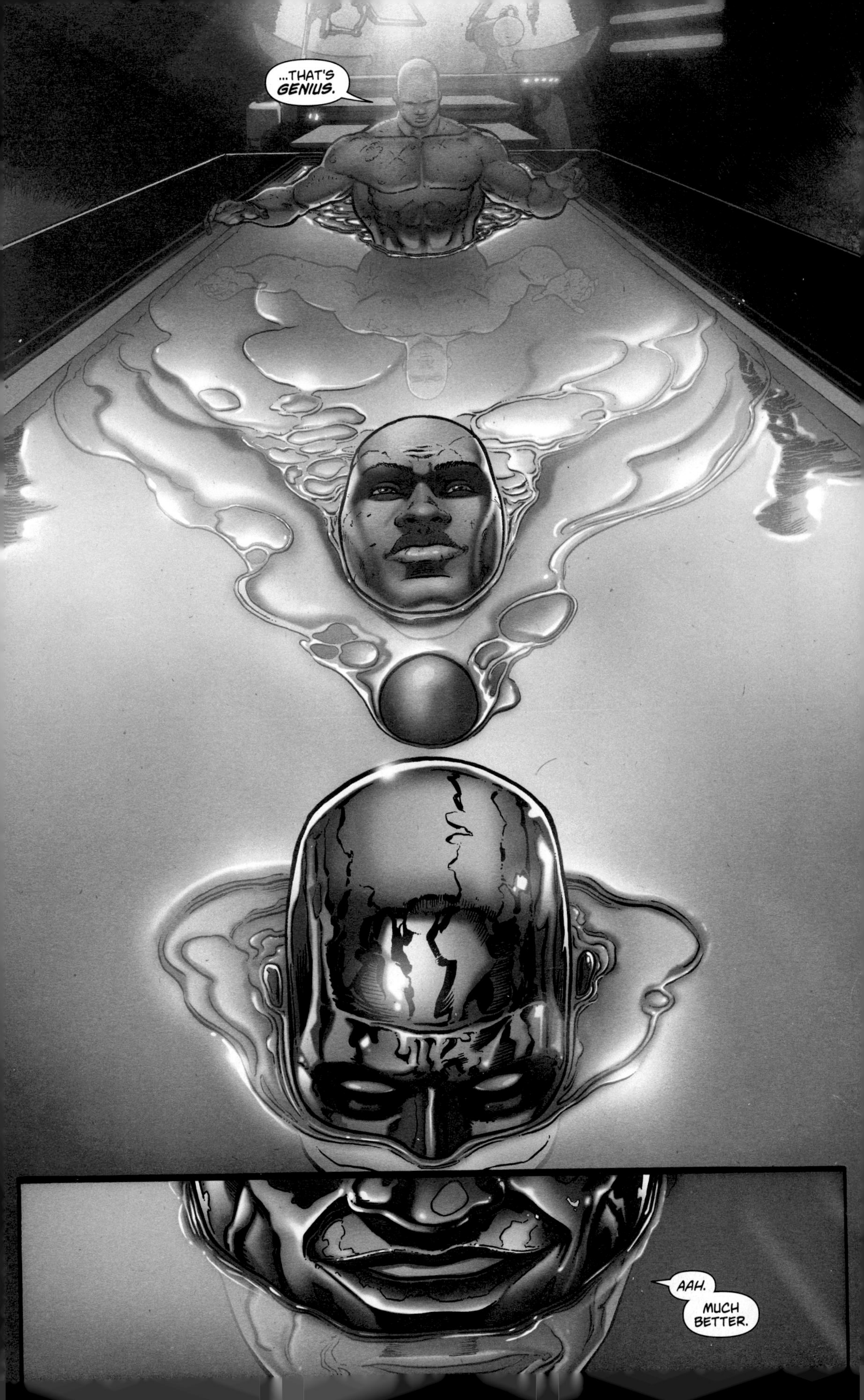
...THAT'S GENIUS.
AAH.
MUCH BETTER.

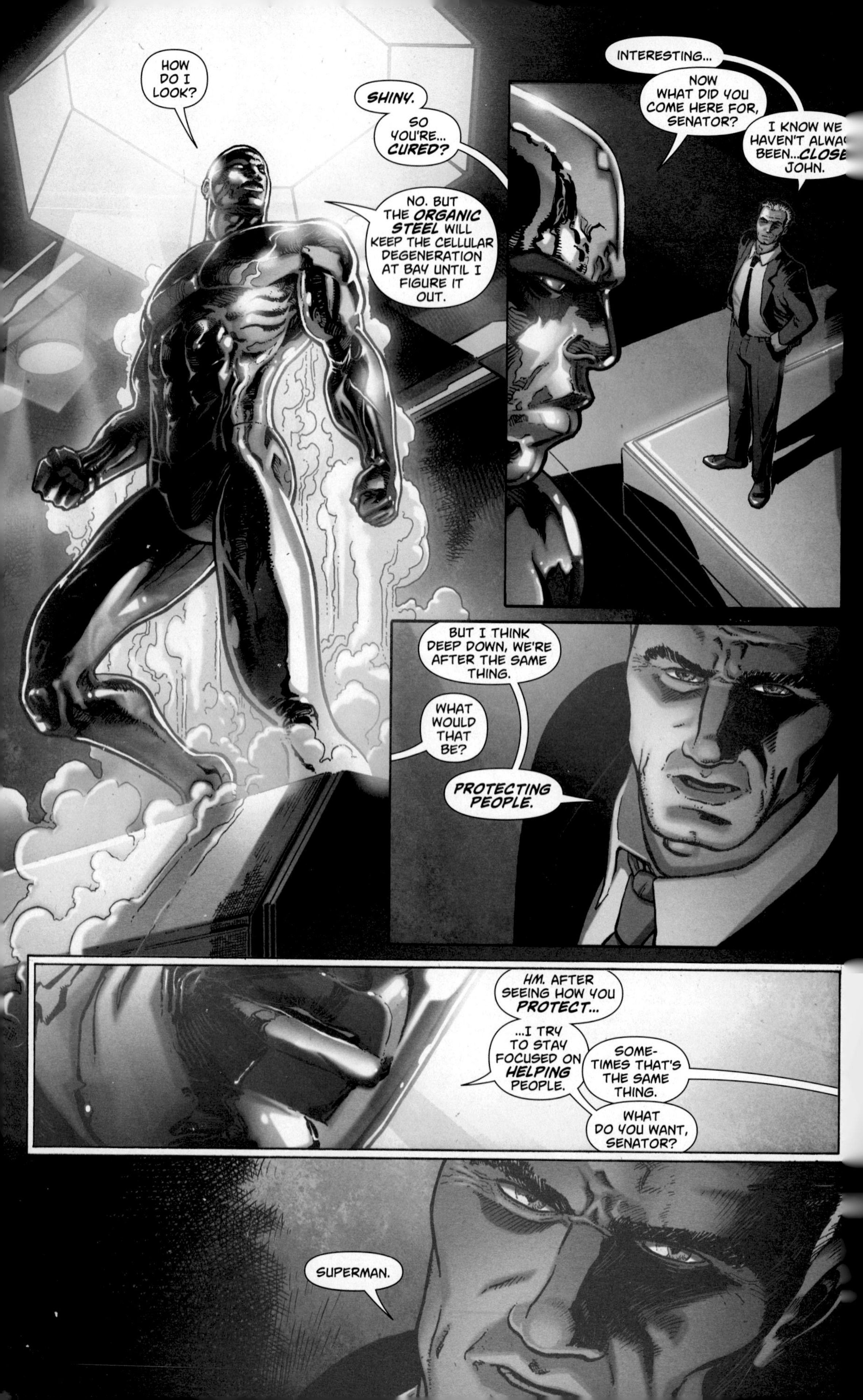
HOW DO I LOOK?
SHINY.
SO YOU'RE... CURED?
NO. BUT THE ORGANIC STEEL WILL KEEP THE CELLULAR DEGENERATION AT BAY UNTIL I FIGURE IT OUT.
INTERESTING...
NOW WHAT DID YOU COME HERE FOR, SENATOR?
I KNOW WE HAVEN'T ALWA BEEN...CLOSE JOHN.
BUT I THINK DEEP DOWN, WE'RE AFTER THE SAME THING.
WHAT WOULD THAT BE?
PROTECTING PEOPLE.
HM. AFTER SEEING HOW YOU PROTECT...
...I TRY TO STAY FOCUSED ON HELPING PEOPLE.
SOME-TIMES THAT'S THE SAME THING.
WHAT DO YOU WANT, SENATOR?
SUPERMAN.

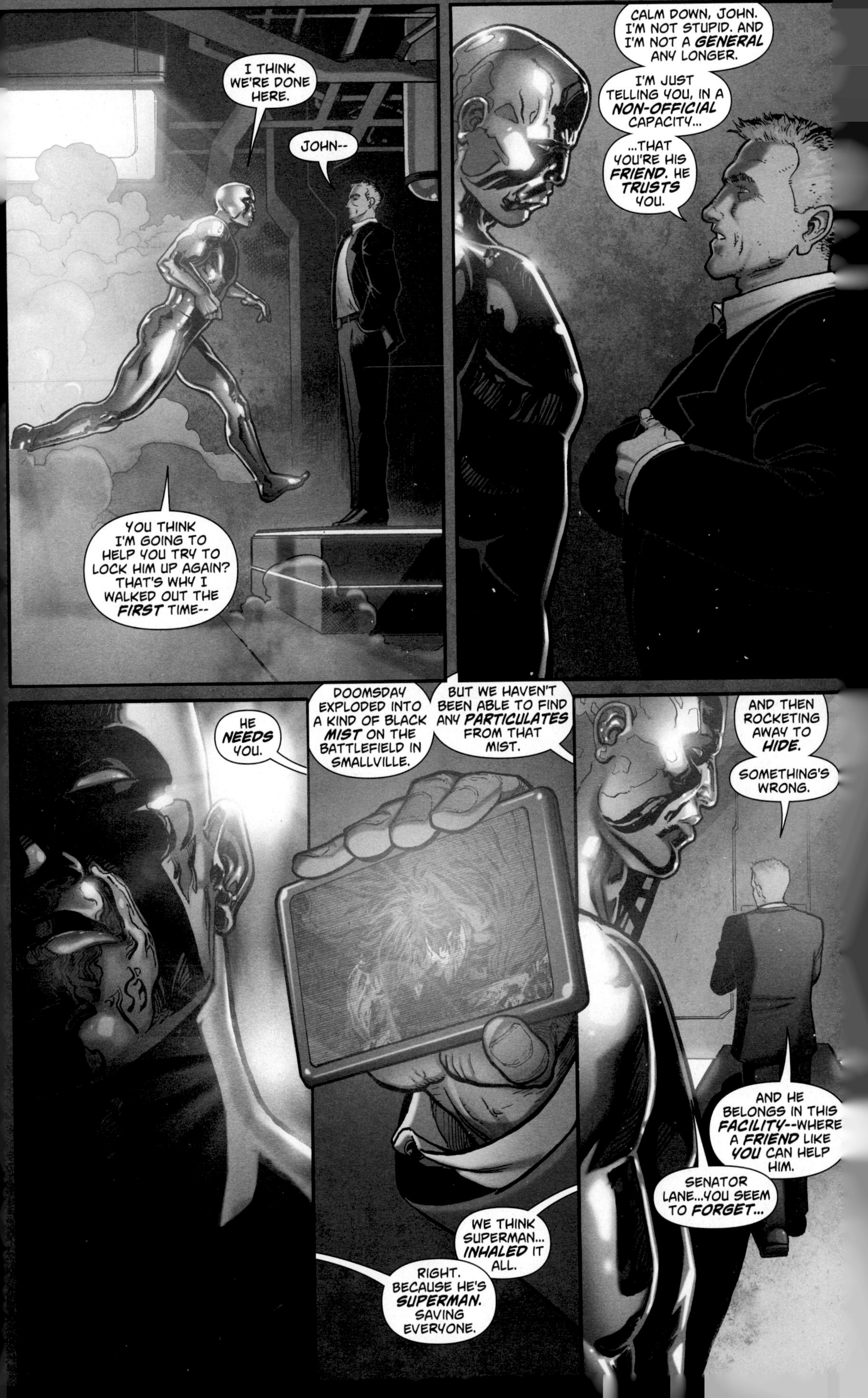
I THINK WE'RE DONE HERE.
JOHN--
YOU THINK I'M GOING TO HELP YOU TRY TO LOCK HIM UP AGAIN? THAT'S WHY I WALKED OUT THE FIRST TIME--
CALM DOWN, JOHN. I'M NOT STUPID. AND I'M NOT A GENERAL ANY LONGER.
I'M JUST TELLING YOU, IN A NON-OFFICIAL CAPACITY...
...THAT YOU'RE HIS FRIEND. HE TRUSTS YOU.
HE NEEDS YOU.
DOOMSDAY EXPLODED INTO A KIND OF BLACK MIST ON THE BATTLEFIELD IN SMALLVILLE.
BUT WE HAVEN'T BEEN ABLE TO FIND ANY PARTICULATES FROM THAT MIST.
WE THINK SUPERMAN... INHALED IT ALL.
RIGHT. BECAUSE HE'S SUPERMAN. SAVING EVERYONE.
AND THEN ROCKETING AWAY TO HIDE.
SOMETHING'S WRONG.
AND HE BELONGS IN THIS FACILITY--WHERE A FRIEND LIKE YOU CAN HELP HIM.
SENATOR LANE...YOU SEEM TO FORGET...

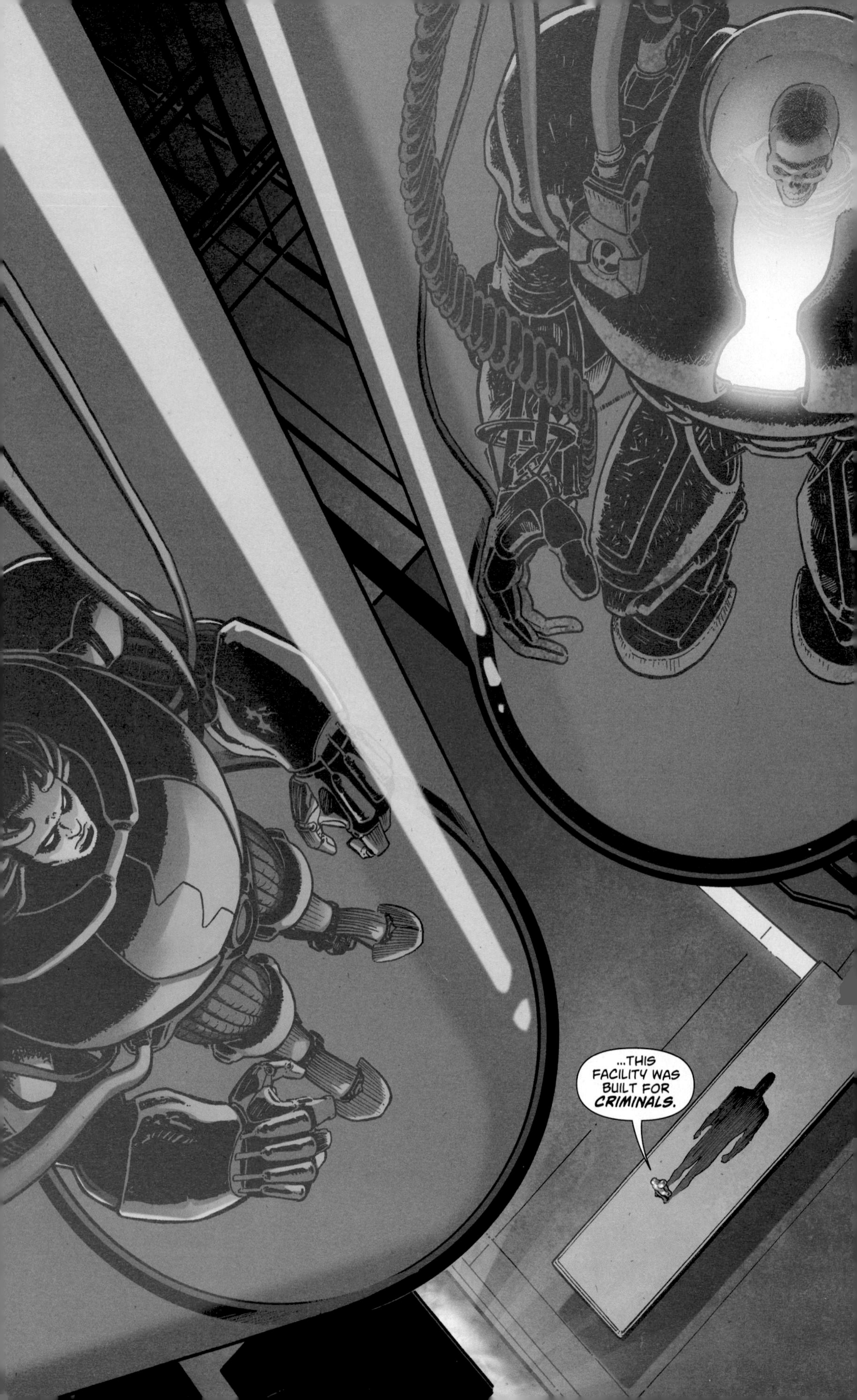
...THIS FACILITY WAS BUILT FOR CRIMINALS.

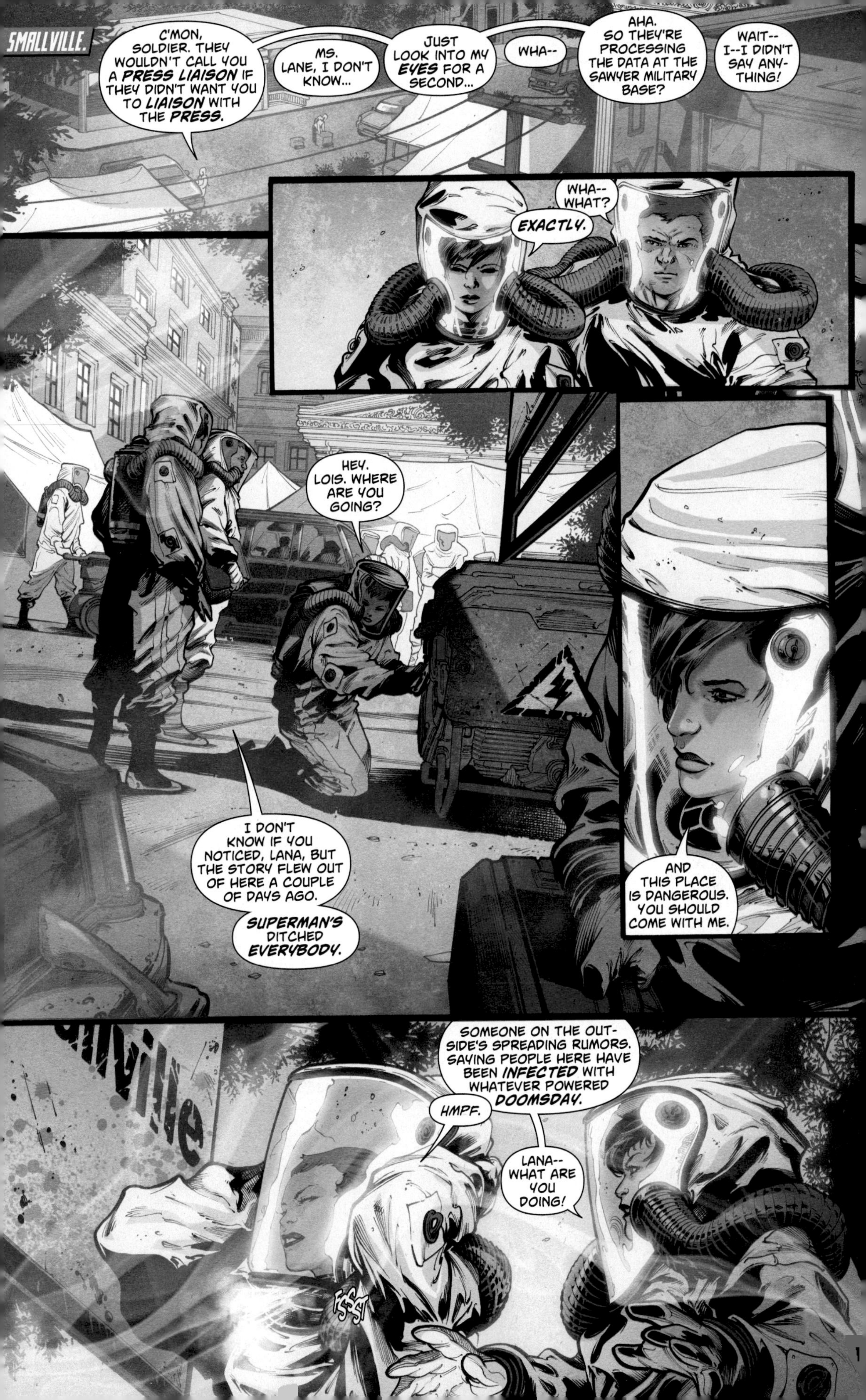
SMALLVILLE.
C'MON, SOLDIER. THEY WOULDN'T CALL YOU A PRESS LIAISON IF THEY DIDN'T WANT YOU TO LIAISON WITH THE PRESS.
MS. LANE, I DON'T KNOW...
JUST LOOK INTO MY EYES FOR A SECOND...
WHA--
AHA. SO THEY'RE PROCESSING THE DATA AT THE SAWYER MILITARY BASE?
WAIT-- I--I DIDN'T SAY ANY-THING!
WHA-- WHAT?
EXACTLY.
HEY. LOIS. WHERE ARE YOU GOING?
I DON'T KNOW IF YOU NOTICED, LANA, BUT THE STORY FLEW OUT OF HERE A COUPLE OF DAYS AGO.
SUPERMAN'S DITCHED EVERYBODY.
AND THIS PLACE IS DANGEROUS. YOU SHOULD COME WITH ME.
SOMEONE ON THE OUT-SIDE'S SPREADING RUMORS. SAYING PEOPLE HERE HAVE BEEN INFECTED WITH WHATEVER POWERED DOOMSDAY.
HMPF.
LANA-- WHAT ARE YOU DOING!

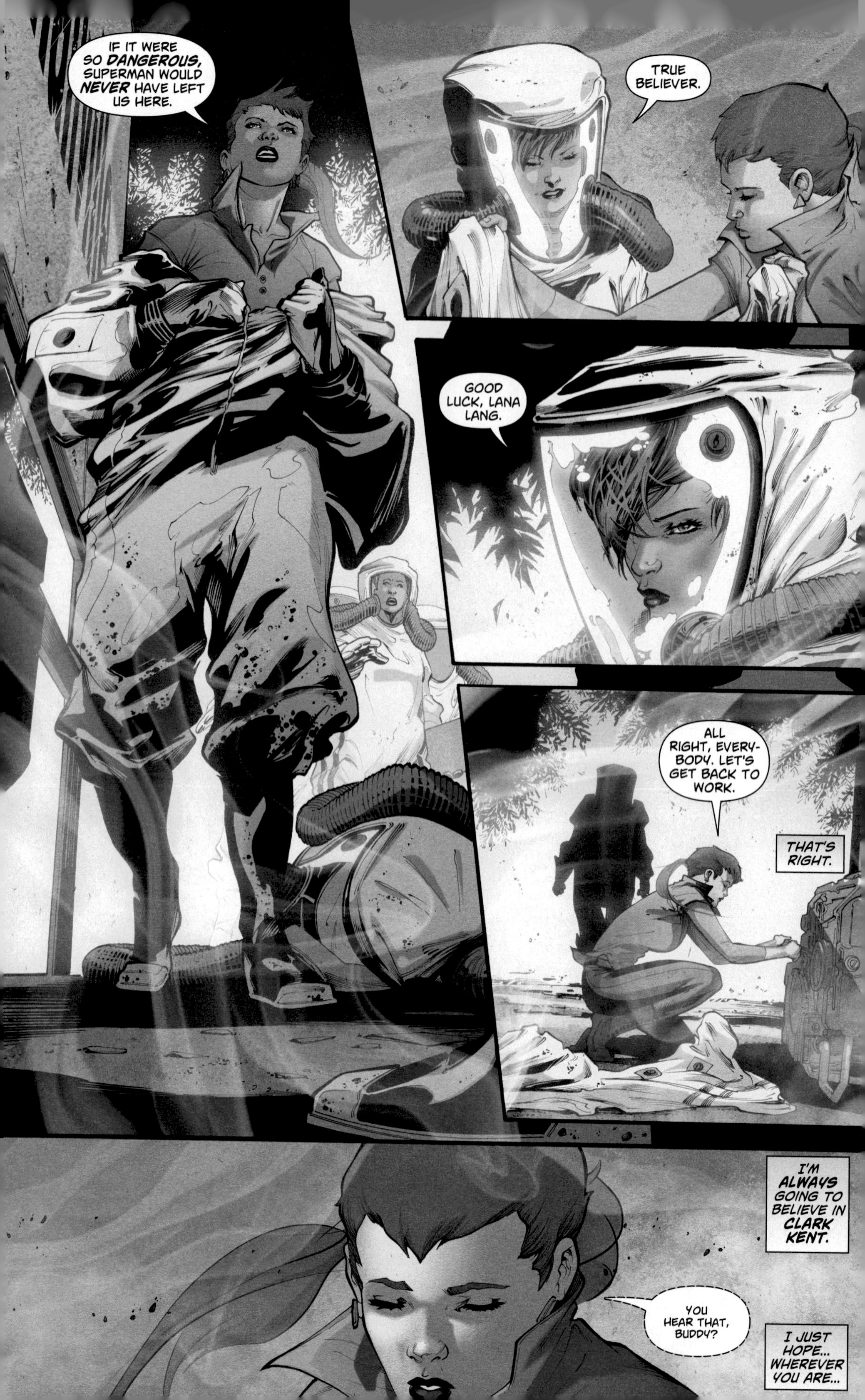
IF IT WERE SO DANGEROUS, SUPERMAN WOULD NEVER HAVE LEFT US HERE.
TRUE BELIEVER.
GOOD LUCK, LANA LANG.
ALL RIGHT, EVERY-BODY. LET'S GET BACK TO WORK.
THAT'S RIGHT.
I'M ALWAYS GOING TO BELIEVE IN CLARK KENT.
YOU HEAR THAT, BUDDY?
I JUST HOPE... WHEREVER YOU ARE...

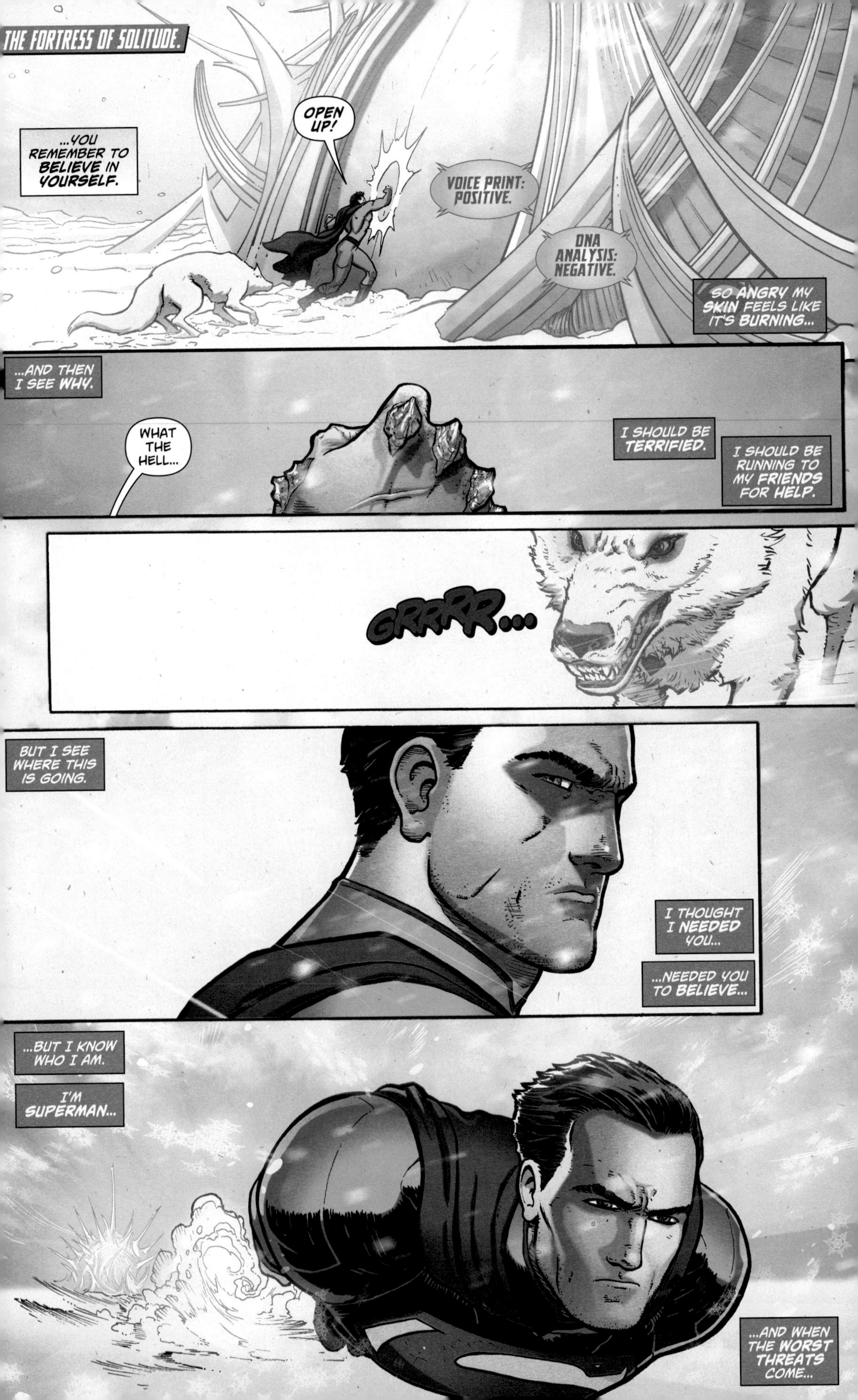
THE FORTRESS OF SOLITUDE.
...YOU REMEMBER TO BELIEVE IN YOURSELF.
OPEN UP!
VOICE PRINT: POSITIVE.
DNA ANALYSIS: NEGATIVE.
SO ANGRY MY SKIN FEELS LIKE IT'S BURNING...
...AND THEN I SEE WHY.
WHAT THE HELL...
I SHOULD BE TERRIFIED.
I SHOULD BE RUNNING TO MY FRIENDS FOR HELP.
GRRRR...
BUT I SEE WHERE THIS IS GOING.
I THOUGHT I NEEDED YOU...
...NEEDED YOU TO BELIEVE...
...BUT I KNOW WHO I AM.
I'M SUPERMAN...
...AND WHEN THE WORST THREATS COME...

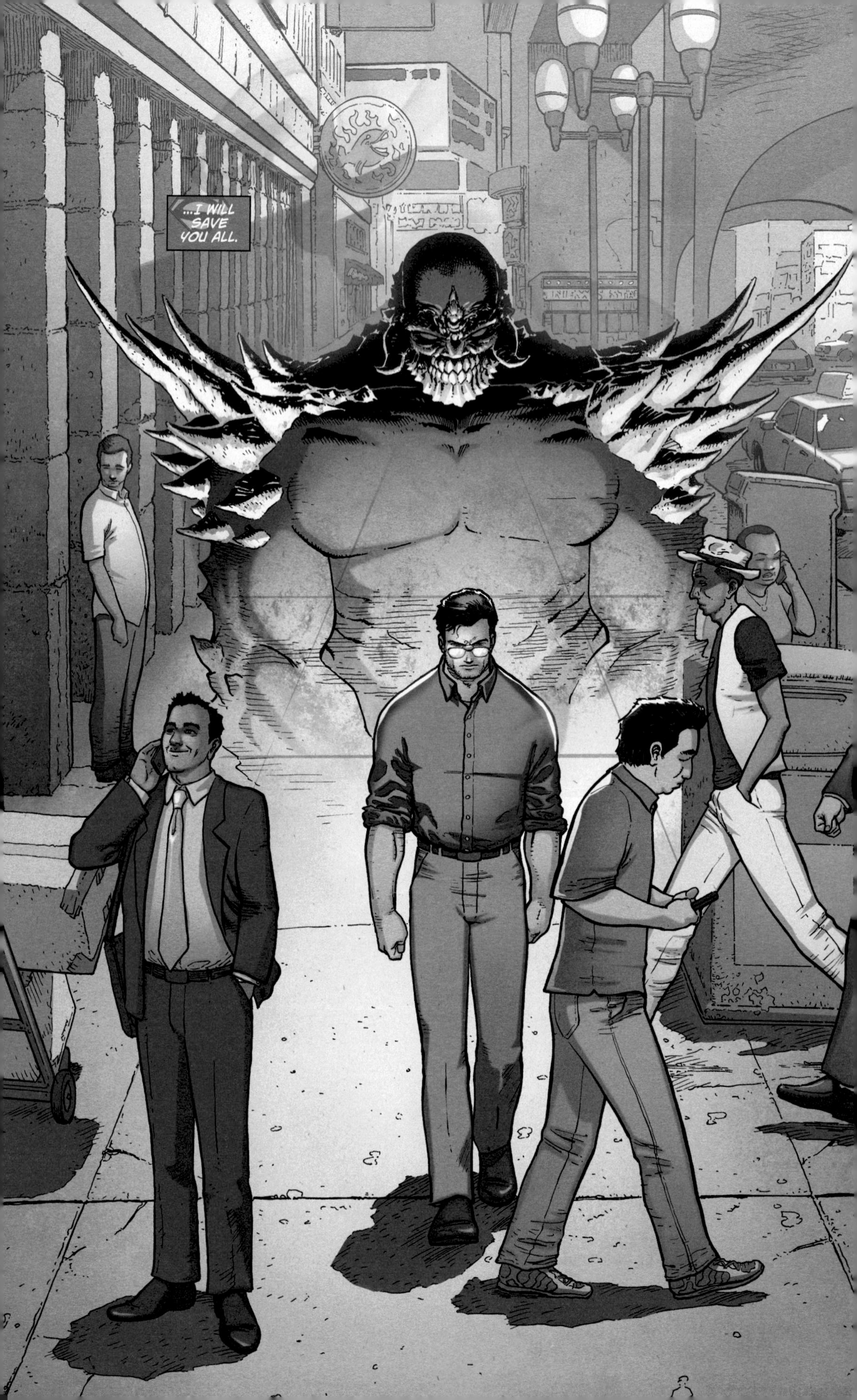
...I WILL SAVE YOU ALL.

"NIGHTMARE"

GREG PAK writer   SCOTT KOLINS artist   WIL QUINTANA colorist

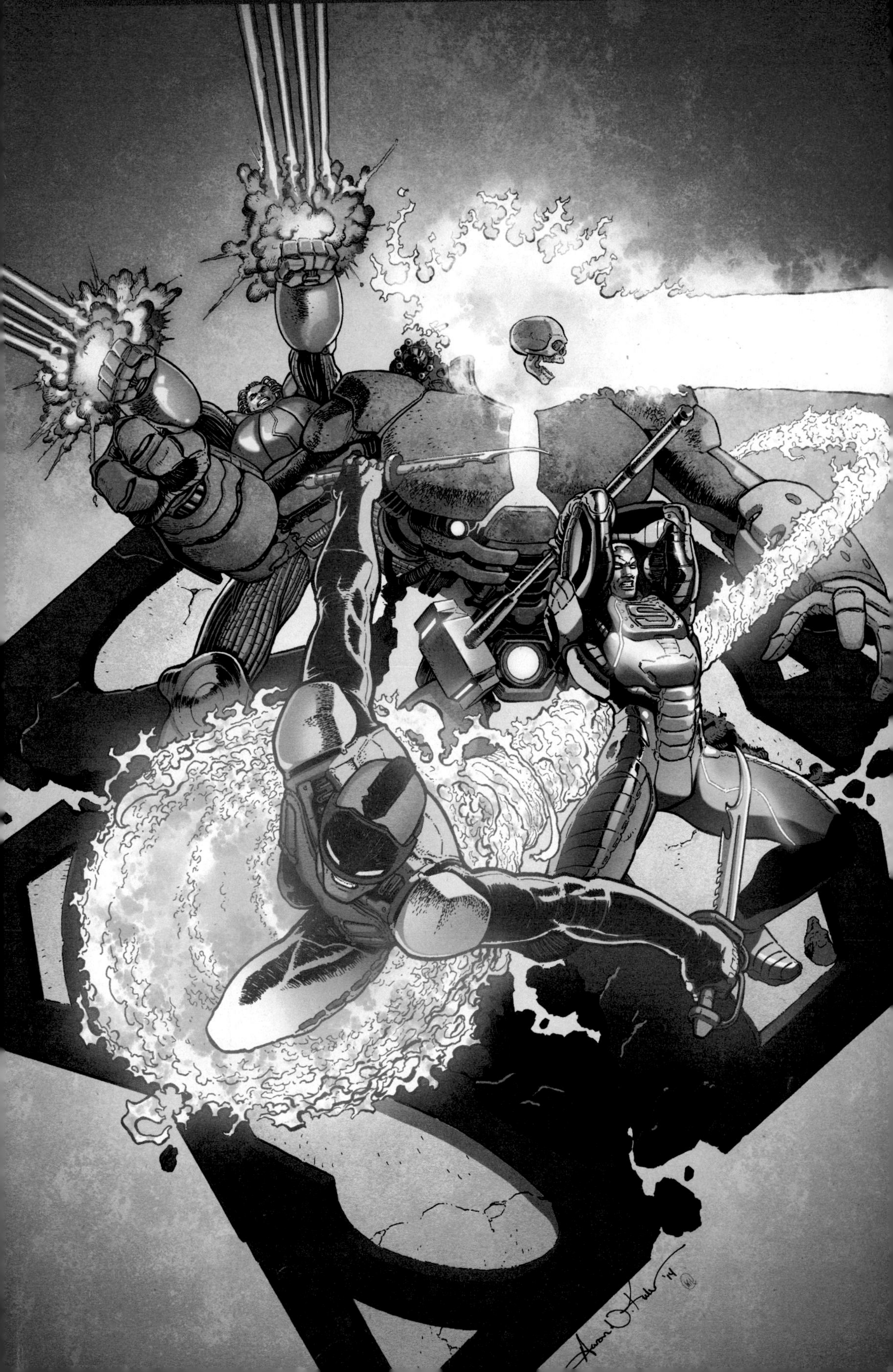

WORLD   U.S.   METROPOLIS   BUSINESS   OPINION   SPORTS   ARTS   STYLE   VIDEO

June 4, 2014

Daily Planet
DAILY PLANET

MY TIME WITH SUPERDOOM

By Lois Lane

I was extremely lucky to be invited by Superman to an undisclosed location where he is being held in hopes that a means can be found to reverse this mutation. Even though the man we all care for is rapidly losing his identity, he still holds true to protecting everyone. The following is from our time speaking together.

Lois Lane: Are you okay?

Superman: I'd like to say "Yes." But I'm afraid that would be a lie. Lois, you should know the risks—

Lois Lane: I'm not afraid, Superman. I just want you to realize… whatever you're going through, I'm rooting for you.

Superman: Lois, I need you to do me a favor.

Lois Lane: Anything.

Superman: I need you… to get the truth out there. I… messed up. I made a mistake. I thought I could take out Doomsday, once and for all, but I realize now… I was wrong. For reasons I don't understand – yet—I'm… I'm becoming Doomsday. I didn't solve the problem, I only changed it.

Lois Lane: What are you saying? What do you want me to do?

Superman: I want you to tell

Photo by James Olsen

the world. To warn the people. I… can't be trusted. Not now. Maybe… never again.

Lois Lane: No one will believe that, Superman. I won't believe you can't get better.

Superman: Warn them. Can you do that for me, Lois?

Lois Lane: Yes, Superman. I can do that for you.

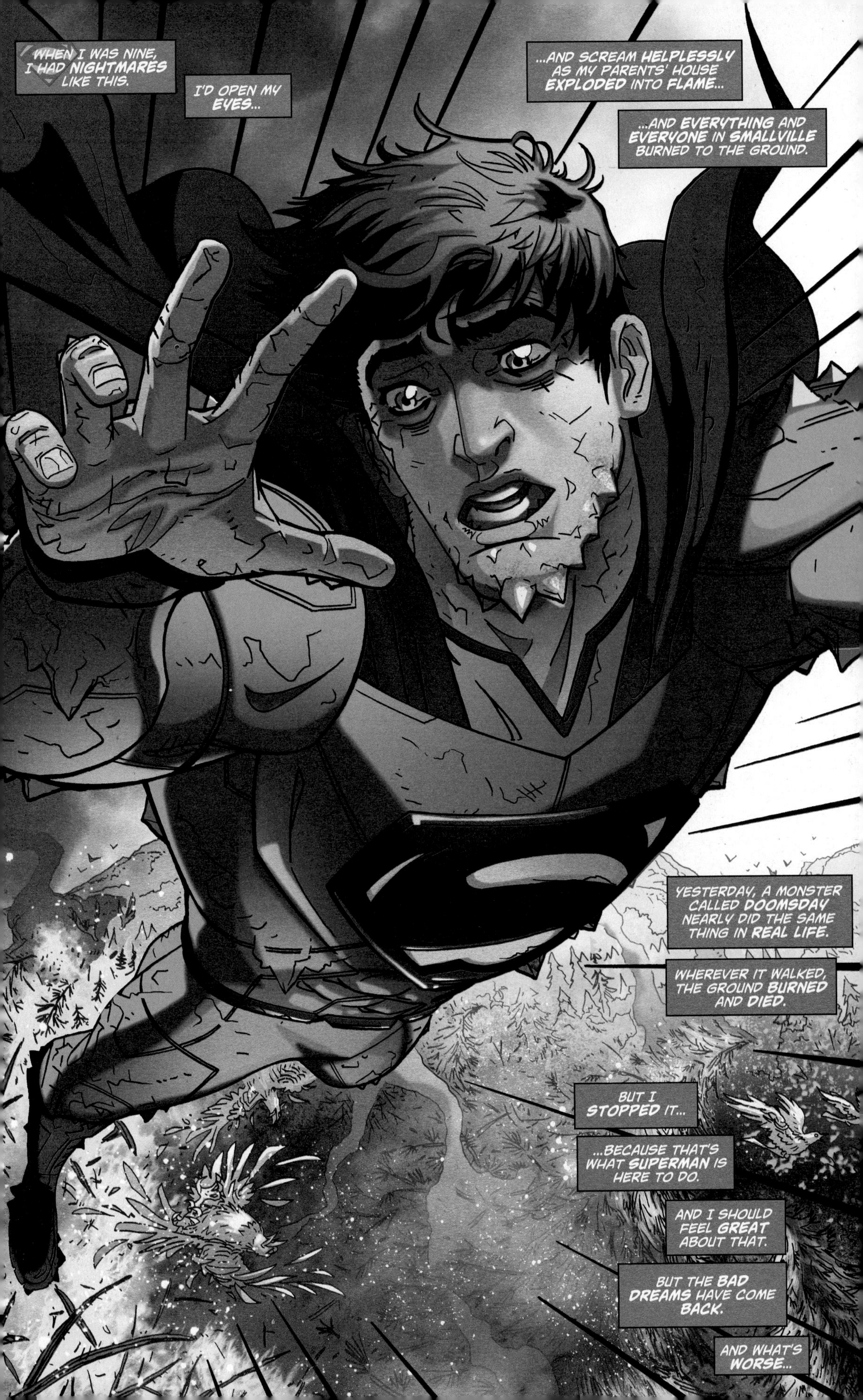
WHEN I WAS NINE, I HAD NIGHTMARES LIKE THIS.
I'D OPEN MY EYES...
...AND SCREAM HELPLESSLY AS MY PARENTS' HOUSE EXPLODED INTO FLAME...
...AND EVERYTHING AND EVERYONE IN SMALLVILLE BURNED TO THE GROUND.
YESTERDAY, A MONSTER CALLED DOOMSDAY NEARLY DID THE SAME THING IN REAL LIFE.
WHEREVER IT WALKED, THE GROUND BURNED AND DIED.
BUT I STOPPED IT...
...BECAUSE THAT'S WHAT SUPERMAN IS HERE TO DO.
AND I SHOULD FEEL GREAT ABOUT THAT.
BUT THE BAD DREAMS HAVE COME BACK.
AND WHAT'S WORSE...

...I DON'T THINK THEY'RE DREAMS.

OH, GOD...

WHEN I KILLED THE THING...

...IT EXPLODED INTO SPORES.

...AND I INHALED THEM ALL.

AND NOW THE TREES CATCH FIRE AS I FLY OVER THEM?

SOMETHING'S HAPPENING TO ME.

I HAVE TO CONCENTRATE, FIGURE OUT HOW TO CONTROL IT BEFORE--

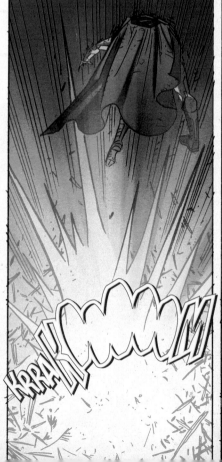

KRRAKBWMMMM

GOVERNMENT BOMBERS.

HOW CAN I BLAME THEM?

IF YOU SEE SOMETHING DO THE THINGS I'M DOING...

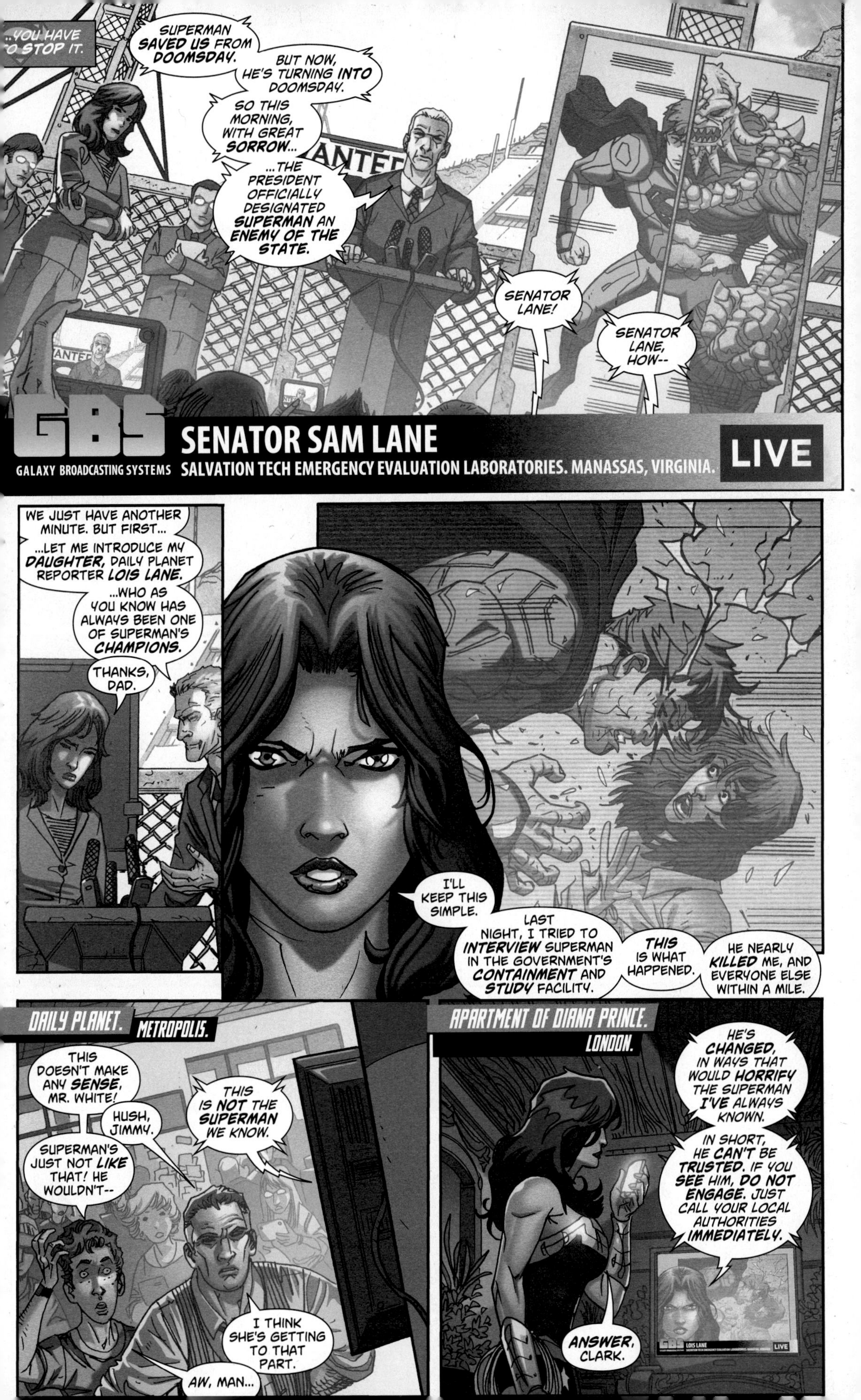
..YOU HAVE TO STOP IT.
SUPERMAN SAVED US FROM DOOMSDAY.
BUT NOW, HE'S TURNING INTO DOOMSDAY.
SO THIS MORNING, WITH GREAT SORROW...
...THE PRESIDENT OFFICIALLY DESIGNATED SUPERMAN AN ENEMY OF THE STATE.
SENATOR LANE!
SENATOR LANE, HOW--
GBS
GALAXY BROADCASTING SYSTEMS
SENATOR SAM LANE
SALVATION TECH EMERGENCY EVALUATION LABORATORIES. MANASSAS, VIRGINIA.
LIVE
WE JUST HAVE ANOTHER MINUTE. BUT FIRST...
...LET ME INTRODUCE MY DAUGHTER, DAILY PLANET REPORTER LOIS LANE.
...WHO AS YOU KNOW HAS ALWAYS BEEN ONE OF SUPERMAN'S CHAMPIONS.
THANKS, DAD.
I'LL KEEP THIS SIMPLE.
LAST NIGHT, I TRIED TO INTERVIEW SUPERMAN IN THE GOVERNMENT'S CONTAINMENT AND STUDY FACILITY.
THIS IS WHAT HAPPENED.
HE NEARLY KILLED ME, AND EVERYONE ELSE WITHIN A MILE.
DAILY PLANET. METROPOLIS.
THIS DOESN'T MAKE ANY SENSE, MR. WHITE!
HUSH, JIMMY.
SUPERMAN'S JUST NOT LIKE THAT! HE WOULDN'T--
THIS IS NOT THE SUPERMAN WE KNOW.
I THINK SHE'S GETTING TO THAT PART.
AW, MAN...
APARTMENT OF DIANA PRINCE. LONDON.
HE'S CHANGED, IN WAYS THAT WOULD HORRIFY THE SUPERMAN I'VE ALWAYS KNOWN.
IN SHORT, HE CAN'T BE TRUSTED. IF YOU SEE HIM, DO NOT ENGAGE. JUST CALL YOUR LOCAL AUTHORITIES IMMEDIATELY.
ANSWER, CLARK.

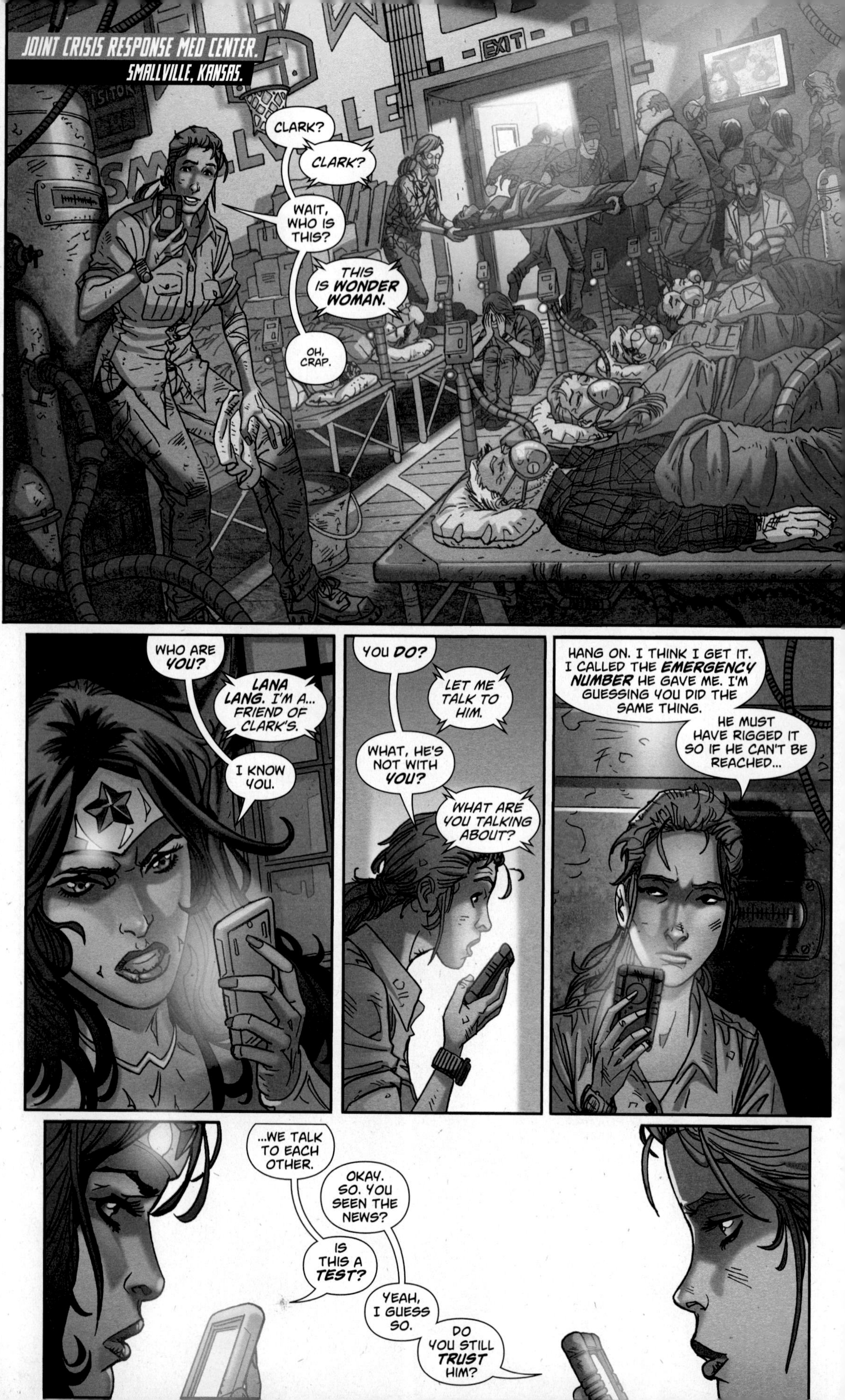
JOINT CRISIS RESPONSE MED CENTER.
SMALLVILLE, KANSAS.
CLARK?
CLARK?
WAIT, WHO IS THIS?
THIS IS WONDER WOMAN.
OH, CRAP.
WHO ARE YOU?
LANA LANG. I'M A... FRIEND OF CLARK'S.
I KNOW YOU.
YOU DO?
LET ME TALK TO HIM.
WHAT, HE'S NOT WITH YOU?
WHAT ARE YOU TALKING ABOUT?
HANG ON. I THINK I GET IT. I CALLED THE EMERGENCY NUMBER HE GAVE ME. I'M GUESSING YOU DID THE SAME THING.
HE MUST HAVE RIGGED IT SO IF HE CAN'T BE REACHED...
...WE TALK TO EACH OTHER.
OKAY. SO. YOU SEEN THE NEWS?
IS THIS A TEST?
YEAH, I GUESS SO.
DO YOU STILL TRUST HIM?

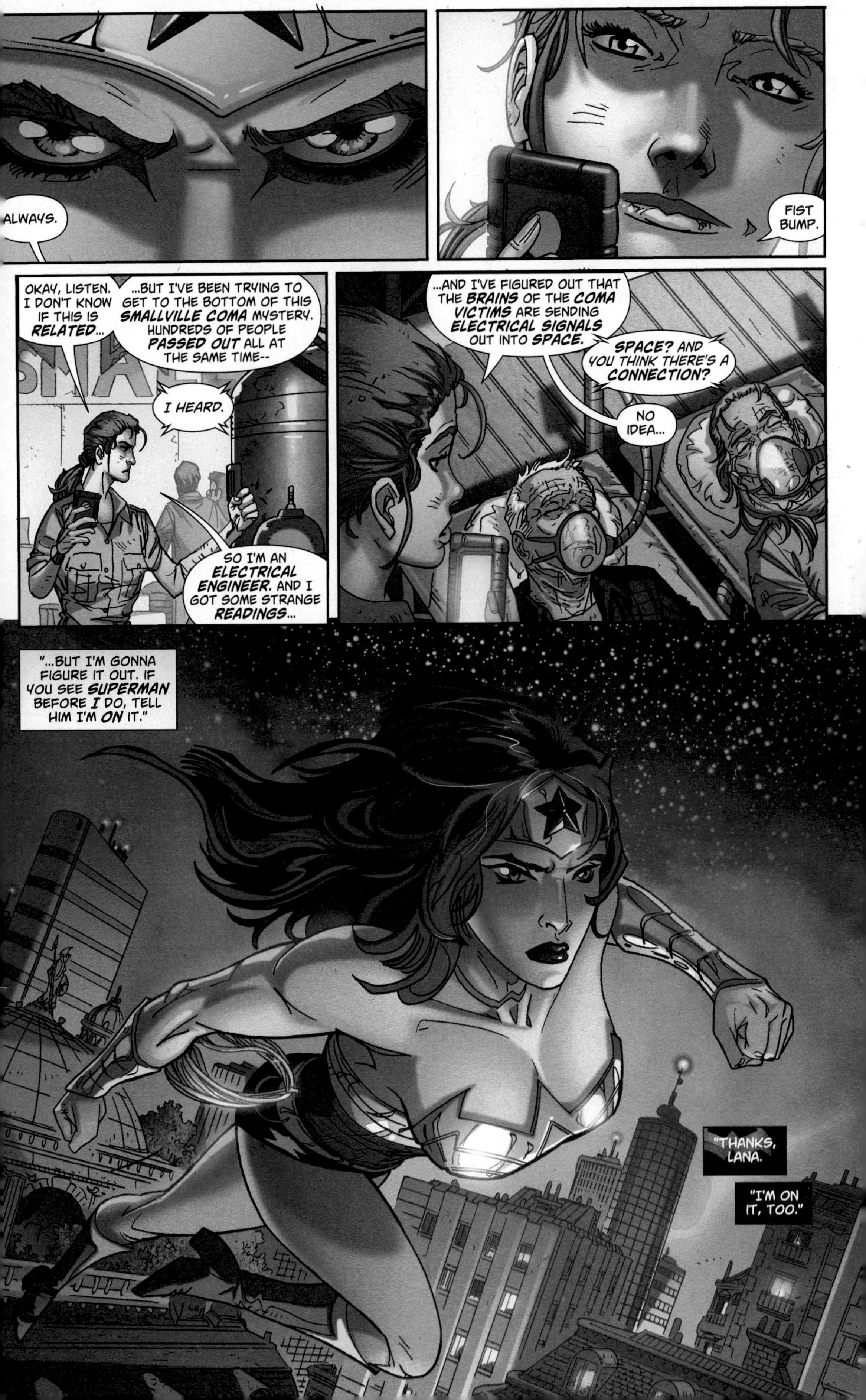
ALWAYS.
FIST BUMP.
OKAY, LISTEN. I DON'T KNOW IF THIS IS RELATED...
...BUT I'VE BEEN TRYING TO GET TO THE BOTTOM OF THIS SMALLVILLE COMA MYSTERY. HUNDREDS OF PEOPLE PASSED OUT ALL AT THE SAME TIME--
I HEARD.
SO I'M AN ELECTRICAL ENGINEER. AND I GOT SOME STRANGE READINGS...
...AND I'VE FIGURED OUT THAT THE BRAINS OF THE COMA VICTIMS ARE SENDING ELECTRICAL SIGNALS OUT INTO SPACE.
SPACE? AND YOU THINK THERE'S A CONNECTION?
NO IDEA...
"...BUT I'M GONNA FIGURE IT OUT. IF YOU SEE SUPERMAN BEFORE I DO, TELL HIM I'M ON IT."
"THANKS, LANA.
"I'M ON IT, TOO."

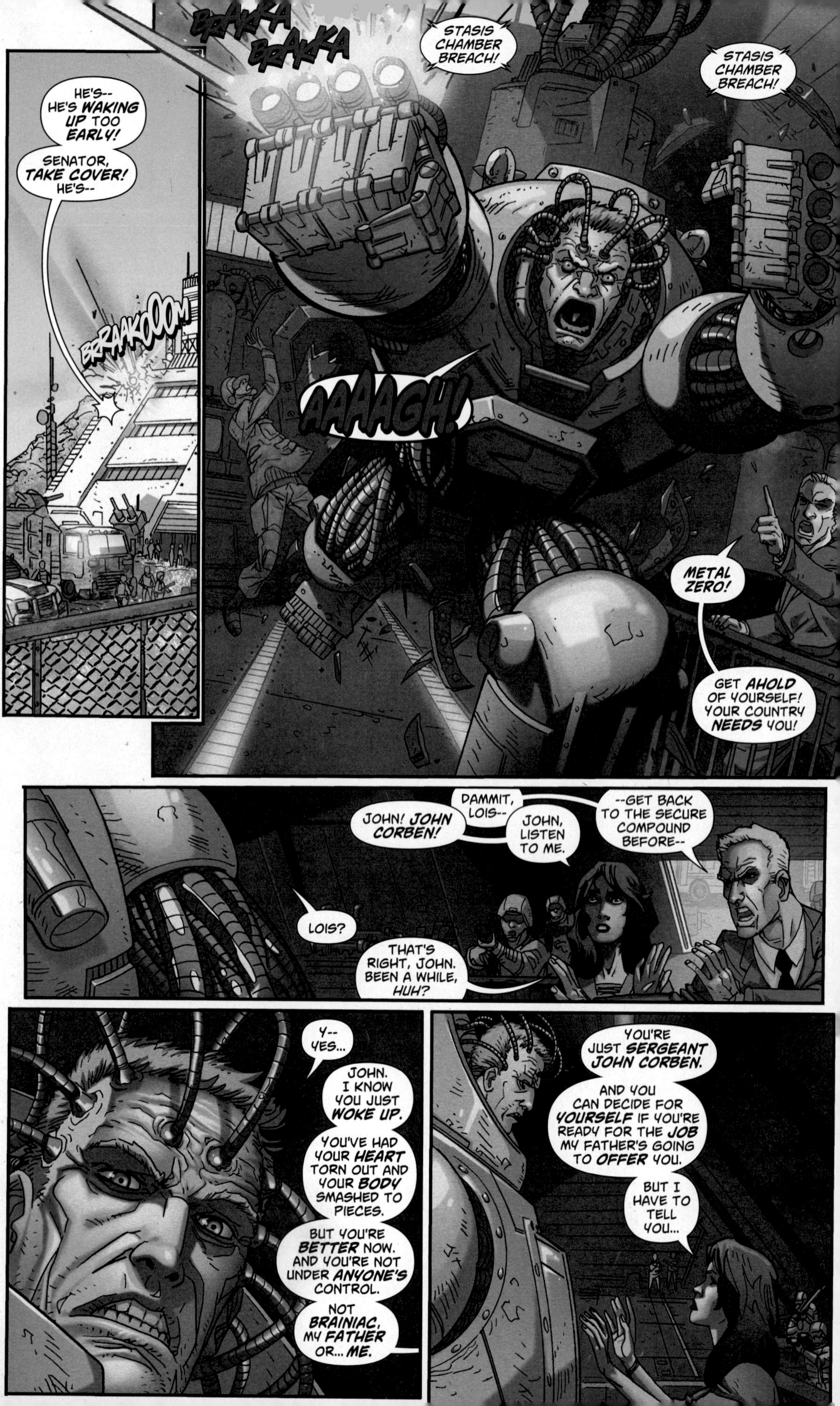

HE'S-- HE'S WAKING UP TOO EARLY!
SENATOR, TAKE COVER! HE'S--
BRRAAKOOOM
BRAKKA BRAKKA
STASIS CHAMBER BREACH!
STASIS CHAMBER BREACH!
AAAAGH!
METAL ZERO!
GET AHOLD OF YOURSELF! YOUR COUNTRY NEEDS YOU!
JOHN! JOHN CORBEN!
DAMMIT, LOIS--
JOHN, LISTEN TO ME.
--GET BACK TO THE SECURE COMPOUND BEFORE--
LOIS?
THAT'S RIGHT, JOHN. BEEN A WHILE, HUH?
Y-- YES...
JOHN. I KNOW YOU JUST WOKE UP.
YOU'VE HAD YOUR HEART TORN OUT AND YOUR BODY SMASHED TO PIECES.
BUT YOU'RE BETTER NOW. AND YOU'RE NOT UNDER ANYONE'S CONTROL.
NOT BRAINIAC, MY FATHER OR... ME.
YOU'RE JUST SERGEANT JOHN CORBEN.
AND YOU CAN DECIDE FOR YOURSELF IF YOU'RE READY FOR THE JOB MY FATHER'S GOING TO OFFER YOU.
BUT I HAVE TO TELL YOU...

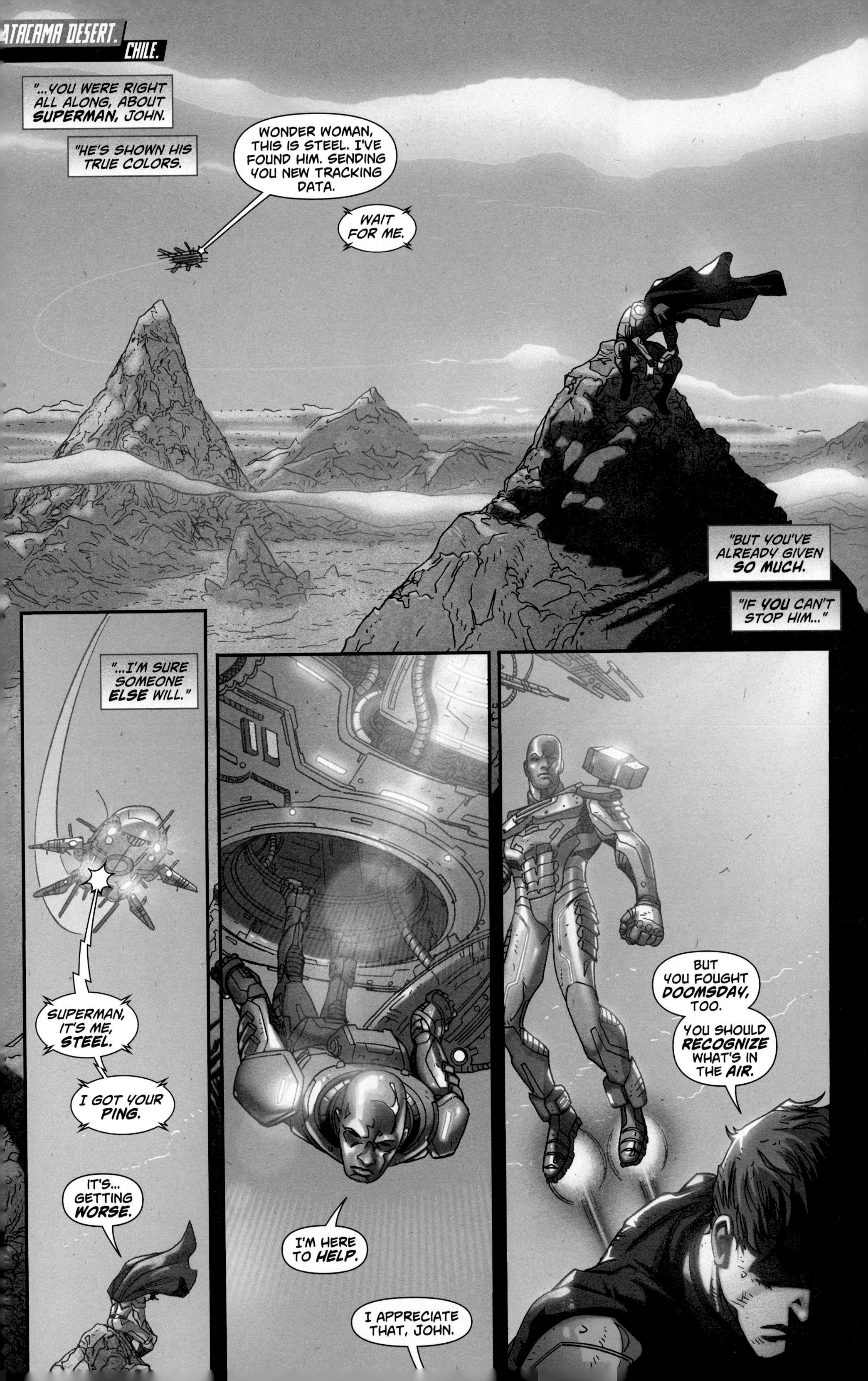
ATACAMA DESERT. CHILE.
"...YOU WERE RIGHT ALL ALONG, ABOUT SUPERMAN, JOHN.
"HE'S SHOWN HIS TRUE COLORS.
WONDER WOMAN, THIS IS STEEL. I'VE FOUND HIM. SENDING YOU NEW TRACKING DATA.
WAIT FOR ME.
"BUT YOU'VE ALREADY GIVEN SO MUCH.
"IF YOU CAN'T STOP HIM..."
"...I'M SURE SOMEONE ELSE WILL."
SUPERMAN, IT'S ME, STEEL.
I GOT YOUR PING.
IT'S... GETTING WORSE.
I'M HERE TO HELP.
I APPRECIATE THAT, JOHN.
BUT YOU FOUGHT DOOMSDAY, TOO.
YOU SHOULD RECOGNIZE WHAT'S IN THE AIR.

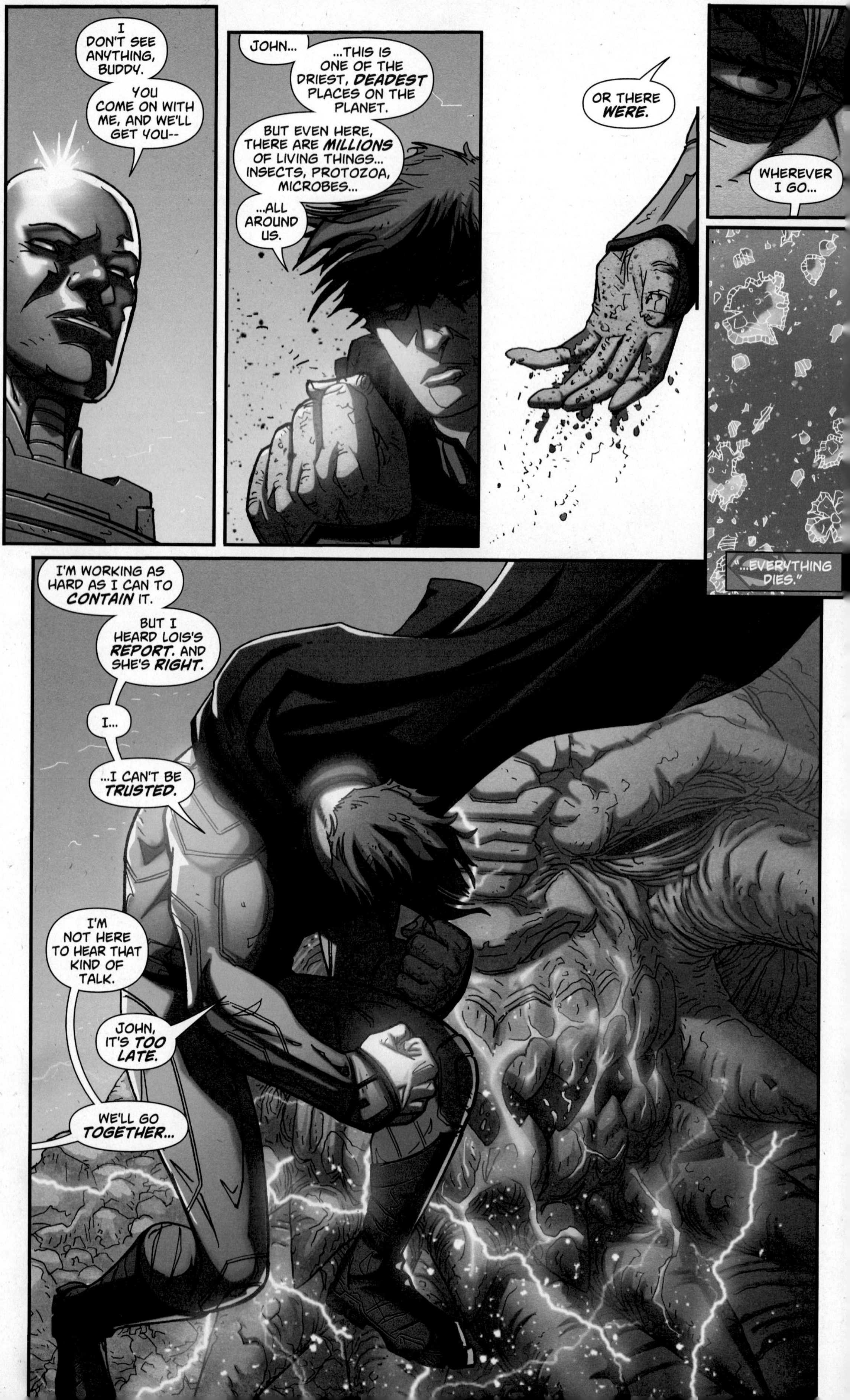
I DON'T SEE ANYTHING, BUDDY.
YOU COME ON WITH ME, AND WE'LL GET YOU--
JOHN...
...THIS IS ONE OF THE DRIEST, DEADEST PLACES ON THE PLANET.
BUT EVEN HERE, THERE ARE MILLIONS OF LIVING THINGS... INSECTS, PROTOZOA, MICROBES...
...ALL AROUND US.
OR THERE WERE.
WHEREVER I GO...
"...EVERYTHING DIES."
I'M WORKING AS HARD AS I CAN TO CONTAIN IT.
BUT I HEARD LOIS'S REPORT. AND SHE'S RIGHT.
I...
...I CAN'T BE TRUSTED.
I'M NOT HERE TO HEAR THAT KIND OF TALK.
JOHN, IT'S TOO LATE.
WE'LL GO TOGETHER...

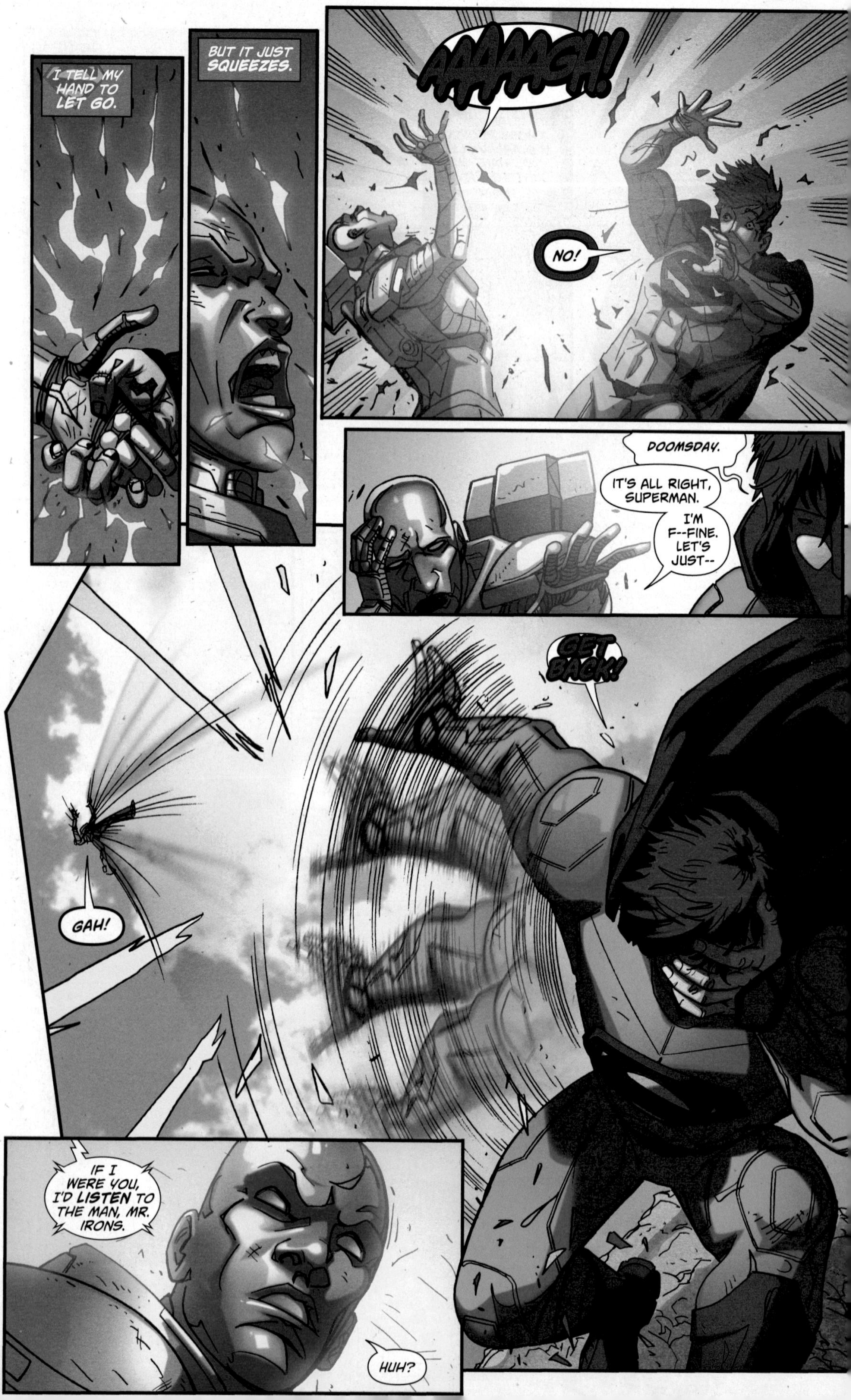
I TELL MY HAND TO LET GO.
BUT IT JUST SQUEEZES.
AAAAAAGH!
NO!
DOOMSDAY.
IT'S ALL RIGHT, SUPERMAN.
I'M F--FINE. LET'S JUST--
GET BACK!
GAH!
IF I WERE YOU, I'D LISTEN TO THE MAN, MR. IRONS.
HUH?

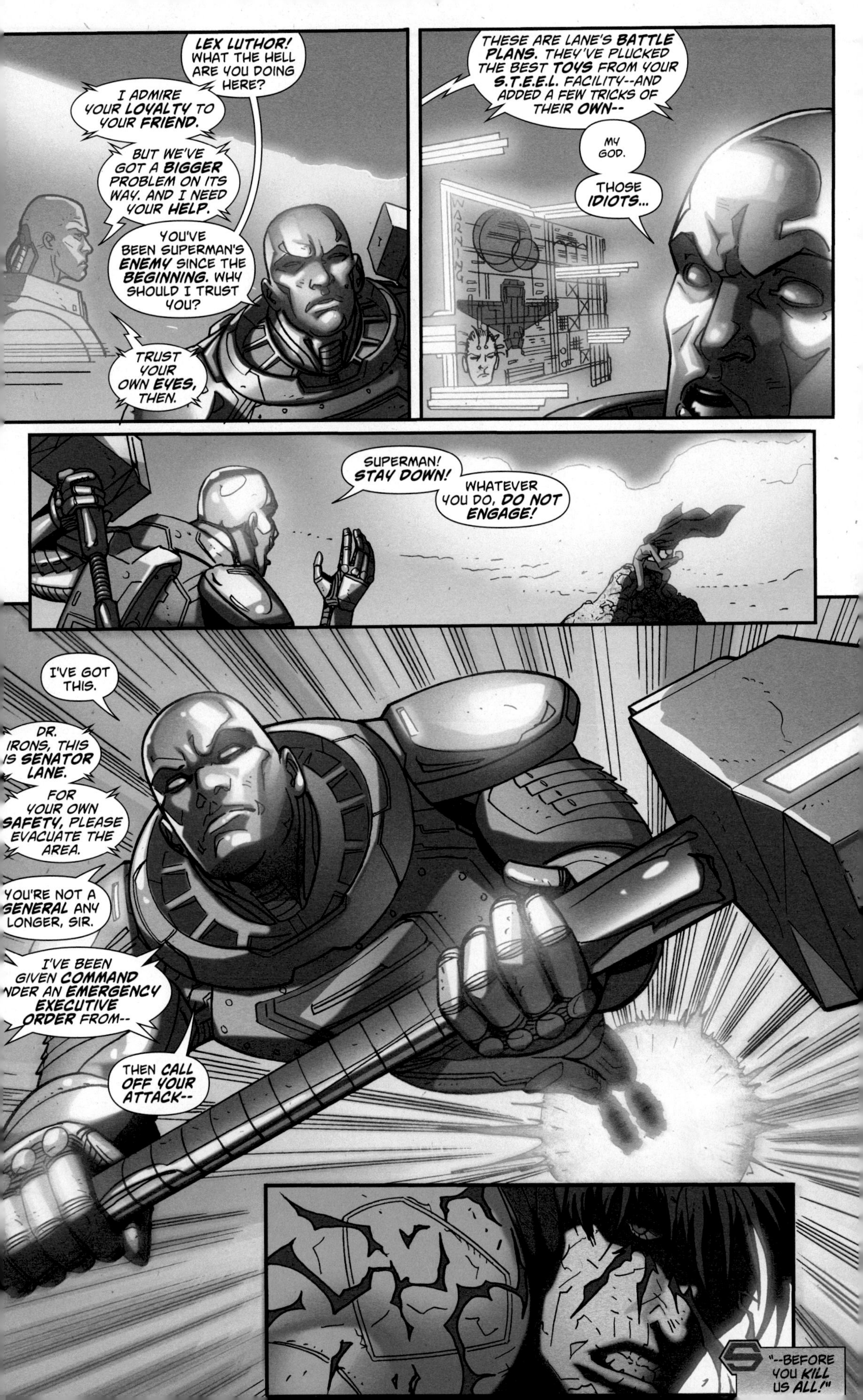

LEX LUTHOR! WHAT THE HELL ARE YOU DOING HERE?
I ADMIRE YOUR LOYALTY TO YOUR FRIEND.
BUT WE'VE GOT A BIGGER PROBLEM ON ITS WAY. AND I NEED YOUR HELP.
YOU'VE BEEN SUPERMAN'S ENEMY SINCE THE BEGINNING. WHY SHOULD I TRUST YOU?
TRUST YOUR OWN EYES, THEN.
THESE ARE LANE'S BATTLE PLANS. THEY'VE PLUCKED THE BEST TOYS FROM YOUR S.T.E.E.L. FACILITY--AND ADDED A FEW TRICKS OF THEIR OWN--
MY GOD.
THOSE IDIOTS...
WARNING
SUPERMAN! STAY DOWN!
WHATEVER YOU DO, DO NOT ENGAGE!
I'VE GOT THIS.
DR. IRONS, THIS IS SENATOR LANE.
FOR YOUR OWN SAFETY, PLEASE EVACUATE THE AREA.
YOU'RE NOT A GENERAL ANY LONGER, SIR.
I'VE BEEN GIVEN COMMAND NDER AN EMERGENCY EXECUTIVE ORDER FROM--
THEN CALL OFF YOUR ATTACK--
"--BEFORE YOU KILL US ALL!"

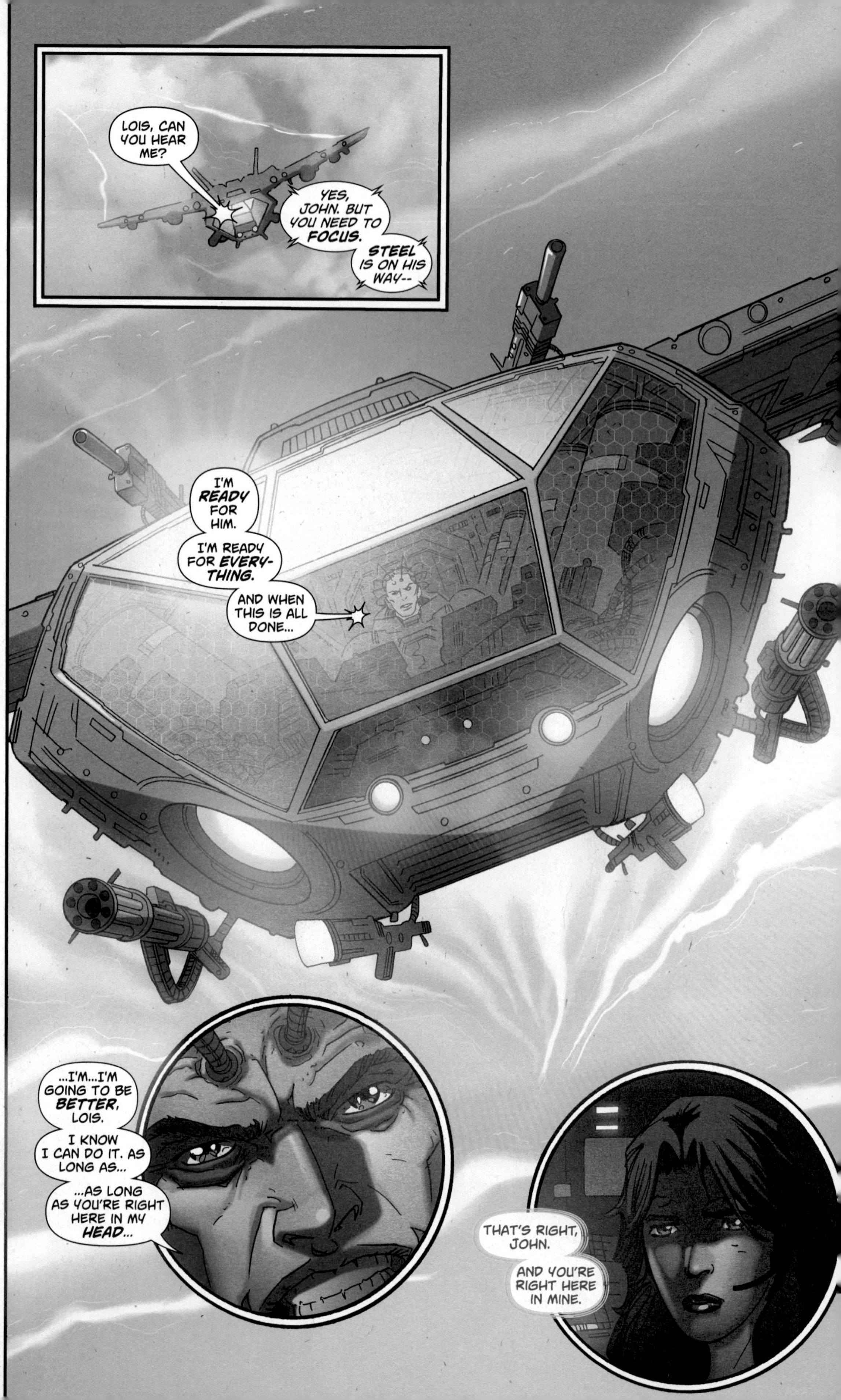
LOIS, CAN YOU HEAR ME?
YES, JOHN. BUT YOU NEED TO FOCUS.
STEEL IS ON HIS WAY--
I'M READY FOR HIM.
I'M READY FOR EVERY-THING.
AND WHEN THIS IS ALL DONE...
...I'M...I'M GOING TO BE BETTER, LOIS.
I KNOW I CAN DO IT. AS LONG AS...
...AS LONG AS YOU'RE RIGHT HERE IN MY HEAD...
THAT'S RIGHT, JOHN.
AND YOU'RE RIGHT HERE IN MINE.

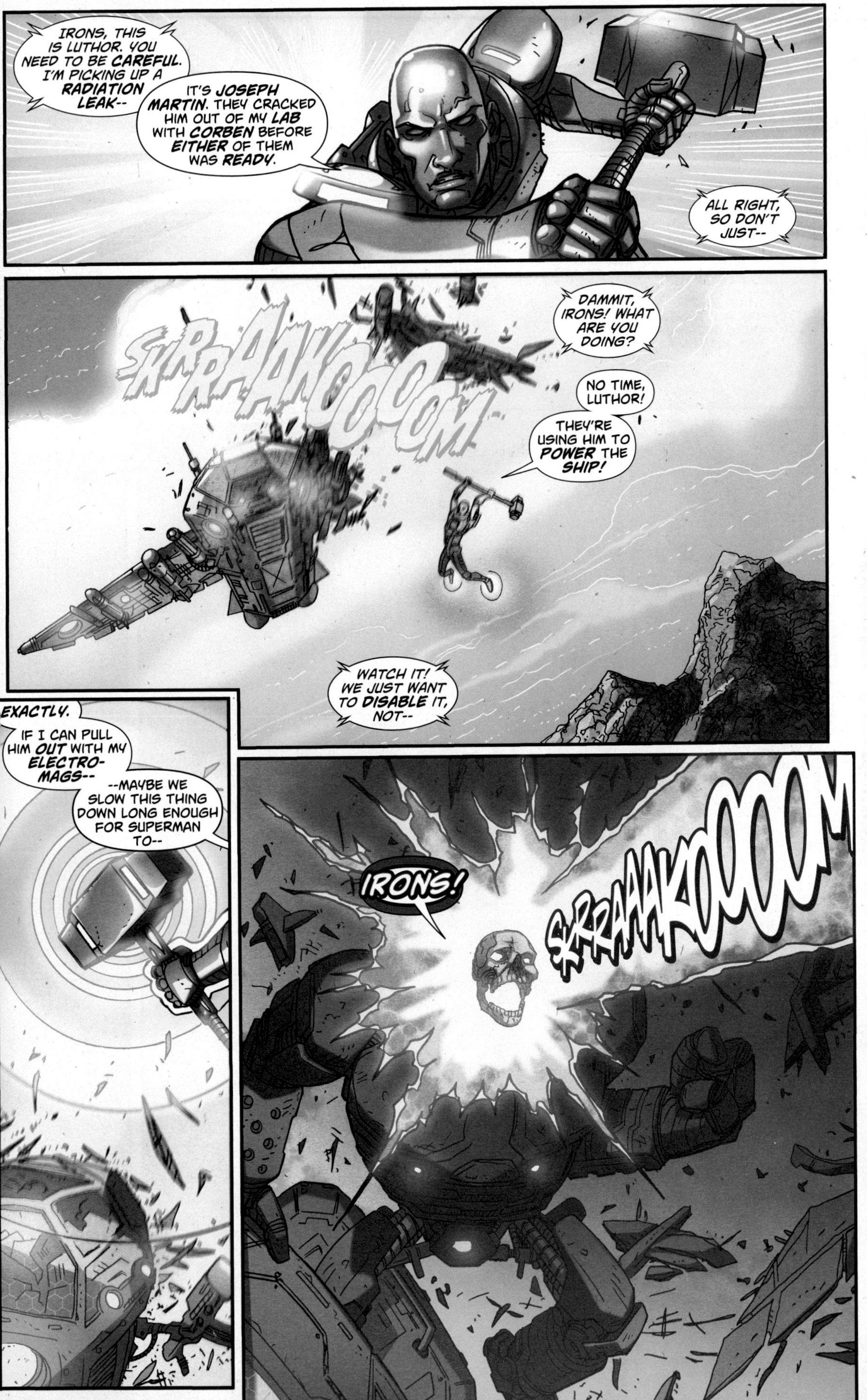
IRONS, THIS IS LUTHOR. YOU NEED TO BE CAREFUL. I'M PICKING UP A RADIATION LEAK--
IT'S JOSEPH MARTIN. THEY CRACKED HIM OUT OF MY LAB WITH CORBEN BEFORE EITHER OF THEM WAS READY.
ALL RIGHT, SO DON'T JUST--
SKRRAAKOOOOM
DAMMIT, IRONS! WHAT ARE YOU DOING?
NO TIME, LUTHOR!
THEY'RE USING HIM TO POWER THE SHIP!
WATCH IT! WE JUST WANT TO DISABLE IT, NOT--
EXACTLY.
IF I CAN PULL HIM OUT WITH MY ELECTRO-MAGS--
--MAYBE WE SLOW THIS THING DOWN LONG ENOUGH FOR SUPERMAN TO--
IRONS!
SKRRAAKOOOOM

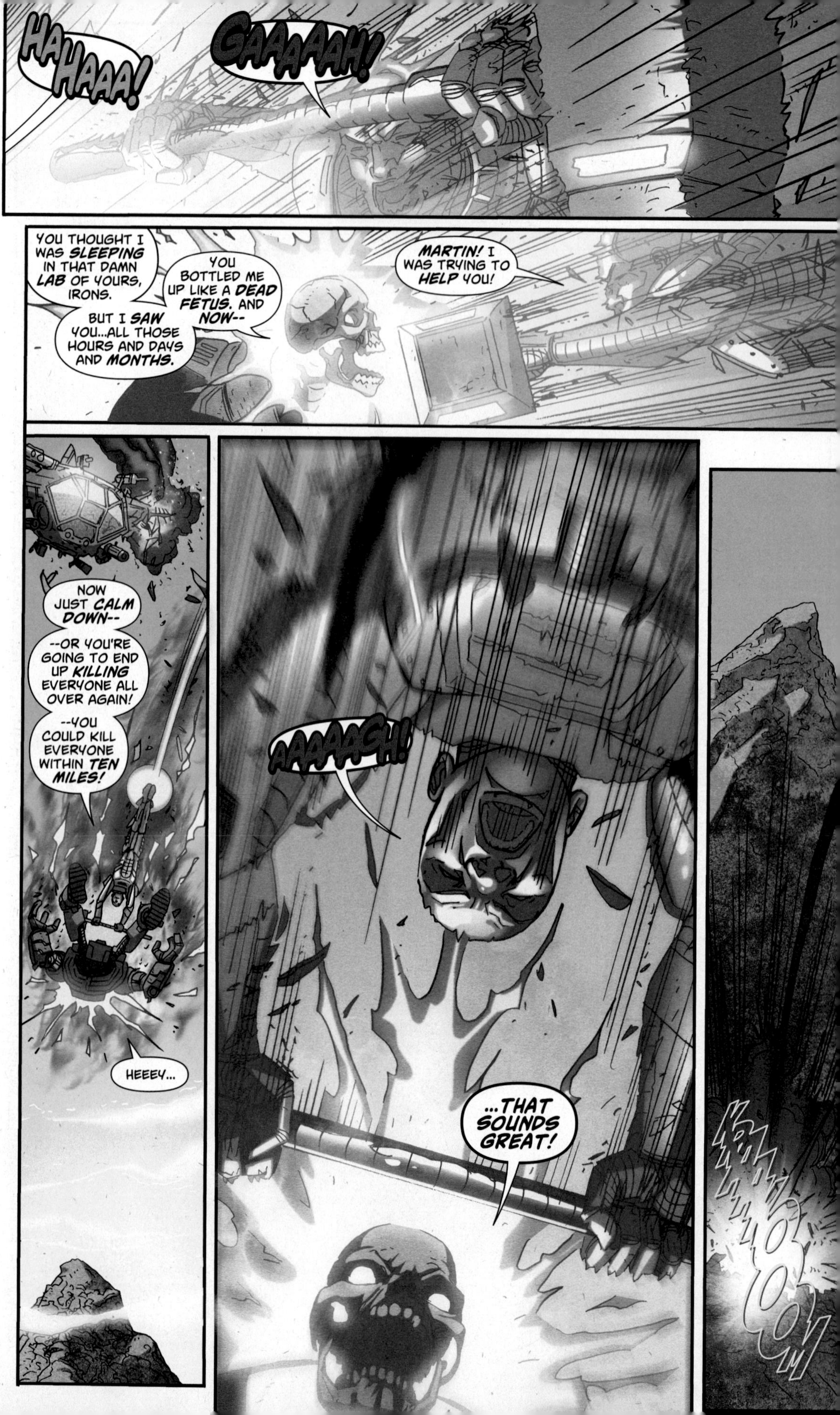
HA HAAA!
GAAAAAH!
YOU THOUGHT I WAS SLEEPING IN THAT DAMN LAB OF YOURS, IRONS.
BUT I SAW YOU...ALL THOSE HOURS AND DAYS AND MONTHS.
YOU BOTTLED ME UP LIKE A DEAD FETUS. AND NOW--
MARTIN! I WAS TRYING TO HELP YOU!
NOW JUST CALM DOWN--
--OR YOU'RE GOING TO END UP KILLING EVERYONE ALL OVER AGAIN!
--YOU COULD KILL EVERYONE WITHIN TEN MILES!
HEEEY...
AAAAAGH!
...THAT SOUNDS GREAT!

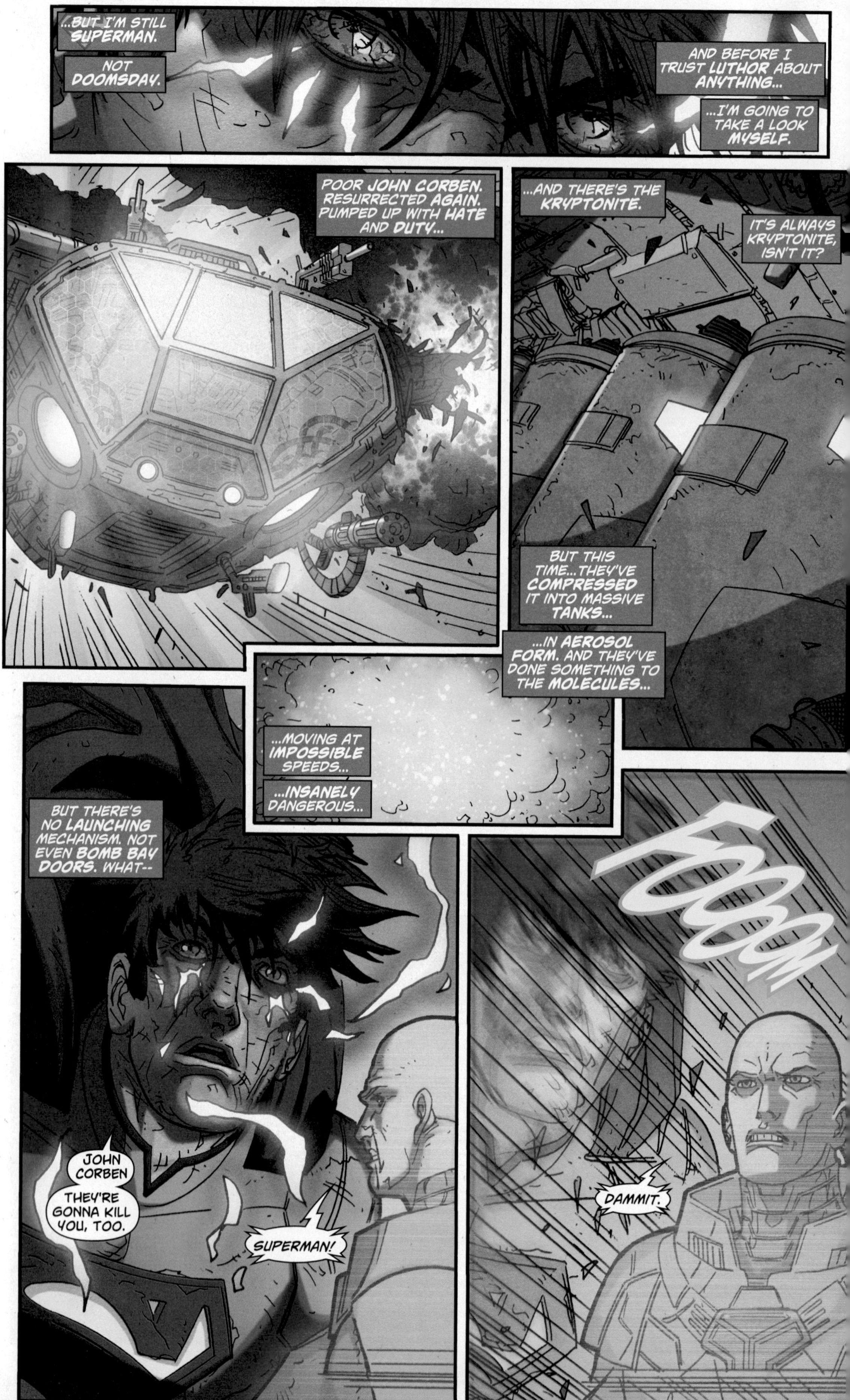
...BUT I'M STILL SUPERMAN.
NOT DOOMSDAY.
AND BEFORE I TRUST LUTHOR ABOUT ANYTHING...
...I'M GOING TO TAKE A LOOK MYSELF.
POOR JOHN CORBEN. RESURRECTED AGAIN. PUMPED UP WITH HATE AND DUTY...
...AND THERE'S THE KRYPTONITE.
IT'S ALWAYS KRYPTONITE, ISN'T IT?
BUT THIS TIME...THEY'VE COMPRESSED IT INTO MASSIVE TANKS...
...IN AEROSOL FORM. AND THEY'VE DONE SOMETHING TO THE MOLECULES...
...MOVING AT IMPOSSIBLE SPEEDS...
...INSANELY DANGEROUS...
BUT THERE'S NO LAUNCHING MECHANISM. NOT EVEN BOMB BAY DOORS. WHAT--
JOHN CORBEN
THEY'RE GONNA KILL YOU, TOO.
SUPERMAN!
FOOOM
DAMMIT.

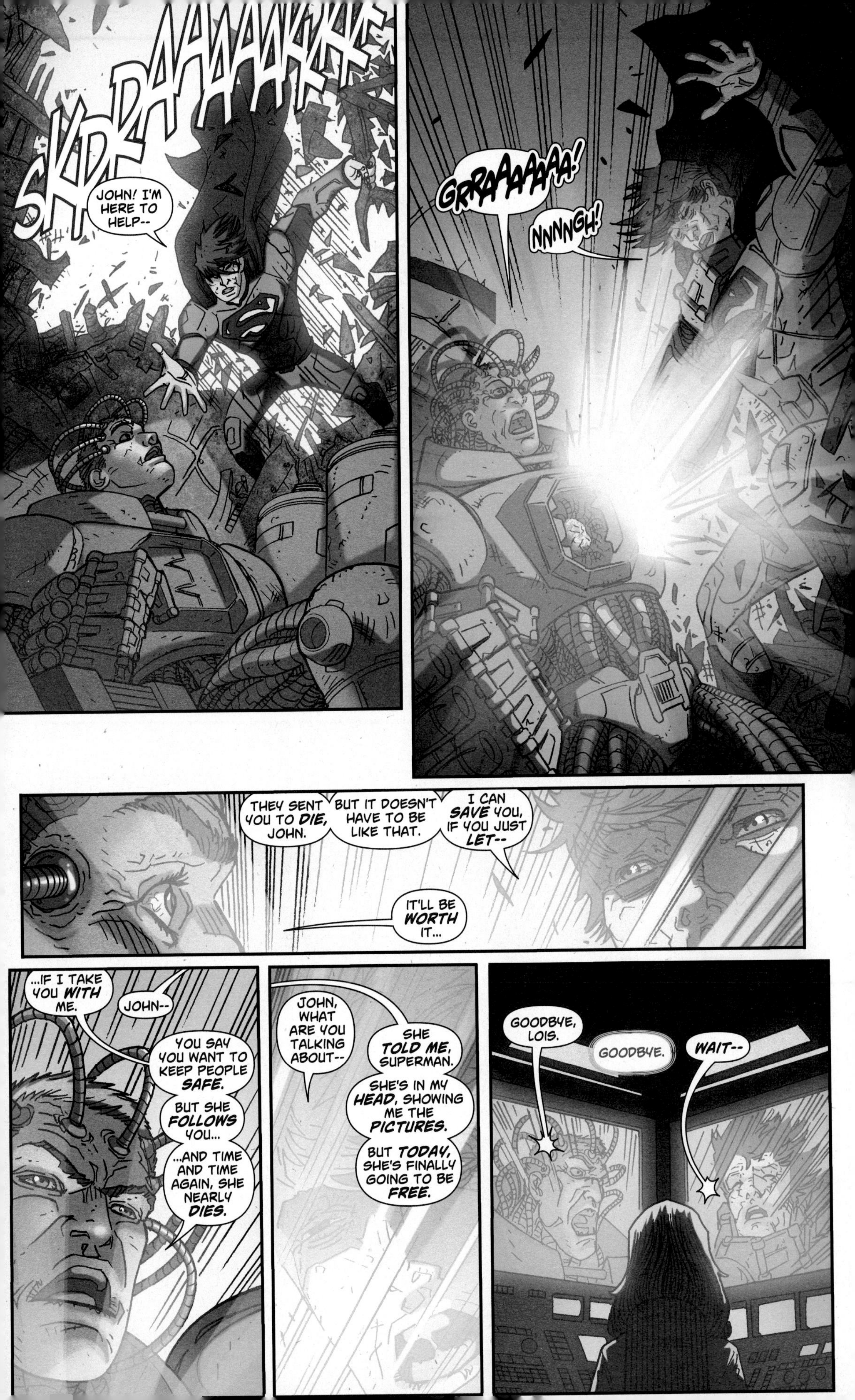
SKDRAAAAKKKK
JOHN! I'M HERE TO HELP--
GRRAAAAAAA!
NNNNGH!
THEY SENT YOU TO DIE, JOHN.
BUT IT DOESN'T HAVE TO BE LIKE THAT.
I CAN SAVE YOU, IF YOU JUST LET--
IT'LL BE WORTH IT...
...IF I TAKE YOU WITH ME.
JOHN--
YOU SAY YOU WANT TO KEEP PEOPLE SAFE.
BUT SHE FOLLOWS YOU...
...AND TIME AND TIME AGAIN, SHE NEARLY DIES.
JOHN, WHAT ARE YOU TALKING ABOUT--
SHE TOLD ME, SUPERMAN.
SHE'S IN MY HEAD, SHOWING ME THE PICTURES.
BUT TODAY, SHE'S FINALLY GOING TO BE FREE.
GOODBYE, LOIS.
GOODBYE.
WAIT--

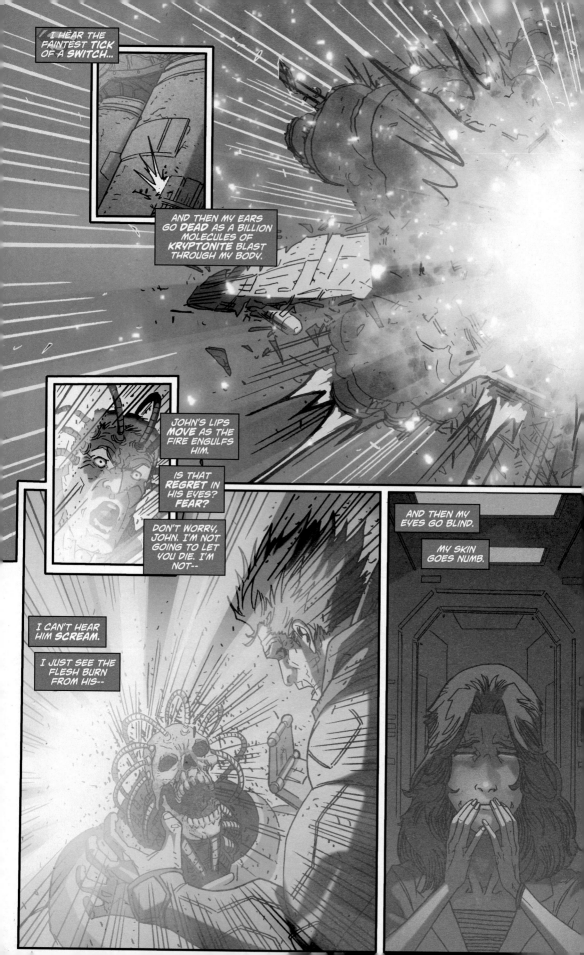

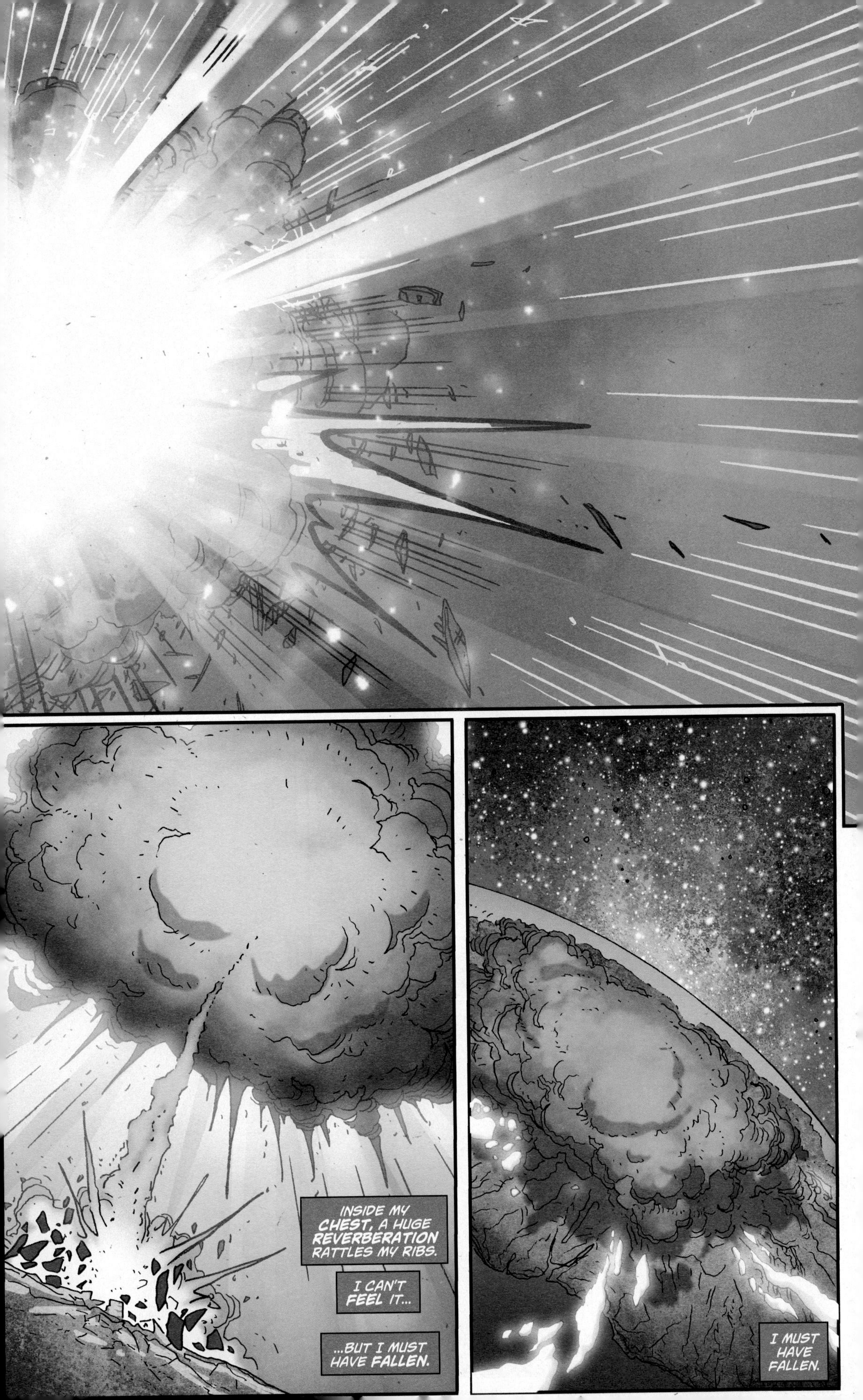
INSIDE MY CHEST, A HUGE REVERBERATION RATTLES MY RIBS.
I CAN'T FEEL IT...
...BUT I MUST HAVE FALLEN.
I MUST HAVE FALLEN.

THE ARCTIC.

GRRAAAOOOO!

SMALLVILLE.

CLARK...

HYDE PARK.

GODS...

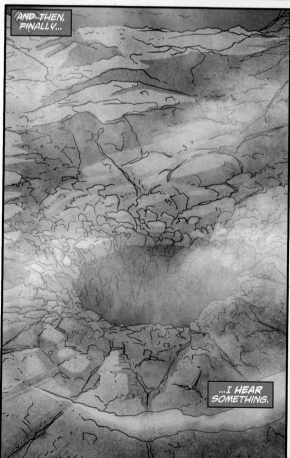

AND THEN, FINALLY...

...I HEAR SOMETHING.

AND I KNOW IT'S OVER.

GET UP.

NO.

THIS ISN'T THE END.

THIS IS JUST THE BEGINNING.

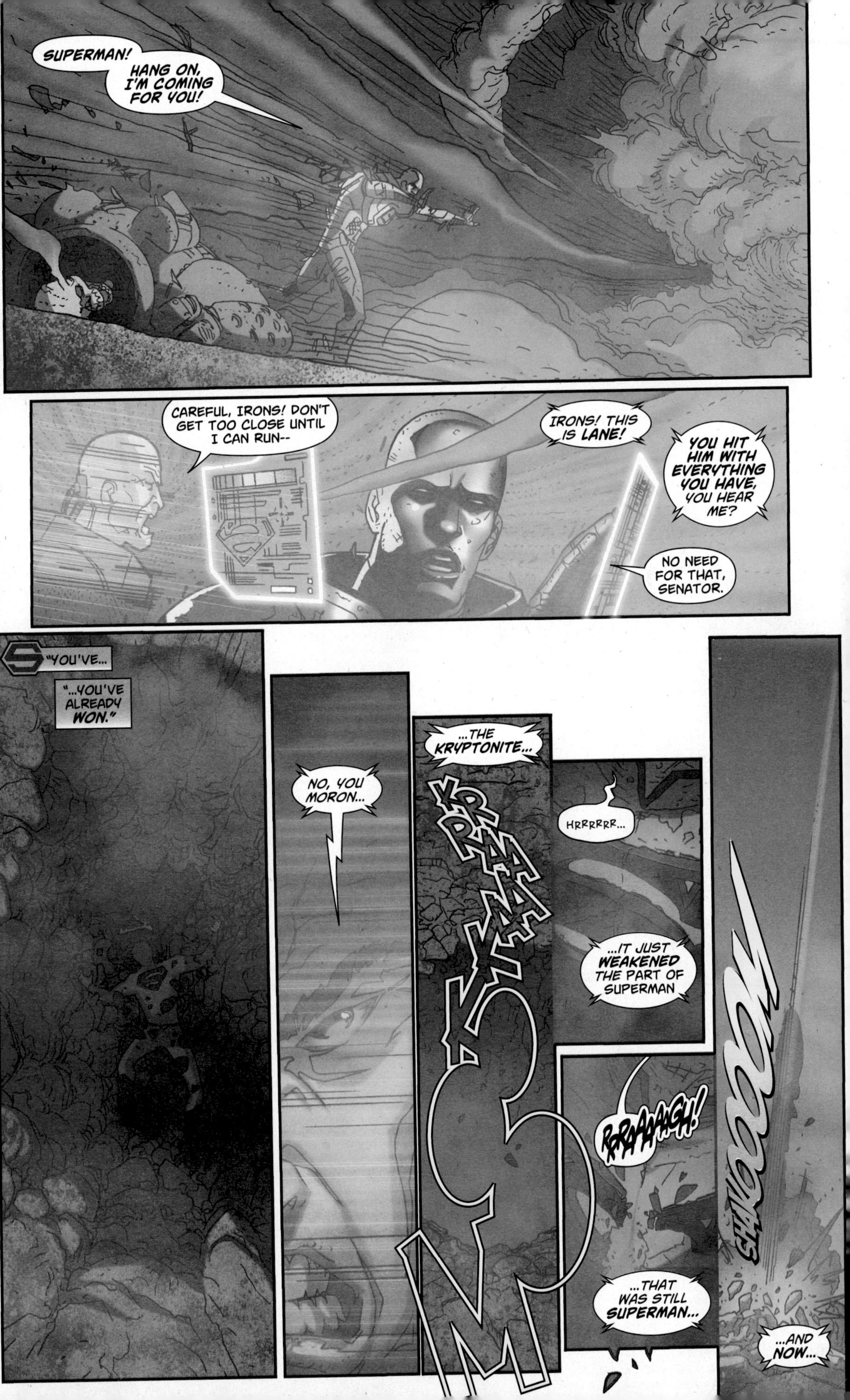

SUPERMAN! HANG ON, I'M COMING FOR YOU!
CAREFUL, IRONS! DON'T GET TOO CLOSE UNTIL I CAN RUN--
IRONS! THIS IS LANE!
YOU HIT HIM WITH EVERYTHING YOU HAVE, YOU HEAR ME?
NO NEED FOR THAT, SENATOR.
"YOU'VE...
"...YOU'VE ALREADY WON."
NO, YOU MORON...
...THE KRYPTONITE...
KRRAAAAKKA
HRRRRRR...
...IT JUST WEAKENED THE PART OF SUPERMAN
RRRAAAAAGH!
...THAT WAS STILL SUPERMAN...
SHHHOOOOOM
...AND NOW...

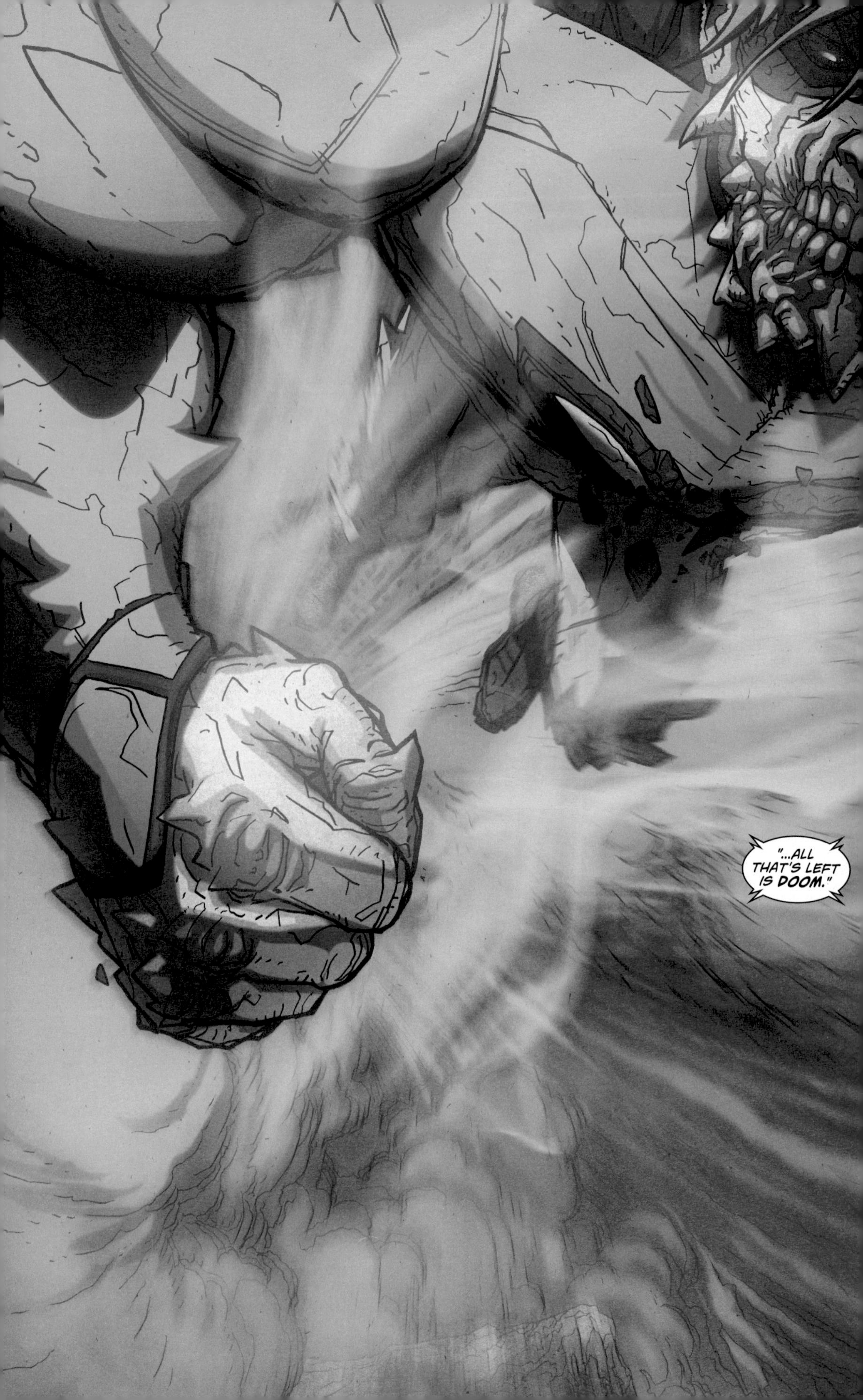
"...ALL THAT'S LEFT IS DOOM."

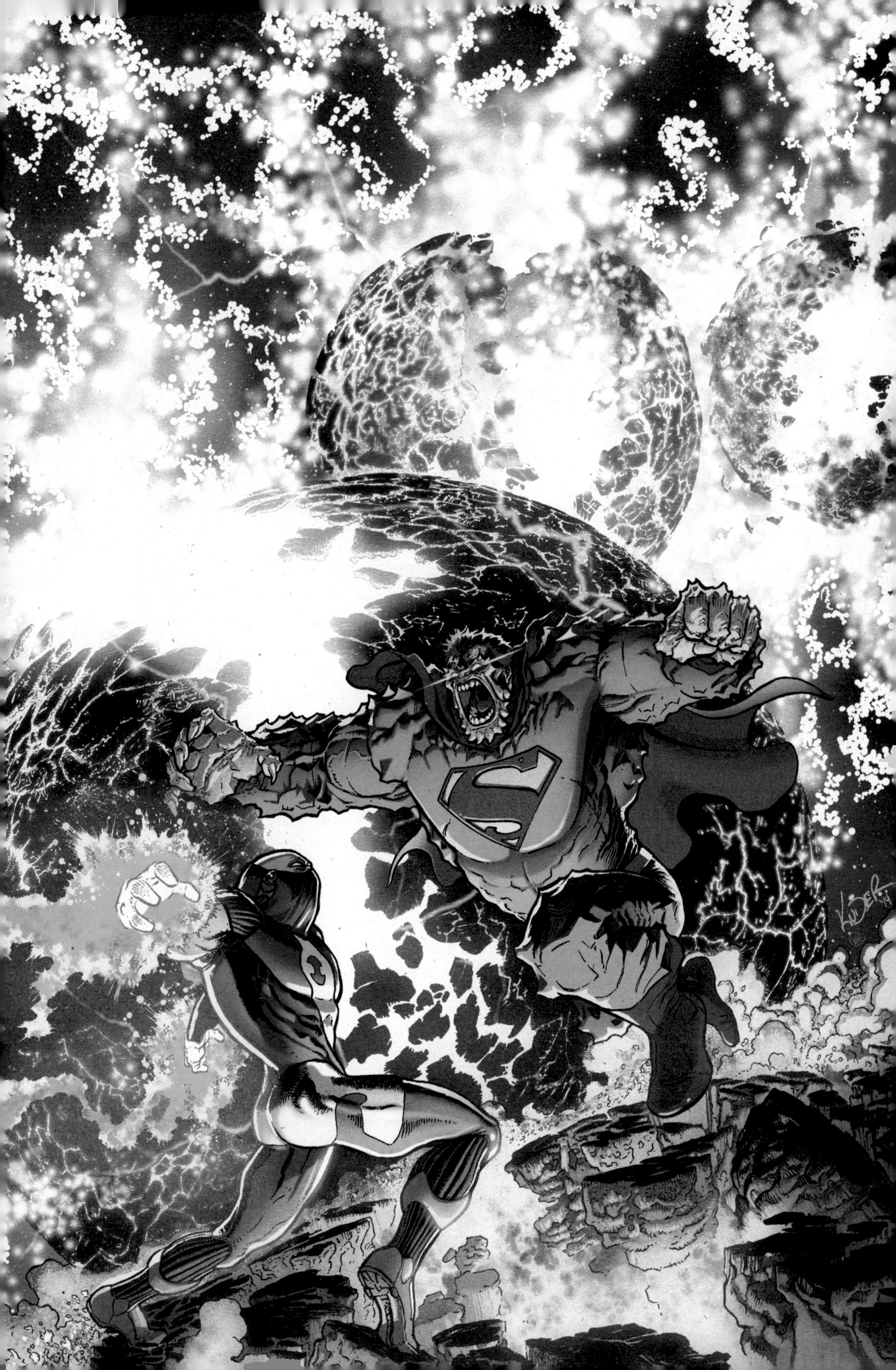

WORLD   U.S. METROPOLIS   BUSINESS   OPINION   SPORTS   ARTS   STYLE   VIDEO

Daily Planet

DAILY PLANET

July 7, 201

Superman or SuperMENACE?

By Lois Lane

It looks as if Metropolis and the world may finally find itself free of the Man of Steel's recent erratic and dangerous behavior.

After a bloody battle with the monster known as Doomsday in Smallville, Kansas, Superman has grown increasingly unpredictable and destructive. As the Teen Titans were heard to say, "There's something wrong with Superman."

Looking more and more like the monster he just defeated, an increasingly dangerous Superman has forced the government to deploy a Kryptonite bomb, which has left the Earth covered in material that we have been assured is not lethal to humans.

Most recently the Last Son of Krypton was spotted in Brazil, where witnesses claimed he first fought an unknown armored, female warrior, who was later joined by Wonder Woman.

Onlookers claim Wonder Woman pulled the Super-Monster

Photo by Daily Planet Satellite

into the upper atmosphere, only to return moments later in a battle with a trio of Red Lanterns and the Super-creature.

According to witnesses, Super-

man finally left the planet of his own accord, but his destination and when he might return are unknown. We will all just have to look up in the sky and pray he does not come back.

How will this all affect Supergirl?
Smallville still under quarantine—
— no change in victims
What is the Justice League's response?
Weather—Mostly Cloudy Green

Real-time satellite video of
the green atmosphere

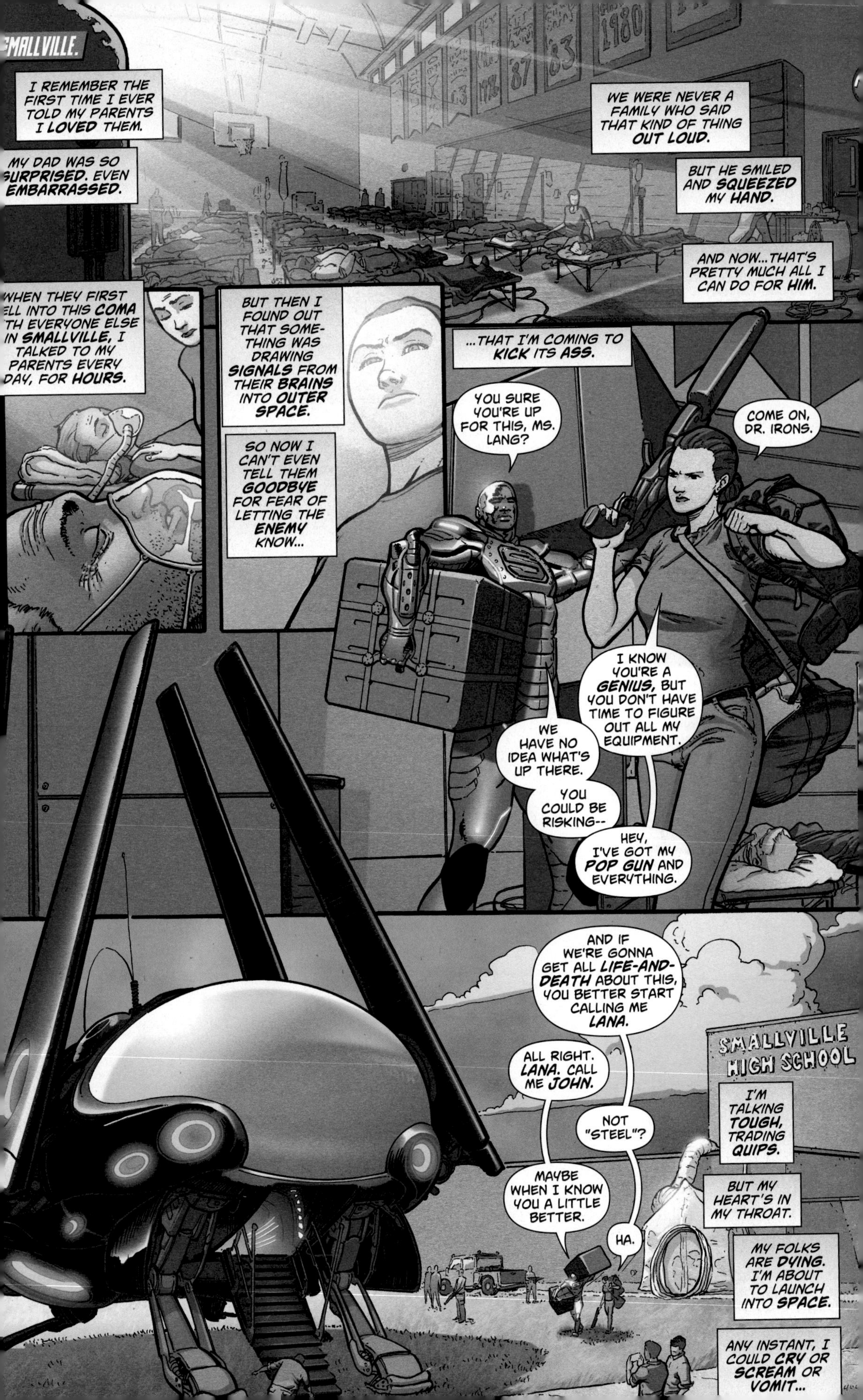
SMALLVILLE.
I REMEMBER THE FIRST TIME I EVER TOLD MY PARENTS I LOVED THEM.
MY DAD WAS SO SURPRISED. EVEN EMBARRASSED.
WE WERE NEVER A FAMILY WHO SAID THAT KIND OF THING OUT LOUD.
BUT HE SMILED AND SQUEEZED MY HAND.
AND NOW...THAT'S PRETTY MUCH ALL I CAN DO FOR HIM.
WHEN THEY FIRST ELL INTO THIS COMA TH EVERYONE ELSE IN SMALLVILLE, I TALKED TO MY PARENTS EVERY DAY, FOR HOURS.
BUT THEN I FOUND OUT THAT SOMETHING WAS DRAWING SIGNALS FROM THEIR BRAINS INTO OUTER SPACE.
SO NOW I CAN'T EVEN TELL THEM GOODBYE FOR FEAR OF LETTING THE ENEMY KNOW...
...THAT I'M COMING TO KICK ITS ASS.
YOU SURE YOU'RE UP FOR THIS, MS. LANG?
COME ON, DR. IRONS.
I KNOW YOU'RE A GENIUS, BUT YOU DON'T HAVE TIME TO FIGURE OUT ALL MY EQUIPMENT.
WE HAVE NO IDEA WHAT'S UP THERE.
YOU COULD BE RISKING--
HEY, I'VE GOT MY POP GUN AND EVERYTHING.
AND IF WE'RE GONNA GET ALL LIFE-AND-DEATH ABOUT THIS, YOU BETTER START CALLING ME LANA.
ALL RIGHT. LANA. CALL ME JOHN.
NOT "STEEL"?
MAYBE WHEN I KNOW YOU A LITTLE BETTER.
HA.
SMALLVILLE HIGH SCHOOL
I'M TALKING TOUGH, TRADING QUIPS.
BUT MY HEART'S IN MY THROAT.
MY FOLKS ARE DYING. I'M ABOUT TO LAUNCH INTO SPACE.
ANY INSTANT, I COULD CRY OR SCREAM OR VOMIT...

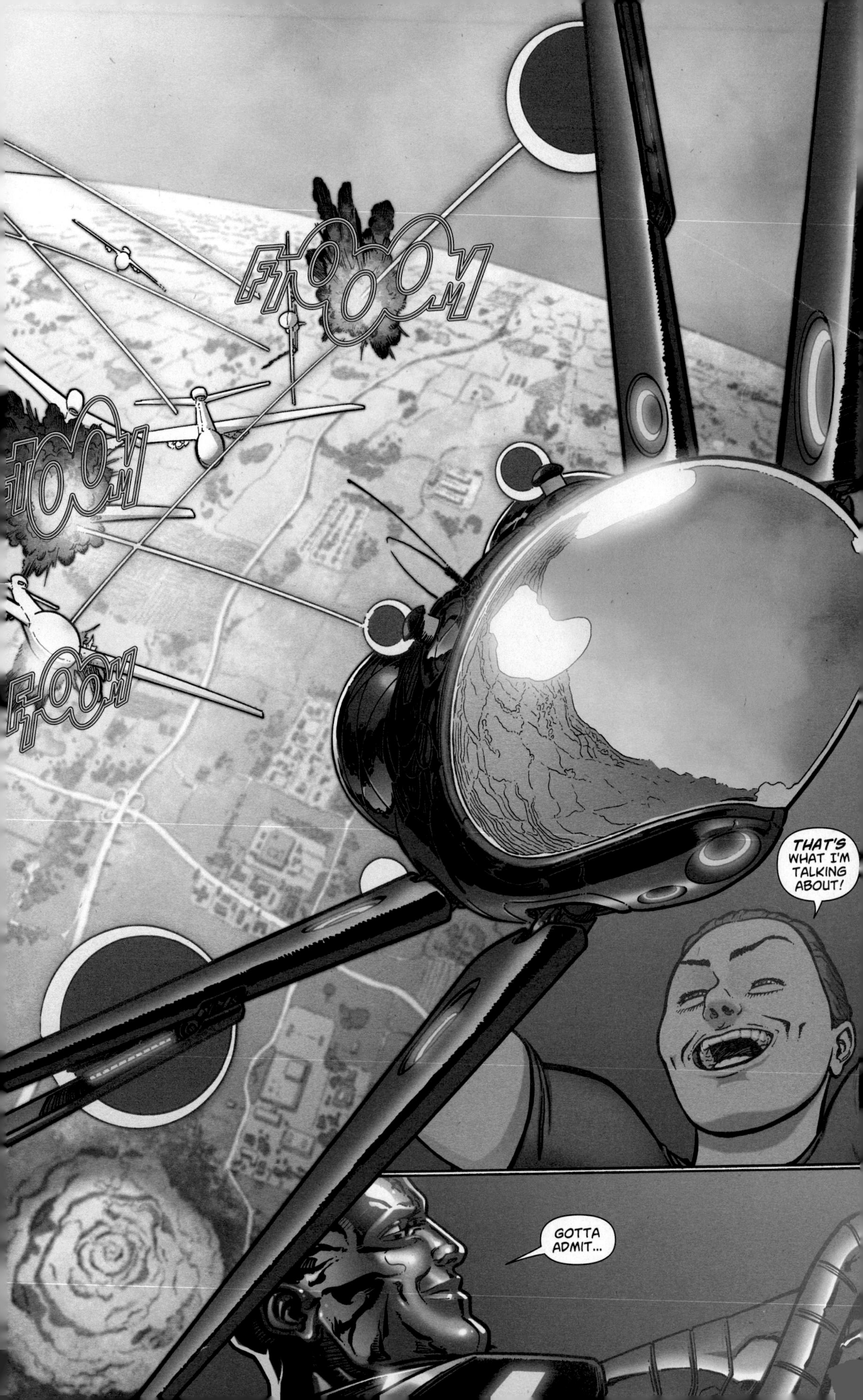
FTOOOM
FTOOOM
FTOOOM
THAT'S WHAT I'M TALKING ABOUT!
GOTTA ADMIT...

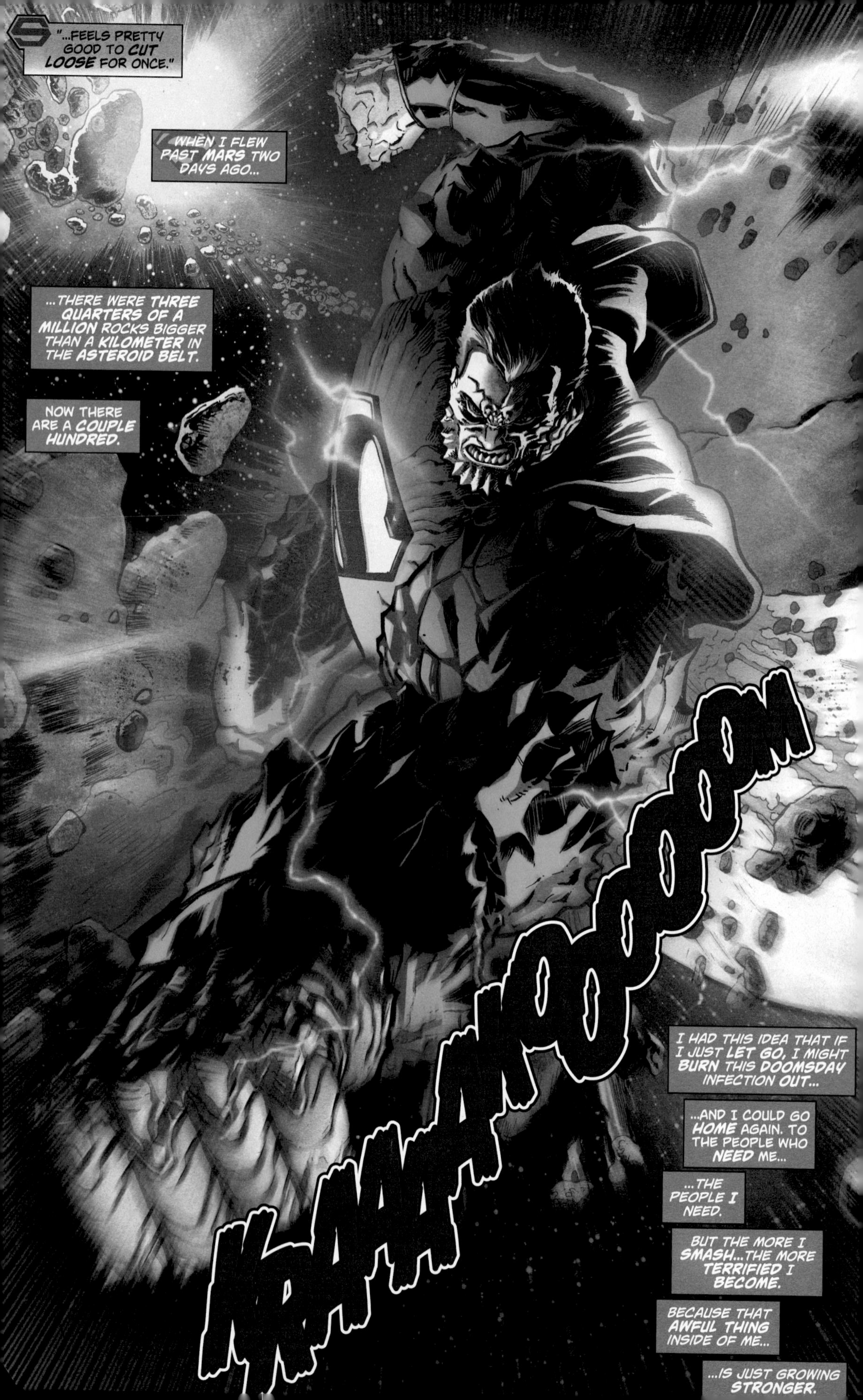
"...FEELS PRETTY GOOD TO CUT LOOSE FOR ONCE."
WHEN I FLEW PAST MARS TWO DAYS AGO...
...THERE WERE THREE QUARTERS OF A MILLION ROCKS BIGGER THAN A KILOMETER IN THE ASTEROID BELT.
NOW THERE ARE A COUPLE HUNDRED.
KRAAAKOOOOOOOM
I HAD THIS IDEA THAT IF I JUST LET GO, I MIGHT BURN THIS DOOMSDAY INFECTION OUT...
...AND I COULD GO HOME AGAIN. TO THE PEOPLE WHO NEED ME...
...THE PEOPLE I NEED.
BUT THE MORE I SMASH...THE MORE TERRIFIED I BECOME.
BECAUSE THAT AWFUL THING INSIDE OF ME...
...IS JUST GROWING STRONGER.

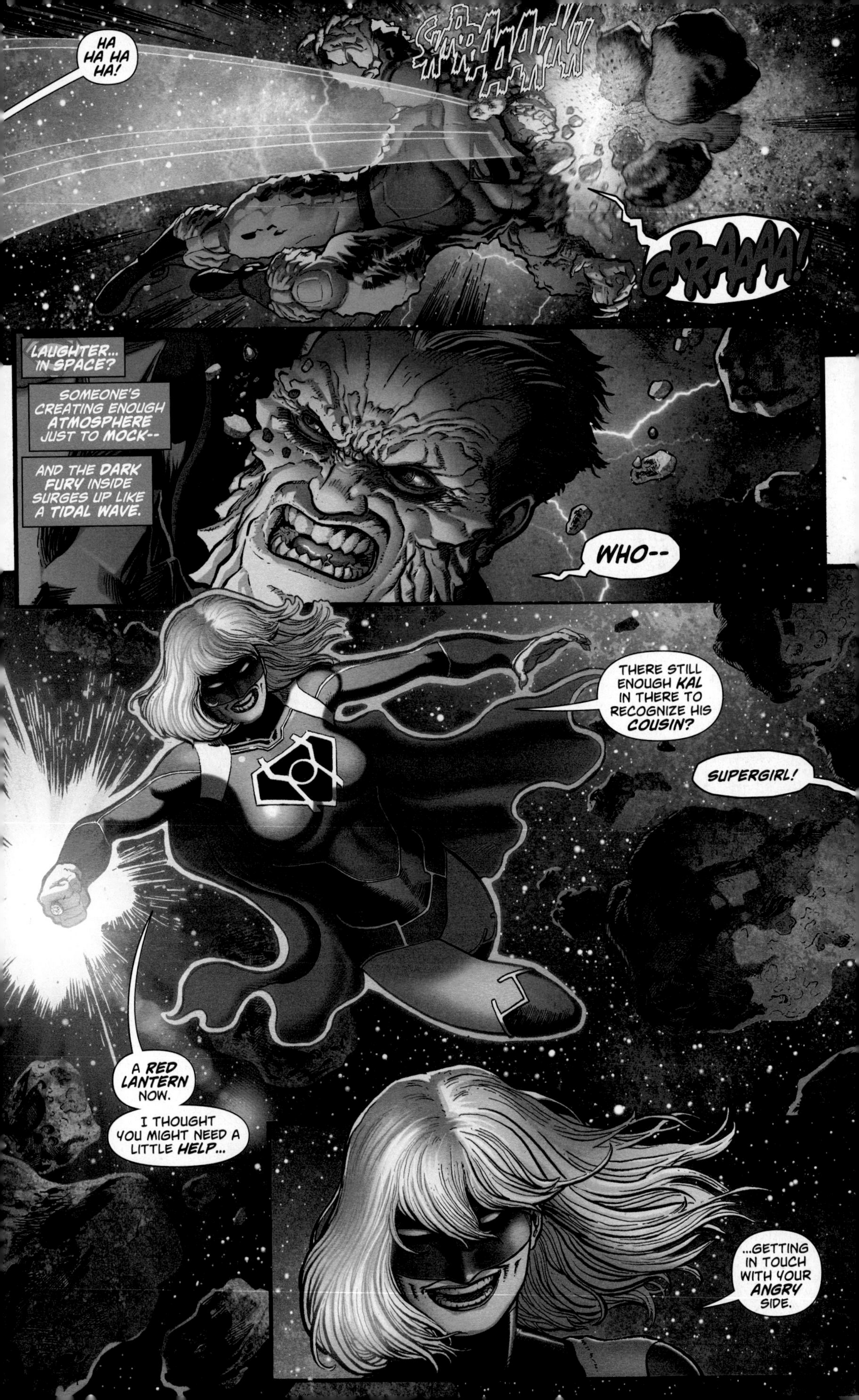
HA HA HA HA!
SKRAAAKK
GRRAAAA!
LAUGHTER... IN SPACE?
SOMEONE'S CREATING ENOUGH ATMOSPHERE JUST TO MOCK--
AND THE DARK FURY INSIDE SURGES UP LIKE A TIDAL WAVE.
WHO--
THERE STILL ENOUGH KAL IN THERE TO RECOGNIZE HIS COUSIN?
SUPERGIRL!
A RED LANTERN NOW.
I THOUGHT YOU MIGHT NEED A LITTLE HELP...
...GETTING IN TOUCH WITH YOUR ANGRY SIDE.

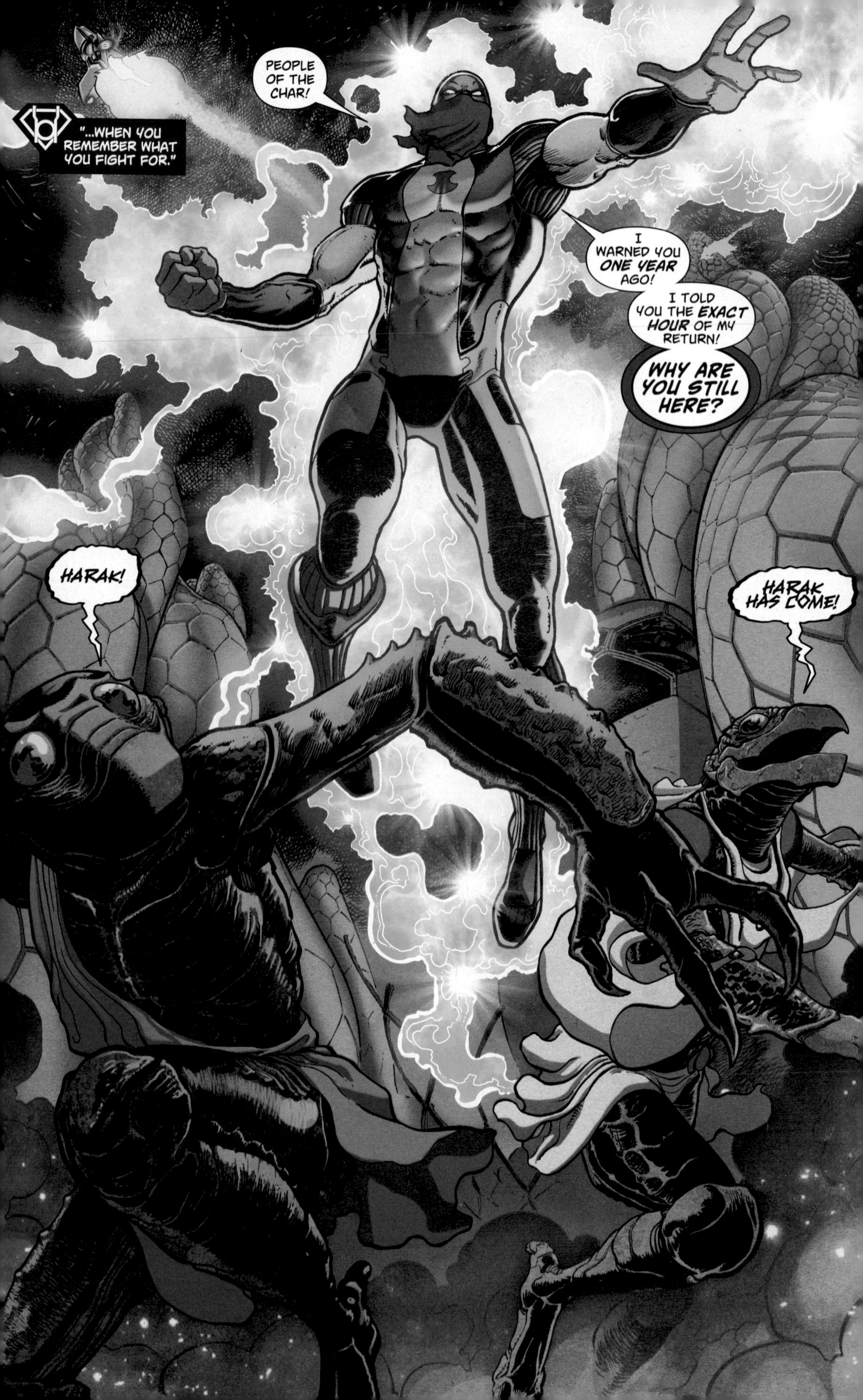
"...WHEN YOU REMEMBER WHAT YOU FIGHT FOR."
PEOPLE OF THE CHAR!
I WARNED YOU ONE YEAR AGO!
I TOLD YOU THE EXACT HOUR OF MY RETURN!
WHY ARE YOU STILL HERE?
HARAK!
HARAK HAS COME!

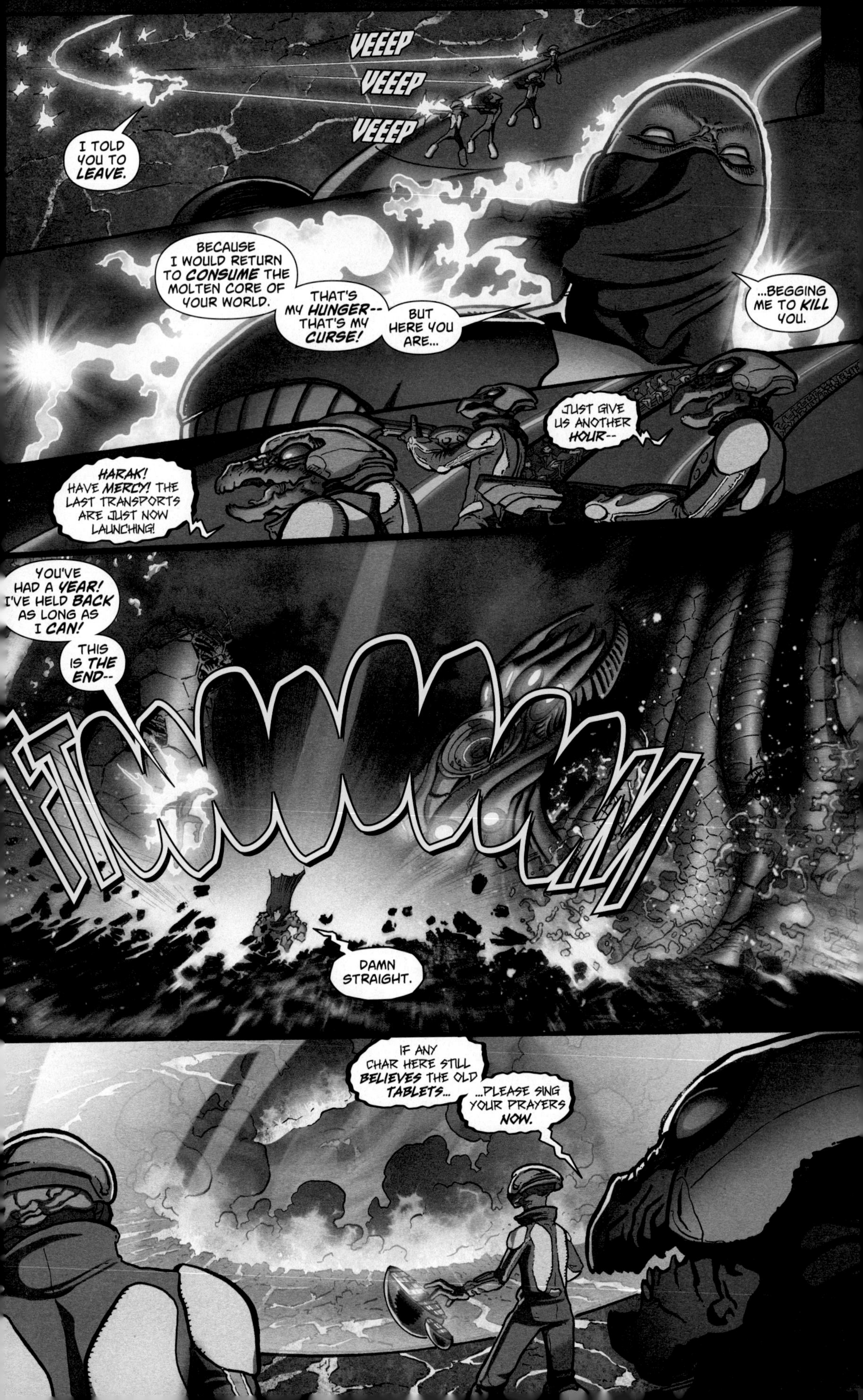
VEEEP
VEEEP
VEEEP
I TOLD YOU TO LEAVE.
BECAUSE I WOULD RETURN TO CONSUME THE MOLTEN CORE OF YOUR WORLD.
THAT'S MY HUNGER-- THAT'S MY CURSE!
BUT HERE YOU ARE...
...BEGGING ME TO KILL YOU.
HARAK! HAVE MERCY! THE LAST TRANSPORTS ARE JUST NOW LAUNCHING!
JUST GIVE US ANOTHER HOUR--
YOU'VE HAD A YEAR! I'VE HELD BACK AS LONG AS I CAN!
THIS IS THE END--
DAMN STRAIGHT.
IF ANY CHAR HERE STILL BELIEVES THE OLD TABLETS...
...PLEASE SING YOUR PRAYERS NOW.

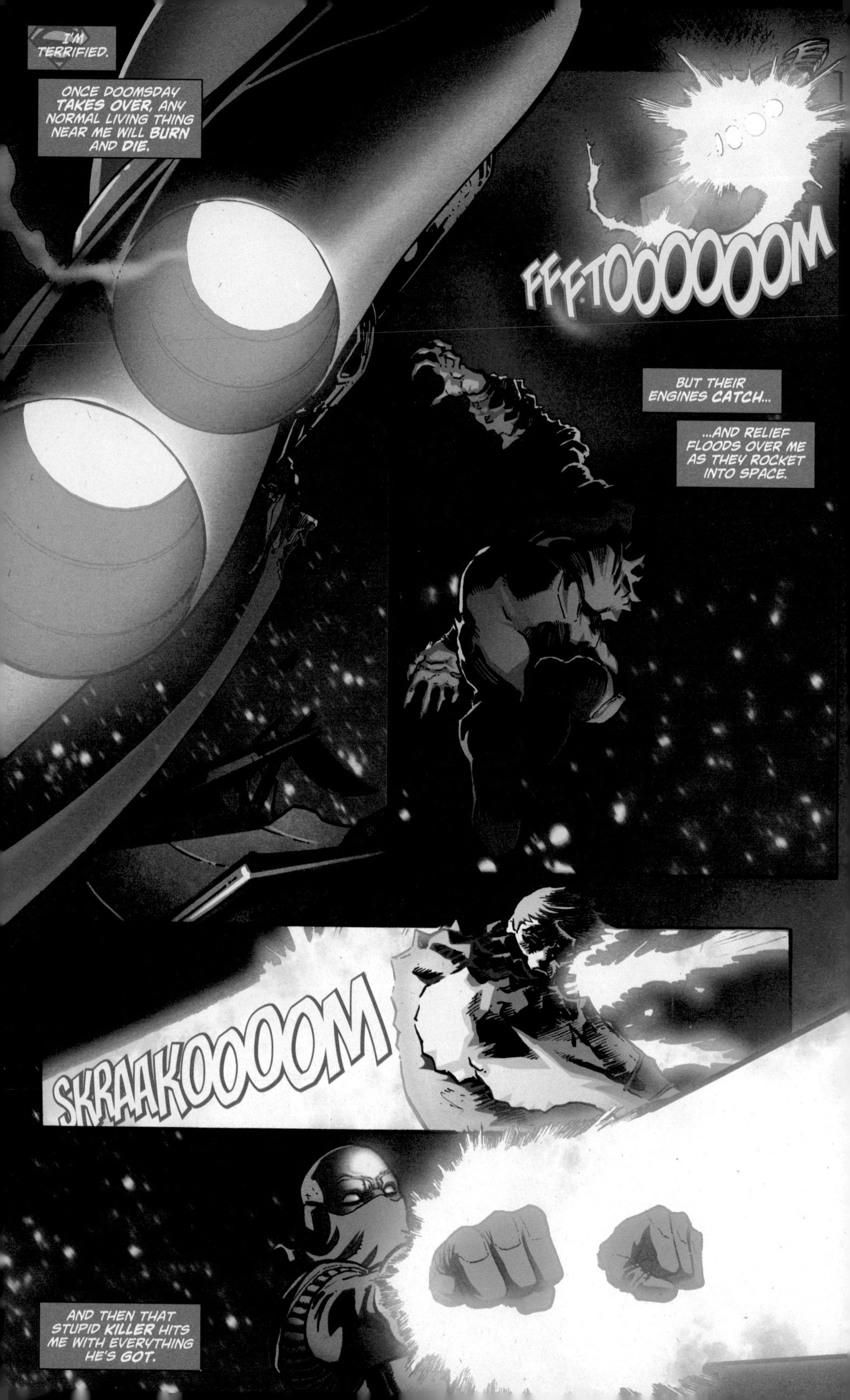
I'M TERRIFIED.
ONCE DOOMSDAY TAKES OVER, ANY NORMAL LIVING THING NEAR ME WILL BURN AND DIE.
FFFTOOOOOOOM
BUT THEIR ENGINES CATCH...
...AND RELIEF FLOODS OVER ME AS THEY ROCKET INTO SPACE.
SKRAAKOOOOM
AND THEN THAT STUPID KILLER HITS ME WITH EVERYTHING HE'S GOT.

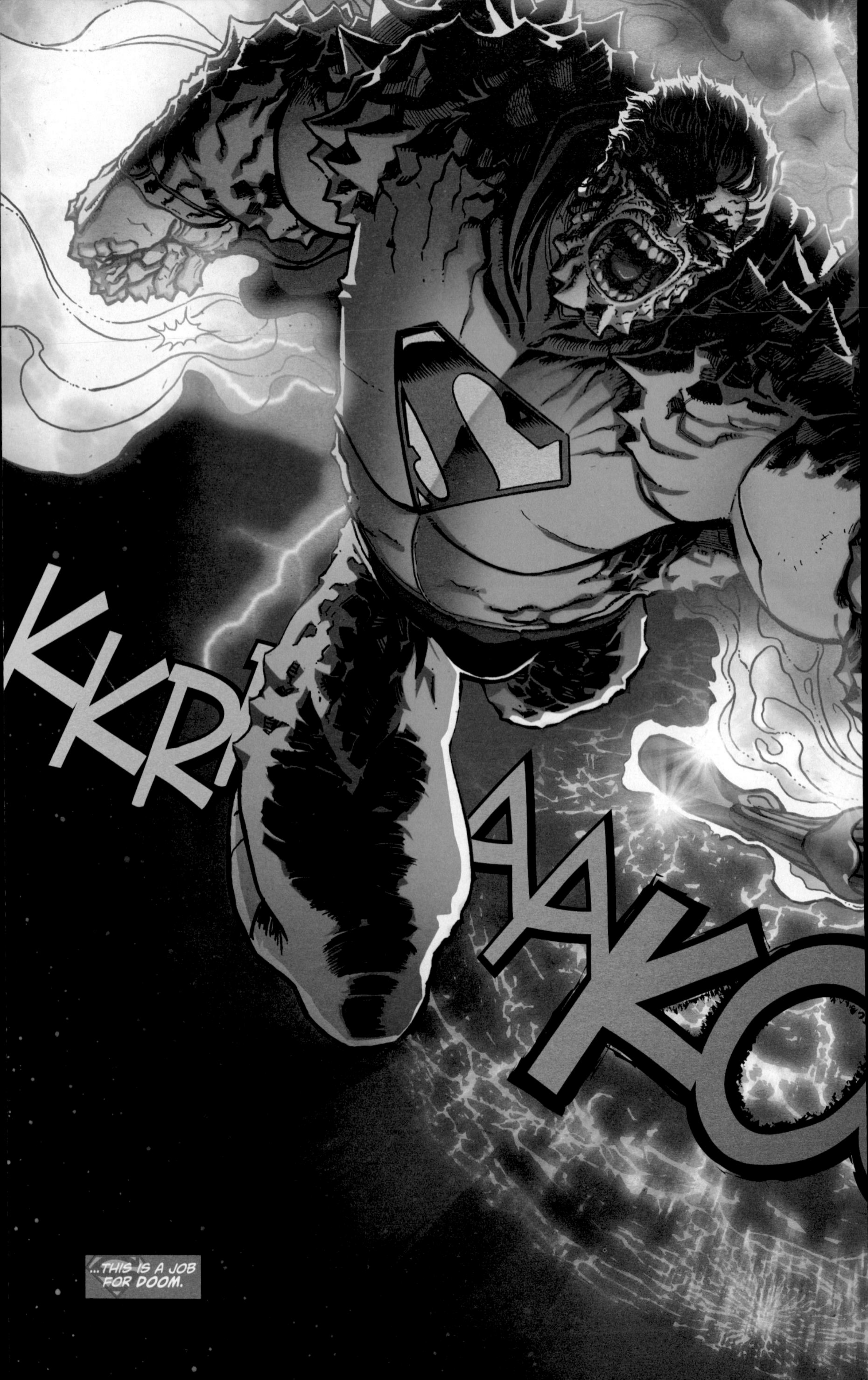
KKRAAKOO
...THIS IS A JOB FOR DOOM.

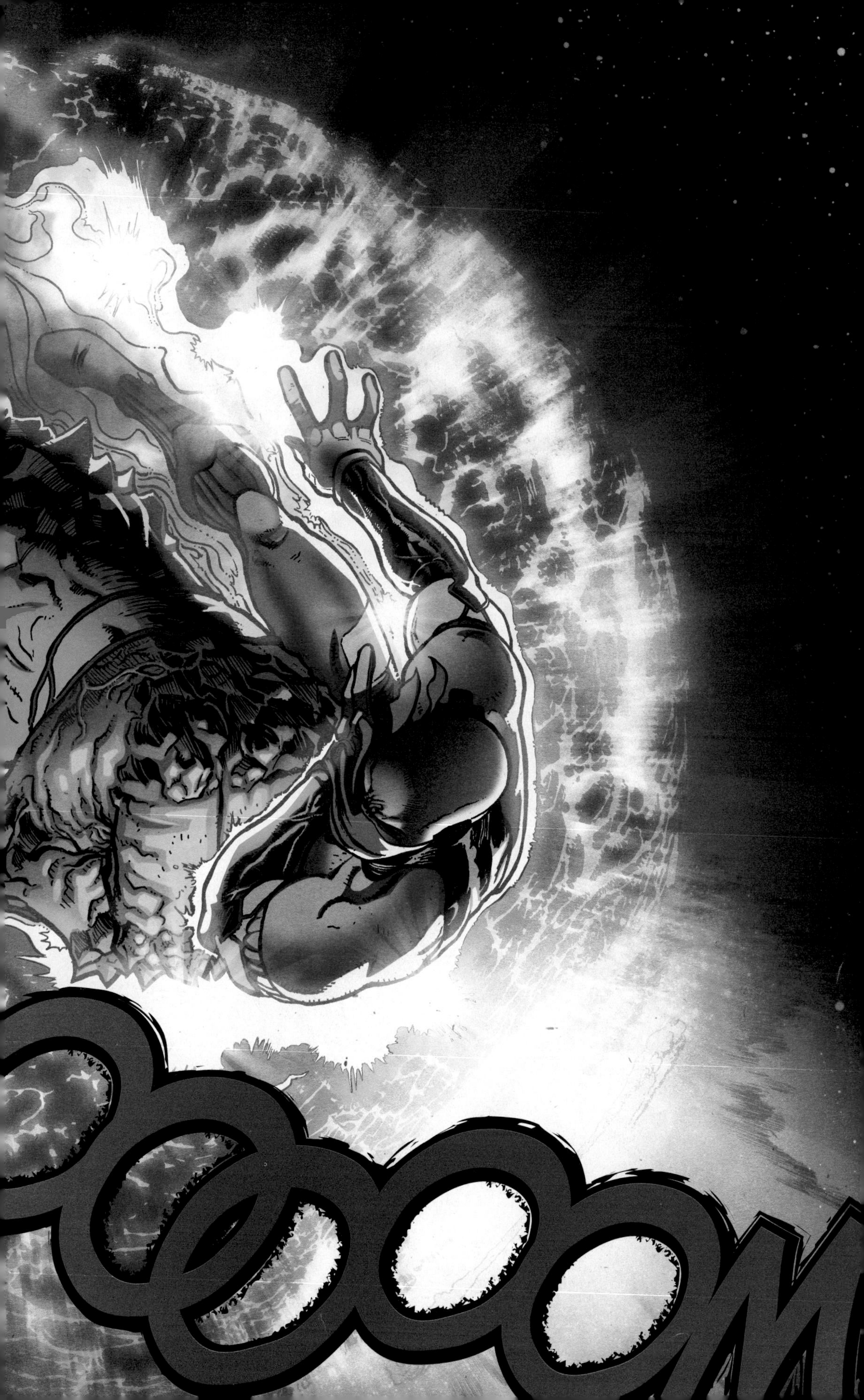
OOOOM

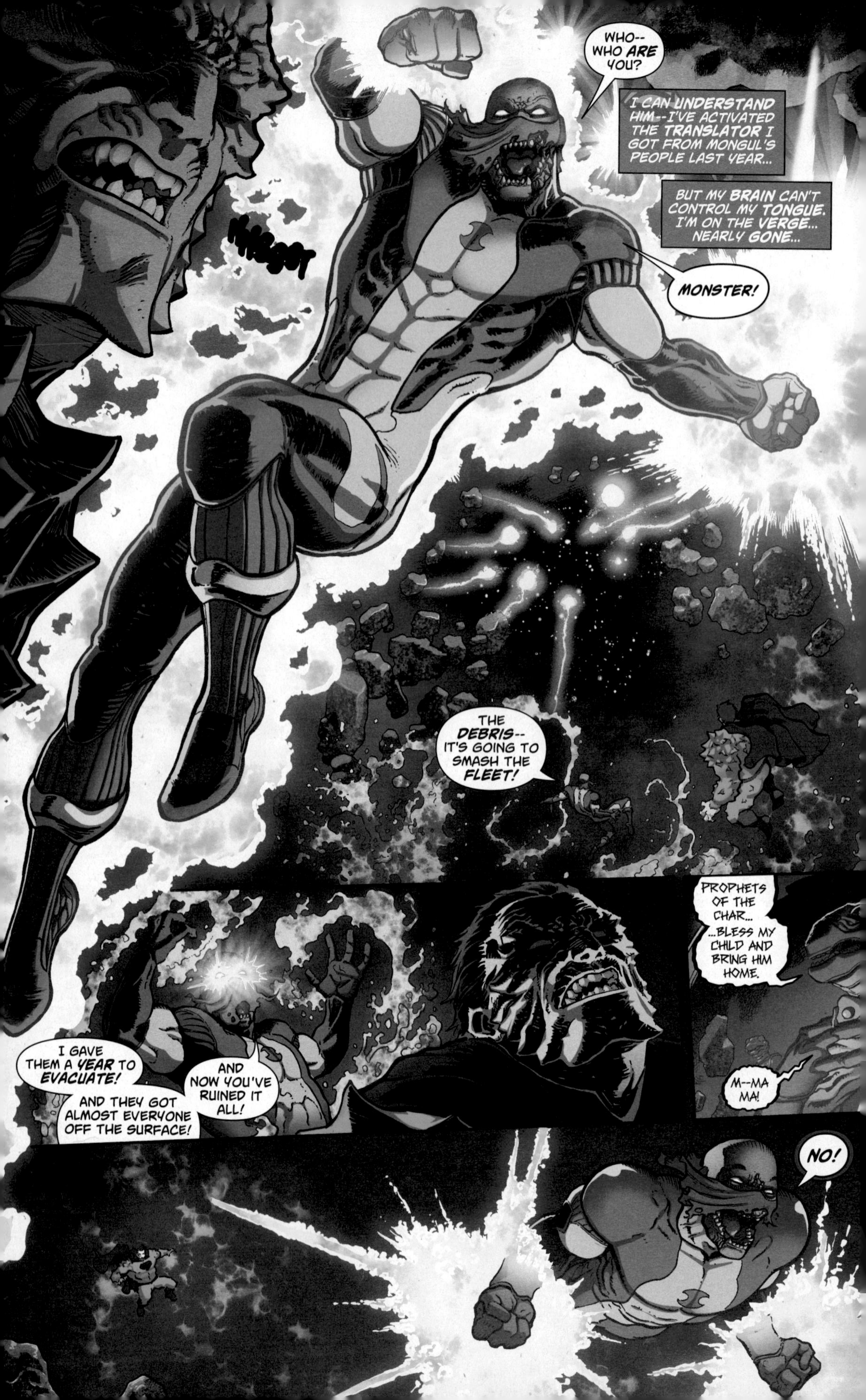
WHO--
WHO ARE YOU?
I CAN UNDERSTAND HIM--I'VE ACTIVATED THE TRANSLATOR I GOT FROM MONGUL'S PEOPLE LAST YEAR...
BUT MY BRAIN CAN'T CONTROL MY TONGUE. I'M ON THE VERGE... NEARLY GONE...
MONSTER!
THE DEBRIS-- IT'S GOING TO SMASH THE FLEET!
I GAVE THEM A YEAR TO EVACUATE!
AND THEY GOT ALMOST EVERYONE OFF THE SURFACE!
AND NOW YOU'VE RUINED IT ALL!
PROPHETS OF THE CHAR... ...BLESS MY CHILD AND BRING HIM HOME.
M--MA MA!
NO!

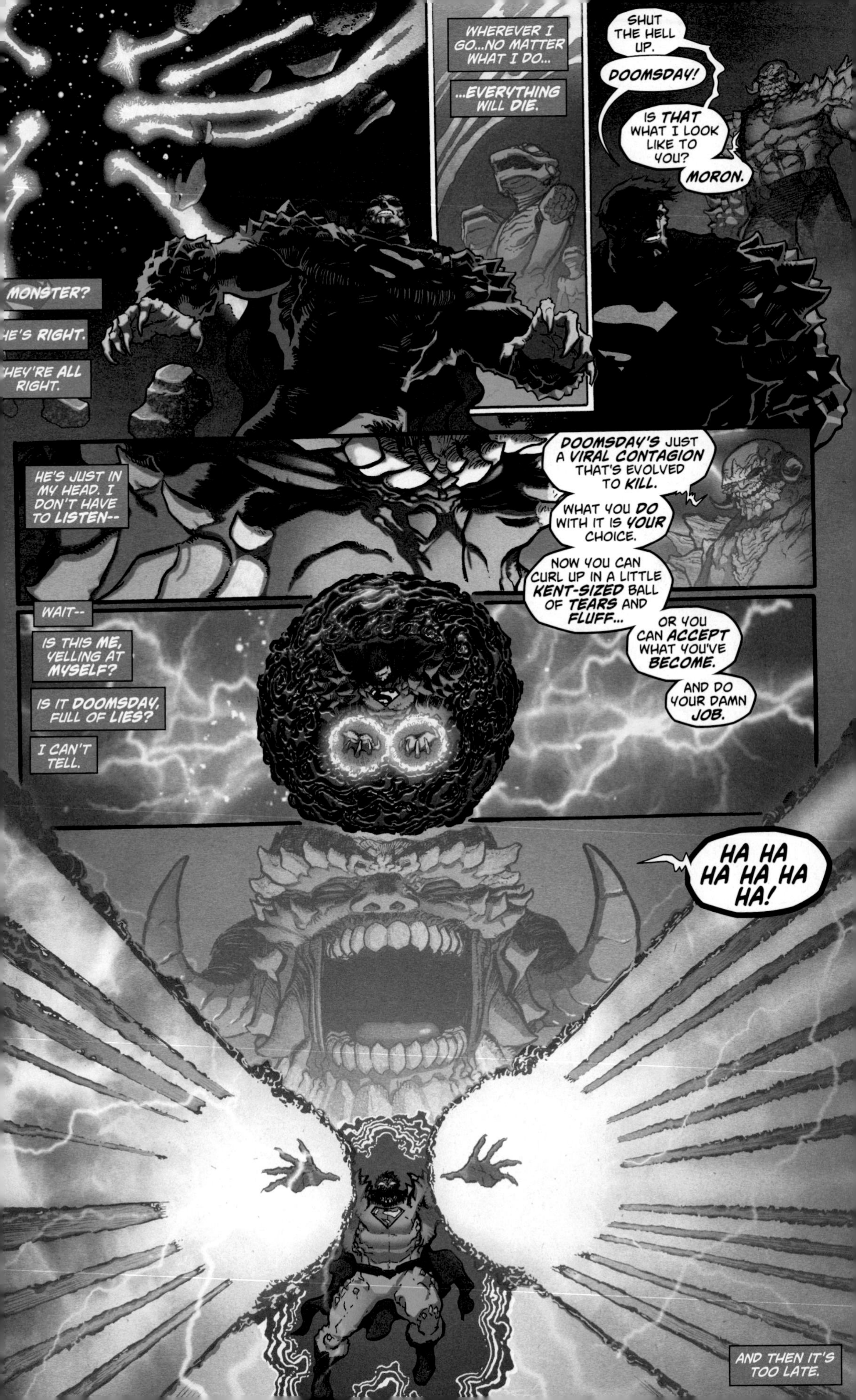
WHEREVER I GO...NO MATTER WHAT I DO...
...EVERYTHING WILL DIE.
SHUT THE HELL UP.
DOOMSDAY!
IS THAT WHAT I LOOK LIKE TO YOU?
MORON.
MONSTER?
HE'S RIGHT.
THEY'RE ALL RIGHT.
HE'S JUST IN MY HEAD. I DON'T HAVE TO LISTEN--
DOOMSDAY'S JUST A VIRAL CONTAGION THAT'S EVOLVED TO KILL.
WHAT YOU DO WITH IT IS YOUR CHOICE.
NOW YOU CAN CURL UP IN A LITTLE KENT-SIZED BALL OF TEARS AND FLUFF...
OR YOU CAN ACCEPT WHAT YOU'VE BECOME.
AND DO YOUR DAMN JOB.
WAIT--
IS THIS ME, YELLING AT MYSELF?
IS IT DOOMSDAY, FULL OF LIES?
I CAN'T TELL.
HA HA HA HA HA HA!
AND THEN IT'S TOO LATE.

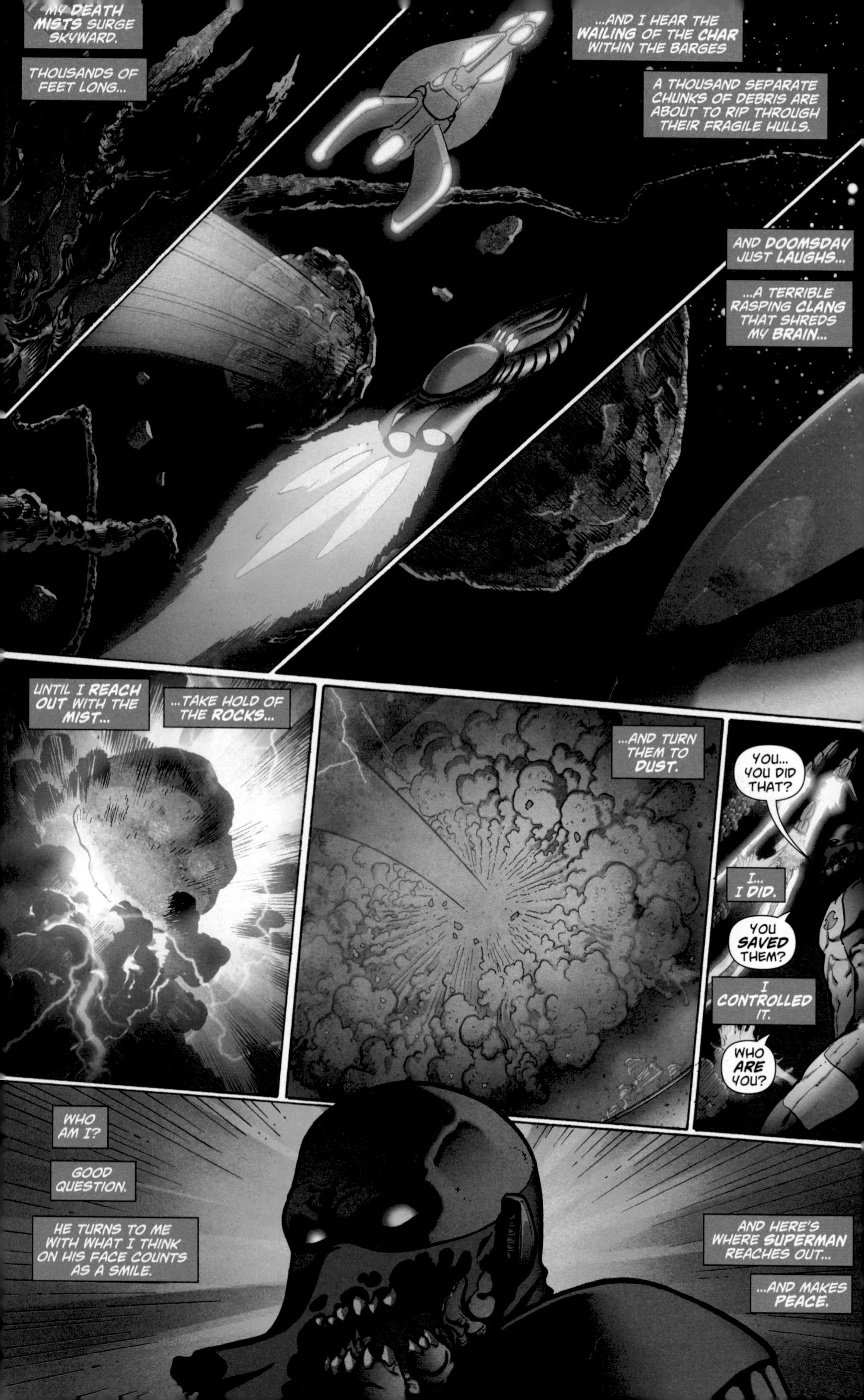
MY DEATH MISTS SURGE SKYWARD.
THOUSANDS OF FEET LONG...
...AND I HEAR THE WAILING OF THE CHAR WITHIN THE BARGES
A THOUSAND SEPARATE CHUNKS OF DEBRIS ARE ABOUT TO RIP THROUGH THEIR FRAGILE HULLS.
AND DOOMSDAY JUST LAUGHS...
...A TERRIBLE RASPING CLANG THAT SHREDS MY BRAIN...
UNTIL I REACH OUT WITH THE MIST...
...TAKE HOLD OF THE ROCKS...
...AND TURN THEM TO DUST.
YOU... YOU DID THAT?
I... I DID.
YOU SAVED THEM?
I CONTROLLED IT.
WHO ARE YOU?
WHO AM I?
GOOD QUESTION.
HE TURNS TO ME WITH WHAT I THINK ON HIS FACE COUNTS AS A SMILE.
AND HERE'S WHERE SUPERMAN REACHES OUT...
...AND MAKES PEACE.

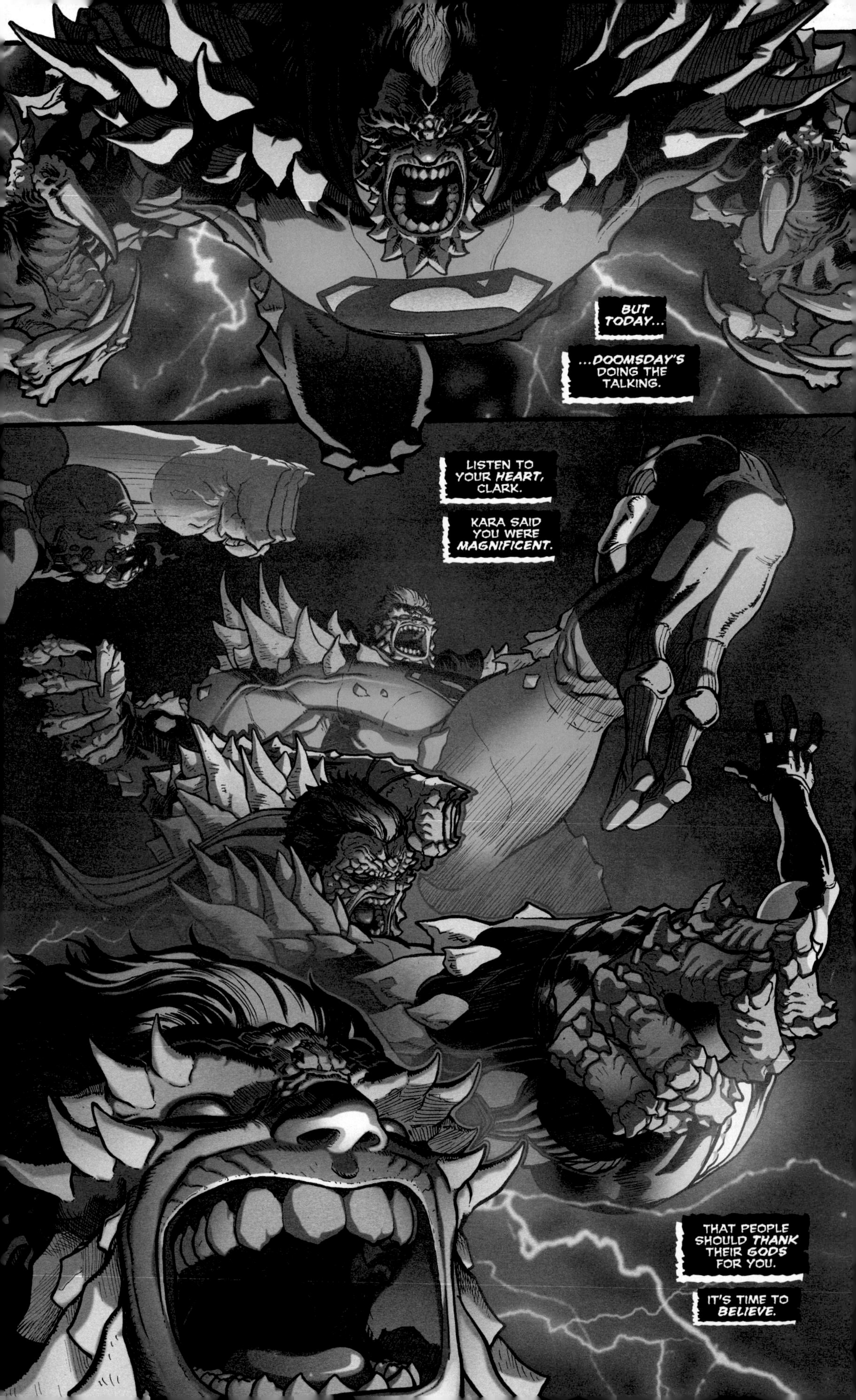
BUT TODAY...
...DOOMSDAY'S DOING THE TALKING.
LISTEN TO YOUR HEART, CLARK.
KARA SAID YOU WERE MAGNIFICENT.
THAT PEOPLE SHOULD THANK THEIR GODS FOR YOU.
IT'S TIME TO BELIEVE.

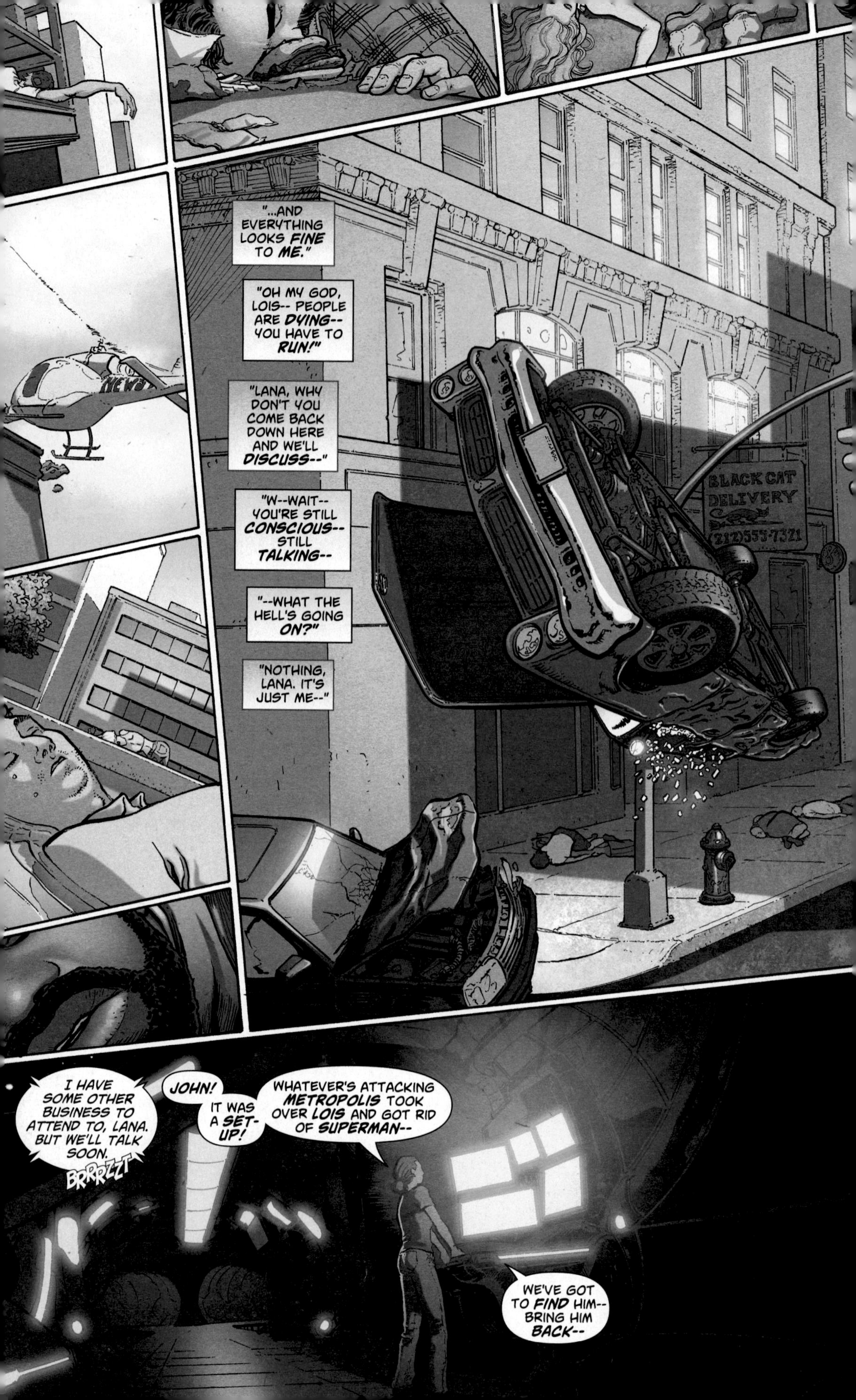
"...AND EVERYTHING LOOKS FINE TO ME."
"OH MY GOD, LOIS-- PEOPLE ARE DYING-- YOU HAVE TO RUN!"
"LANA, WHY DON'T YOU COME BACK DOWN HERE AND WE'LL DISCUSS--"
"W--WAIT-- YOU'RE STILL CONSCIOUS-- STILL TALKING--
"--WHAT THE HELL'S GOING ON?"
"NOTHING, LANA. IT'S JUST ME--"
BLACK CAT DELIVERY
(212)555-7321
I HAVE SOME OTHER BUSINESS TO ATTEND TO, LANA. BUT WE'LL TALK SOON.
BRRRZZT
JOHN!
IT WAS A SET-UP!
WHATEVER'S ATTACKING METROPOLIS TOOK OVER LOIS AND GOT RID OF SUPERMAN--
WE'VE GOT TO FIND HIM-- BRING HIM BACK--

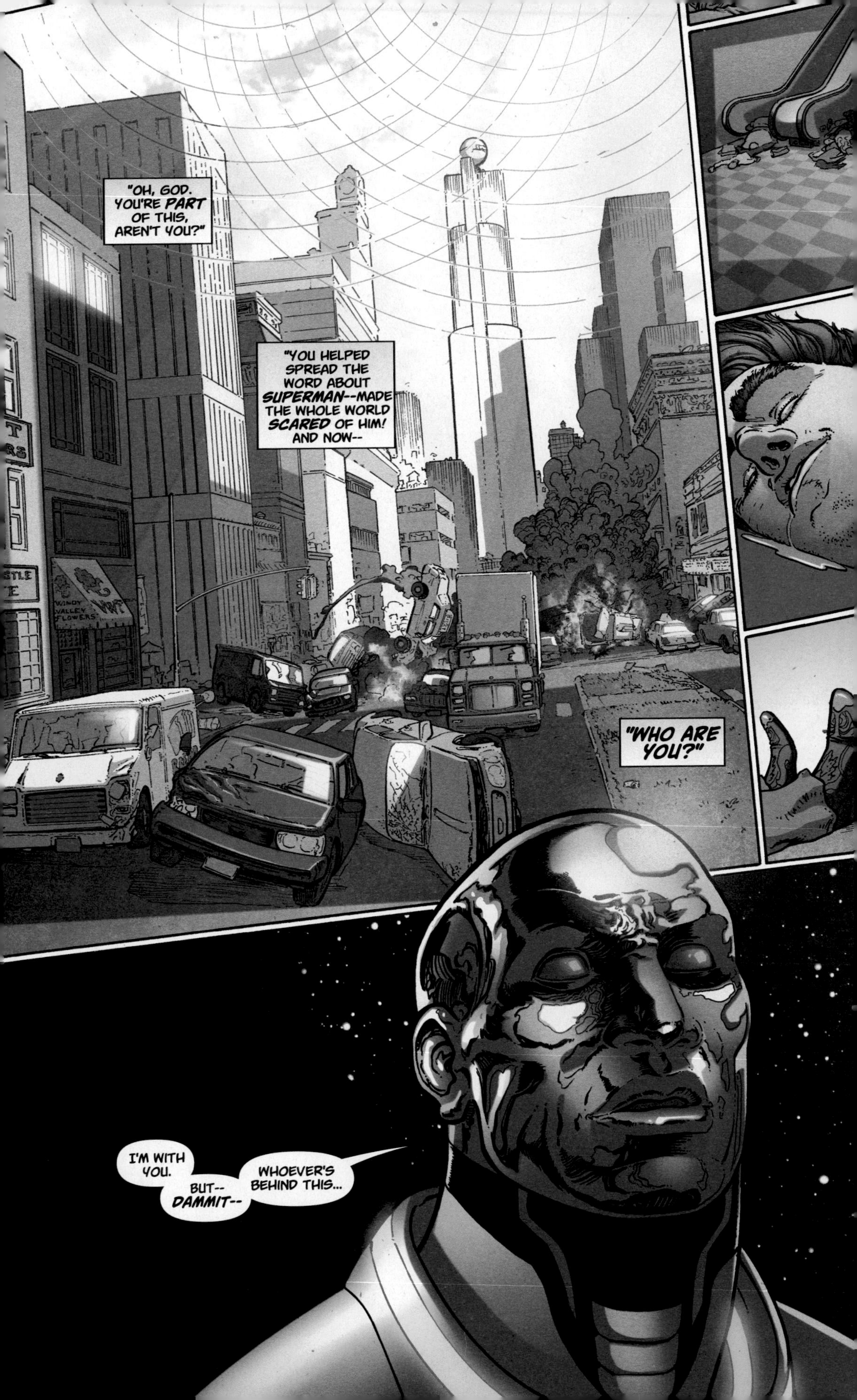
"OH, GOD. YOU'RE PART OF THIS, AREN'T YOU?"
"YOU HELPED SPREAD THE WORD ABOUT SUPERMAN--MADE THE WHOLE WORLD SCARED OF HIM! AND NOW--
WINDY VALLEY FLOWERS
"WHO ARE YOU?"
I'M WITH YOU.
BUT-- DAMMIT--
WHOEVER'S BEHIND THIS...

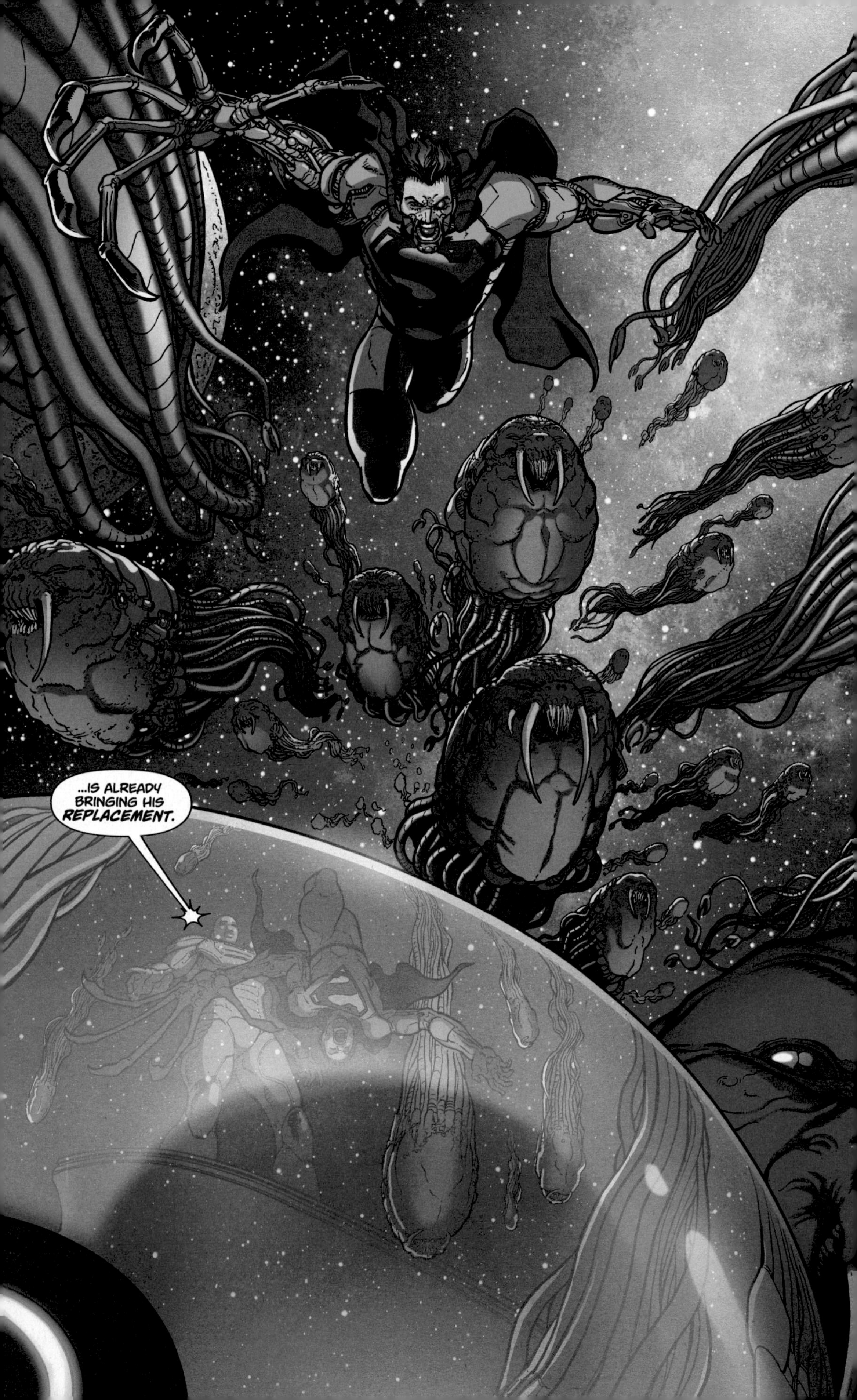
...IS ALREADY BRINGING HIS *REPLACEMENT*.

GREG PAK writer KEN LASHLEY AARON KUDER JACK HERBERT CLIFF RICHARDS
JULIUS GOPEZ WILL CONRAD PASCAL ALIXE artists VICENTE CIFUENTES inker ULISES ARREOLA colorist

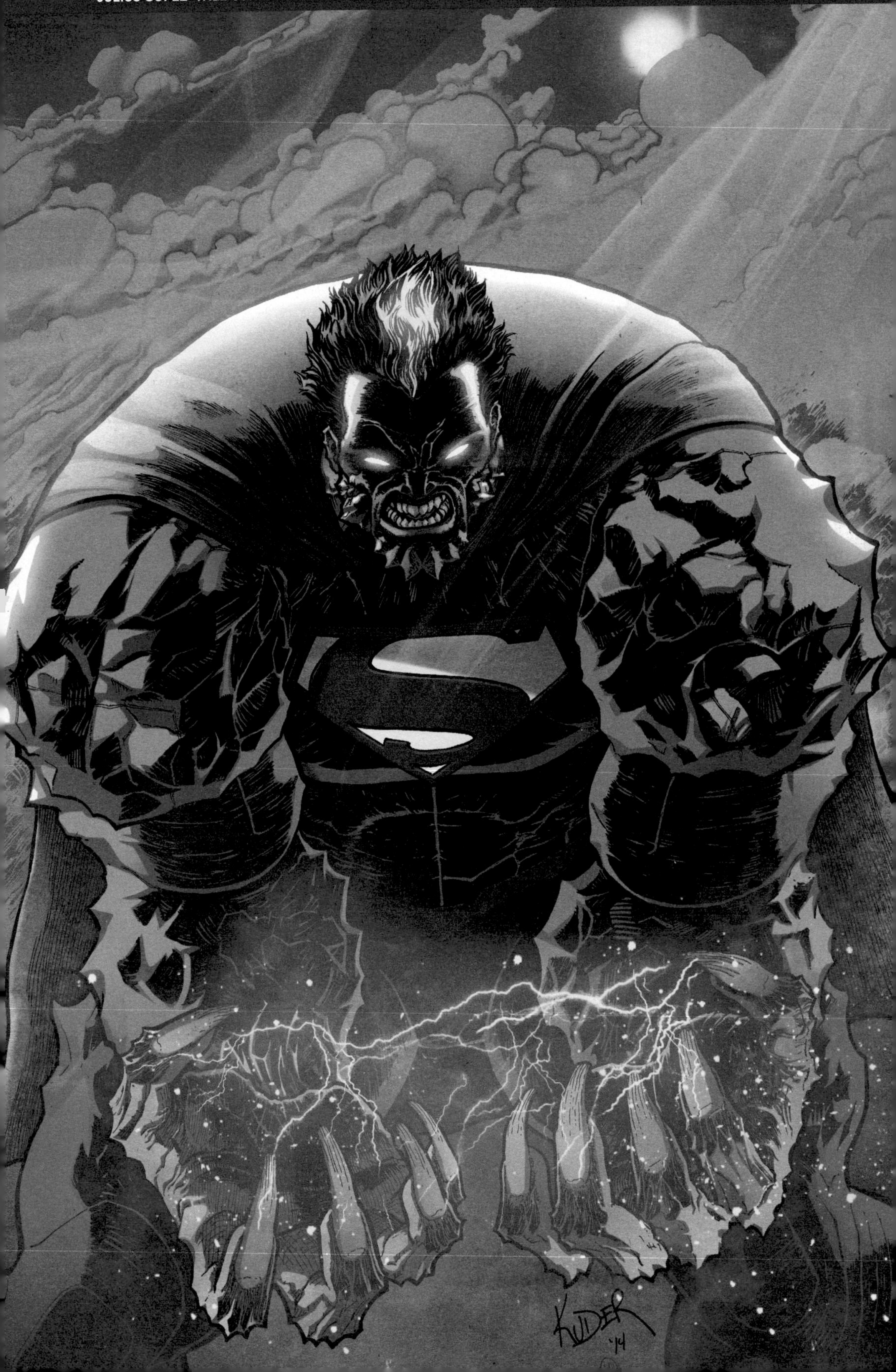
KUDER '14

WORLD   U.S. METROPOLIS   BUSINESS   OPINION   SPORTS   ARTS   STYLE   VIDEO

July 30 201

Daily Planet

DAILY PLANET

HELP!

By Lois Lane

I don't know if this will reach anyone, but I want to let someone know that as strange as it sounds, my body has become a cage for me. I am trapped doing the bidding of another; and, I have done terrible, horrible things in the name of the one known as the Collector—that is just one of the many names, one of the many aspects of this being. But to know Brainwyrm, Mind2, Abbakus or Brainiac is to be witness to the end of your world.

I fear that I have brought about our end. It started with my investigation into "the Twenty," individuals who went missing after Metropolis was shrunken and taken by Brainiac 5 years ago. My leads eventually led me to Senator Milton Hume and my demise. I died at his hands as his mind passed on to me the 12 level intellect that he had been burdened with from our encounter with Brainiac. I was reborn with unlimited mental abilities, and I began

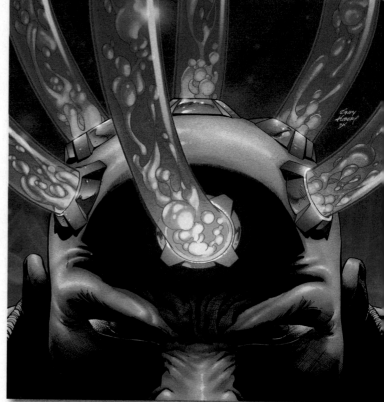

Artis Rendering : Andy Kube

what became known as the Psi-War in an effort to control every other Psi'ss on Earth. Erroneously, I believed Superman to have saved me and freed me from this curse, but he had just caused the powers to become dormant, waiting until He was ready to summon me.

I have cleared the path for Him. His machines come to prepare our world for collection.

Is there anyone out there that can save us?

Stop me?

Superman, where are you?

X

Slideshow - Superdoom's Path of Destruction

404 Error
404 Error
404 Error

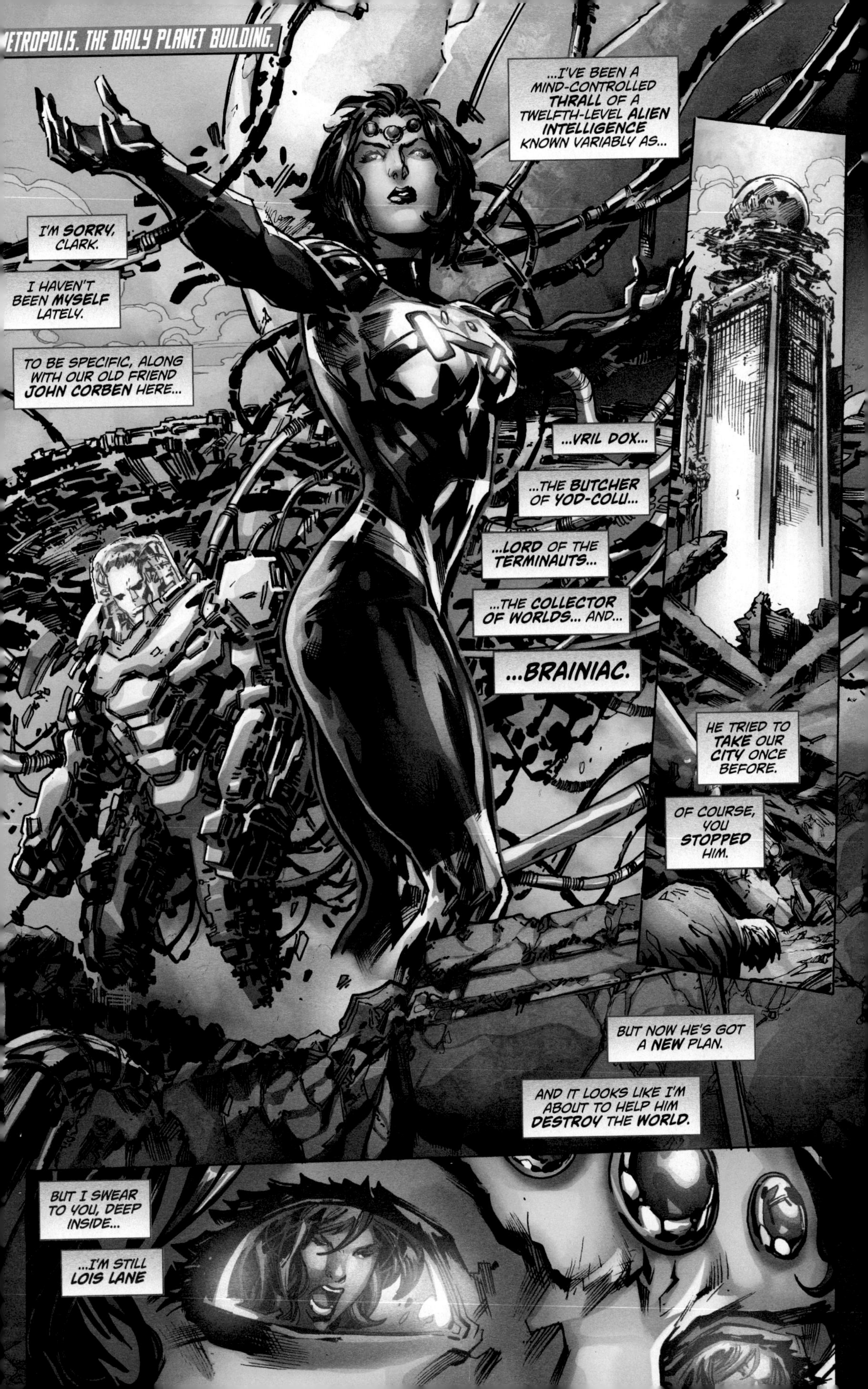
ETROPOLIS. THE DAILY PLANET BUILDING.
I'M SORRY, CLARK.
I HAVEN'T BEEN MYSELF LATELY.
TO BE SPECIFIC, ALONG WITH OUR OLD FRIEND JOHN CORBEN HERE...
...I'VE BEEN A MIND-CONTROLLED THRALL OF A TWELFTH-LEVEL ALIEN INTELLIGENCE KNOWN VARIABLY AS...
...VRIL DOX...
...THE BUTCHER OF YOD-COLU...
...LORD OF THE TERMINAUTS...
...THE COLLECTOR OF WORLDS... AND...
...BRAINIAC.
HE TRIED TO TAKE OUR CITY ONCE BEFORE.
OF COURSE, YOU STOPPED HIM.
BUT NOW HE'S GOT A NEW PLAN.
AND IT LOOKS LIKE I'M ABOUT TO HELP HIM DESTROY THE WORLD.
BUT I SWEAR TO YOU, DEEP INSIDE...
...I'M STILL LOIS LANE

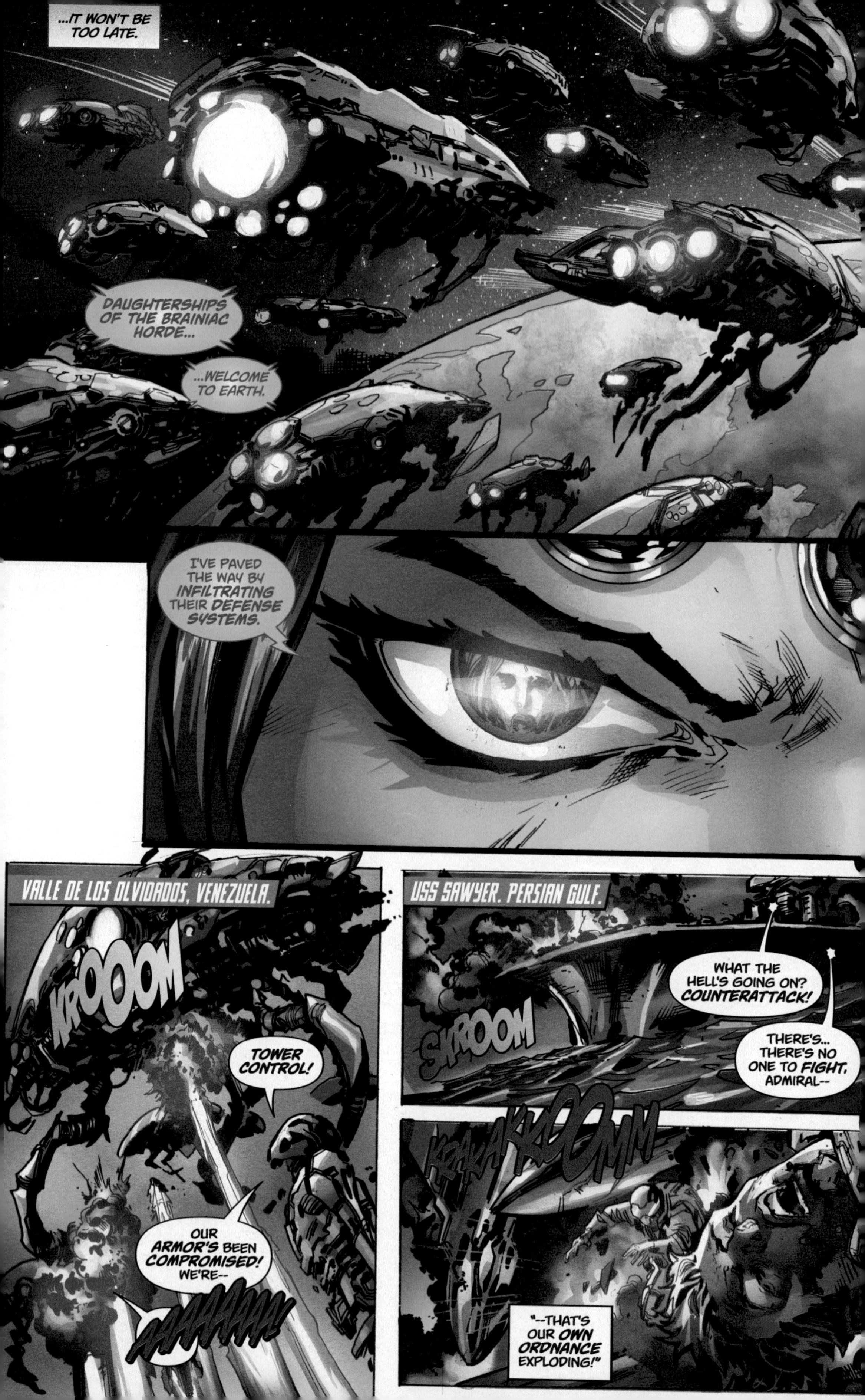
...IT WON'T BE TOO LATE.
DAUGHTERSHIPS OF THE BRAINIAC HORDE...
...WELCOME TO EARTH.
I'VE PAVED THE WAY BY INFILTRATING THEIR DEFENSE SYSTEMS.
VALLE DE LOS OLVIDADOS, VENEZUELA.
KROOOM
TOWER CONTROL!
OUR ARMOR'S BEEN COMPROMISED! WE'RE--
AAAAAAAA!
USS SAWYER. PERSIAN GULF.
SKROOM
WHAT THE HELL'S GOING ON? COUNTERATTACK!
THERE'S... THERE'S NO ONE TO FIGHT, ADMIRAL--
KRAKAKKOOMM
"--THAT'S OUR OWN ORDNANCE EXPLODING!"

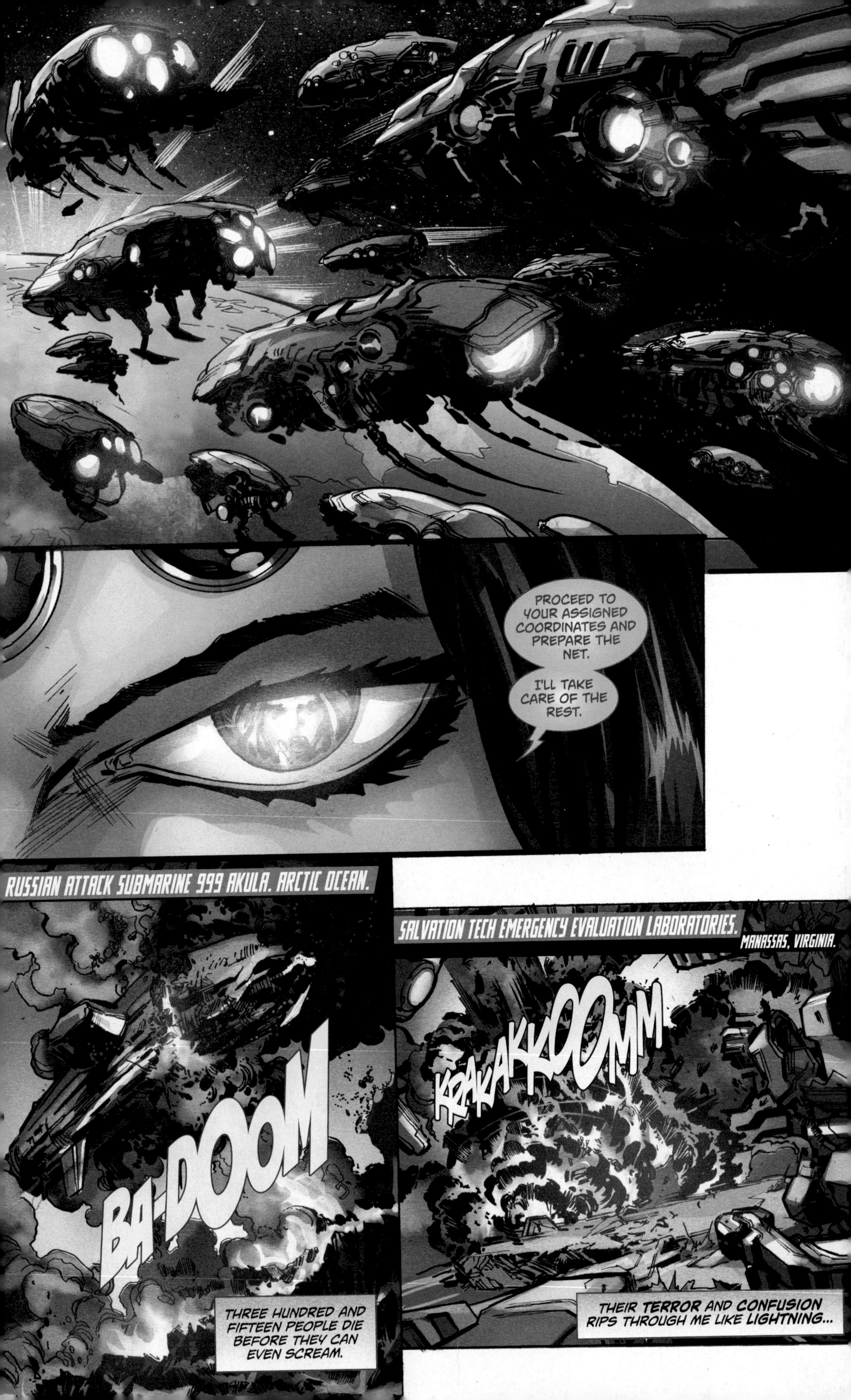
PROCEED TO YOUR ASSIGNED COORDINATES AND PREPARE THE NET.
I'LL TAKE CARE OF THE REST.
RUSSIAN ATTACK SUBMARINE 999 AKULA. ARCTIC OCEAN.
BA-DOOM
THREE HUNDRED AND FIFTEEN PEOPLE DIE BEFORE THEY CAN EVEN SCREAM.
SALVATION TECH EMERGENCY EVALUATION LABORATORIES.
MANASSAS, VIRGINIA.
KRAKAKKOOMM
THEIR TERROR AND CONFUSION RIPS THROUGH ME LIKE LIGHTNING...

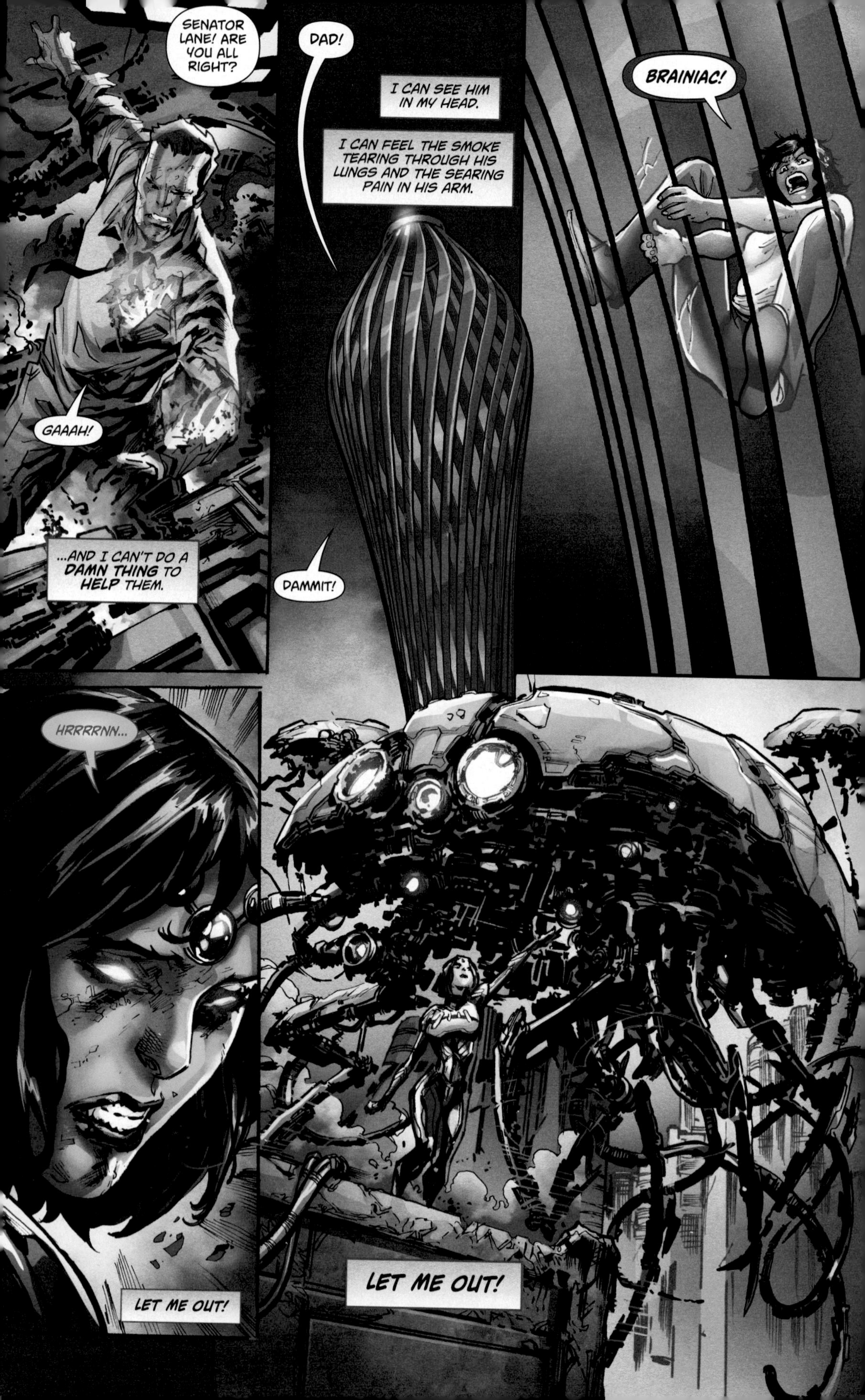
SENATOR LANE! ARE YOU ALL RIGHT?
GAAAH!
...AND I CAN'T DO A DAMN THING TO HELP THEM.
DAD!
I CAN SEE HIM IN MY HEAD.
I CAN FEEL THE SMOKE TEARING THROUGH HIS LUNGS AND THE SEARING PAIN IN HIS ARM.
DAMMIT!
BRAINIAC!
HRRRRNN...
LET ME OUT!
LET ME OUT!

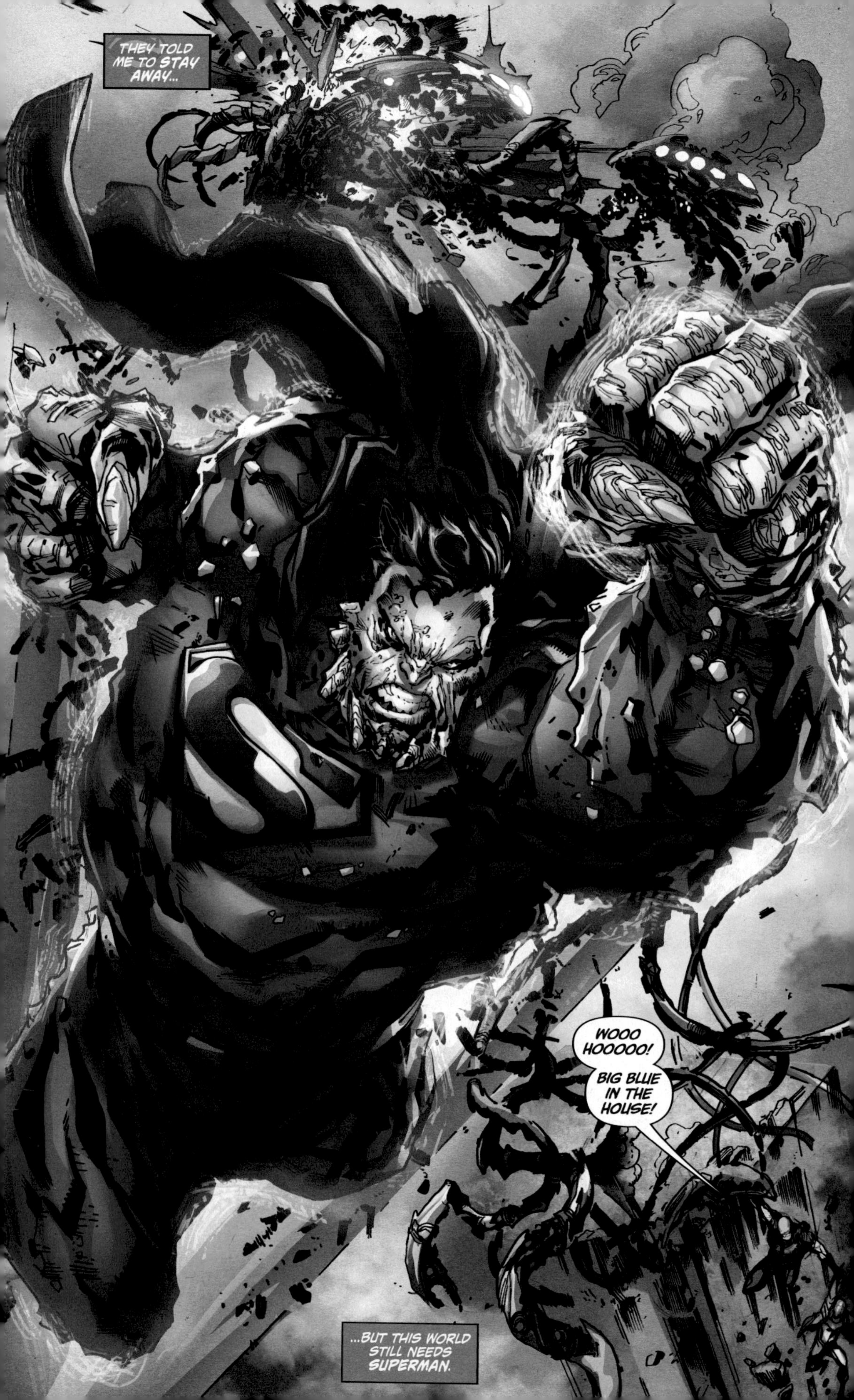
THEY TOLD ME TO STAY AWAY...
WOOO HOOOOO!
BIG BLUE IN THE HOUSE!
...BUT THIS WORLD STILL NEEDS SUPERMAN.

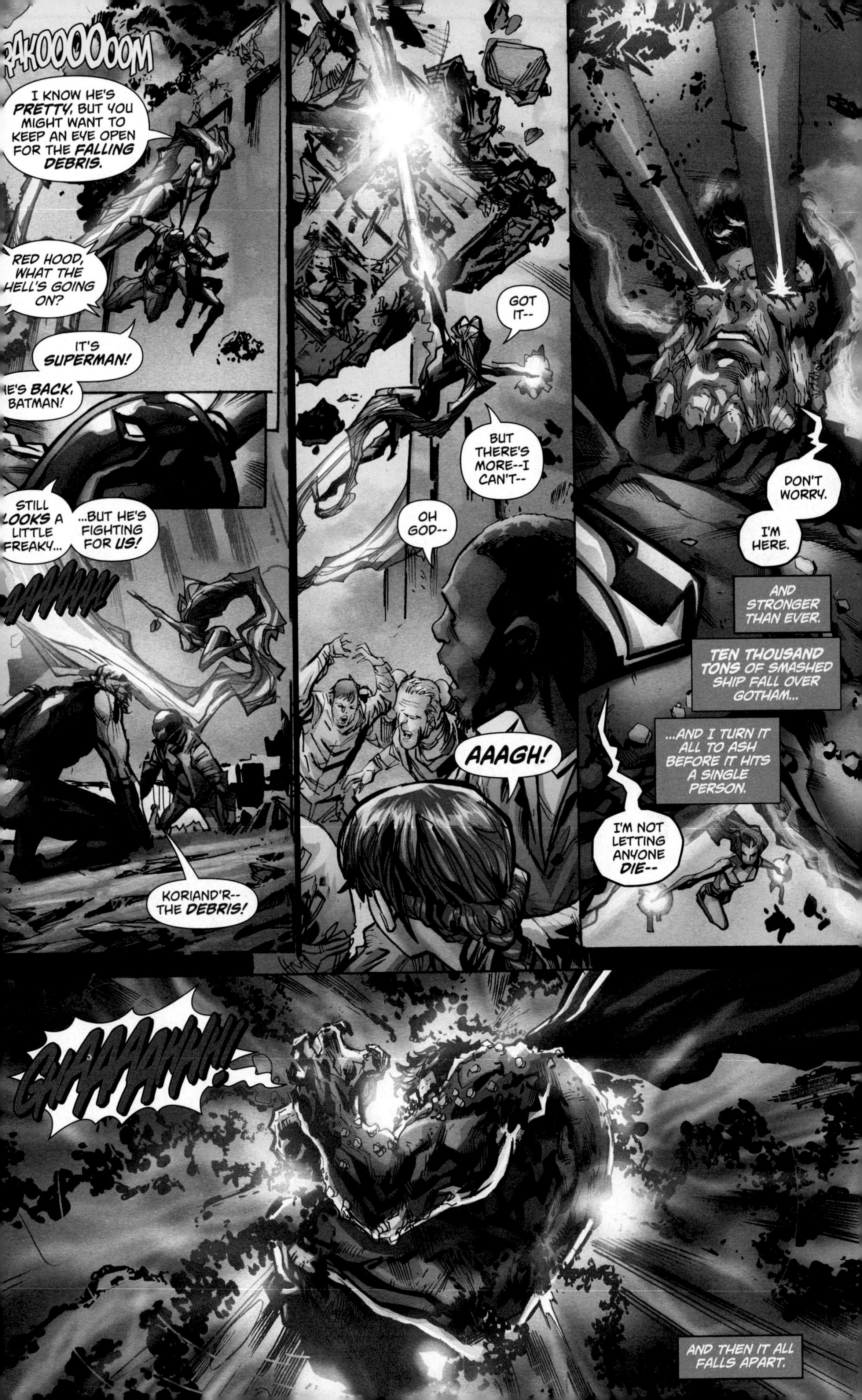

RAKOOOOOOM
I KNOW HE'S PRETTY, BUT YOU MIGHT WANT TO KEEP AN EYE OPEN FOR THE FALLING DEBRIS.
RED HOOD, WHAT THE HELL'S GOING ON?
IT'S SUPERMAN!
HE'S BACK, BATMAN!
STILL LOOKS A LITTLE FREAKY...
...BUT HE'S FIGHTING FOR US!
KORIAND'R-- THE DEBRIS!
GOT IT--
BUT THERE'S MORE--I CAN'T--
OH GOD--
AAAGH!
DON'T WORRY.
I'M HERE.
AND STRONGER THAN EVER.
TEN THOUSAND TONS OF SMASHED SHIP FALL OVER GOTHAM...
...AND I TURN IT ALL TO ASH BEFORE IT HITS A SINGLE PERSON.
I'M NOT LETTING ANYONE DIE--
AND THEN IT ALL FALLS APART.

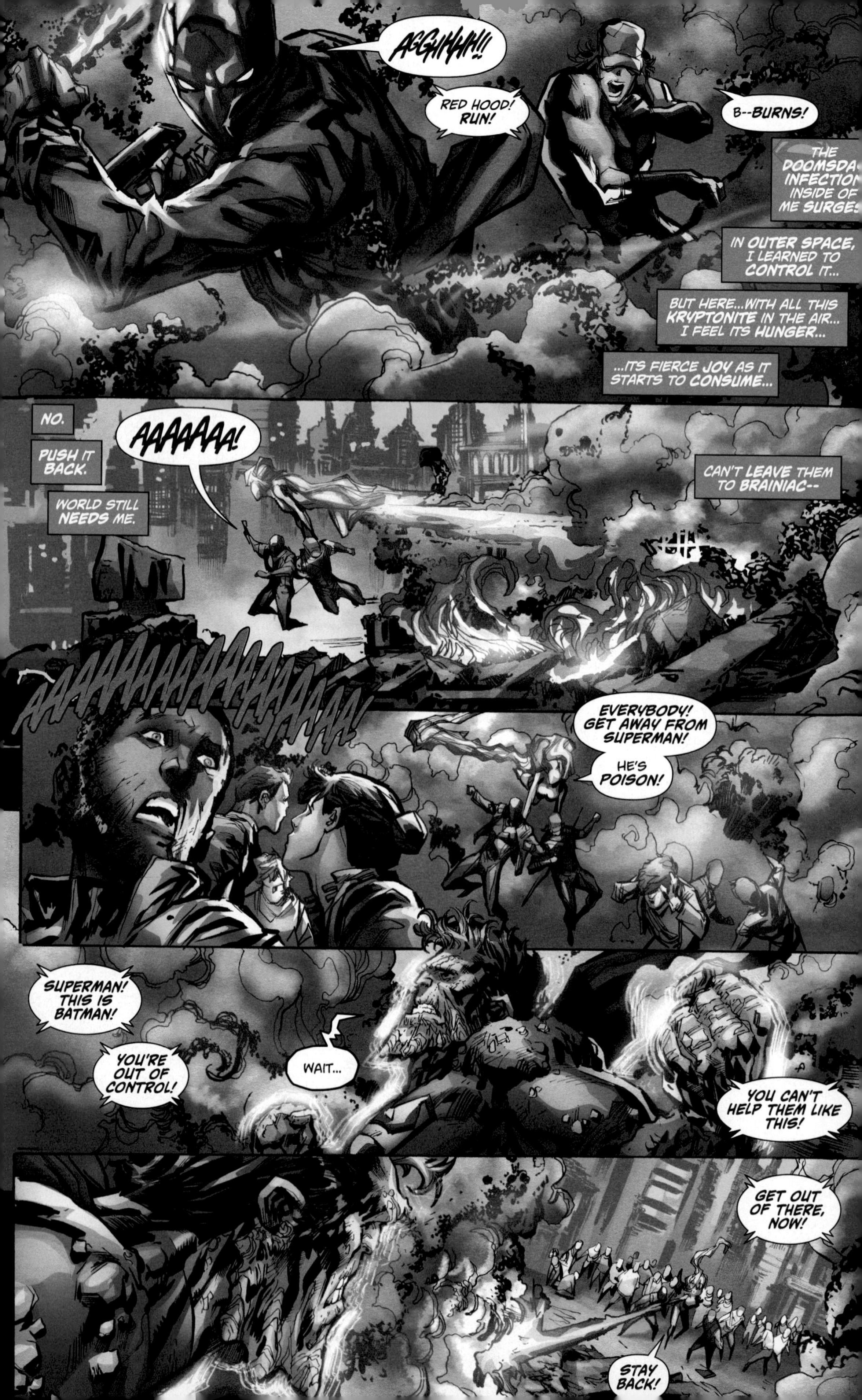

AGGHHH!!
RED HOOD! RUN!
B--BURNS!
THE DOOMSDA INFECTIO INSIDE OF ME SURGE
IN OUTER SPACE, I LEARNED TO CONTROL IT...
BUT HERE...WITH ALL THIS KRYPTONITE IN THE AIR... I FEEL ITS HUNGER...
...ITS FIERCE JOY AS IT STARTS TO CONSUME...
NO.
PUSH IT BACK.
WORLD STILL NEEDS ME.
AAAAAAA!
CAN'T LEAVE THEM TO BRAINIAC--
AAAAAAAAAAAAAAAAAAAA!
EVERYBODY! GET AWAY FROM SUPERMAN!
HE'S POISON!
SUPERMAN! THIS IS BATMAN!
YOU'RE OUT OF CONTROL!
WAIT...
YOU CAN'T HELP THEM LIKE THIS!
GET OUT OF THERE, NOW!
STAY BACK!

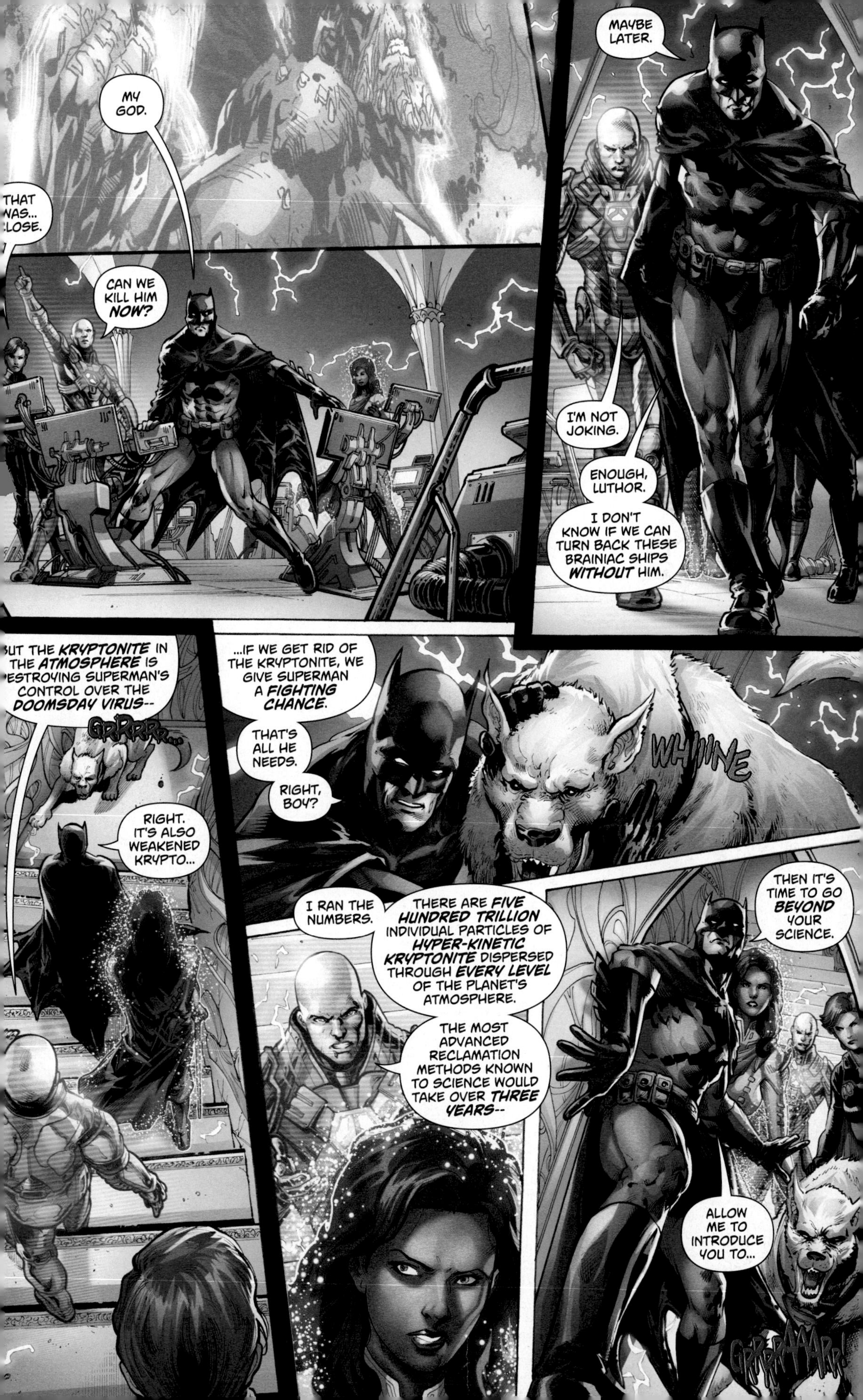

THAT WAS... CLOSE.
MY GOD.
CAN WE KILL HIM NOW?
MAYBE LATER.
I'M NOT JOKING.
ENOUGH, LUTHOR.
I DON'T KNOW IF WE CAN TURN BACK THESE BRAINIAC SHIPS WITHOUT HIM.
BUT THE KRYPTONITE IN THE ATMOSPHERE IS DESTROYING SUPERMAN'S CONTROL OVER THE DOOMSDAY VIRUS--
GRRRRR...
RIGHT. IT'S ALSO WEAKENED KRYPTO...
...IF WE GET RID OF THE KRYPTONITE, WE GIVE SUPERMAN A FIGHTING CHANCE.
THAT'S ALL HE NEEDS.
RIGHT, BOY?
WHIIINE
I RAN THE NUMBERS.
THERE ARE FIVE HUNDRED TRILLION INDIVIDUAL PARTICLES OF HYPER-KINETIC KRYPTONITE DISPERSED THROUGH EVERY LEVEL OF THE PLANET'S ATMOSPHERE.
THE MOST ADVANCED RECLAMATION METHODS KNOWN TO SCIENCE WOULD TAKE OVER THREE YEARS--
THEN IT'S TIME TO GO BEYOND YOUR SCIENCE.
ALLOW ME TO INTRODUCE YOU TO...
GRRRRAAARR!

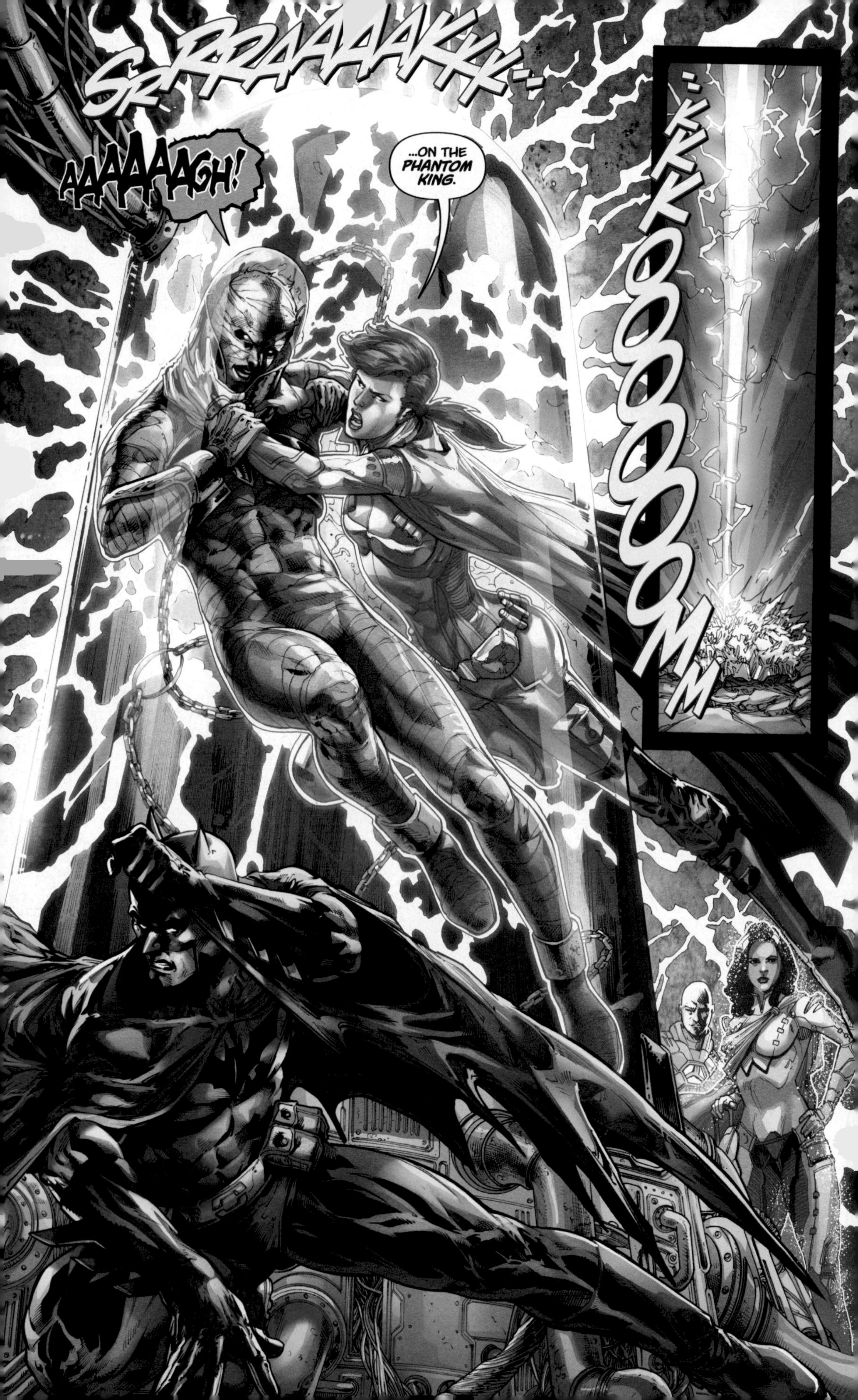
SRRRAAAAKKK--
AAAAAAAGH!
...ON THE PHANTOM KING.
--KKKOOOOOOOMM

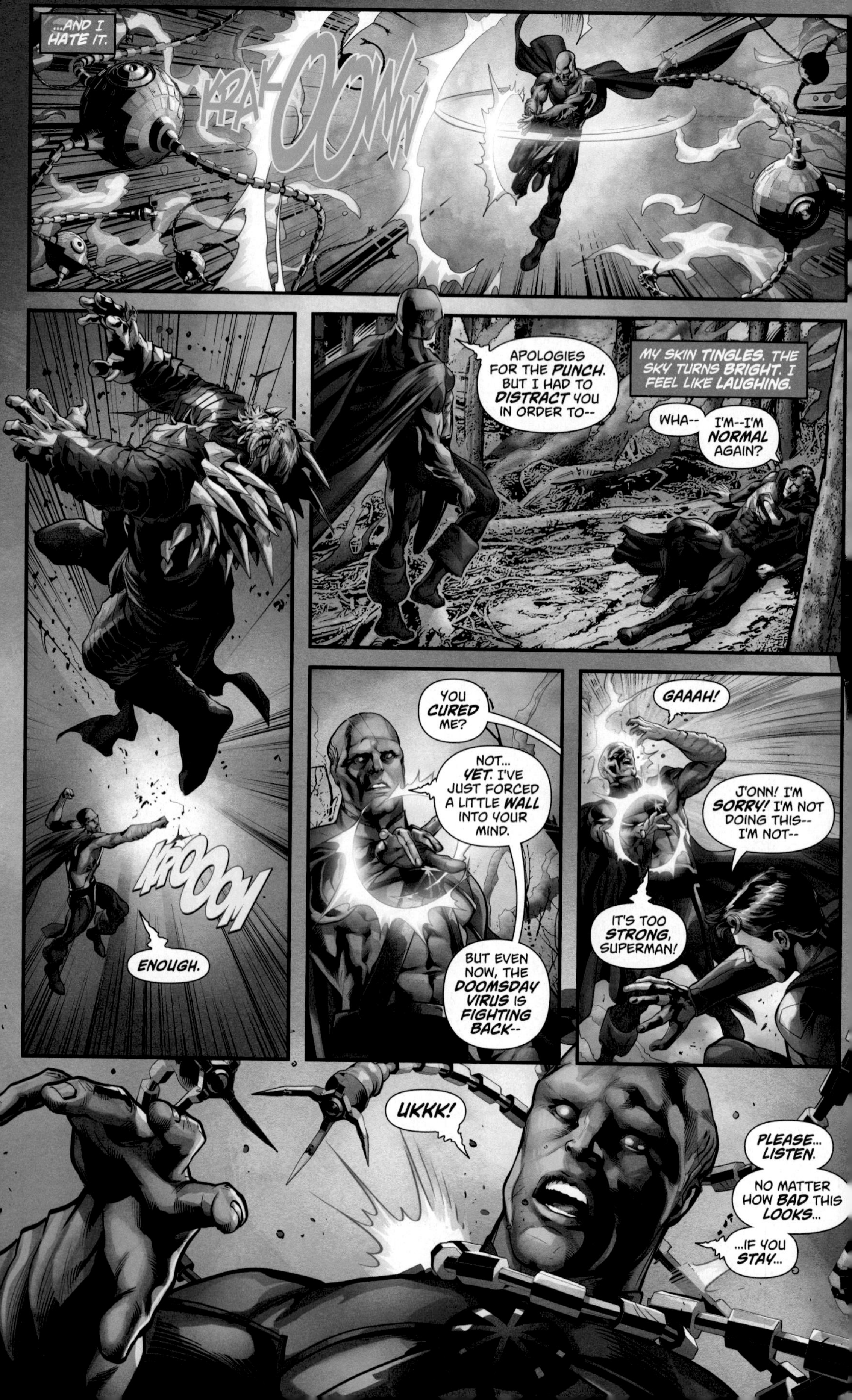

...AND I HATE IT.
APOLOGIES FOR THE PUNCH. BUT I HAD TO DISTRACT YOU IN ORDER TO--
MY SKIN TINGLES. THE SKY TURNS BRIGHT. I FEEL LIKE LAUGHING.
WHA--
I'M--I'M NORMAL AGAIN?
KROOOM
ENOUGH.
YOU CURED ME?
NOT... YET. I'VE JUST FORCED A LITTLE WALL INTO YOUR MIND.
BUT EVEN NOW, THE DOOMSDAY VIRUS IS FIGHTING BACK--
GAAAH!
J'ONN! I'M SORRY! I'M NOT DOING THIS-- I'M NOT--
IT'S TOO STRONG, SUPERMAN!
UKKK!
PLEASE... LISTEN.
NO MATTER HOW BAD THIS LOOKS...
...IF YOU STAY...

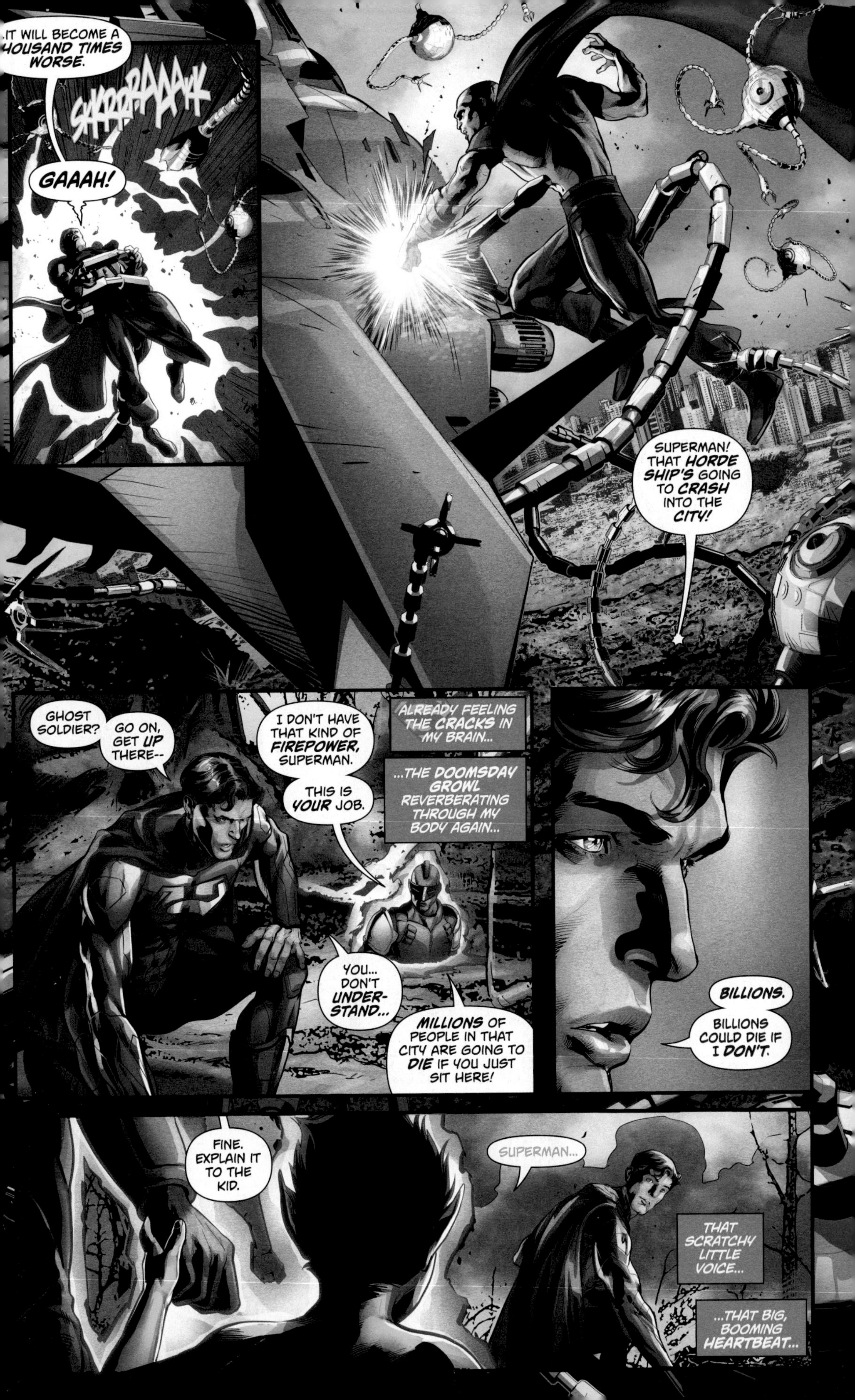

IT WILL BECOME A THOUSAND TIMES WORSE.
SKRRRAAAKK
GAAAH!
SUPERMAN! THAT HORDE SHIP'S GOING TO CRASH INTO THE CITY!
GHOST SOLDIER?
GO ON, GET UP THERE--
I DON'T HAVE THAT KIND OF FIREPOWER, SUPERMAN.
THIS IS YOUR JOB.
ALREADY FEELING THE CRACKS IN MY BRAIN...
...THE DOOMSDAY GROWL REVERBERATING THROUGH MY BODY AGAIN...
YOU... DON'T UNDER-STAND...
MILLIONS OF PEOPLE IN THAT CITY ARE GOING TO DIE IF YOU JUST SIT HERE!
BILLIONS.
BILLIONS COULD DIE IF I DON'T.
FINE. EXPLAIN IT TO THE KID.
SUPERMAN...
THAT SCRATCHY LITTLE VOICE...
...THAT BIG, BOOMING HEARTBEAT...

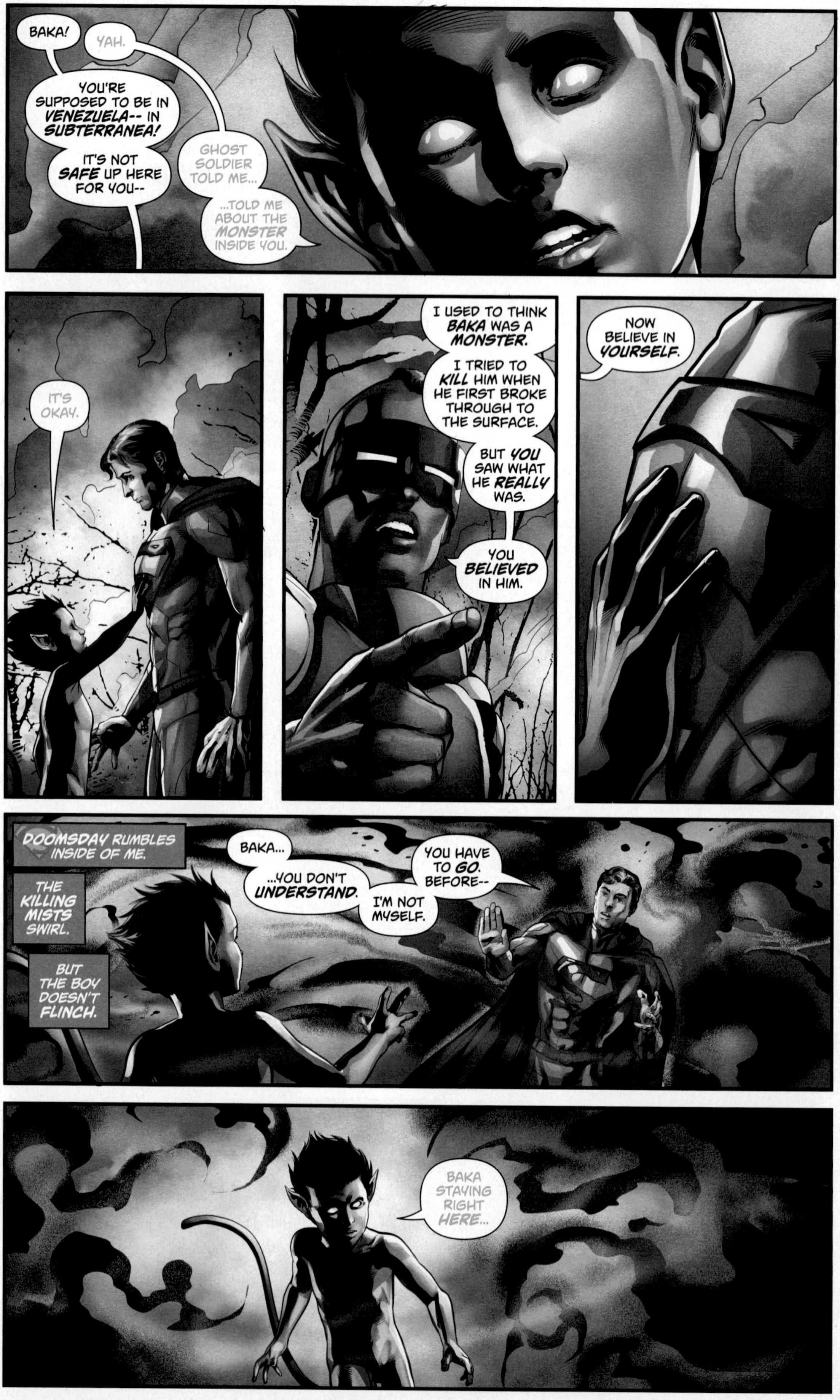
BAKA!
YAH.
YOU'RE SUPPOSED TO BE IN VENEZUELA-- IN SUBTERRANEA!
IT'S NOT SAFE UP HERE FOR YOU--
GHOST SOLDIER TOLD ME...
...TOLD ME ABOUT THE MONSTER INSIDE YOU.
IT'S OKAY.
I USED TO THINK BAKA WAS A MONSTER.
I TRIED TO KILL HIM WHEN HE FIRST BROKE THROUGH TO THE SURFACE.
BUT YOU SAW WHAT HE REALLY WAS.
YOU BELIEVED IN HIM.
NOW BELIEVE IN YOURSELF.
DOOMSDAY RUMBLES INSIDE OF ME.
THE KILLING MISTS SWIRL.
BUT THE BOY DOESN'T FLINCH.
BAKA...
...YOU DON'T UNDERSTAND.
YOU HAVE TO GO. BEFORE--
I'M NOT MYSELF.
BAKA STAYING RIGHT HERE...

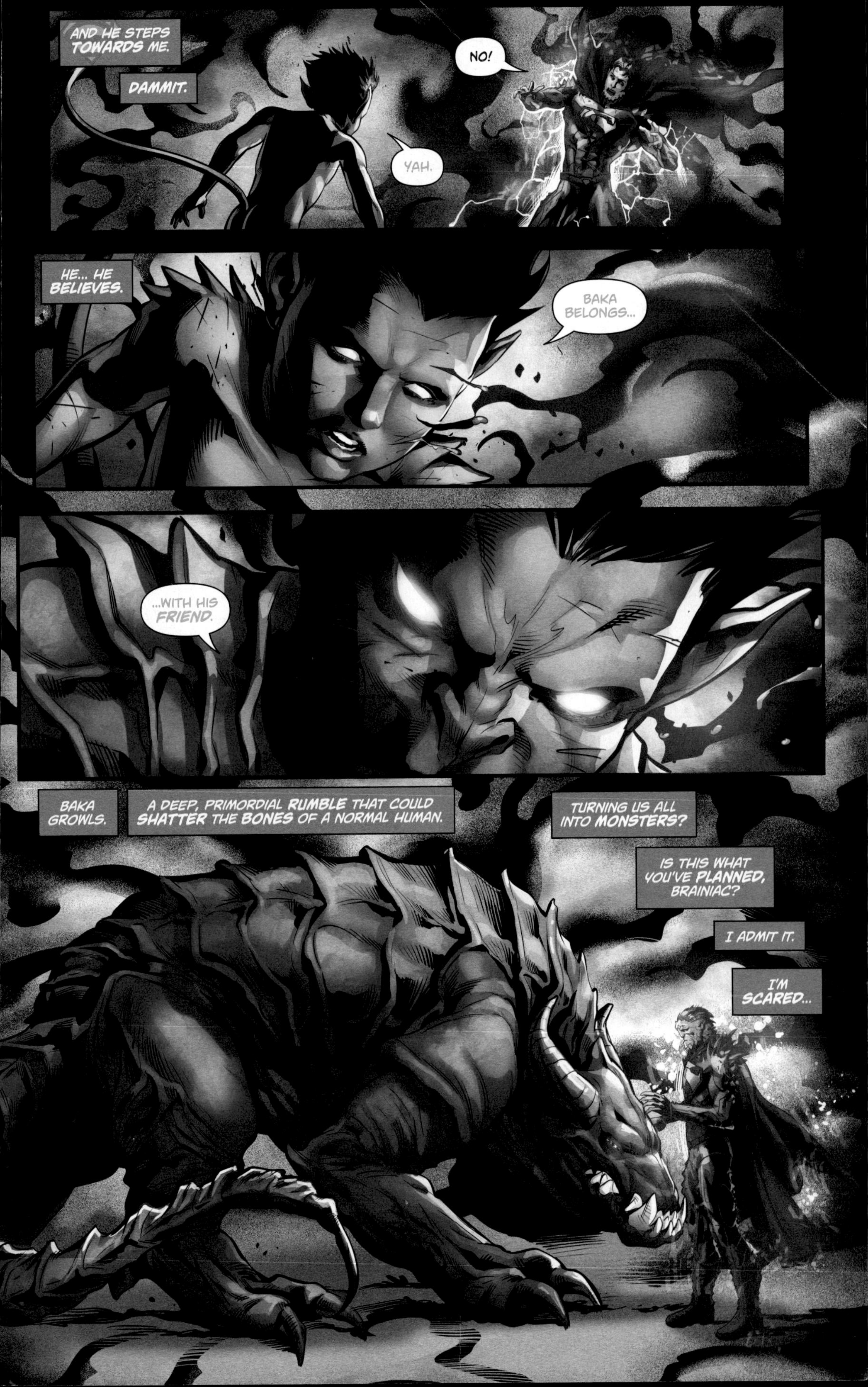
AND HE STEPS TOWARDS ME.
DAMMIT.
NO!
YAH.
HE... HE BELIEVES.
BAKA BELONGS...
...WITH HIS FRIEND.
BAKA GROWLS.
A DEEP, PRIMORDIAL RUMBLE THAT COULD SHATTER THE BONES OF A NORMAL HUMAN.
TURNING US ALL INTO MONSTERS?
IS THIS WHAT YOU'VE PLANNED, BRAINIAC?
I ADMIT IT.
I'M SCARED...

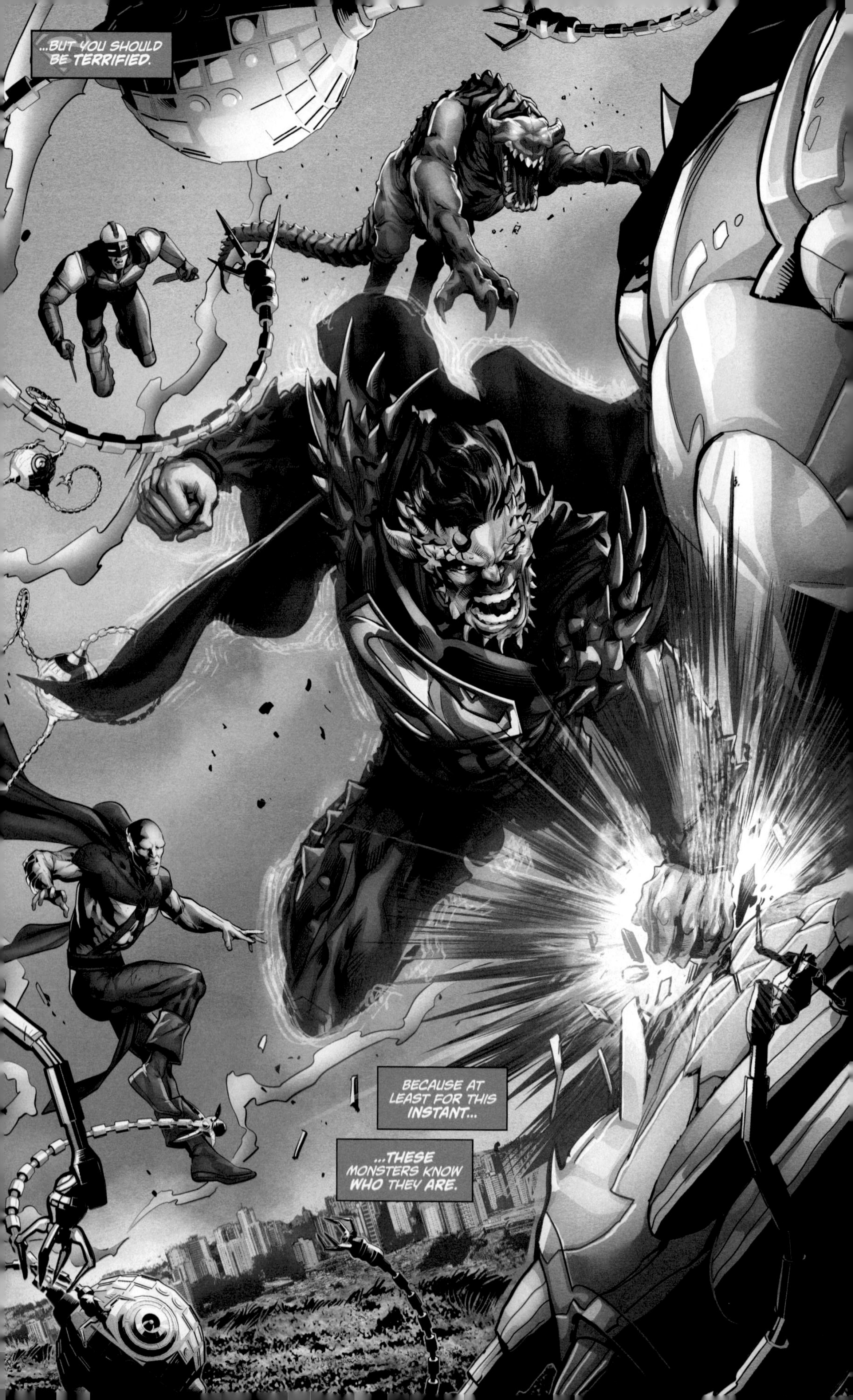
...BUT YOU SHOULD BE TERRIFIED.
BECAUSE AT LEAST FOR THIS INSTANT...
...THESE MONSTERS KNOW WHO THEY ARE.

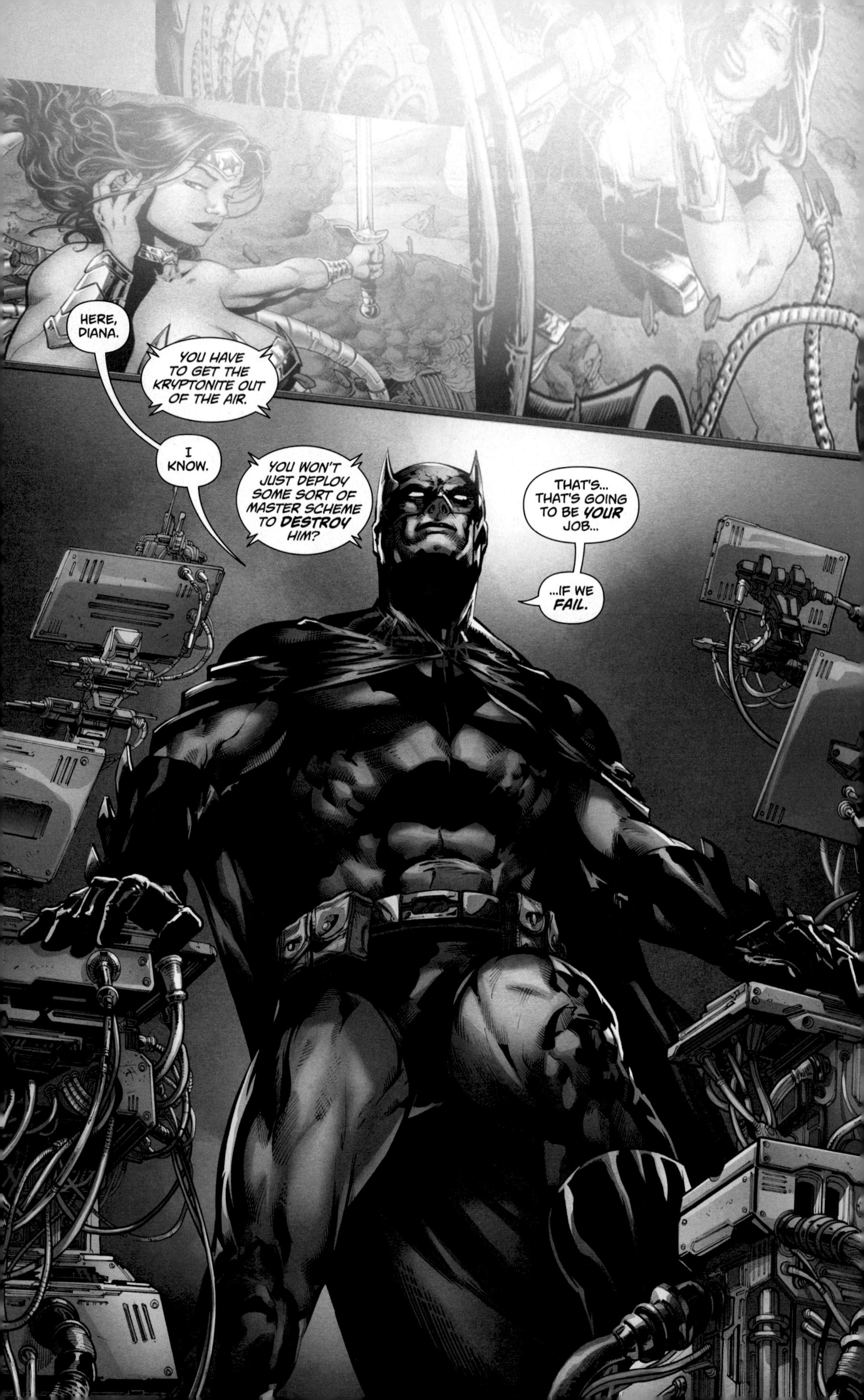
HERE, DIANA.
YOU HAVE TO GET THE KRYPTONITE OUT OF THE AIR.
I KNOW.
YOU WON'T JUST DEPLOY SOME SORT OF MASTER SCHEME TO DESTROY HIM?
THAT'S... THAT'S GOING TO BE YOUR JOB...
...IF WE FAIL.

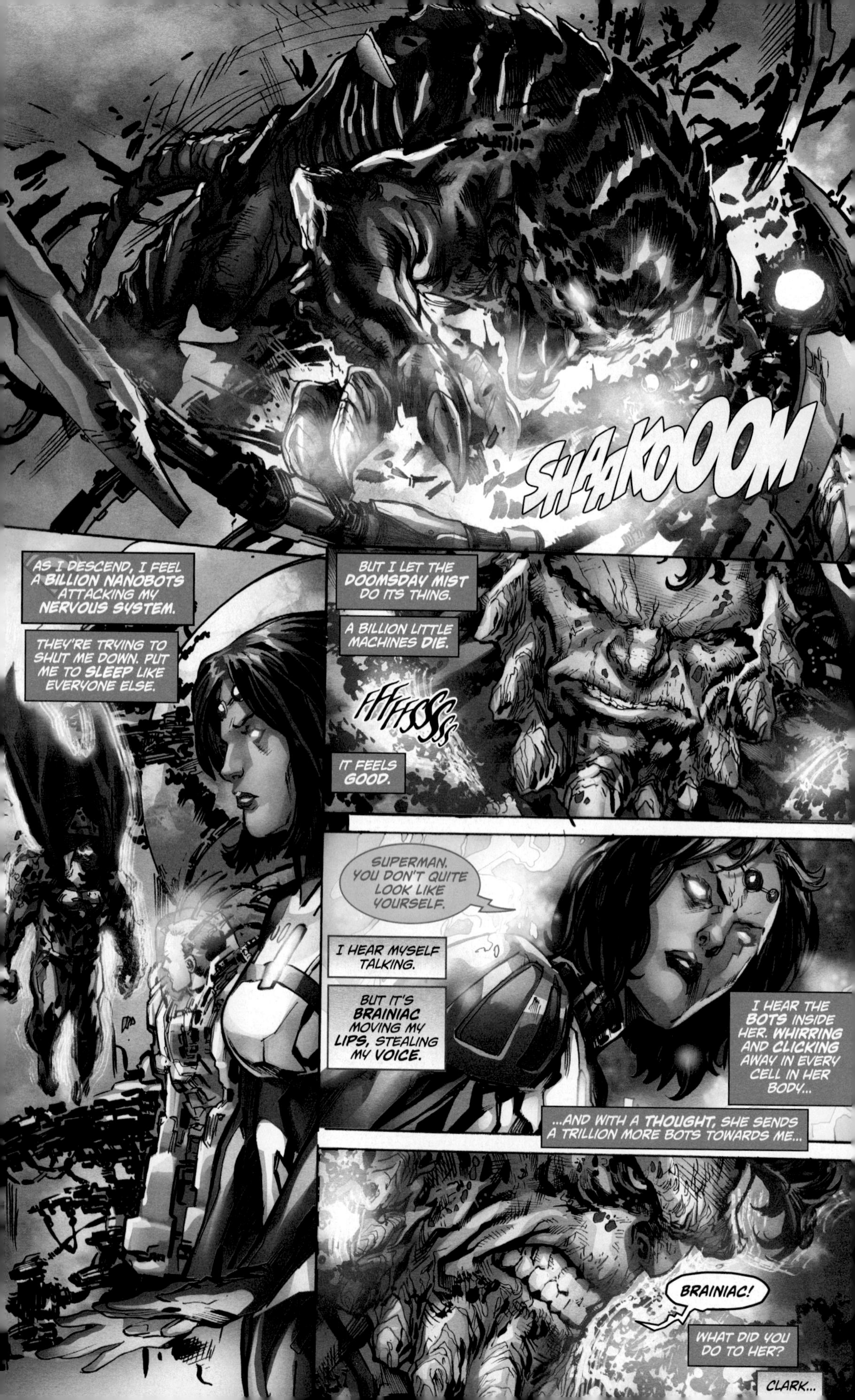
SHAAKOOOM
AS I DESCEND, I FEEL A BILLION NANOBOTS ATTACKING MY NERVOUS SYSTEM.
THEY'RE TRYING TO SHUT ME DOWN. PUT ME TO SLEEP LIKE EVERYONE ELSE.
BUT I LET THE DOOMSDAY MIST DO ITS THING.
A BILLION LITTLE MACHINES DIE.
FFFFSSSSS
IT FEELS GOOD.
SUPERMAN. YOU DON'T QUITE LOOK LIKE YOURSELF.
I HEAR MYSELF TALKING.
BUT IT'S BRAINIAC MOVING MY LIPS, STEALING MY VOICE.
I HEAR THE BOTS INSIDE HER. WHIRRING AND CLICKING AWAY IN EVERY CELL IN HER BODY...
...AND WITH A THOUGHT, SHE SENDS A TRILLION MORE BOTS TOWARDS ME...
BRAINIAC!
WHAT DID YOU DO TO HER?
CLARK...

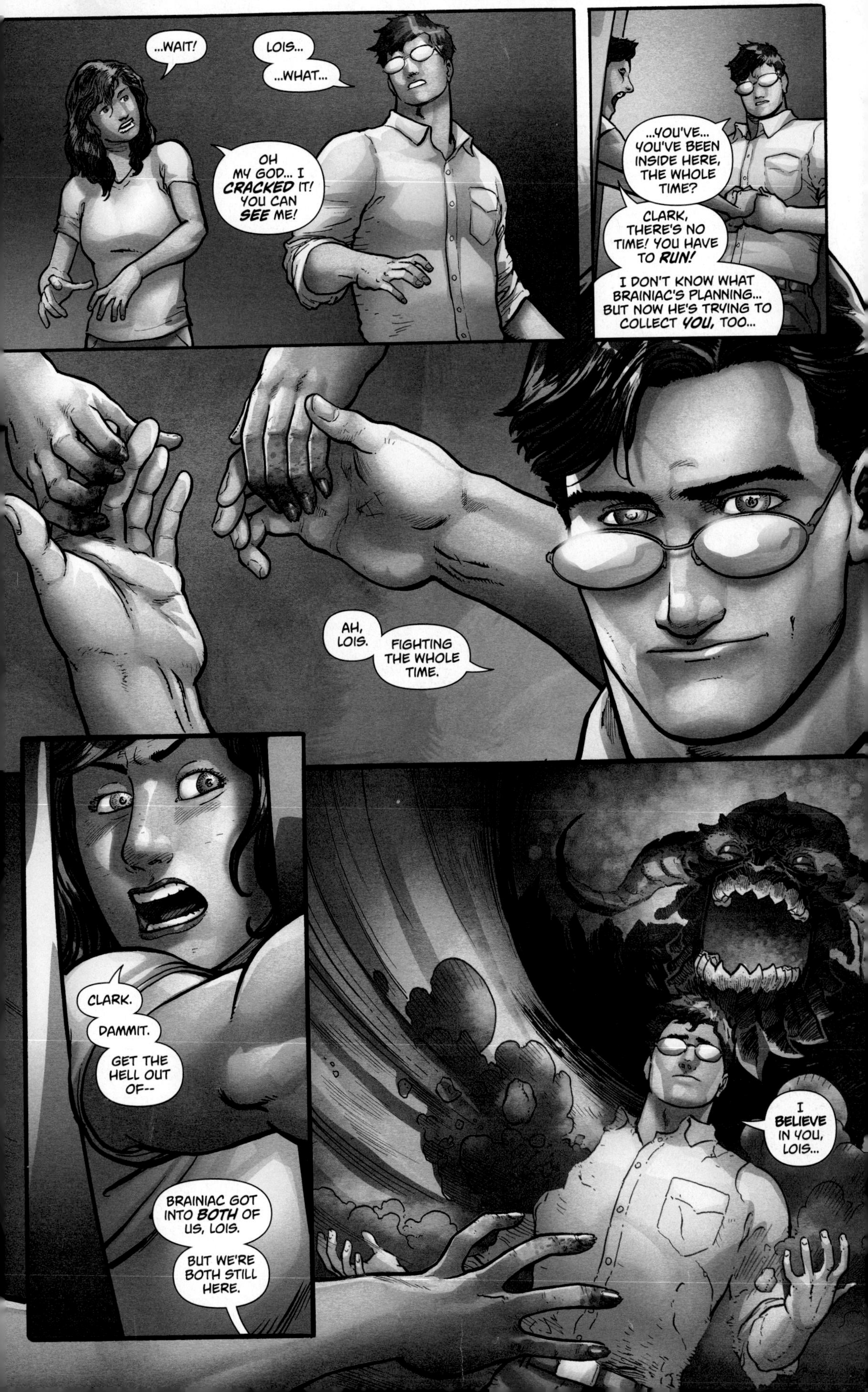
...WAIT!
LOIS...
...WHAT...
OH MY GOD... I CRACKED IT! YOU CAN SEE ME!
...YOU'VE... YOU'VE BEEN INSIDE HERE, THE WHOLE TIME?
CLARK, THERE'S NO TIME! YOU HAVE TO RUN!
I DON'T KNOW WHAT BRAINIAC'S PLANNING... BUT NOW HE'S TRYING TO COLLECT YOU, TOO...
AH, LOIS.
FIGHTING THE WHOLE TIME.
CLARK.
DAMMIT.
GET THE HELL OUT OF--
BRAINIAC GOT INTO BOTH OF US, LOIS.
BUT WE'RE BOTH STILL HERE.
I BELIEVE IN YOU, LOIS...

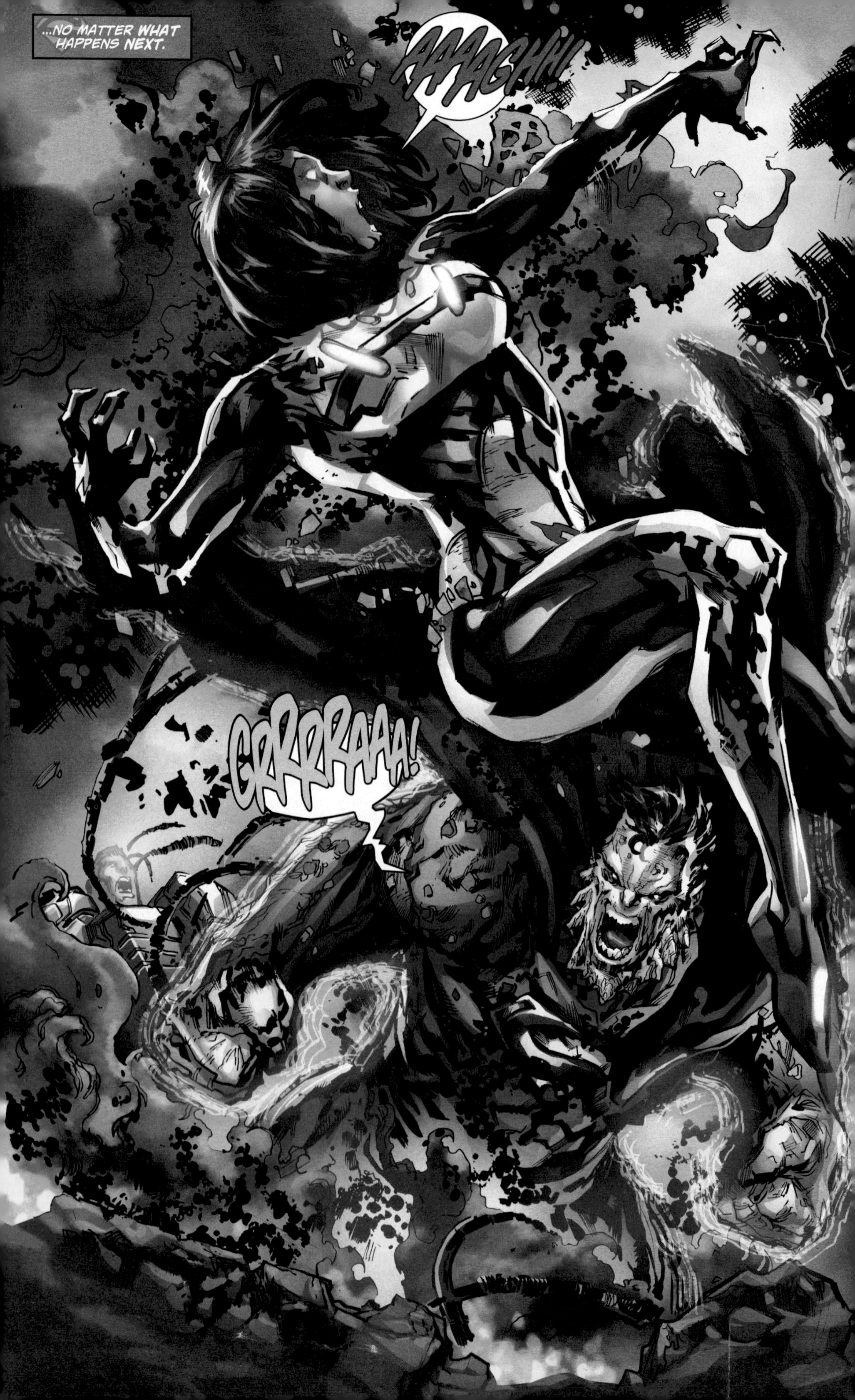
...NO MATTER WHAT HAPPENS NEXT.
AAAAGHH!
GRRRRAAA!

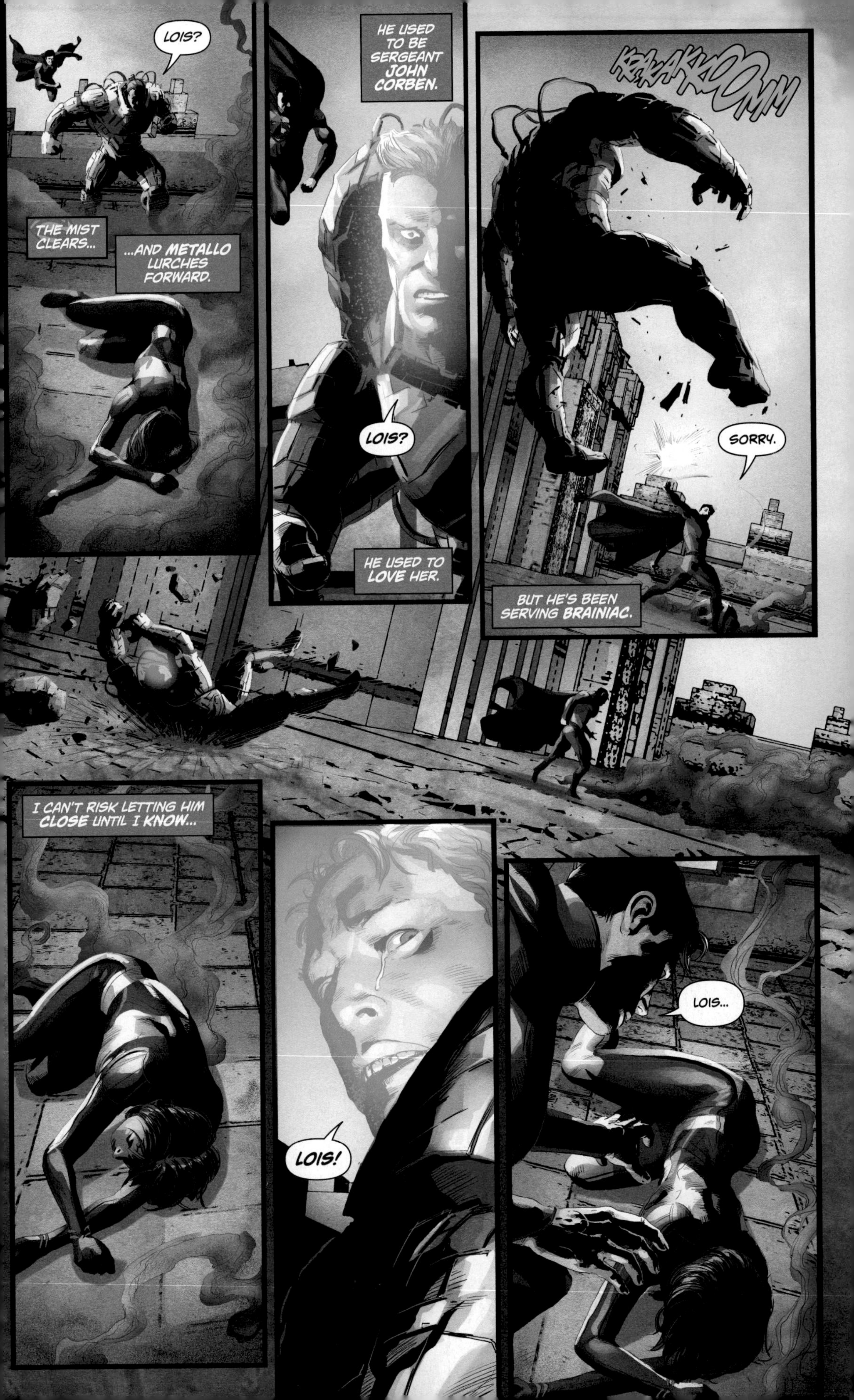
LOIS?
THE MIST CLEARS...
...AND METALLO LURCHES FORWARD.
HE USED TO BE SERGEANT JOHN CORBEN.
LOIS?
HE USED TO LOVE HER.
KRAKAKOOMM
SORRY.
BUT HE'S BEEN SERVING BRAINIAC.
I CAN'T RISK LETTING HIM CLOSE UNTIL I KNOW...
LOIS!
LOIS...

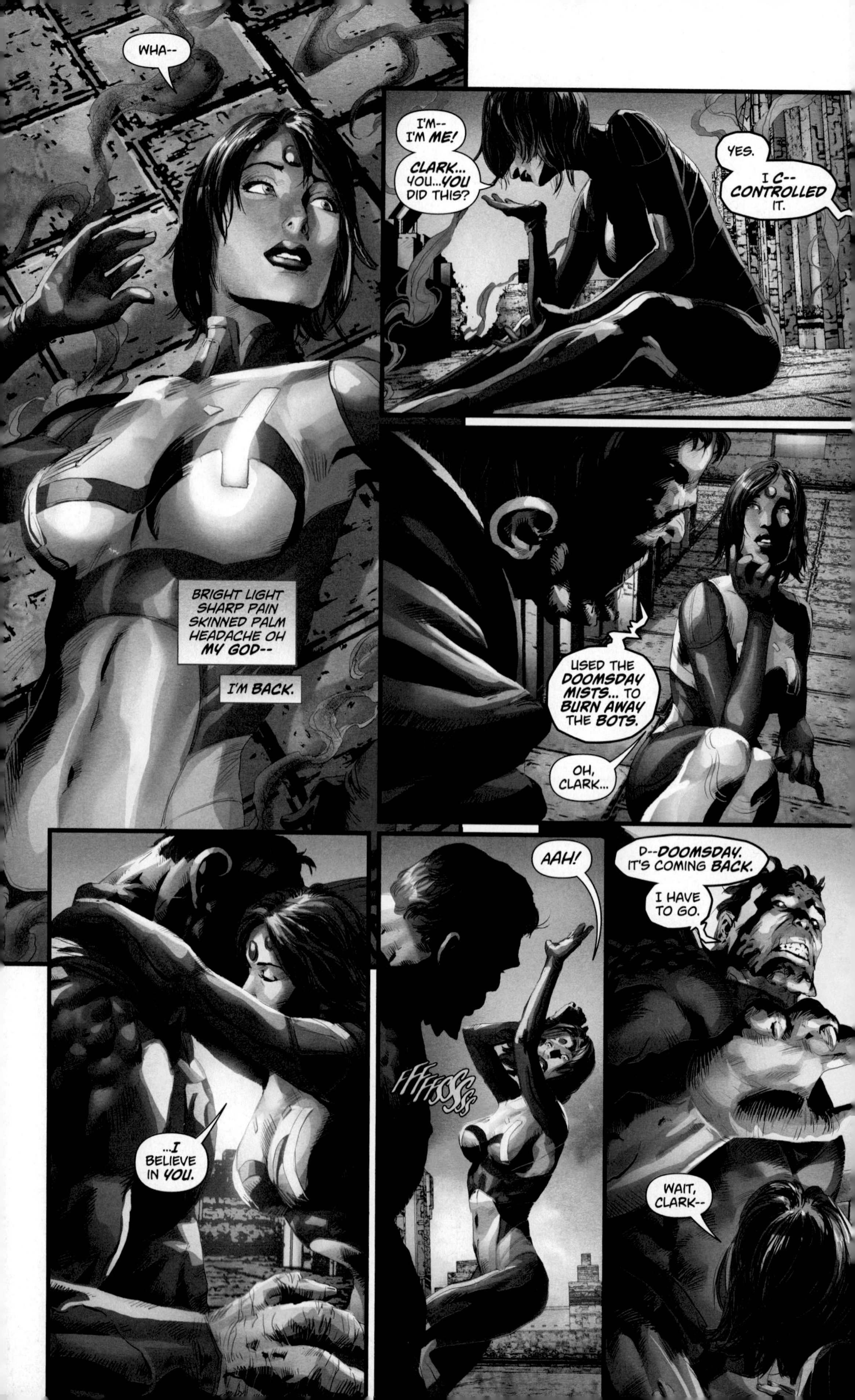
WHA--
BRIGHT LIGHT SHARP PAIN SKINNED PALM HEADACHE OH MY GOD--
I'M BACK.
I'M-- I'M ME!
CLARK... YOU...YOU DID THIS?
YES.
I C-- CONTROLLED IT.
USED THE DOOMSDAY MISTS... TO BURN AWAY THE BOTS.
OH, CLARK...
...I BELIEVE IN YOU.
AAH!
FFFFFOSSSS
D--DOOMSDAY. IT'S COMING BACK.
I HAVE TO GO.
WAIT, CLARK--

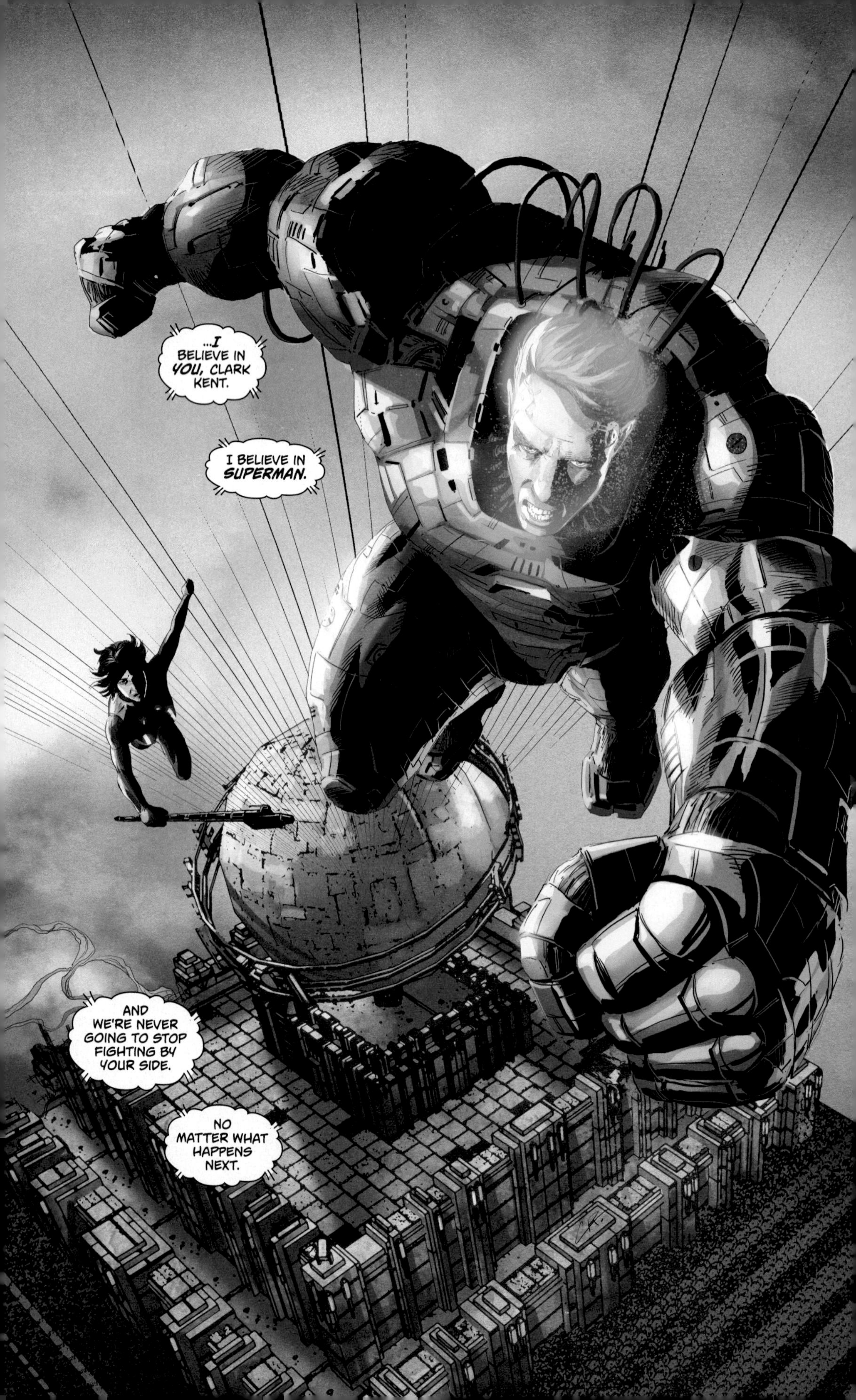
...I BELIEVE IN YOU, CLARK KENT.
I BELIEVE IN SUPERMAN.
AND WE'RE NEVER GOING TO STOP FIGHTING BY YOUR SIDE.
NO MATTER WHAT HAPPENS NEXT.

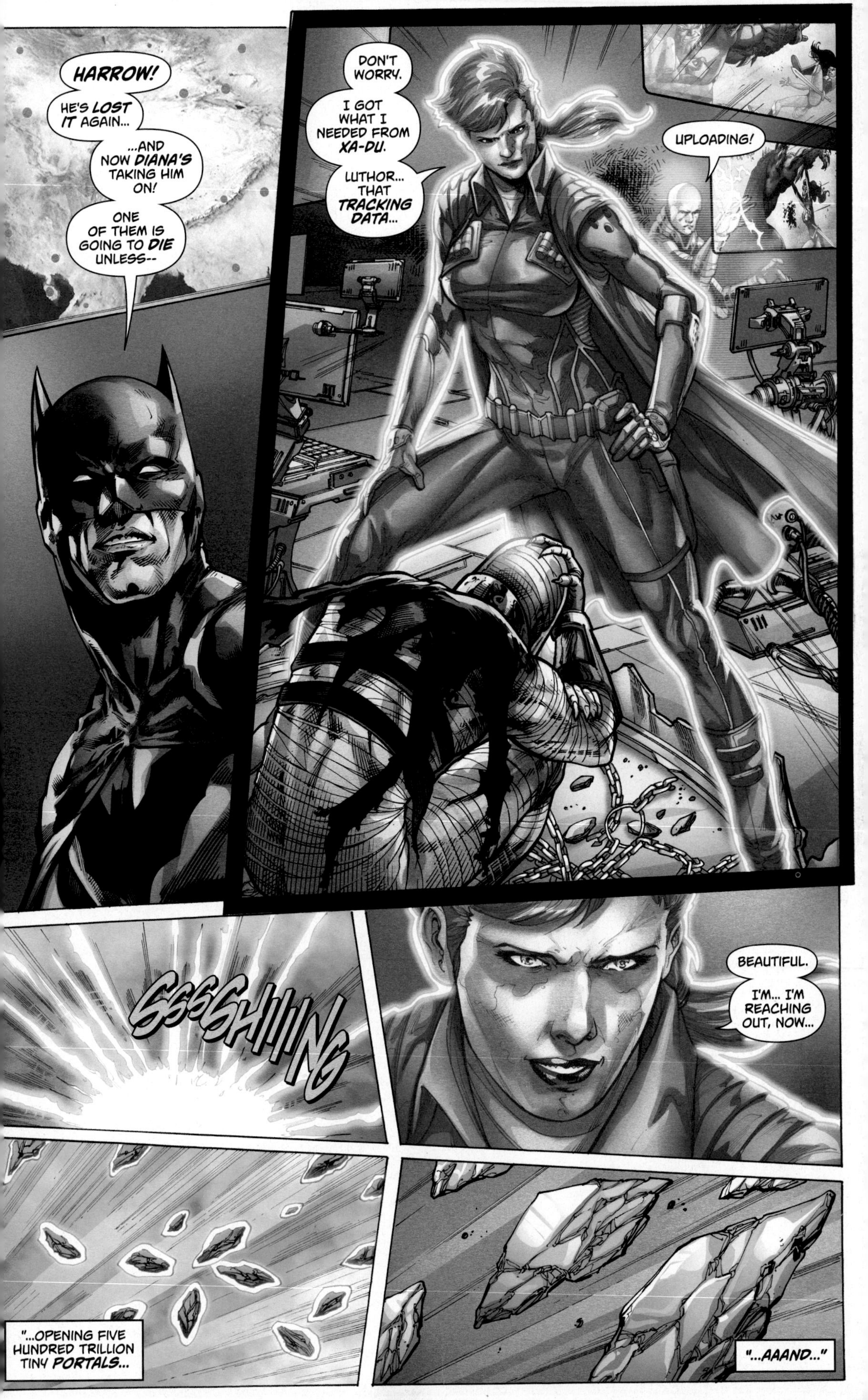
HARROW!
HE'S LOST IT AGAIN...
...AND NOW DIANA'S TAKING HIM ON!
ONE OF THEM IS GOING TO DIE UNLESS--
DON'T WORRY.
I GOT WHAT I NEEDED FROM XA-DU.
LUTHOR... THAT TRACKING DATA...
UPLOADING!
SSSSHIIIING
BEAUTIFUL.
I'M... I'M REACHING OUT, NOW...
"...OPENING FIVE HUNDRED TRILLION TINY PORTALS...
"...AAAND..."

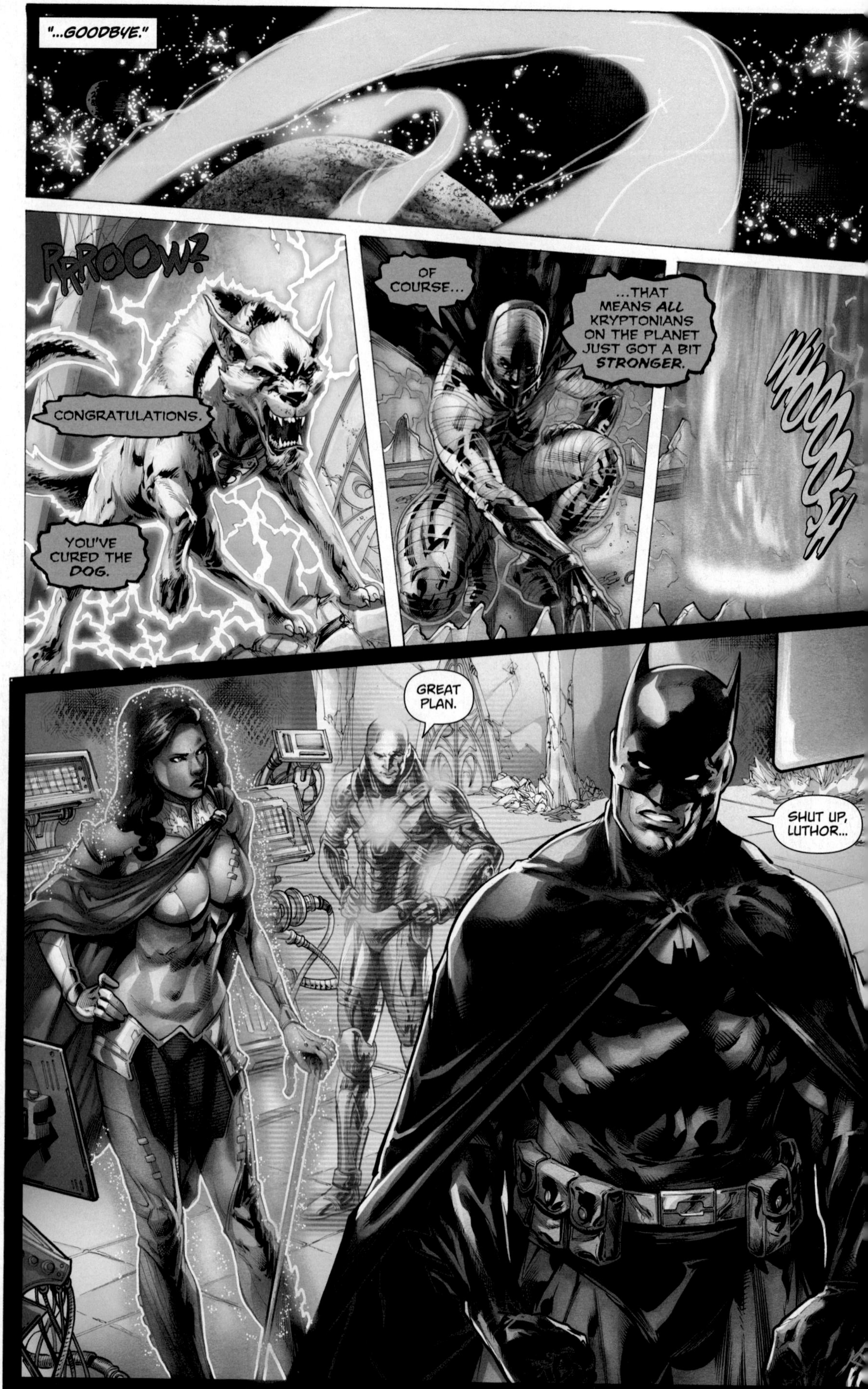
"...GOODBYE."
RRROOOW?
CONGRATULATIONS.
YOU'VE CURED THE DOG.
OF COURSE...
...THAT MEANS ALL KRYPTONIANS ON THE PLANET JUST GOT A BIT STRONGER.
WHOOOOSH
GREAT PLAN.
SHUT UP, LUTHOR...

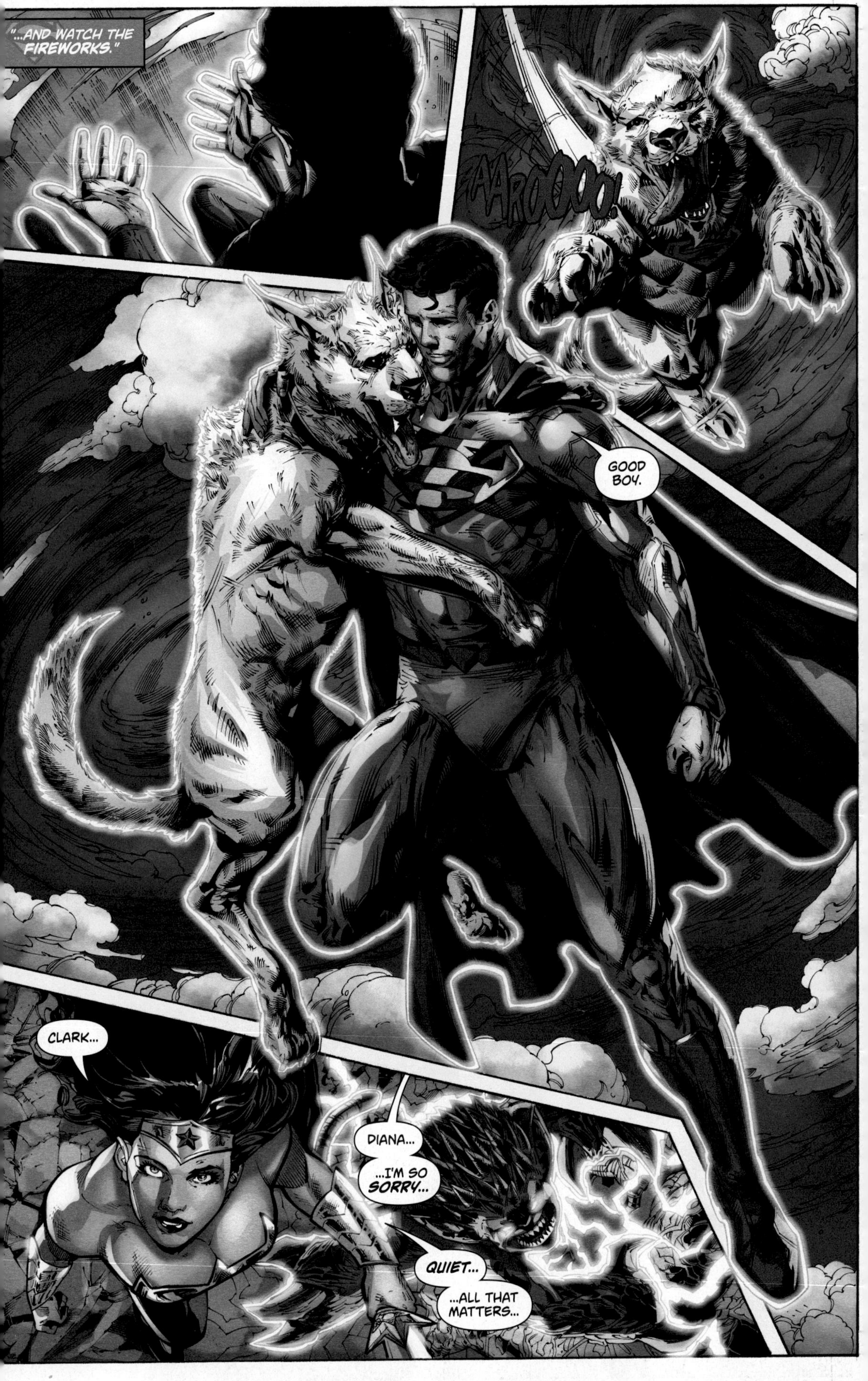
"...AND WATCH THE FIREWORKS."
AAROOOO!
GOOD BOY.
CLARK...
DIANA...
...I'M SO SORRY...
QUIET...
...ALL THAT MATTERS...

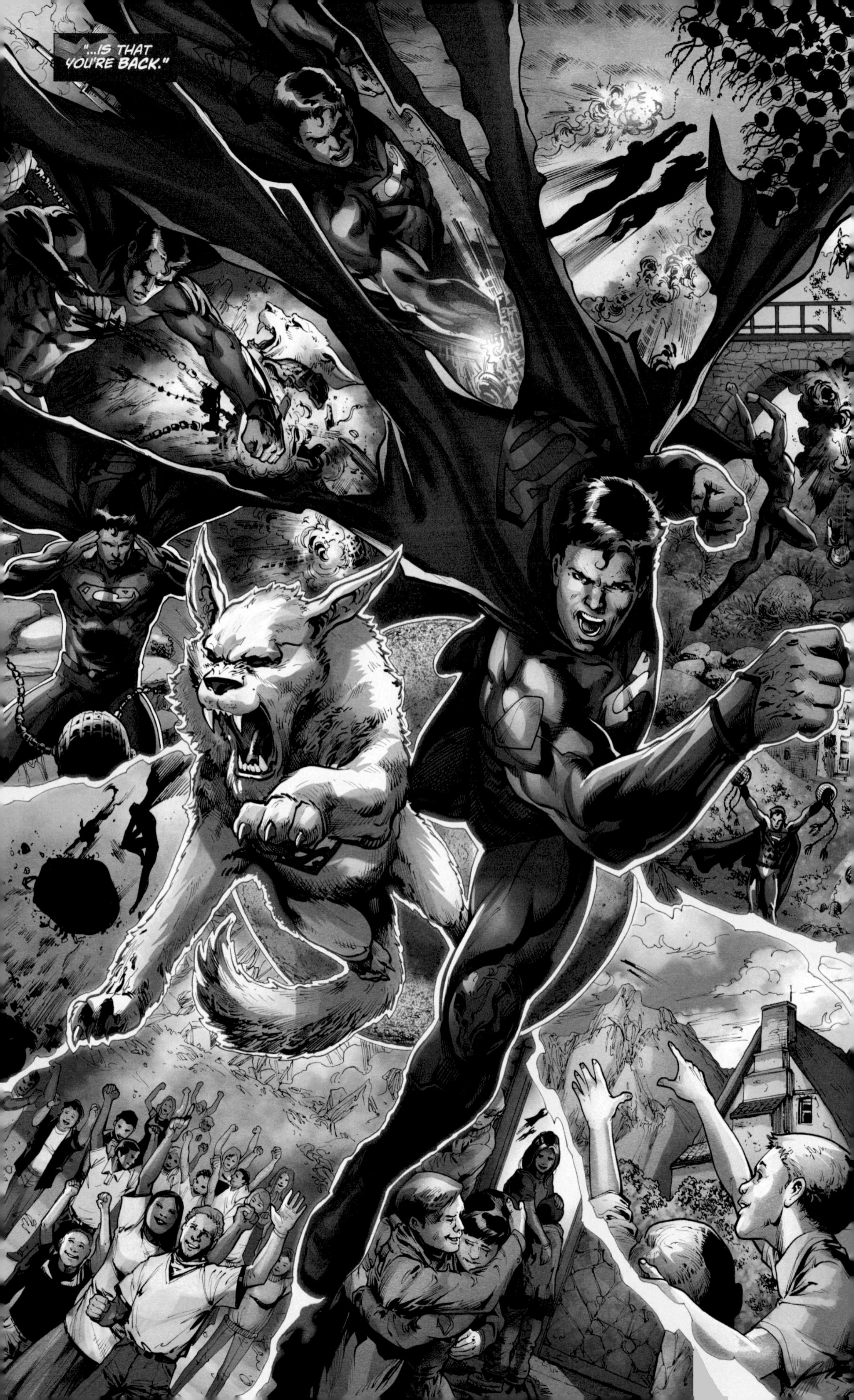
"...IS THAT YOU'RE BACK."

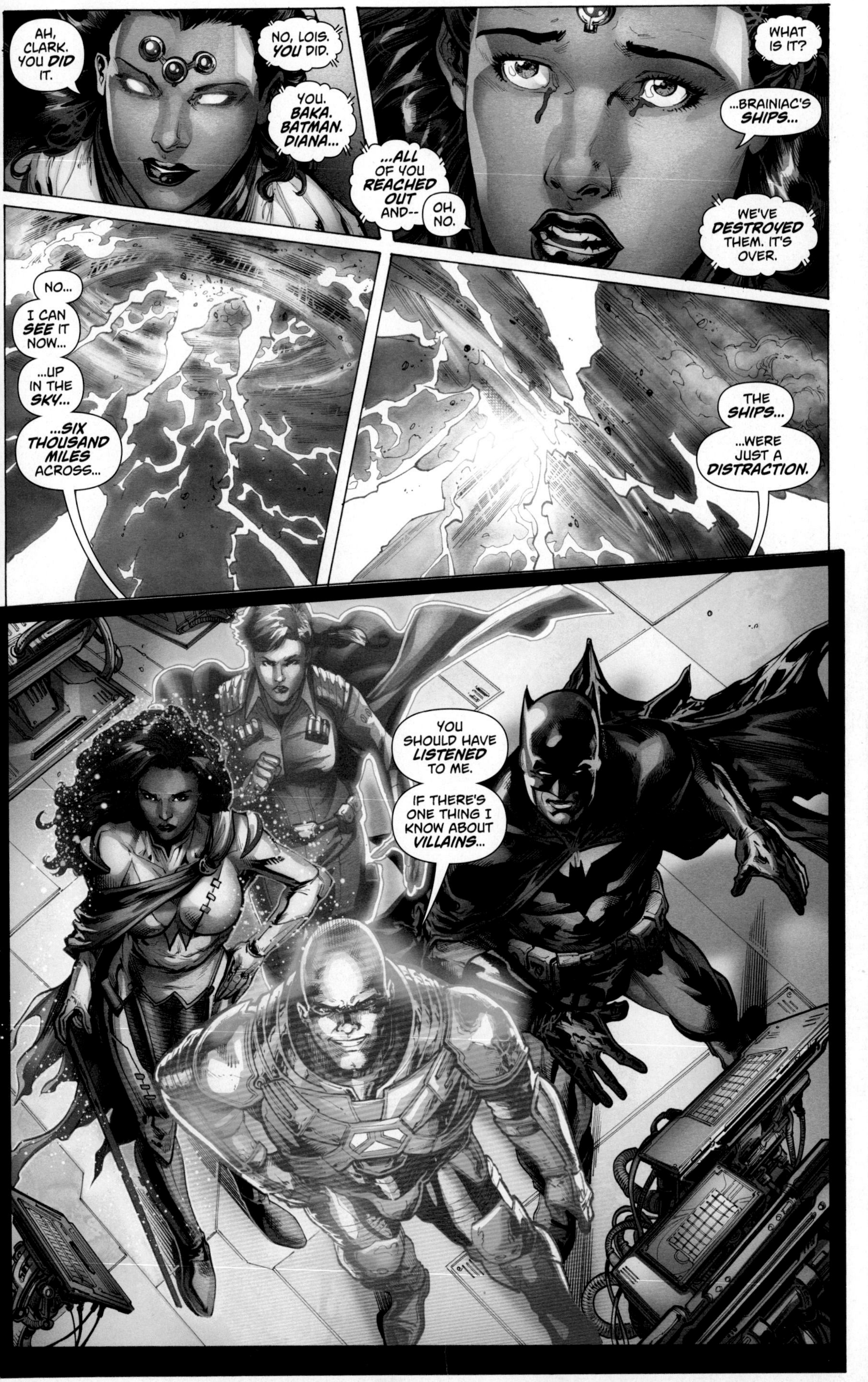
AH, CLARK. YOU DID IT.
NO, LOIS. YOU DID.
YOU. BAKA. BATMAN. DIANA...
...ALL OF YOU REACHED OUT AND--
OH, NO.
WHAT IS IT?
...BRAINIAC'S SHIPS...
WE'VE DESTROYED THEM. IT'S OVER.
NO...
I CAN SEE IT NOW...
...UP IN THE SKY...
...SIX THOUSAND MILES ACROSS...
THE SHIPS...
...WERE JUST A DISTRACTION.
YOU SHOULD HAVE LISTENED TO ME.
IF THERE'S ONE THING I KNOW ABOUT VILLAINS...

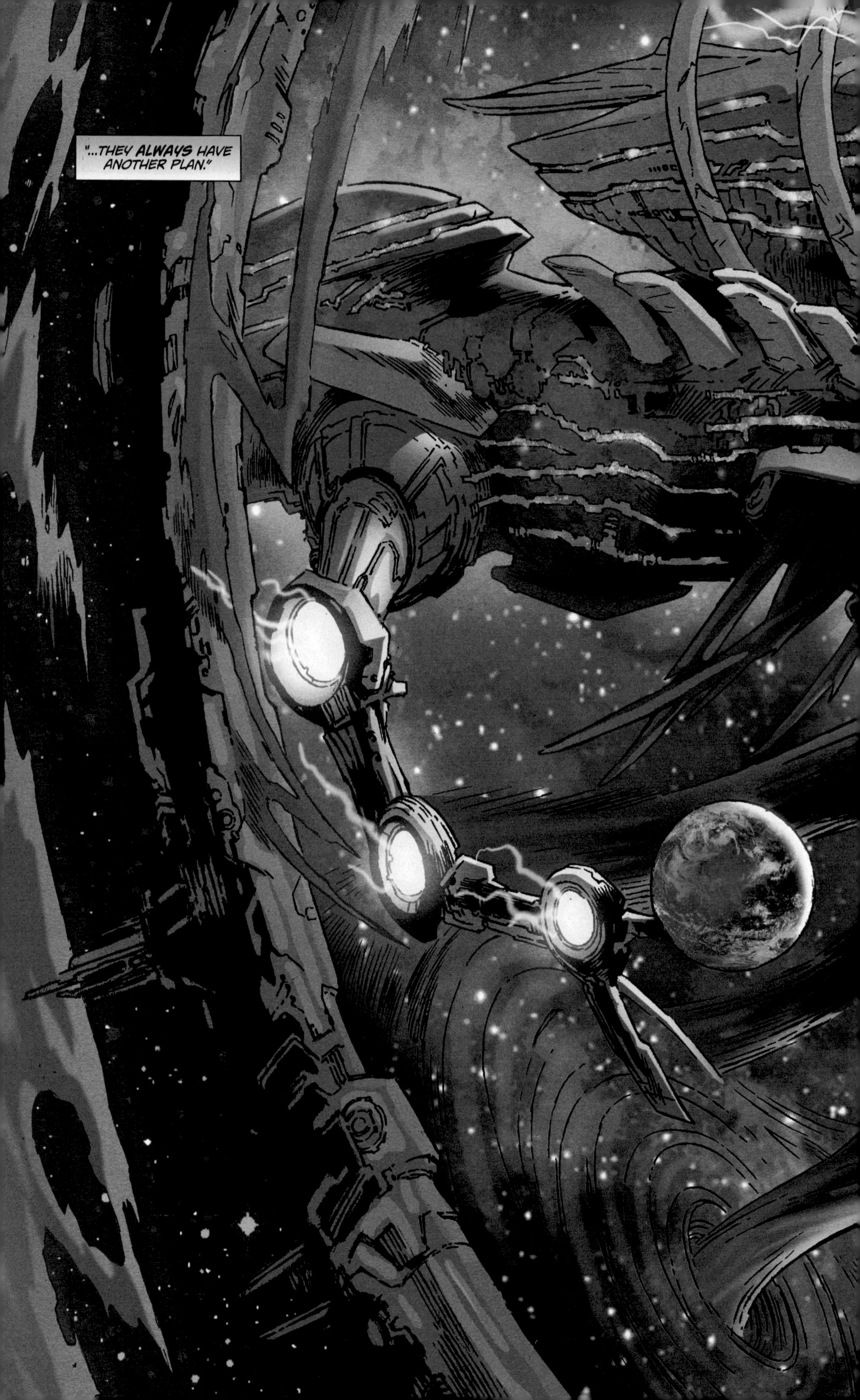
"...THEY ALWAYS HAVE ANOTHER PLAN."

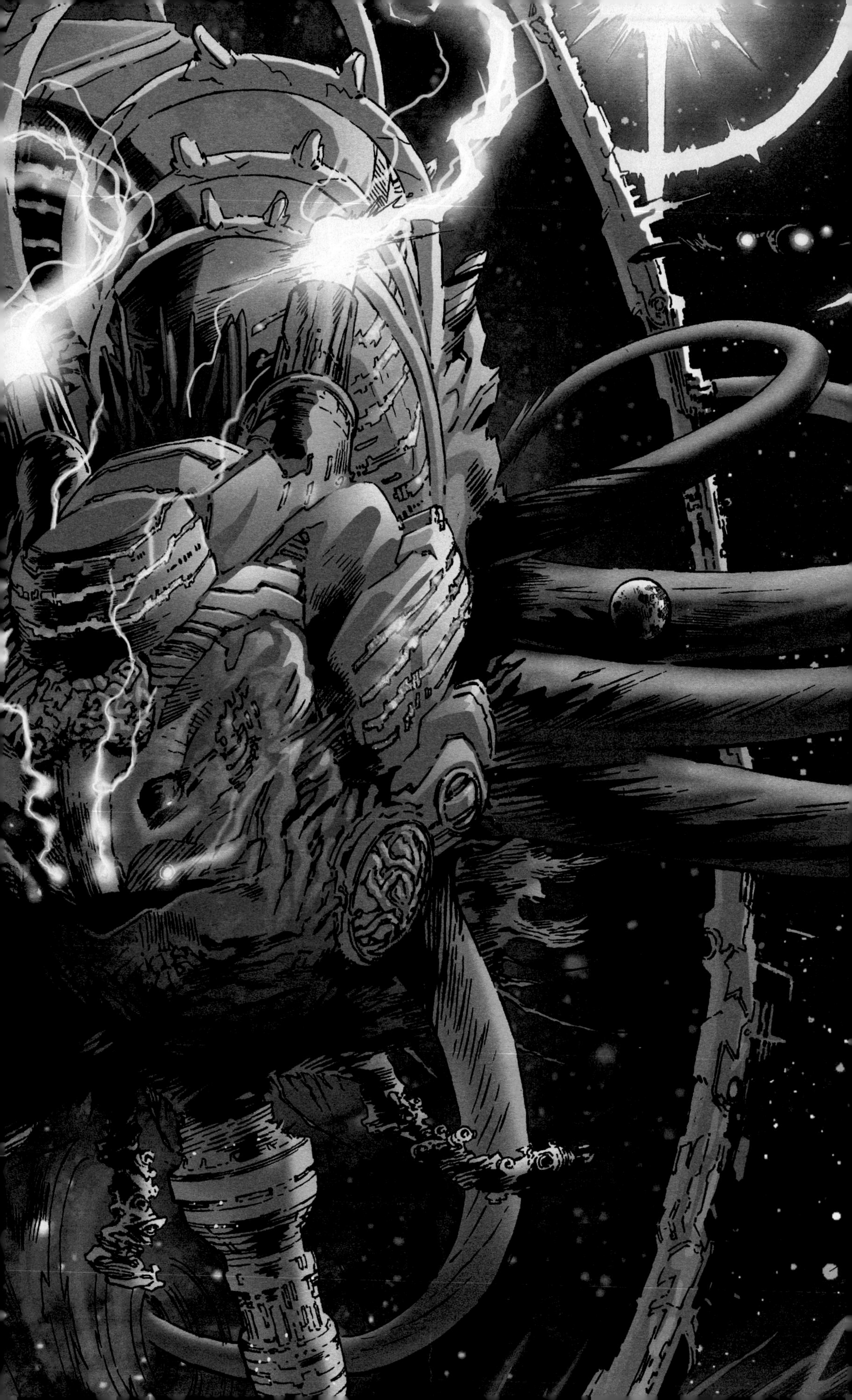

"ASSIMILATION"

GREG PAK writer AARON KUDER SCOTT KOLINS artists WIL QUINTANA colorist

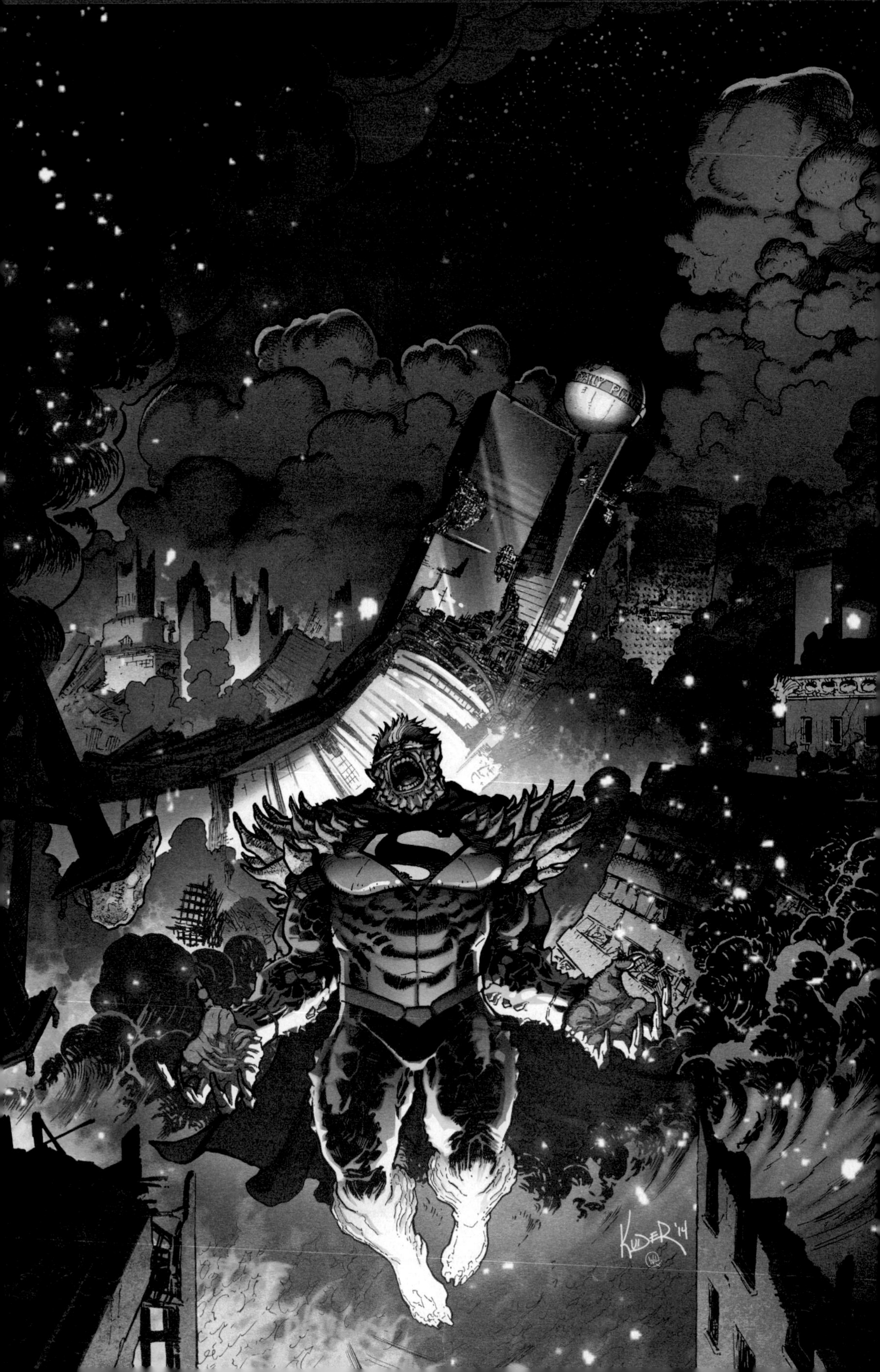
KUDER '14

WORLD   U.S.   METROPOLIS   BUSINESS   OPINION   SPORTS   ARTS   STYLE   VIDEO

Daily Planet

DAILY PLANET

August 06, 2

PANIC IN THE SKY

BY LOIS LANE

The world is still here today. For how much longer I can't say.

Earth was invaded a few hours ago by a fleet of ships, now being referred to as nodes, seeking to link up together here on Earth as they disabled all of the planet's defenses. In command of this armada is what strangely appears to be a Cyborg version of Superman. The Justice League and many others responded to the threat quickly, but their ultimate goal was just that—to be a diversionary tactic allowing a stargate to be built and let what seems to be a planet sized starship through.

We cannot lose hope yet. Superman has returned. Batman and a group that

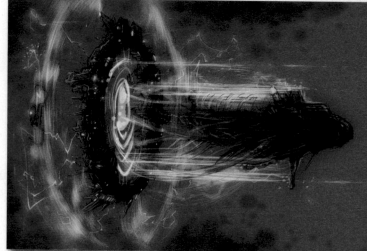

Artis Rendering : Pasco

included Lex Luthor have managed to get rid of the Kryptonite in the atmosphere, allowing the Man of Steel to shed his Doomsday persona and become more himself. My unwitting role in this as a pawn of the true mastermind behind this, Brainiac has been severed. But nothing

has changed for Smallville Metropolis where its citizen still remain in comas.

There are still many that c stand against this new danger. We have to just not stop believing in them. The next move is the enemies...

| X | Slideshow - Superdoom's Path of Destruction | 404 Error
404 Error
404 Error |

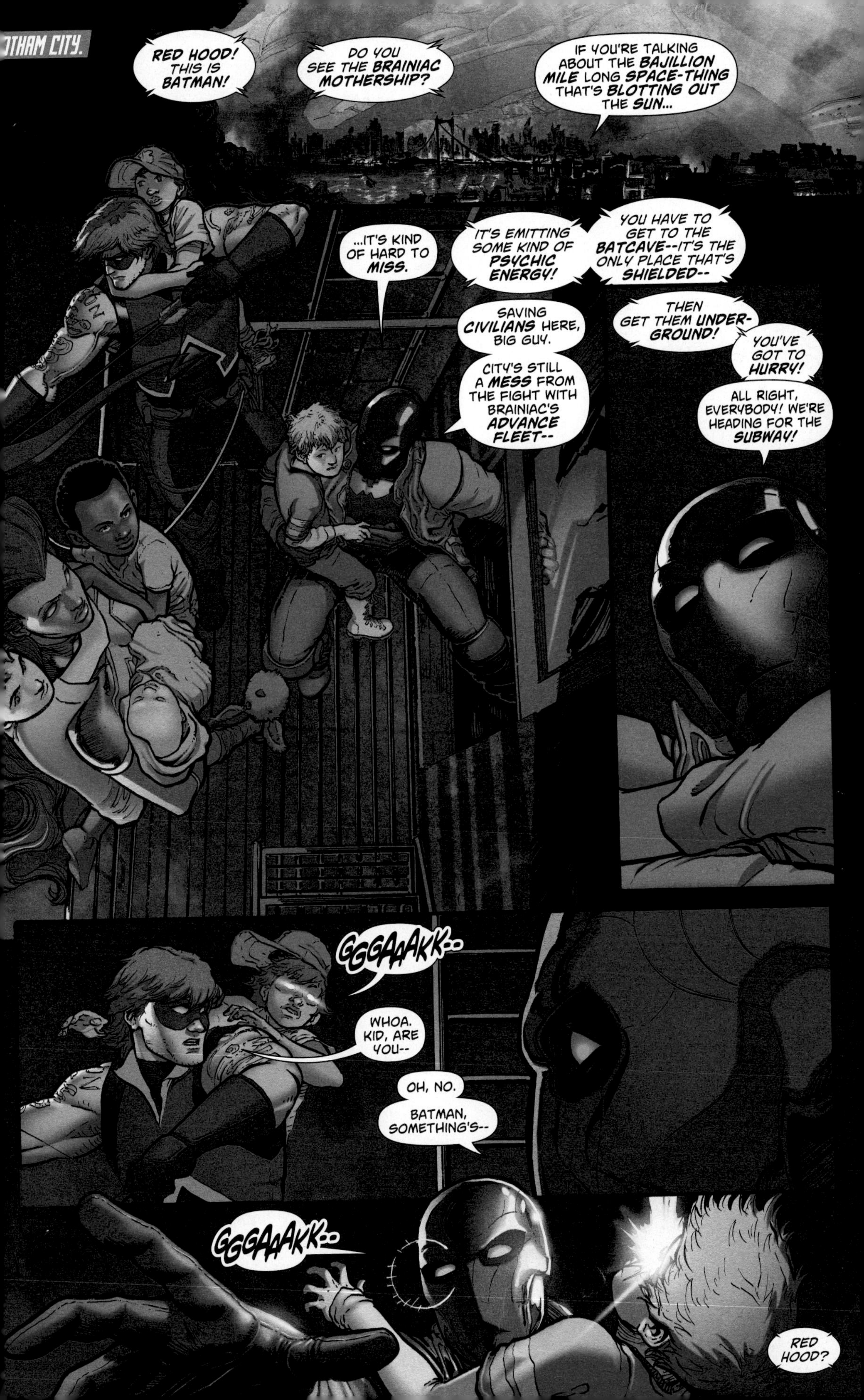

OTHAM CITY.
RED HOOD! THIS IS BATMAN!
DO YOU SEE THE BRAINIAC MOTHERSHIP?
IF YOU'RE TALKING ABOUT THE BAJILLION MILE LONG SPACE-THING THAT'S BLOTTING OUT THE SUN...
...IT'S KIND OF HARD TO MISS.
IT'S EMITTING SOME KIND OF PSYCHIC ENERGY!
YOU HAVE TO GET TO THE BATCAVE--IT'S THE ONLY PLACE THAT'S SHIELDED--
SAVING CIVILIANS HERE, BIG GUY.
CITY'S STILL A MESS FROM THE FIGHT WITH BRAINIAC'S ADVANCE FLEET--
THEN GET THEM UNDERGROUND!
YOU'VE GOT TO HURRY!
ALL RIGHT, EVERYBODY! WE'RE HEADING FOR THE SUBWAY!
GGGAAAKK--
WHOA. KID, ARE YOU--
OH, NO.
BATMAN, SOMETHING'S--
GGGAAAKK--
RED HOOD?

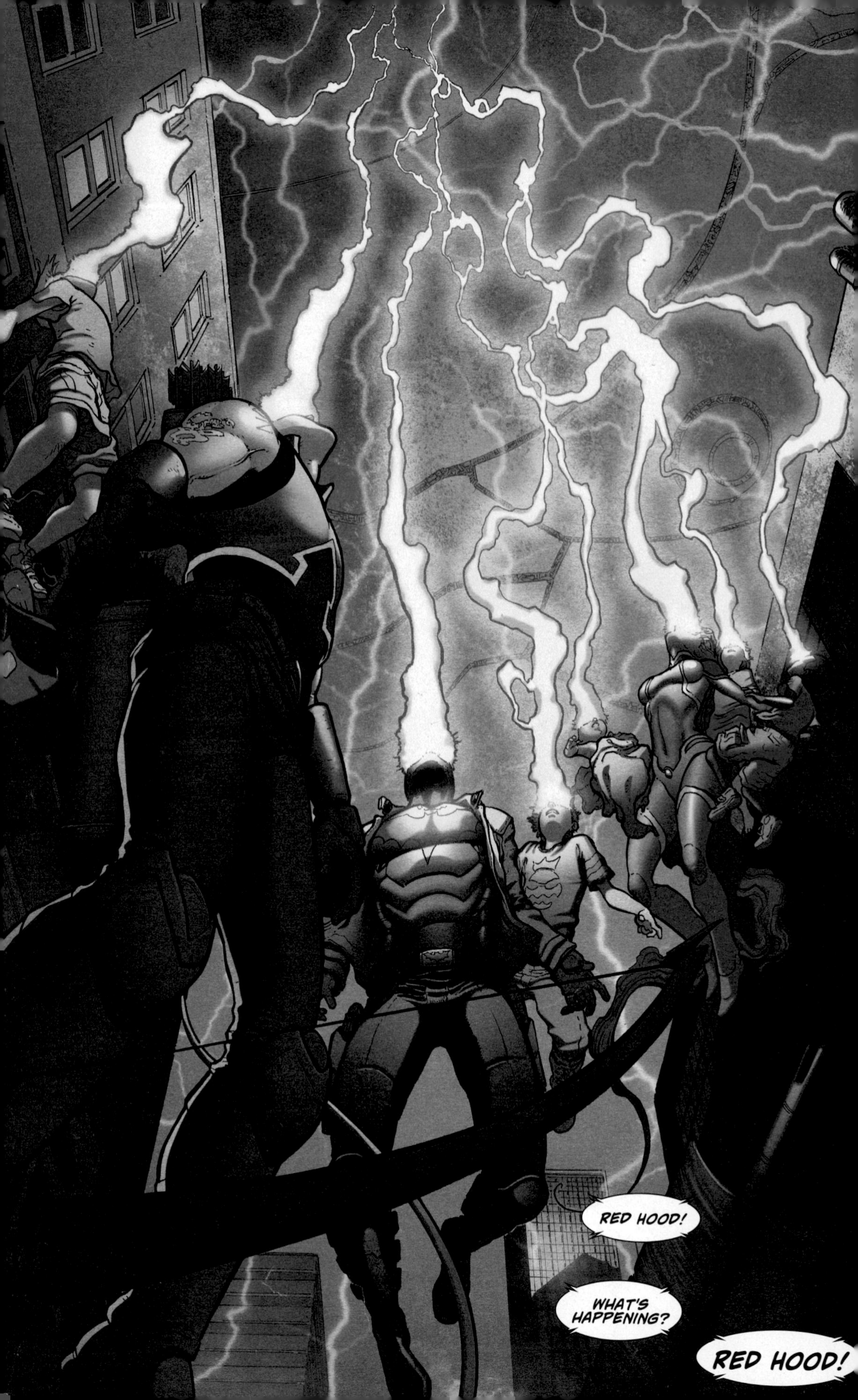
RED HOOD!
WHAT'S HAPPENING?
RED HOOD!

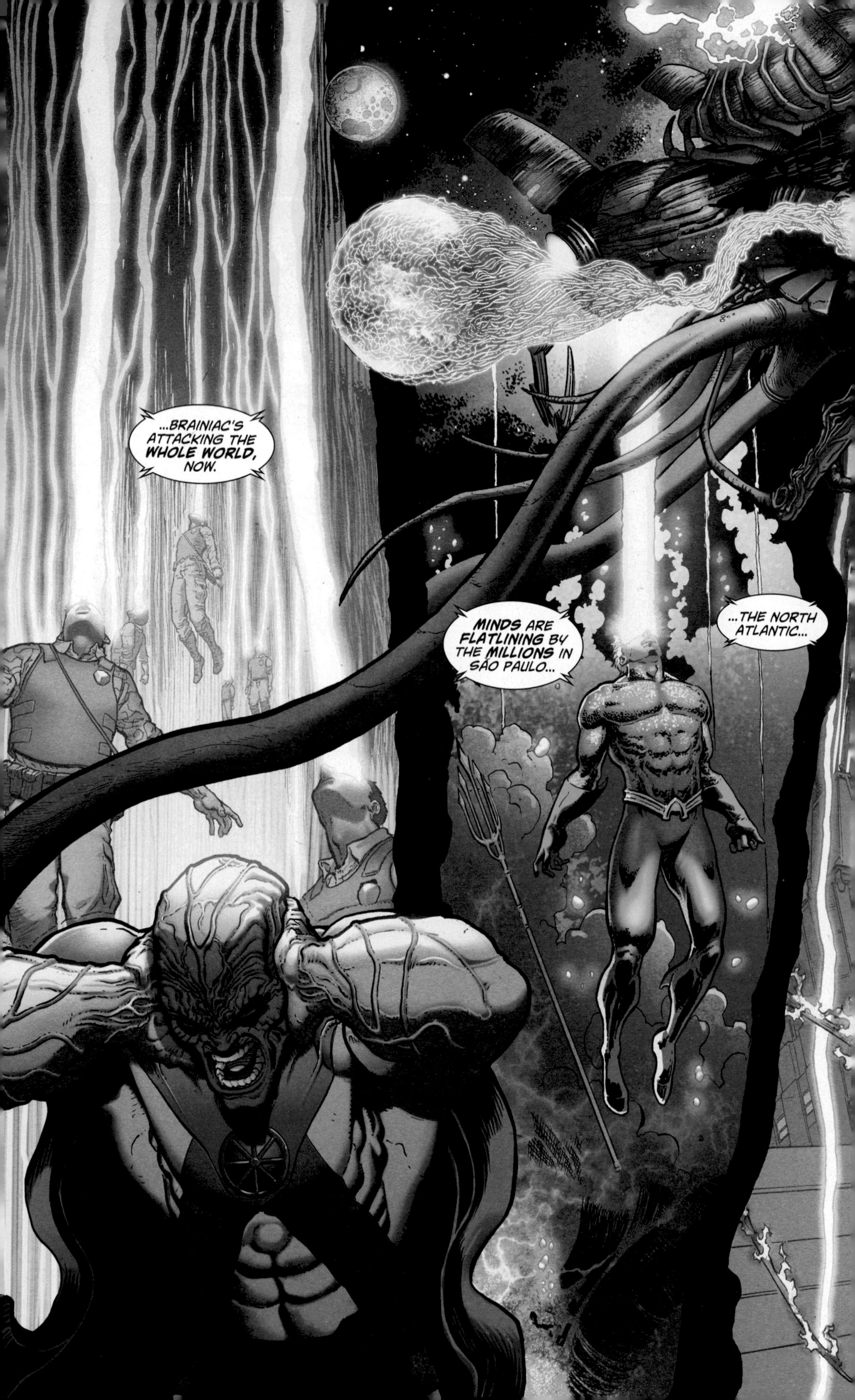
...BRAINIAC'S ATTACKING THE WHOLE WORLD, NOW.
MINDS ARE FLATLINING BY THE MILLIONS IN SÃO PAULO...
...THE NORTH ATLANTIC...

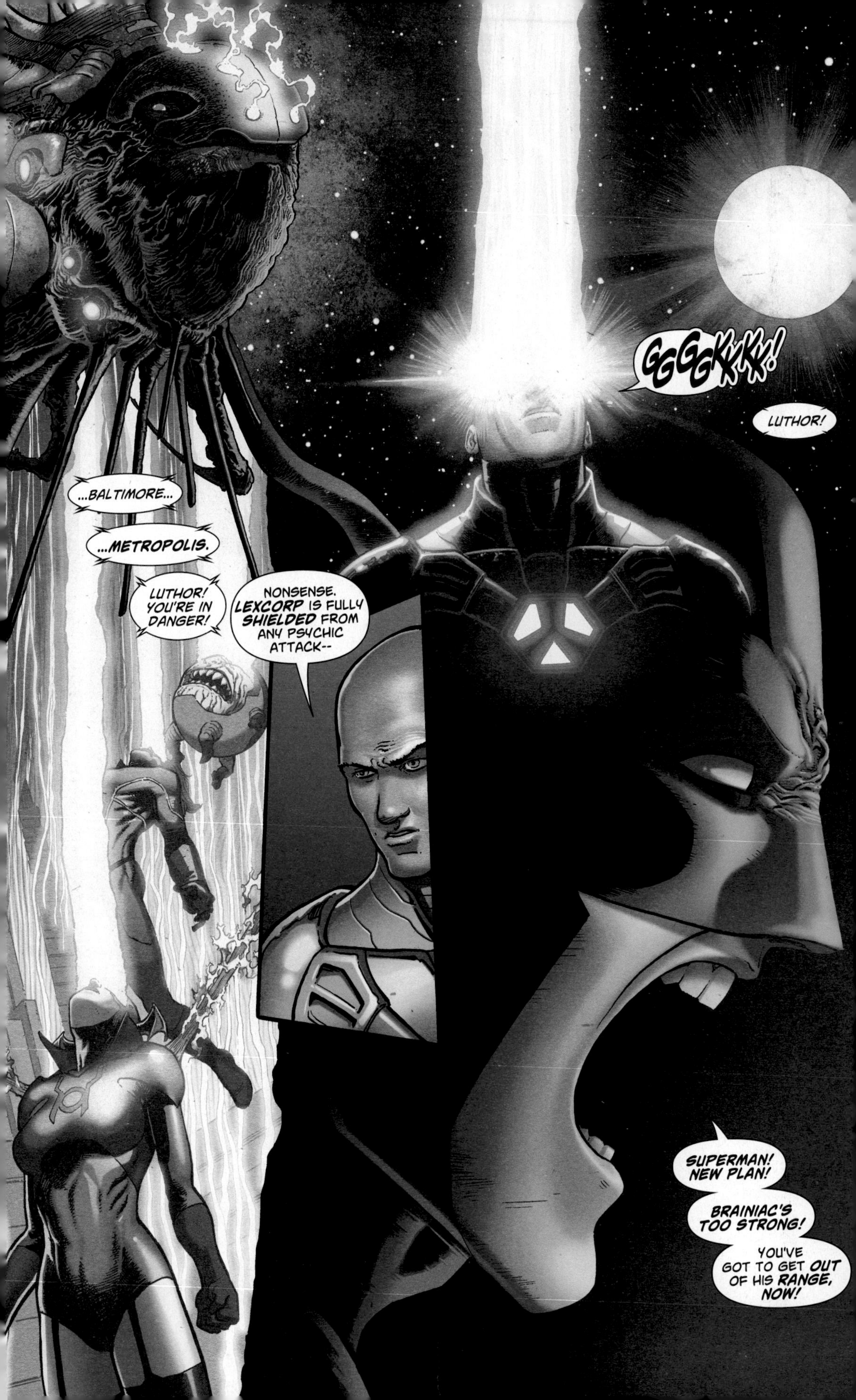
GGGGKKKK!
LUTHOR!
...BALTIMORE...
...METROPOLIS.
LUTHOR! YOU'RE IN DANGER!
NONSENSE. LEXCORP IS FULLY SHIELDED FROM ANY PSYCHIC ATTACK--
SUPERMAN! NEW PLAN!
BRAINIAC'S TOO STRONG!
YOU'VE GOT TO GET OUT OF HIS RANGE, NOW!

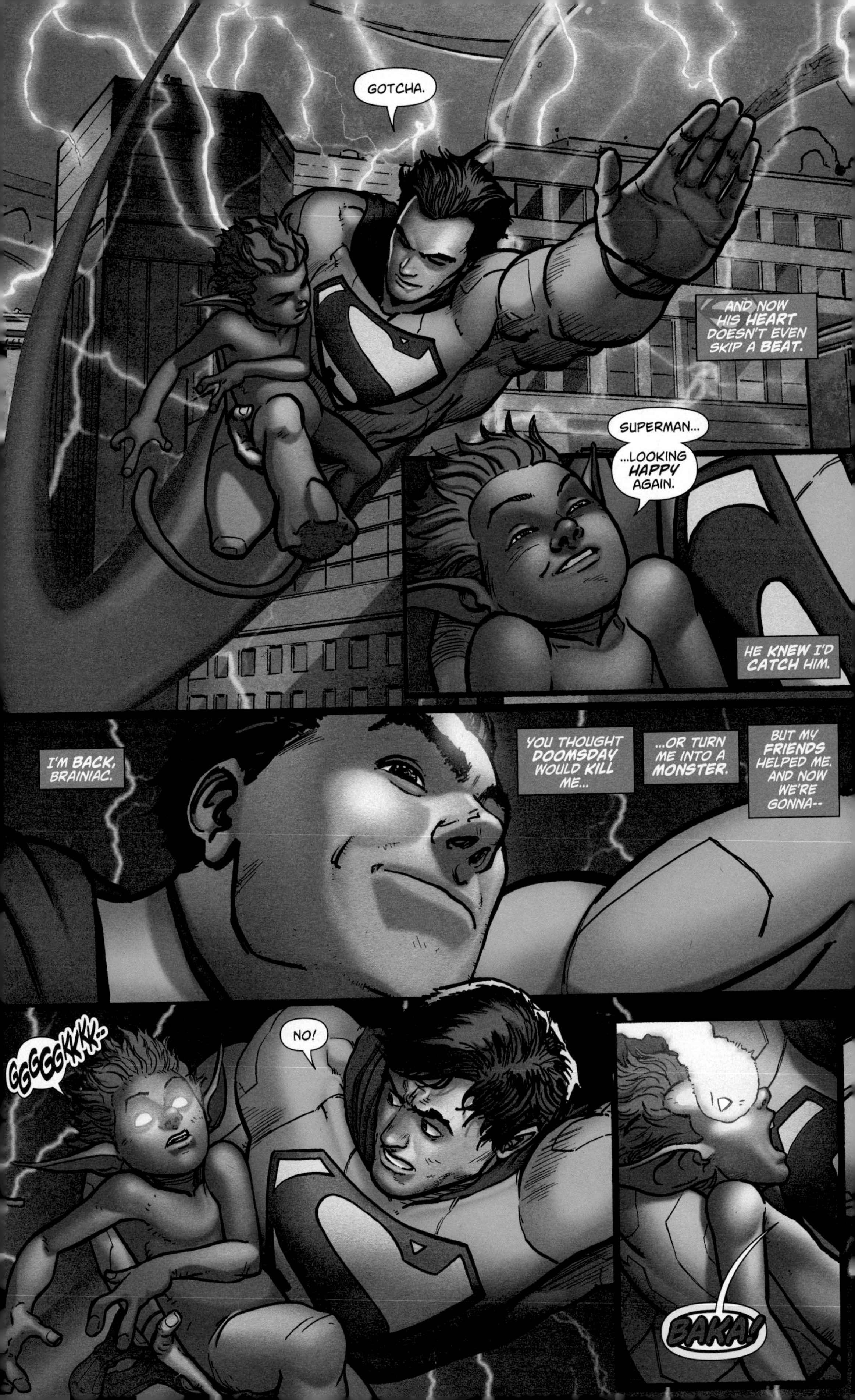
GOTCHA.
AND NOW HIS HEART DOESN'T EVEN SKIP A BEAT.
SUPERMAN...
...LOOKING HAPPY AGAIN.
HE KNEW I'D CATCH HIM.
I'M BACK, BRAINIAC.
YOU THOUGHT DOOMSDAY WOULD KILL ME...
...OR TURN ME INTO A MONSTER.
BUT MY FRIENDS HELPED ME. AND NOW WE'RE GONNA--
GGGGGKKKK-
NO!
BAKA!

HEY, GUYS! LANA LANG, HERE!

I'M GETTING A LOOK AT THIS NEW DATA...

...AND I THINK BRAINIAC'S *NETWORKING* ALL THESE BRAINS!

NETWORKING? BUT I'M NOT PICKING UP ANY *INFORMATION* *EXCHANGE*...

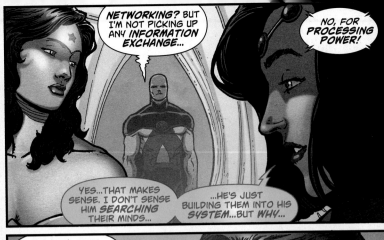
NO, FOR *PROCESSING* *POWER!*

YES...THAT MAKES SENSE. I DON'T SENSE HIM *SEARCHING* THEIR MINDS...

...HE'S JUST BUILDING THEM INTO HIS *SYSTEM*...BUT *WHY*...

MONGUL TRIED SOMETHING LIKE THIS A WHILE BACK.

TAPPED INTO MILLIONS OF BRAINS, TRIED TO TURN THE EARTH INTO A MASSIVE PSYCHIC *WEAPON.*

WE HAD TO THROW HIM INTO THE *PHANTOM* *ZONE* TO STOP HIM.

GUESSING THE *MOTHERSHIP'S* A LITTLE TO *BIG* FOR *THAT* SOLUTION.

BUT WE'VE GOT TO TAKE IT *DOWN.*

HARROW CAN *SUMMON* THE *DEAD.* WE CAN STAY *INTANGIBLE* UNTIL THE LAST MINUTE, WHICH SHOULD HELP US FROM GETTING *ASSIMILATED.*

JUST POINT US TO THE SHIP'S *SOFT* *SPOT* AND--

BELIEVE ME, I'D LOVE TO BREAK ALL OF BRAINIAC'S *TOYS.*

BUT RIGHT NOW, *SEVEN* *BILLION* MINDS ARE LINKED TO THAT MOTHERSHIP.

I...I DON'T KNOW WHAT'LL HAPPEN TO THEM IF WE JUST *SMASH* IT.

HRNN...

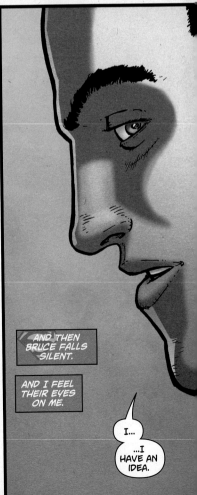
AND THEN BRUCE FALLS SILENT.

AND I FEEL THEIR EYES ON ME.

I...

...I HAVE AN IDEA.

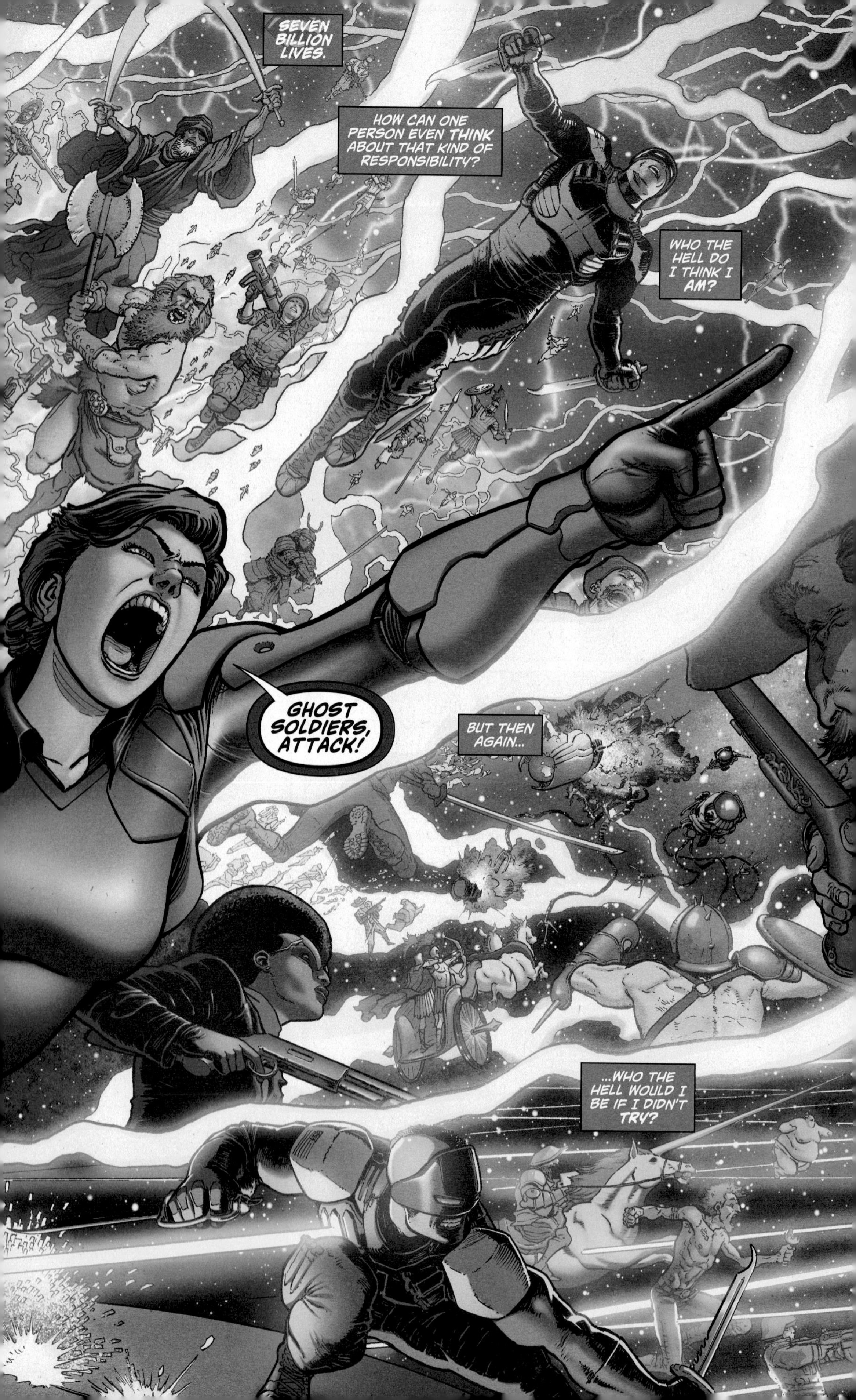
SEVEN BILLION LIVES.
HOW CAN ONE PERSON EVEN THINK ABOUT THAT KIND OF RESPONSIBILITY?
WHO THE HELL DO I THINK I AM?
GHOST SOLDIERS, ATTACK!
BUT THEN AGAIN...
...WHO THE HELL WOULD I BE IF I DIDN'T TRY?

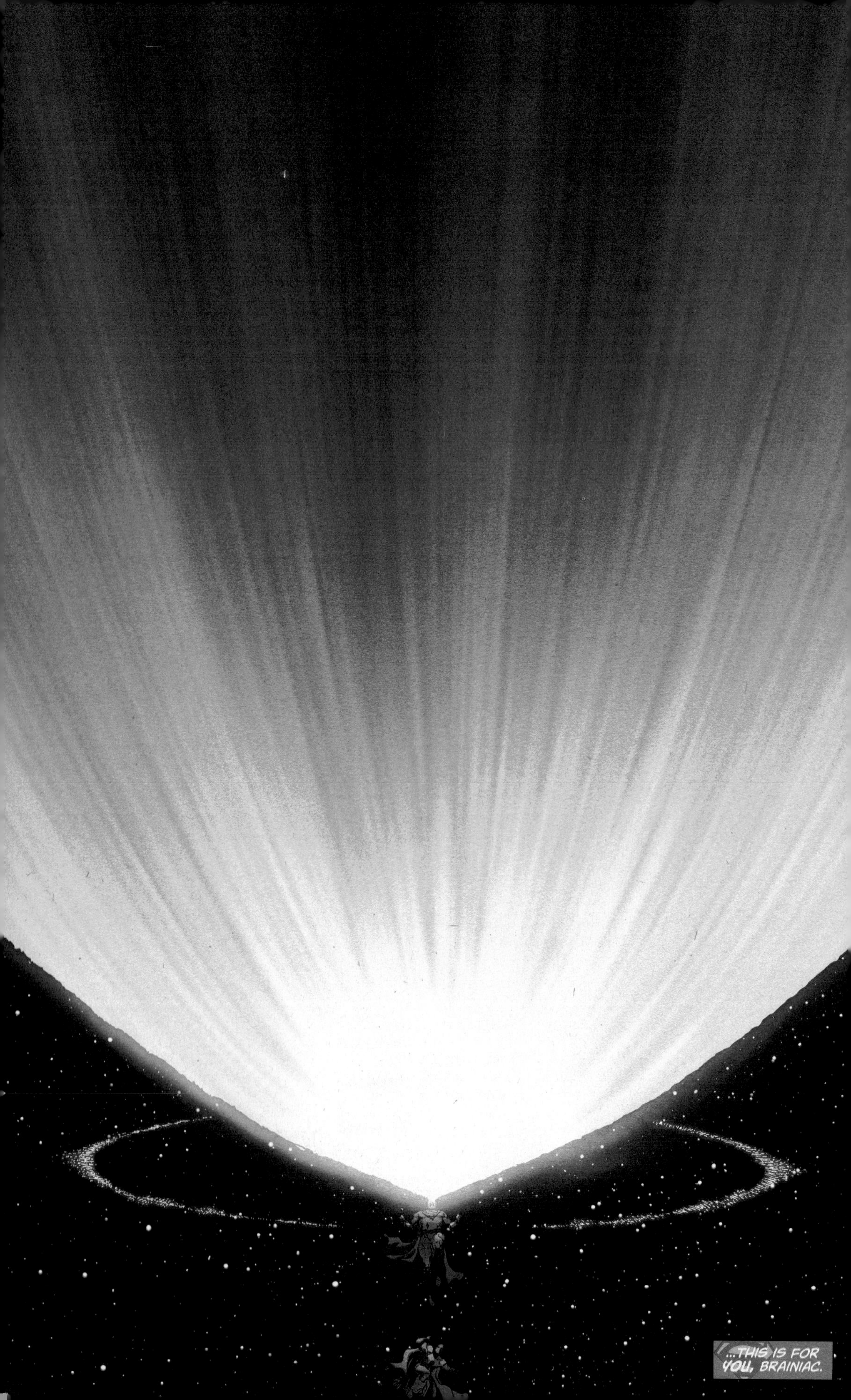
...THIS IS FOR YOU, BRAINIAC.

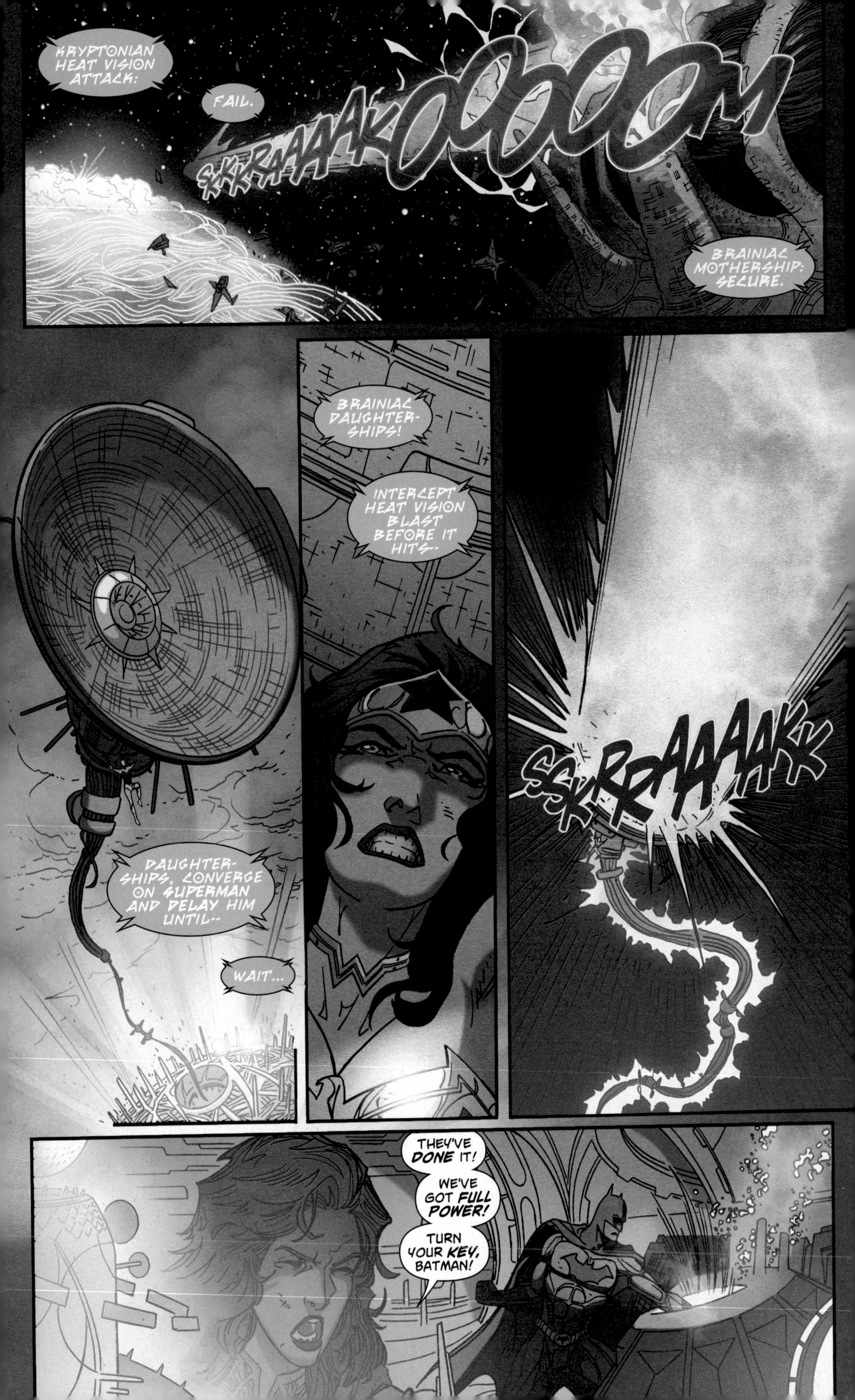
KRYPTONIAN HEAT VISION ATTACK:
FAIL.
SKKRAAAAKOOOOOOM
BRAINIAC MOTHERSHIP: SECURE.
BRAINIAC DAUGHTER-SHIPS!
INTERCEPT HEAT VISION BLAST BEFORE IT HITS--
DAUGHTER-SHIPS, CONVERGE ON SUPERMAN AND DELAY HIM UNTIL--
WAIT...
SSKRRAAAAKK
THEY'VE DONE IT!
WE'VE GOT FULL POWER!
TURN YOUR KEY, BATMAN!

"...NOW I GUESS IT'S TIME FOR *US* TO TRUST *HIM.*"

SECONDARY PHANTOM ENERGY SOURCE DETECTED!

CONVERGING WITH PRIMARY PORTAL!

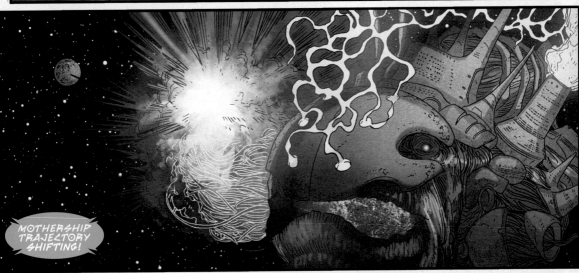

MOTHERSHIP TRAJECTORY SHIFTING!

SHAY.

PLEASE TELL ME SOMETHING *GOOD.*

HAPPY TO *OBLIGE,* SUPERMAN.

IT'S *WORKING.*

WE'RE GOING TO PULL BOTH THE *MOTHER-SHIP...*

...AND THE *ENTIRE* PLANET...

...INTO THE *PHANTOM ZONE...*

...A PLACE WITHOUT *TIME...*

...IN ORDER TO *BUY* THE *TIME* WE NEED TO SAVE *EVERYONE.*

INTRIGUING...

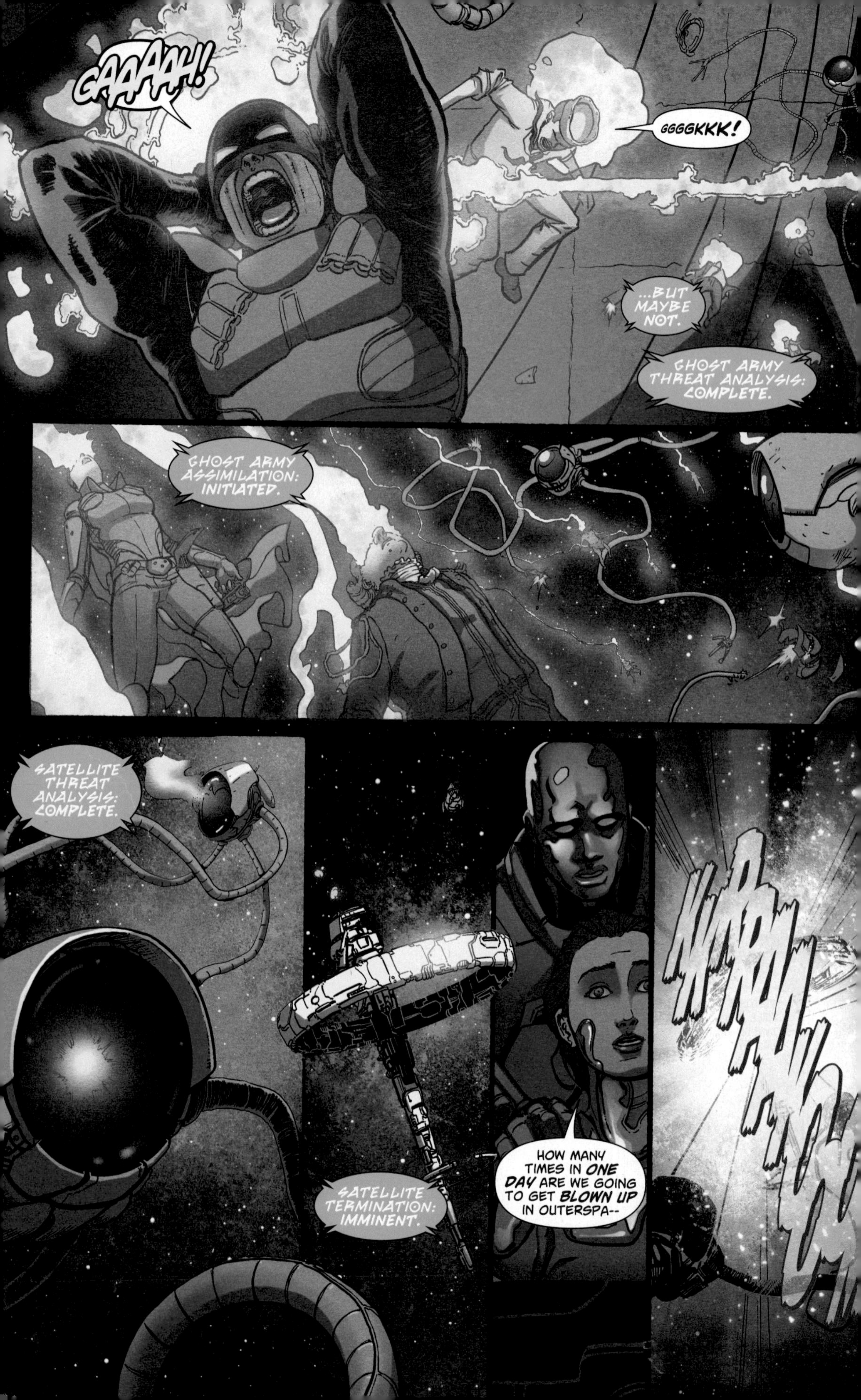
GAAAAH!
GGGGKKK!
...BUT MAYBE NOT.
GHOST ARMY THREAT ANALYSIS: COMPLETE.
GHOST ARMY ASSIMILATION: INITIATED.
SATELLITE THREAT ANALYSIS: COMPLETE.
SATELLITE TERMINATION: IMMINENT.
HOW MANY TIMES IN ONE DAY ARE WE GOING TO GET BLOWN UP IN OUTERSPA--

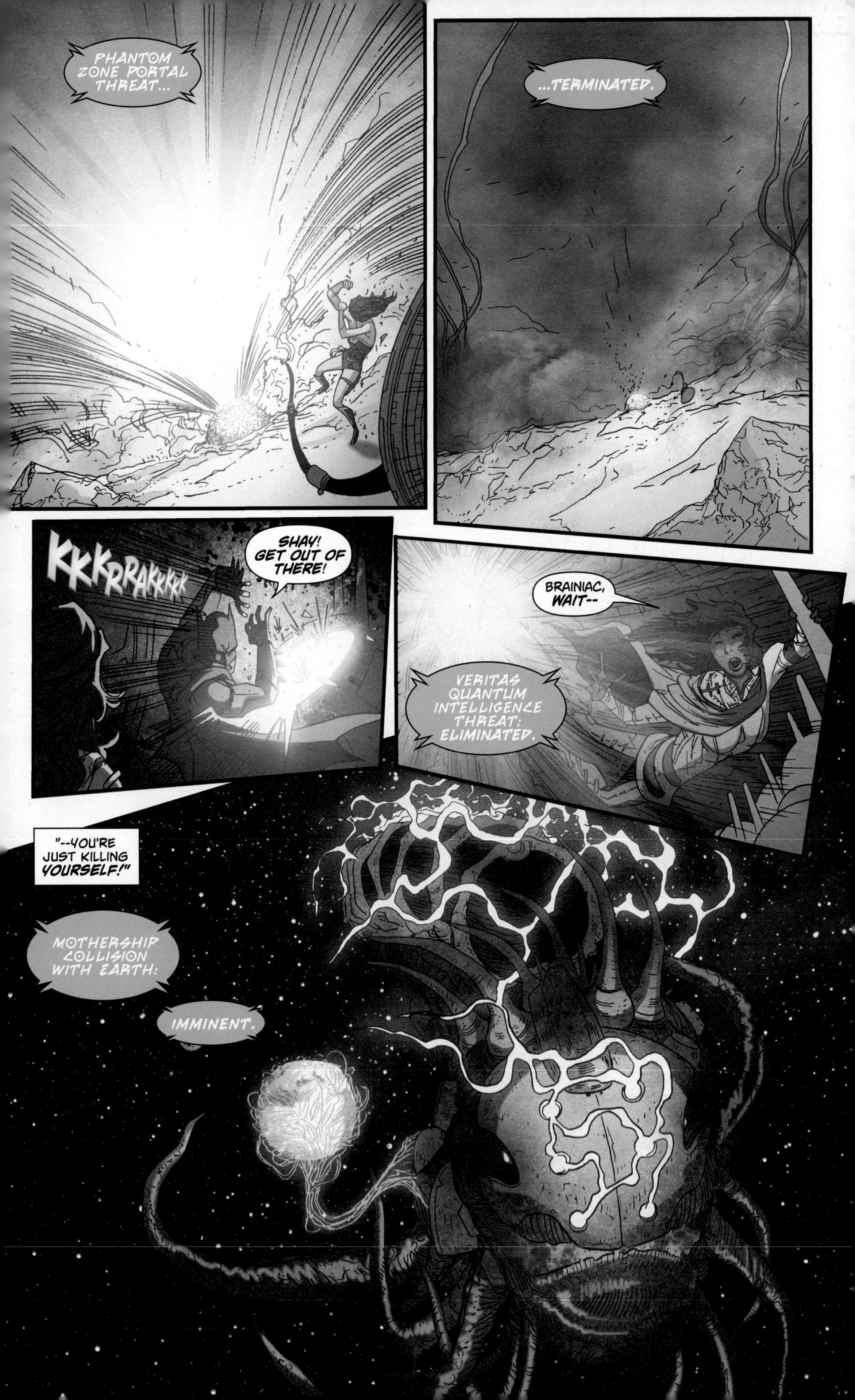
PHANTOM ZONE PORTAL THREAT...
...TERMINATED.
KKKRRAKKKKK
SHAY! GET OUT OF THERE!
BRAINIAC, WAIT--
VERITAS QUANTUM INTELLIGENCE THREAT: ELIMINATED.
"--YOU'RE JUST KILLING YOURSELF!"
MOTHERSHIP COLLISION WITH EARTH:
IMMINENT.

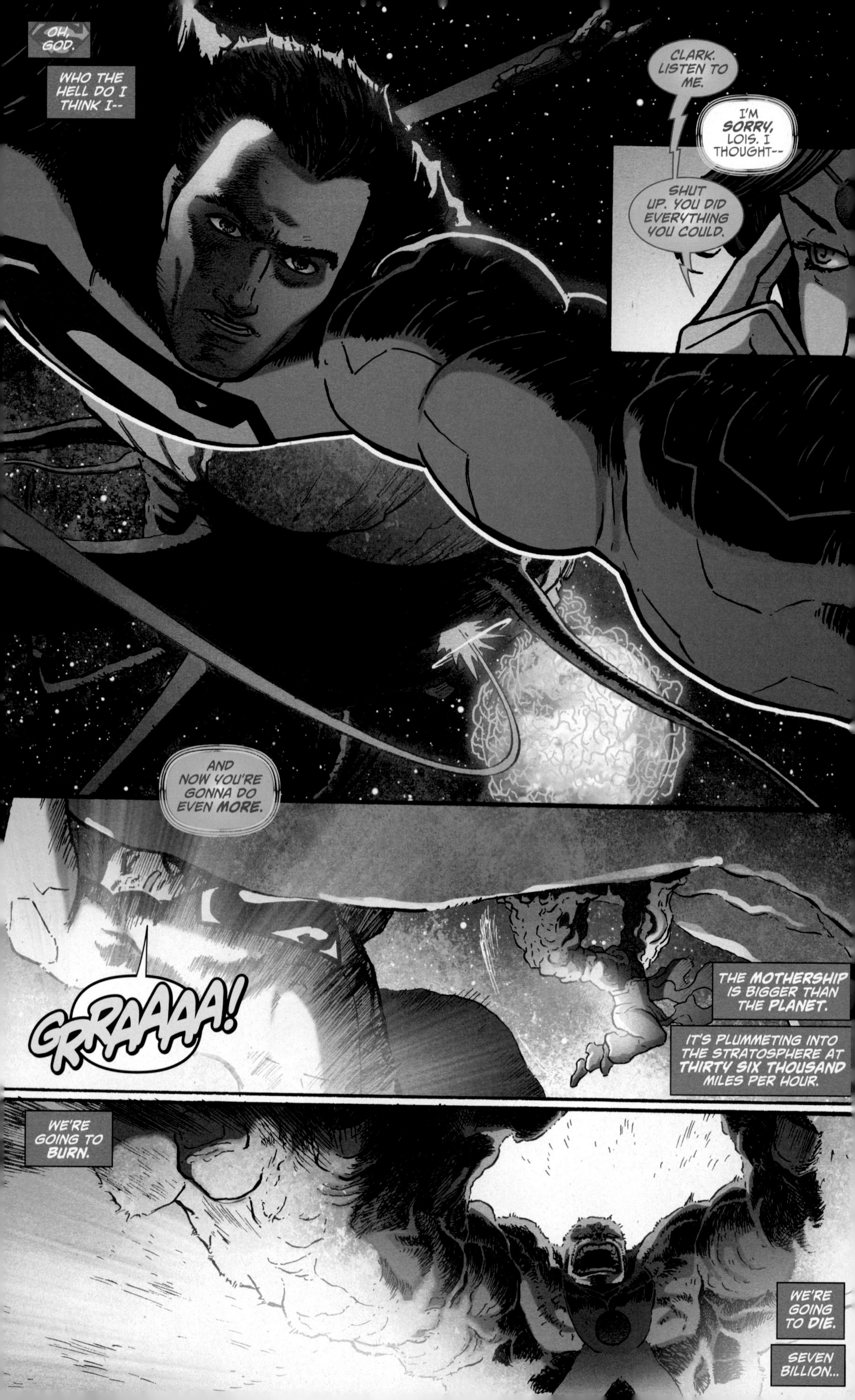

OH, GOD.
WHO THE HELL DO I THINK I--
CLARK. LISTEN TO ME.
I'M SORRY, LOIS. I THOUGHT--
SHUT UP. YOU DID EVERYTHING YOU COULD.
AND NOW YOU'RE GONNA DO EVEN MORE.
GRRAAAA!
THE MOTHERSHIP IS BIGGER THAN THE PLANET.
IT'S PLUMMETING INTO THE STRATOSPHERE AT THIRTY SIX THOUSAND MILES PER HOUR.
WE'RE GOING TO BURN.
WE'RE GOING TO DIE.
SEVEN BILLION...

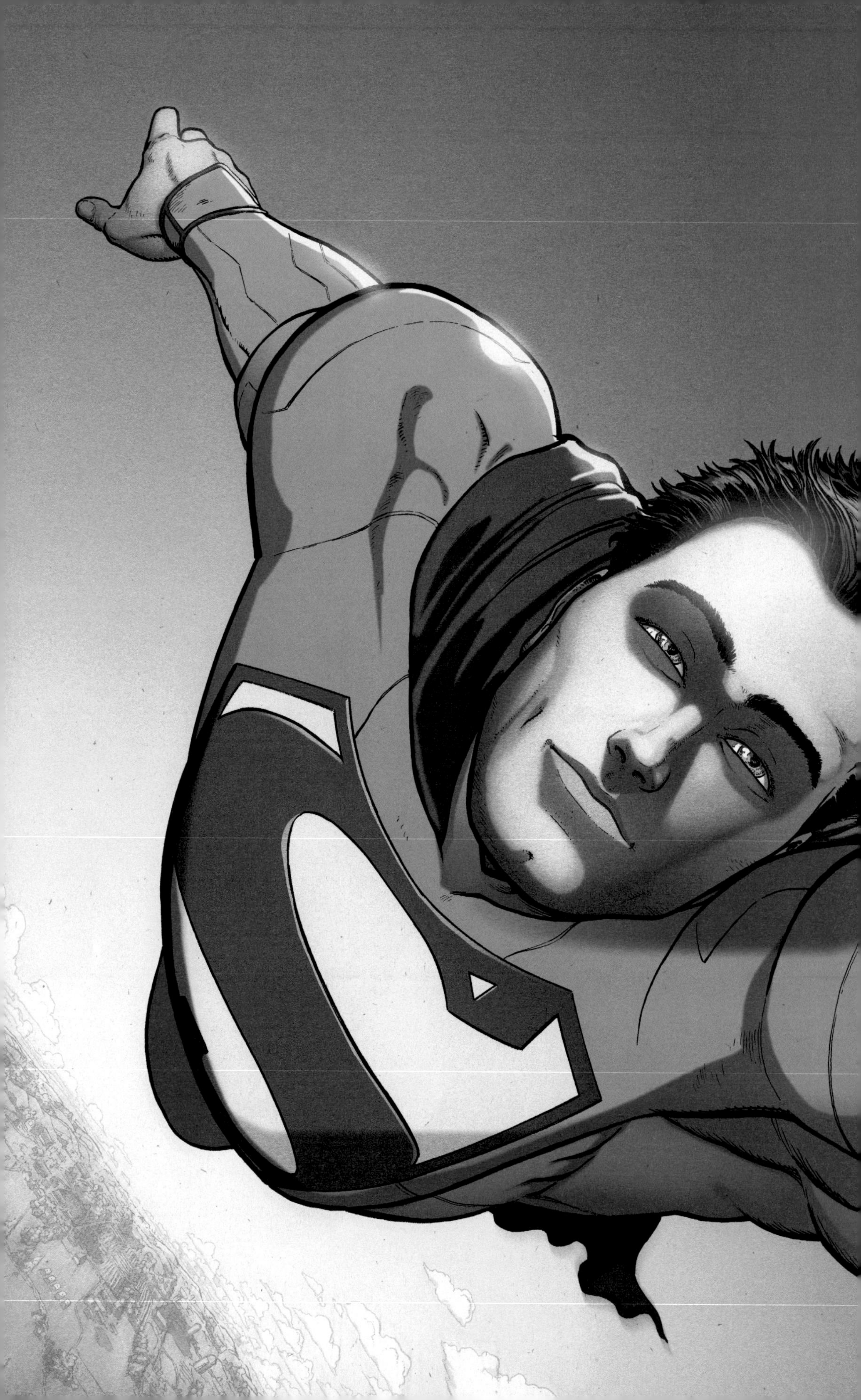

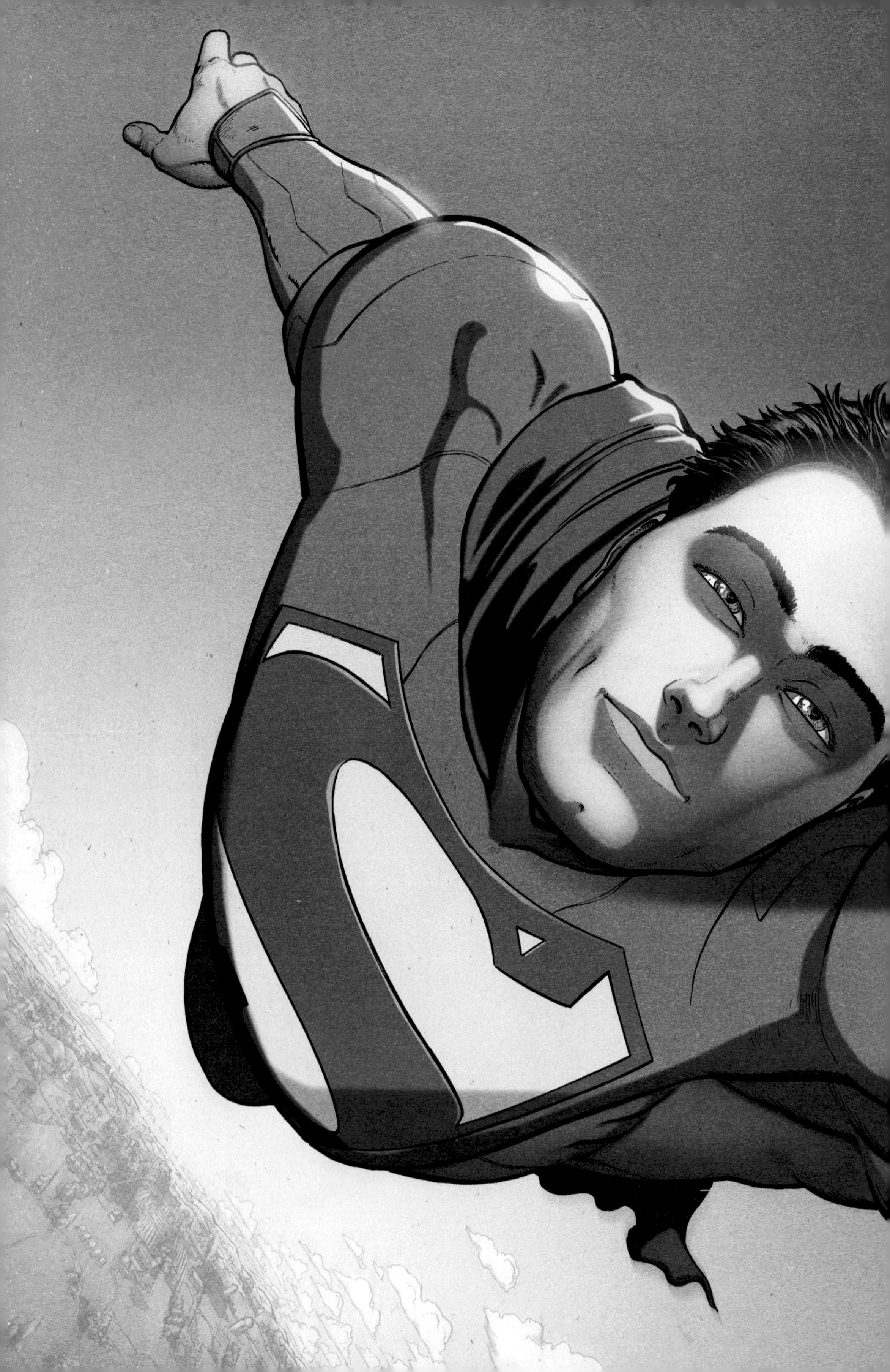

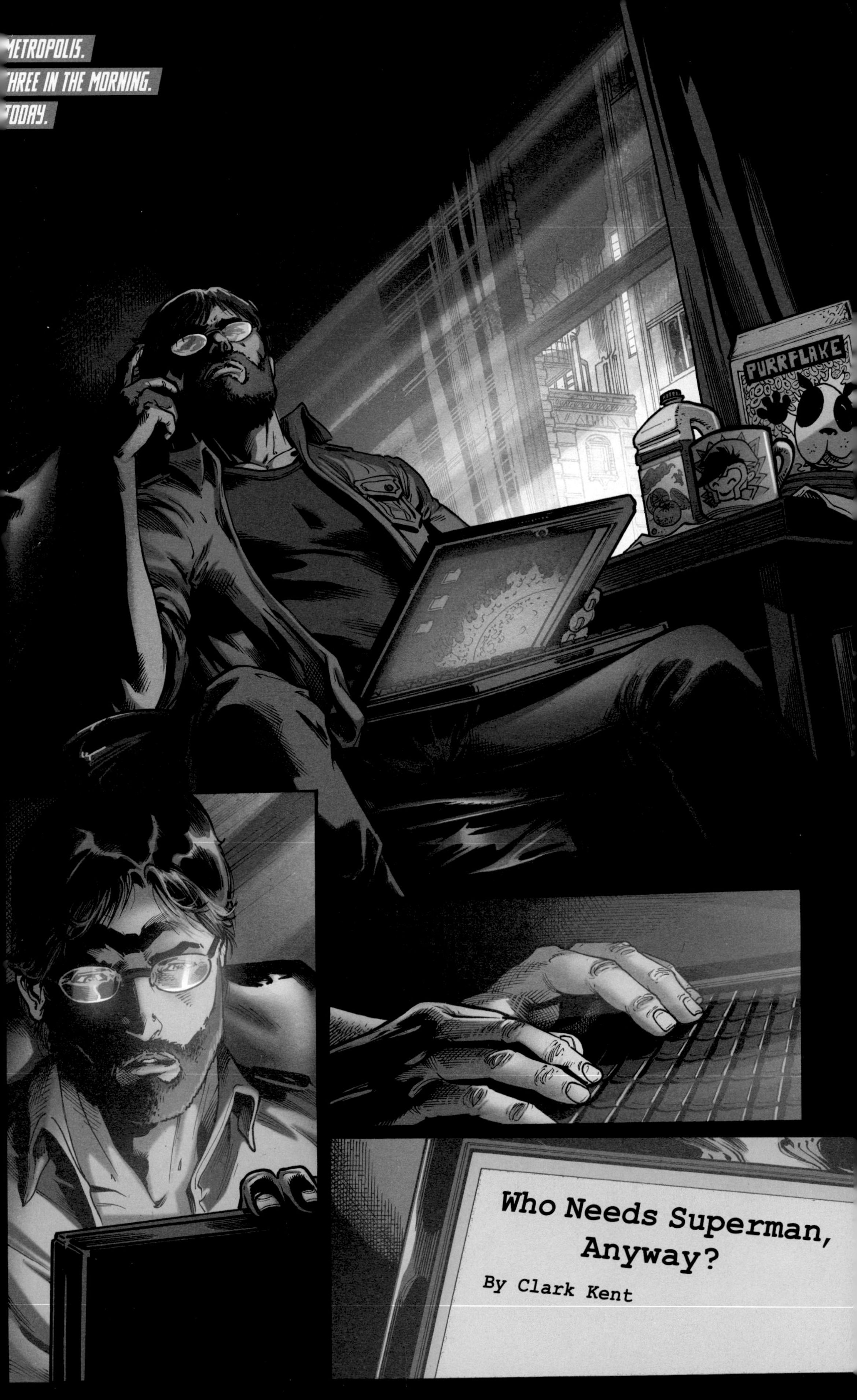

METROPOLIS.
THREE IN THE MORNING.
TODAY.
PURRFLAKE
Who Needs Superman, Anyway?
By Clark Kent

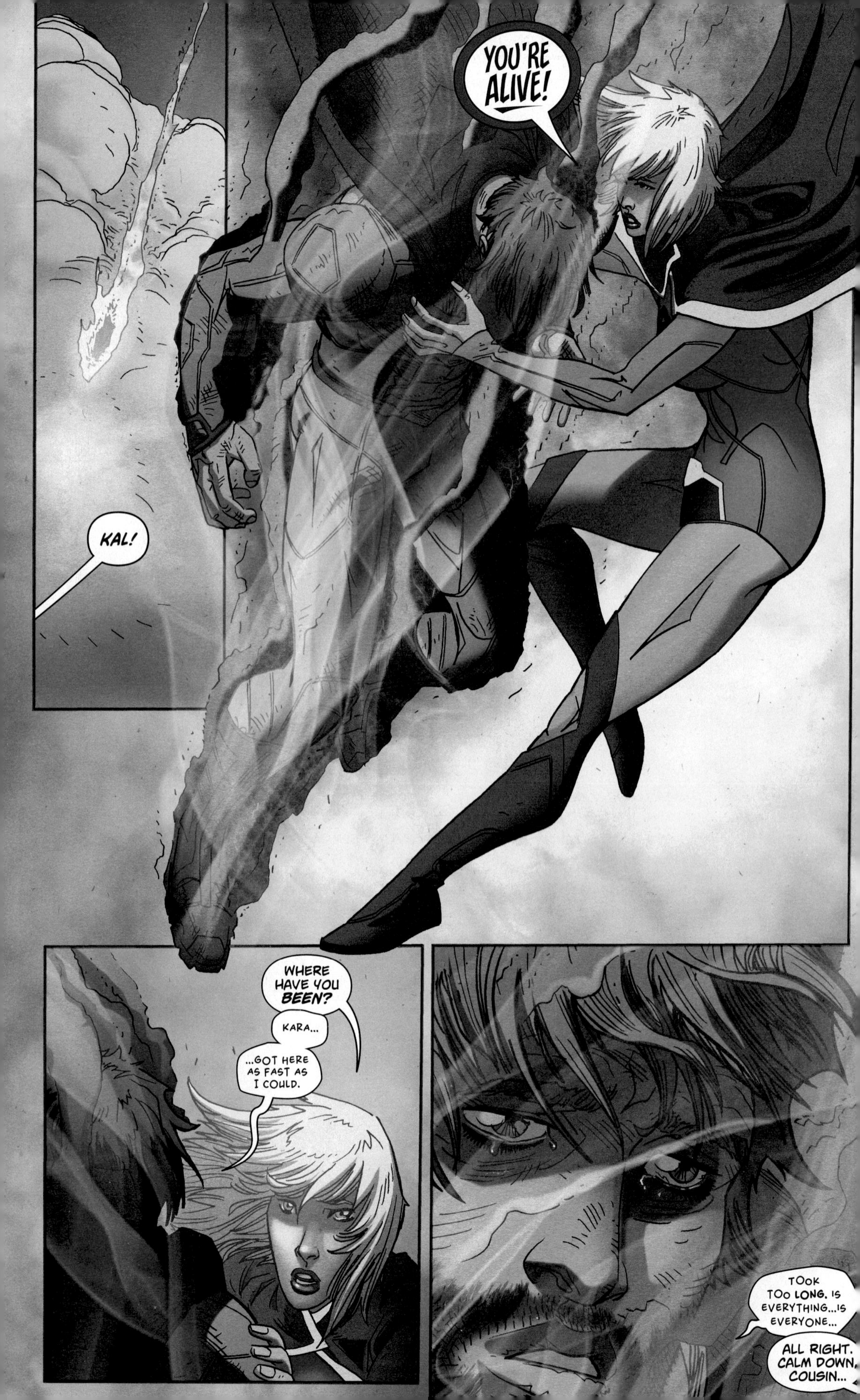
KAL!
YOU'RE ALIVE!
WHERE HAVE YOU BEEN?
KARA...
...GOT HERE AS FAST AS I COULD.
TOOK TOO LONG. IS EVERYTHING...IS EVERYONE...
ALL RIGHT. CALM DOWN, COUSIN...

...THE PLANET'S STILL HERE.

JUST... *LOOK.*

WE BLITZ OVER THE PLANET...

...AND SHE SHOWS ME *SHINING CITIES* AND *BLUE SKIES.*

BUT I'M *WEAK.*

MY SUPER-VISION AND SUPER-HEARING AREN'T STRONG ENOUGH FOR ME TO *TELL...*

AND THIRTEEN THOUSAND SIX HUNDRED AND TWELVE OF THEM *DIED.*

NO...

I...I KNOW.

WE SAVED *BILLIONS...*

KARA. BRAINIAC KNOCKED OUT SEVEN BILLION PEOPLE--

...BUT THERE WERE HEART ATTACKS, HEAT STROKE, CAR WRECKS...

WE DID EVERYTHING WE POSSIBLY *COULD...*

...BUT STILL...

AND NOW I'M JUST...

...JUST TRYING TO FOCUS ON WHAT WE CAN STILL *FIX.*

THE FORTRESS OF SOLITUDE.

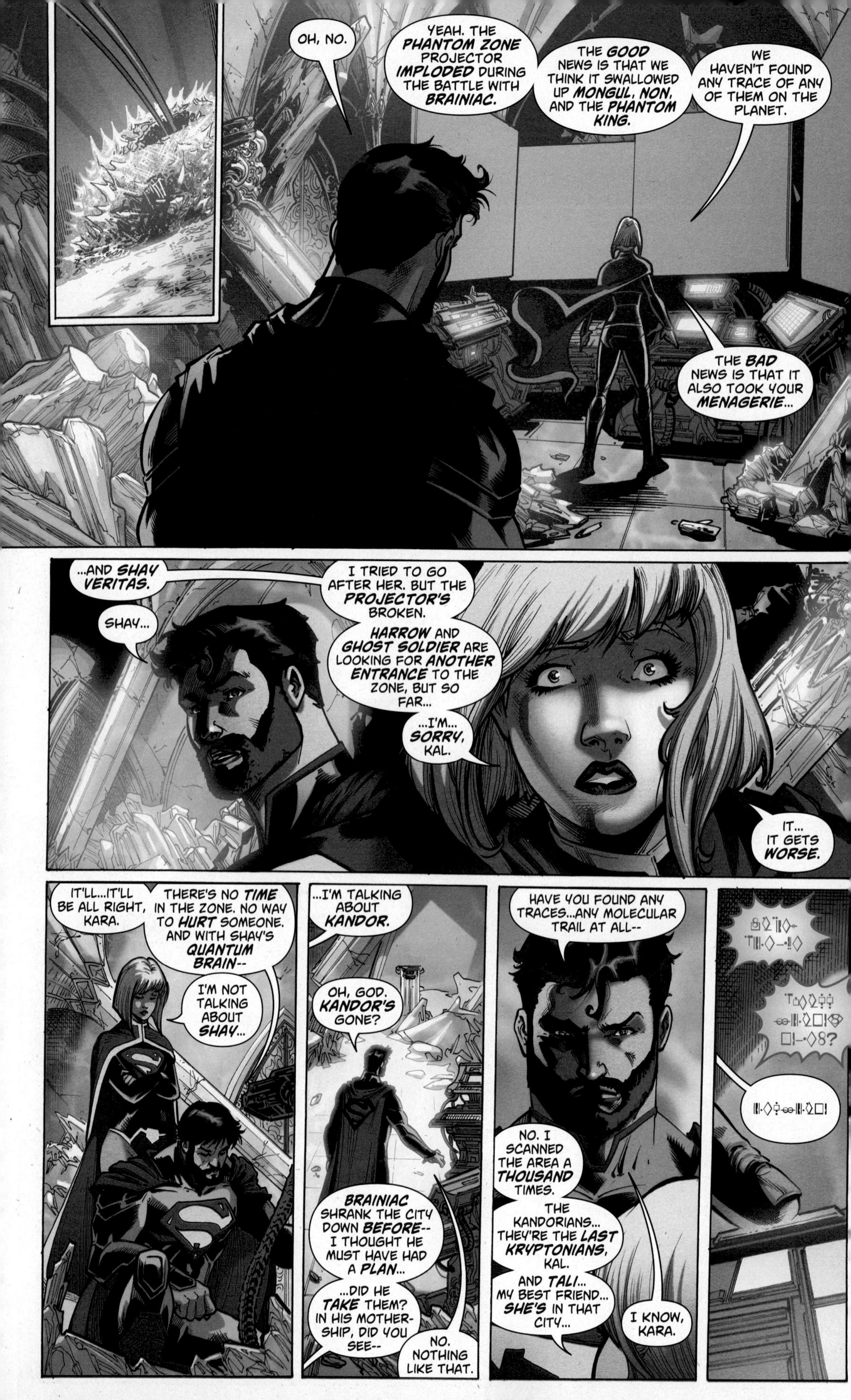
OH, NO.
YEAH. THE PHANTOM ZONE PROJECTOR IMPLODED DURING THE BATTLE WITH BRAINIAC.
THE GOOD NEWS IS THAT WE THINK IT SWALLOWED UP MONGUL, NON, AND THE PHANTOM KING.
WE HAVEN'T FOUND ANY TRACE OF ANY OF THEM ON THE PLANET.
THE BAD NEWS IS THAT IT ALSO TOOK YOUR MENAGERIE...
...AND SHAY VERITAS.
SHAY...
I TRIED TO GO AFTER HER. BUT THE PROJECTOR'S BROKEN.
HARROW AND GHOST SOLDIER ARE LOOKING FOR ANOTHER ENTRANCE TO THE ZONE, BUT SO FAR...
...I'M... SORRY, KAL.
IT... IT GETS WORSE.
IT'LL...IT'LL BE ALL RIGHT, KARA.
THERE'S NO TIME IN THE ZONE. NO WAY TO HURT SOMEONE. AND WITH SHAY'S QUANTUM BRAIN--
I'M NOT TALKING ABOUT SHAY...
...I'M TALKING ABOUT KANDOR.
OH, GOD. KANDOR'S GONE?
BRAINIAC SHRANK THE CITY DOWN BEFORE-- I THOUGHT HE MUST HAVE HAD A PLAN...
...DID HE TAKE THEM? IN HIS MOTHER-SHIP, DID YOU SEE--
NO. NOTHING LIKE THAT.
HAVE YOU FOUND ANY TRACES...ANY MOLECULAR TRAIL AT ALL--
NO. I SCANNED THE AREA A THOUSAND TIMES.
THE KANDORIANS... THEY'RE THE LAST KRYPTONIANS, KAL.
AND TALI... MY BEST FRIEND... SHE'S IN THAT CITY...
I KNOW, KARA.

"...I'LL START AT *HOME*."

THIS WAS THE FIRST PLACE BRAINIAC HIT.

EVERYONE IN THIS TOWN SPENT *THREE MONTHS* IN A *COMA*, STUDIED BY A HUNDRED SCIENTISTS AND QUARANTINED BY FIVE PLATOONS.

BUT NOW THERE ARE JUST A COUPLE OF NATIONAL GUARDSMEN DRINKING *COFFEE* WHERE THE *CHECKPOINTS* USED TO BE.

AND FOLKS SEEM...

...JUST FINE.

HEY, CLARK! THAT *YOU* UNDER THAT BEARD?

HEY, MR. GUNDERSON!

I SHOULD STOP TO *TALK*.

I'M A *REPORTER*. THAT'S HOW YOU GET THE *STORY*.

THIRTEEN THOUSAND.

DEAR GOD.

BUT EVERYTHING'S SO... NORMAL.

...AND IN SPITE OF THAT TERRIBLE *DREAD* EATING AT MY STOMACH...

...I SUDDENLY FEEL ALMOST... *NORMAL*... MYSELF.

AND I JUST HEAD DOWN OLDFIELD DRIVE, LIKE WE DID WHEN WE WERE KIDS...

...WAITING FOR THAT *SLOPE* JUST PAST THE TAKAHARA FARM...

FEELS LIKE FLYING.

AH.

NOSTALGIA

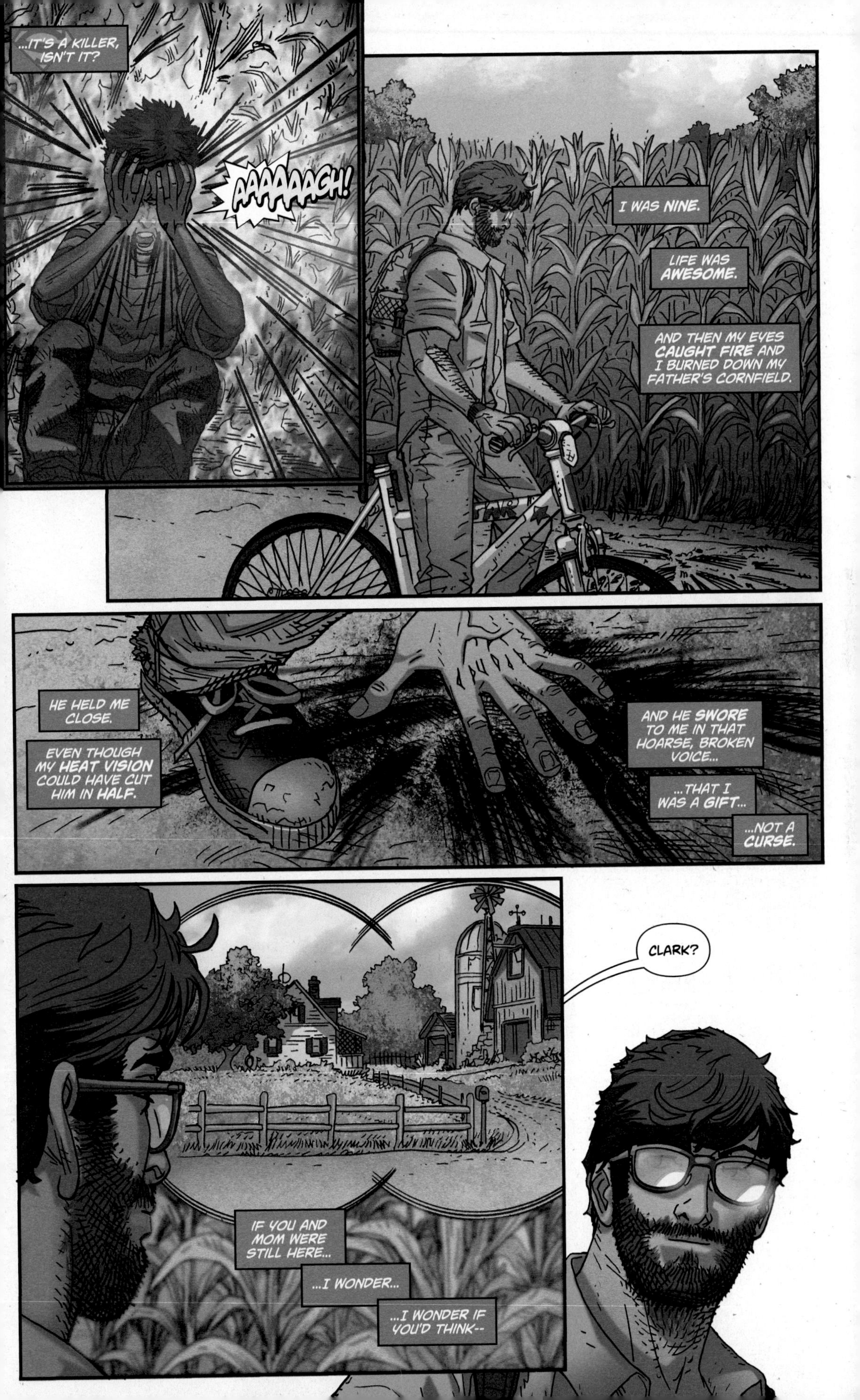
...IT'S A KILLER, ISN'T IT?
AAAAAAGH!
I WAS NINE.
LIFE WAS AWESOME.
AND THEN MY EYES CAUGHT FIRE AND I BURNED DOWN MY FATHER'S CORNFIELD.
HE HELD ME CLOSE.
EVEN THOUGH MY HEAT VISION COULD HAVE CUT HIM IN HALF.
AND HE SWORE TO ME IN THAT HOARSE, BROKEN VOICE...
...THAT I WAS A GIFT...
...NOT A CURSE.
CLARK?
IF YOU AND MOM WERE STILL HERE...
...I WONDER...
...I WONDER IF YOU'D THINK--

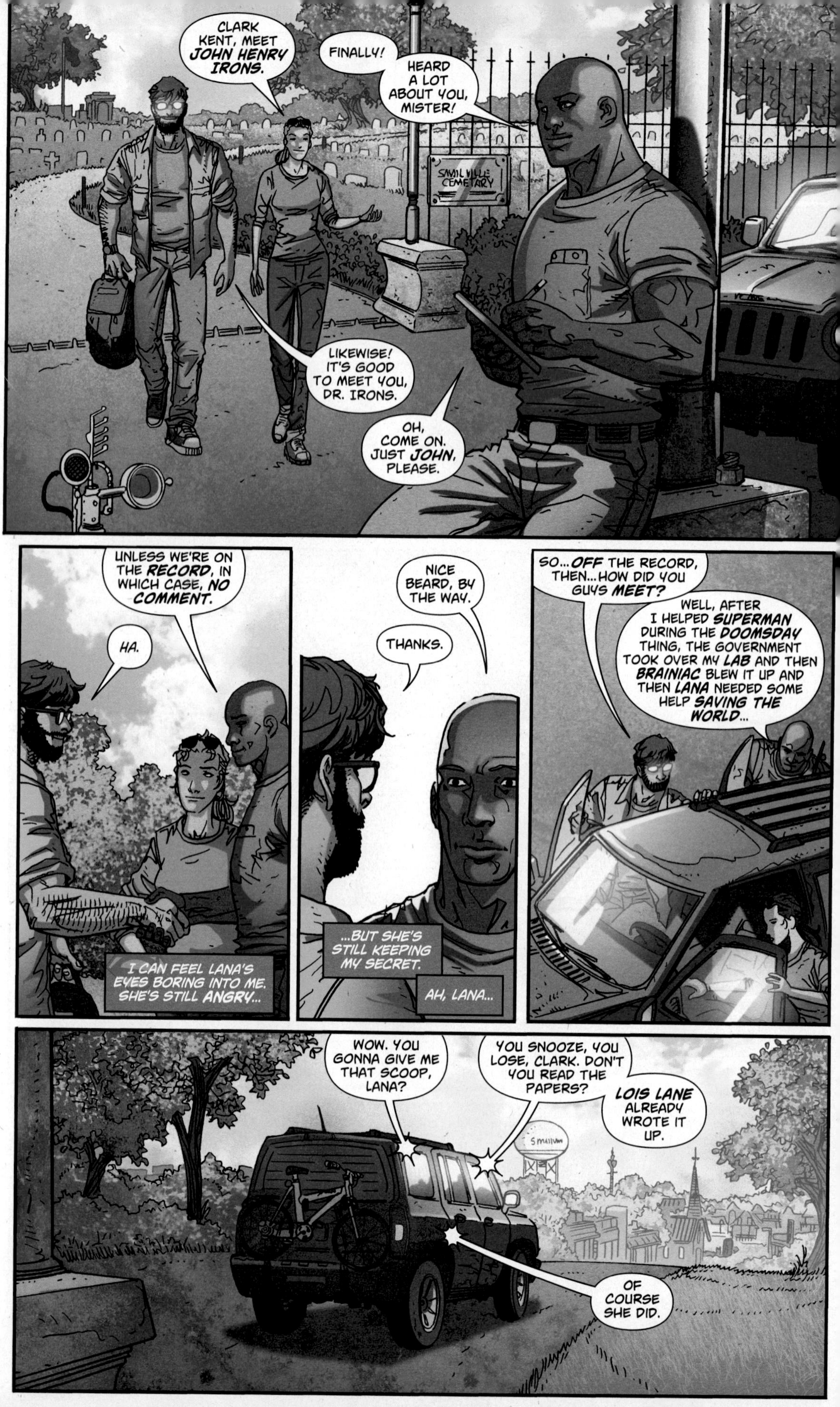

CLARK KENT, MEET JOHN HENRY IRONS.
FINALLY!
HEARD A LOT ABOUT YOU, MISTER!
SAMVILLE CEMETARY
LIKEWISE! IT'S GOOD TO MEET YOU, DR. IRONS.
OH, COME ON. JUST JOHN, PLEASE.
UNLESS WE'RE ON THE RECORD, IN WHICH CASE, NO COMMENT.
HA.
I CAN FEEL LANA'S EYES BORING INTO ME. SHE'S STILL ANGRY...
NICE BEARD, BY THE WAY.
THANKS.
...BUT SHE'S STILL KEEPING MY SECRET.
AH, LANA...
SO... OFF THE RECORD, THEN... HOW DID YOU GUYS MEET?
WELL, AFTER I HELPED SUPERMAN DURING THE DOOMSDAY THING, THE GOVERNMENT TOOK OVER MY LAB AND THEN BRAINIAC BLEW IT UP AND THEN LANA NEEDED SOME HELP SAVING THE WORLD...
WOW. YOU GONNA GIVE ME THAT SCOOP, LANA?
YOU SNOOZE, YOU LOSE, CLARK. DON'T YOU READ THE PAPERS?
LOIS LANE ALREADY WROTE IT UP.
OF COURSE SHE DID.

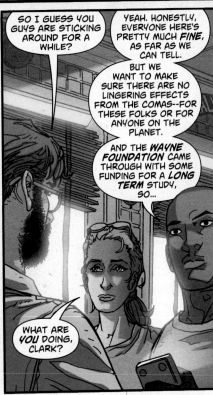

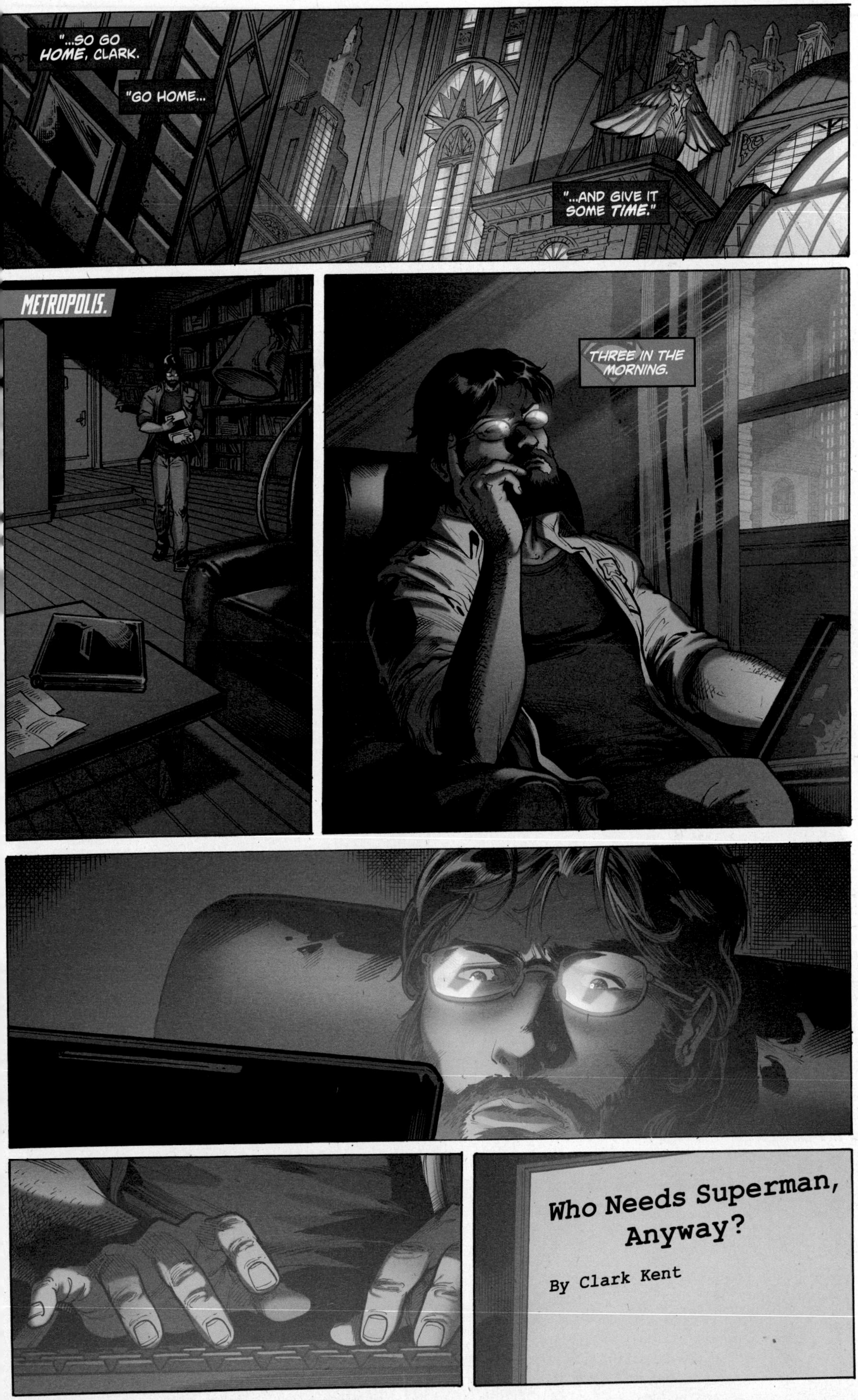

"...SO GO HOME, CLARK.
"GO HOME...
"...AND GIVE IT SOME TIME."
METROPOLIS.
THREE IN THE MORNING.
Who Needs Superman, Anyway?
By Clark Kent

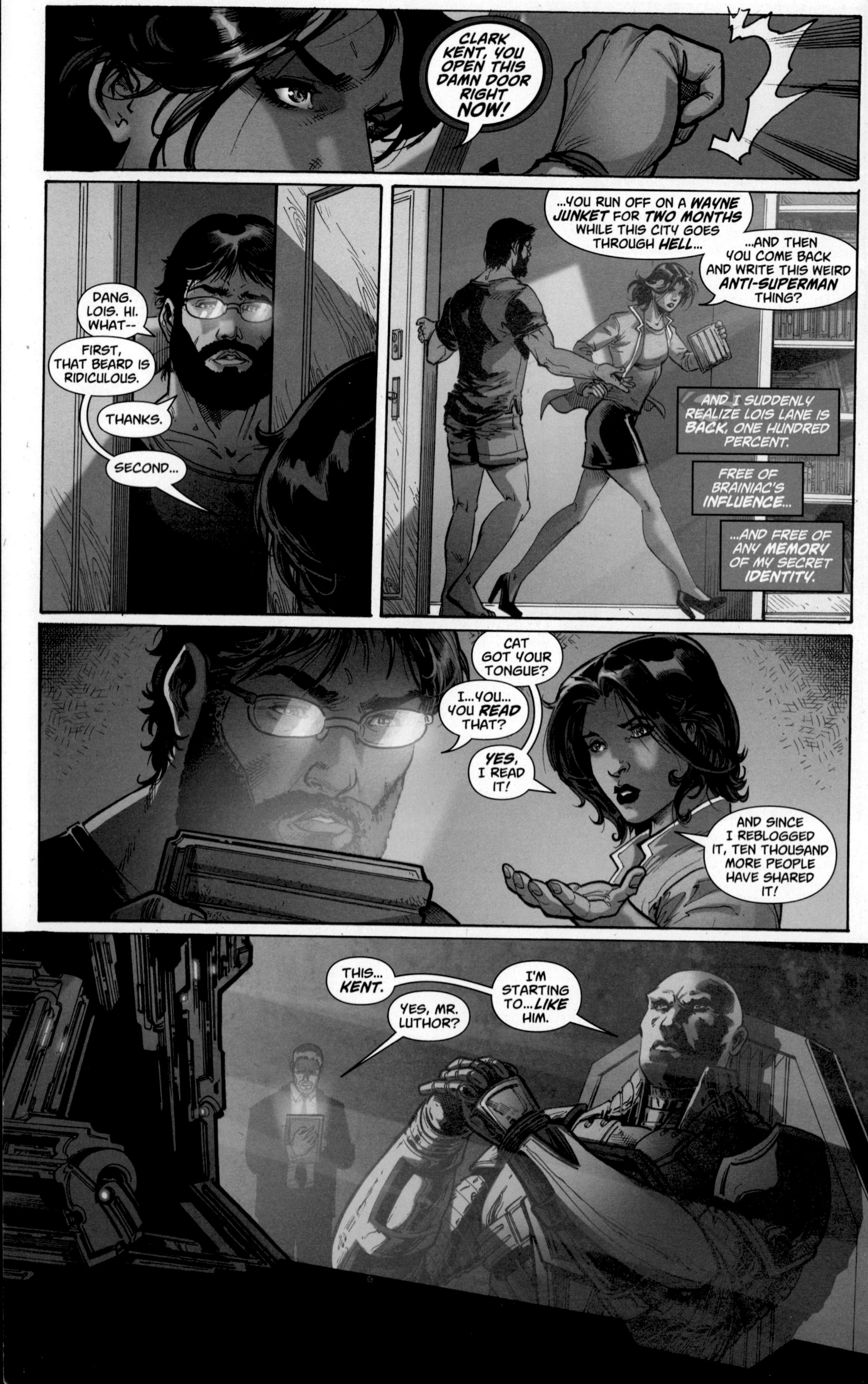
CLARK KENT, YOU OPEN THIS DAMN DOOR RIGHT NOW!
DANG. LOIS. HI. WHAT--
FIRST, THAT BEARD IS RIDICULOUS.
THANKS.
SECOND...
...YOU RUN OFF ON A WAYNE JUNKET FOR TWO MONTHS WHILE THIS CITY GOES THROUGH HELL...
...AND THEN YOU COME BACK AND WRITE THIS WEIRD ANTI-SUPERMAN THING?
AND I SUDDENLY REALIZE LOIS LANE IS BACK, ONE HUNDRED PERCENT.
FREE OF BRAINIAC'S INFLUENCE...
...AND FREE OF ANY MEMORY OF MY SECRET IDENTITY.
CAT GOT YOUR TONGUE?
I...YOU... YOU READ THAT?
YES, I READ IT!
AND SINCE I REBLOGGED IT, TEN THOUSAND MORE PEOPLE HAVE SHARED IT!
THIS... KENT.
YES, MR. LUTHOR?
I'M STARTING TO...LIKE HIM.

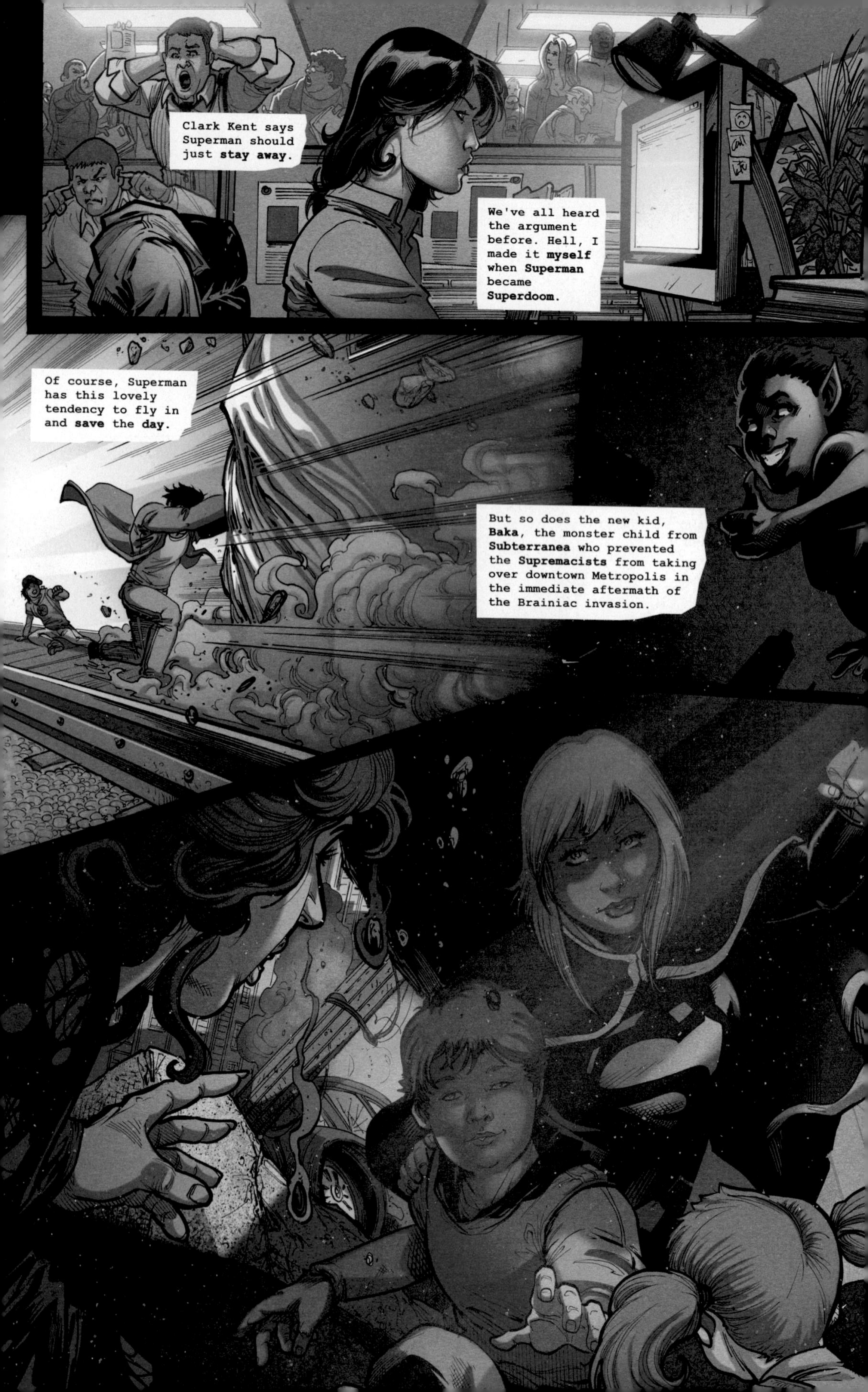
Clark Kent says Superman should just stay away.
We've all heard the argument before. Hell, I made it myself when Superman became Superdoom.
Of course, Superman has this lovely tendency to fly in and save the day.
But so does the new kid, Baka, the monster child from Subterranea who prevented the Supremacists from taking over downtown Metropolis in the immediate aftermath of the Brainiac invasion.

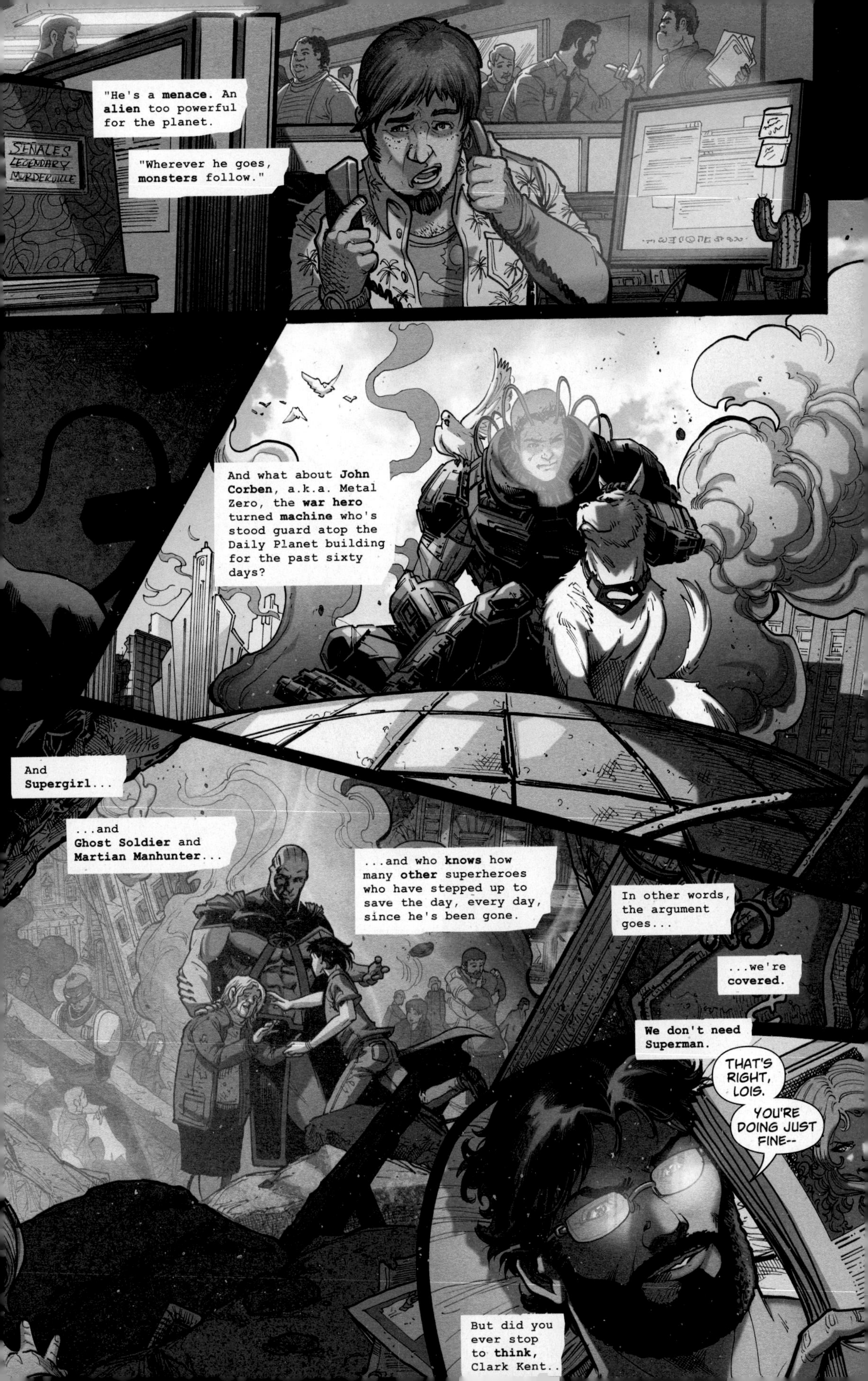
"He's a **menace**. An **alien** too powerful for the planet.
"Wherever he goes, **monsters** follow."
SEÑALES LEGENDARY MURDERVILLE
And what about **John Corben**, a.k.a. Metal Zero, the **war hero** turned **machine** who's stood guard atop the Daily Planet building for the past sixty days?
And **Supergirl**...
...and **Ghost Soldier** and **Martian Manhunter**...
...and who **knows** how many **other** superheroes who have stepped up to save the day, every day, since he's been gone.
In other words, the argument goes...
...we're **covered**.
We don't need Superman.
THAT'S RIGHT, LOIS.
YOU'RE DOING JUST FINE--
But did you ever stop to **think**, Clark Kent..

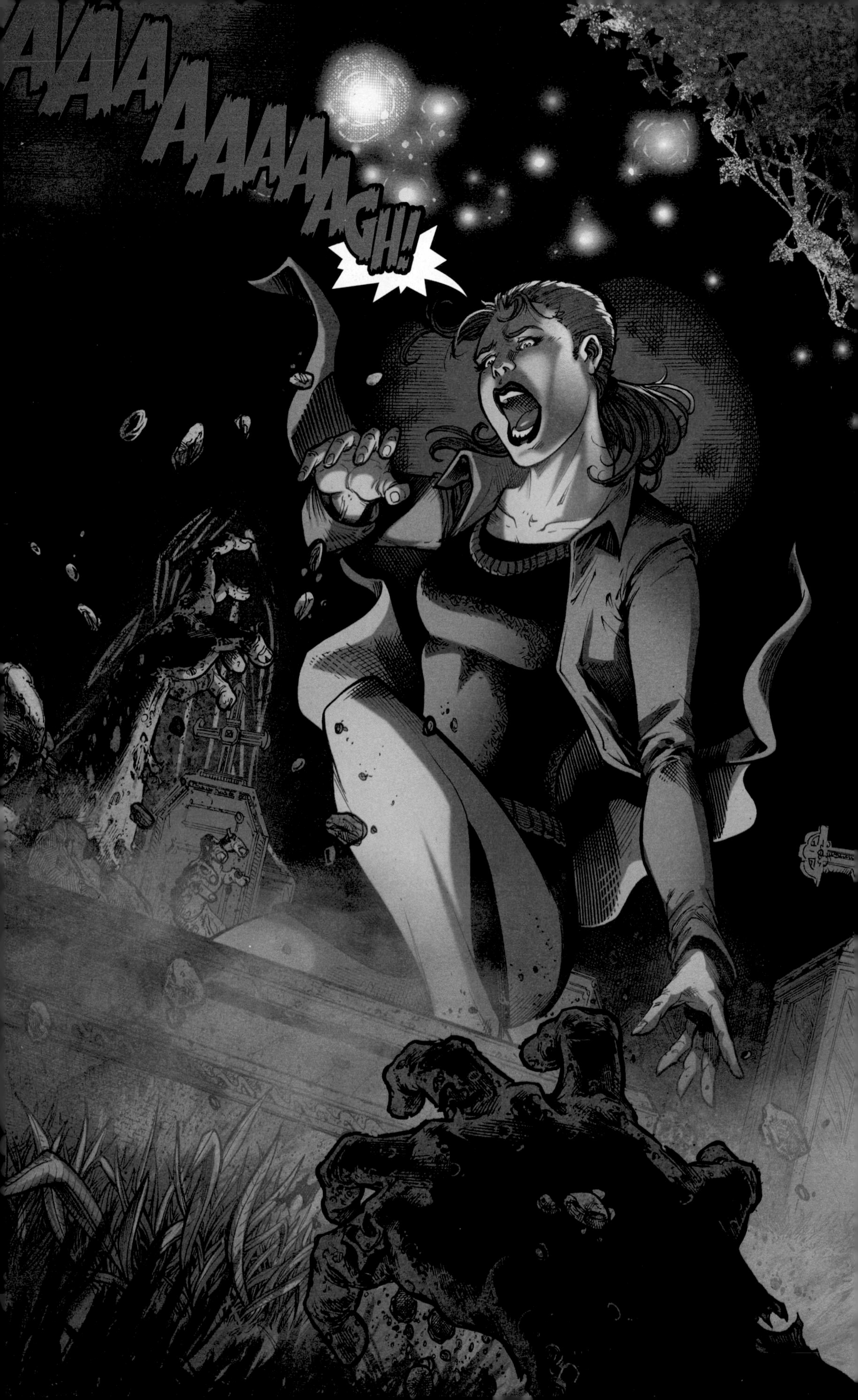
AAAAAAAAAAAGH!!

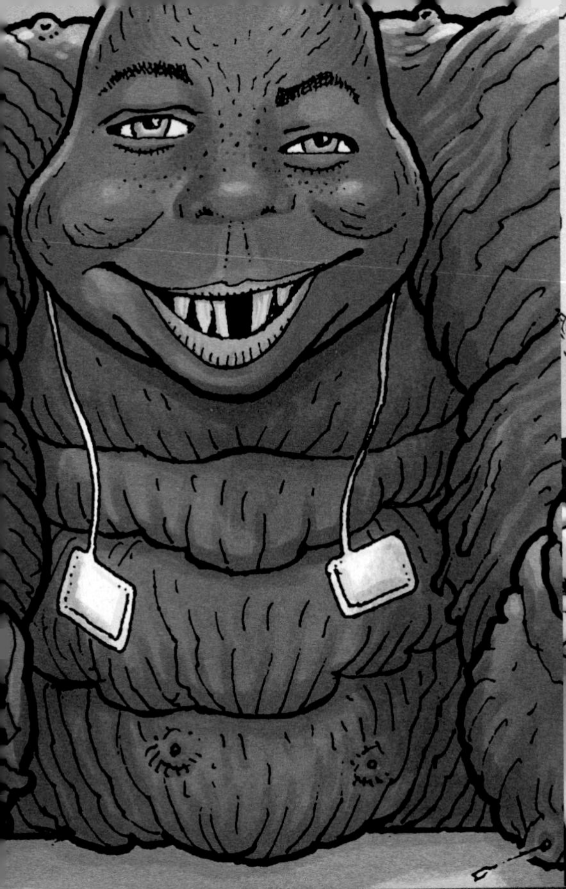
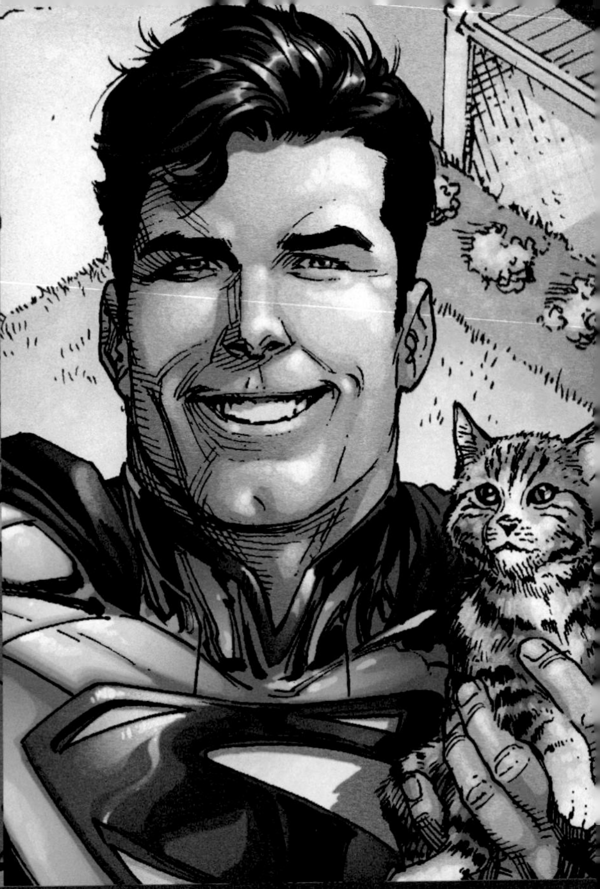

VARIANT COVER GALLERY

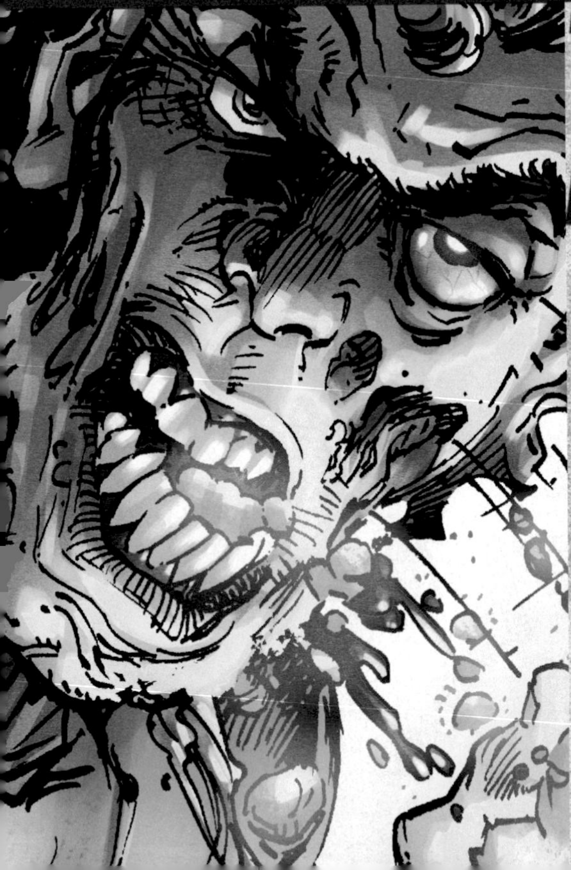
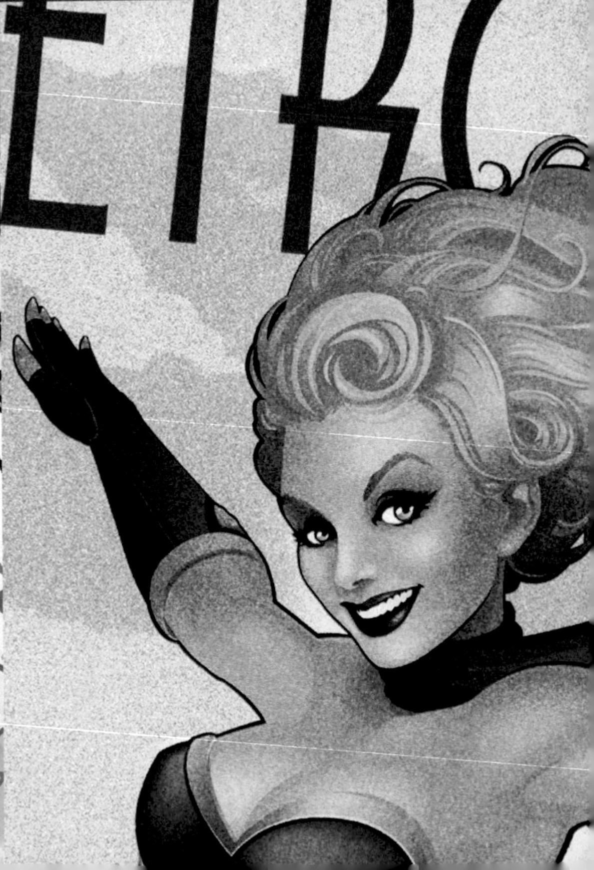

ACTION COMICS #31
BATMAN '66 VARIANT COVER BY MIKE AND LAURA ALLRED

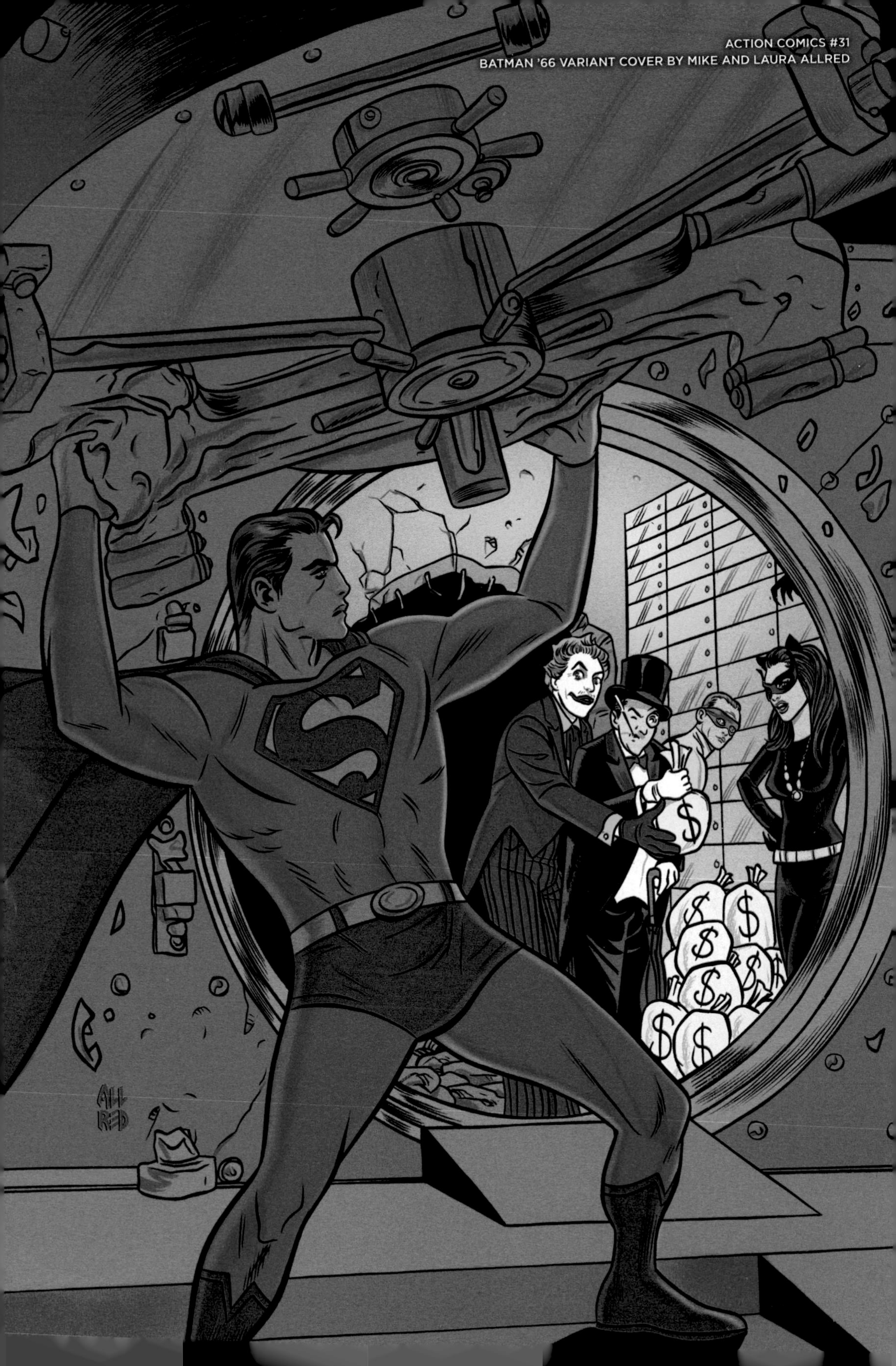

ACTION COMICS #32
BOMBSHELL VARIANT COVER BY ANT LUCIA

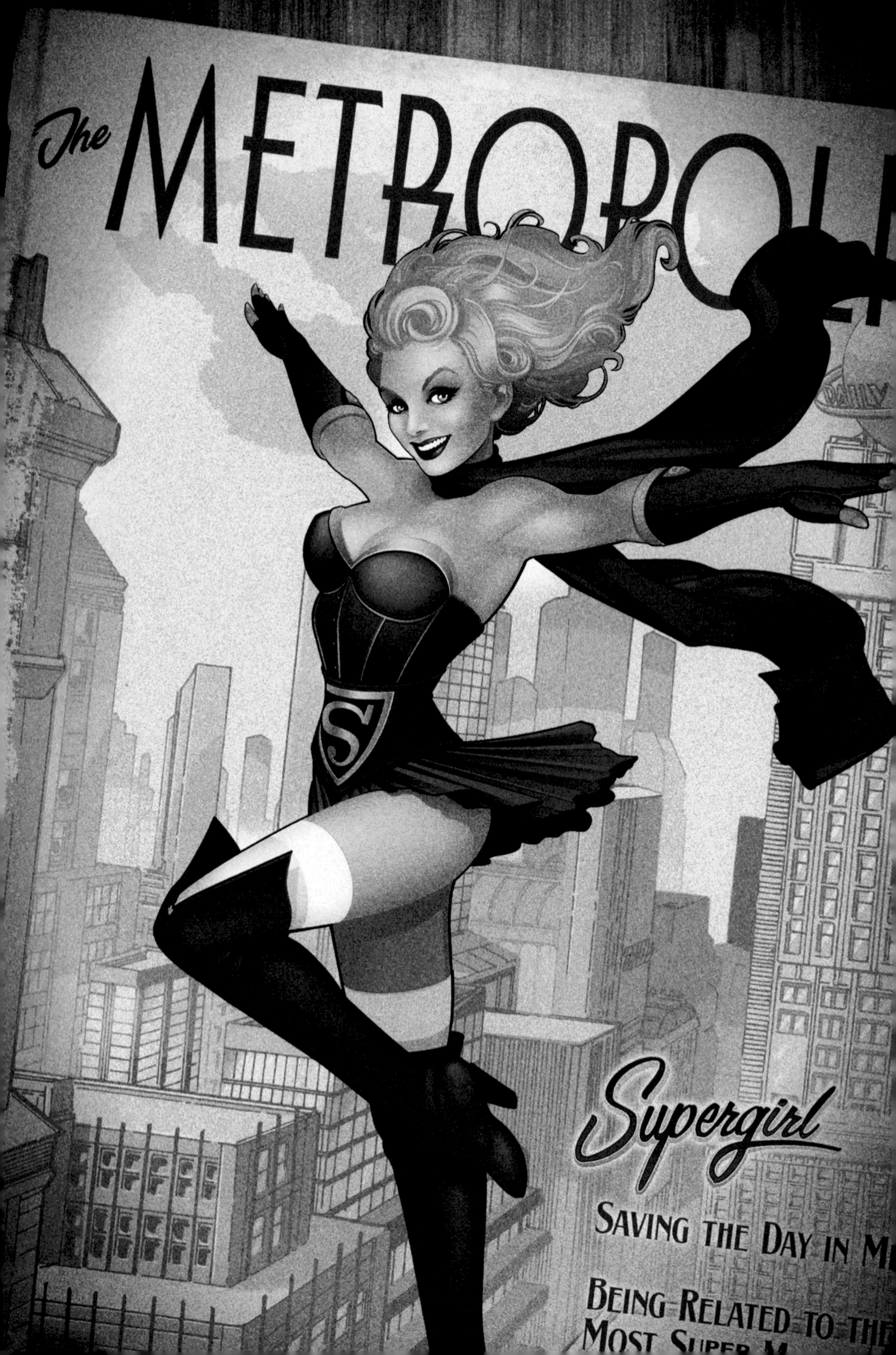

ACTION COMICS #33
BATMAN 75TH ANNIVERSARY VARIANT COVER BY KEVIN NOWLAN

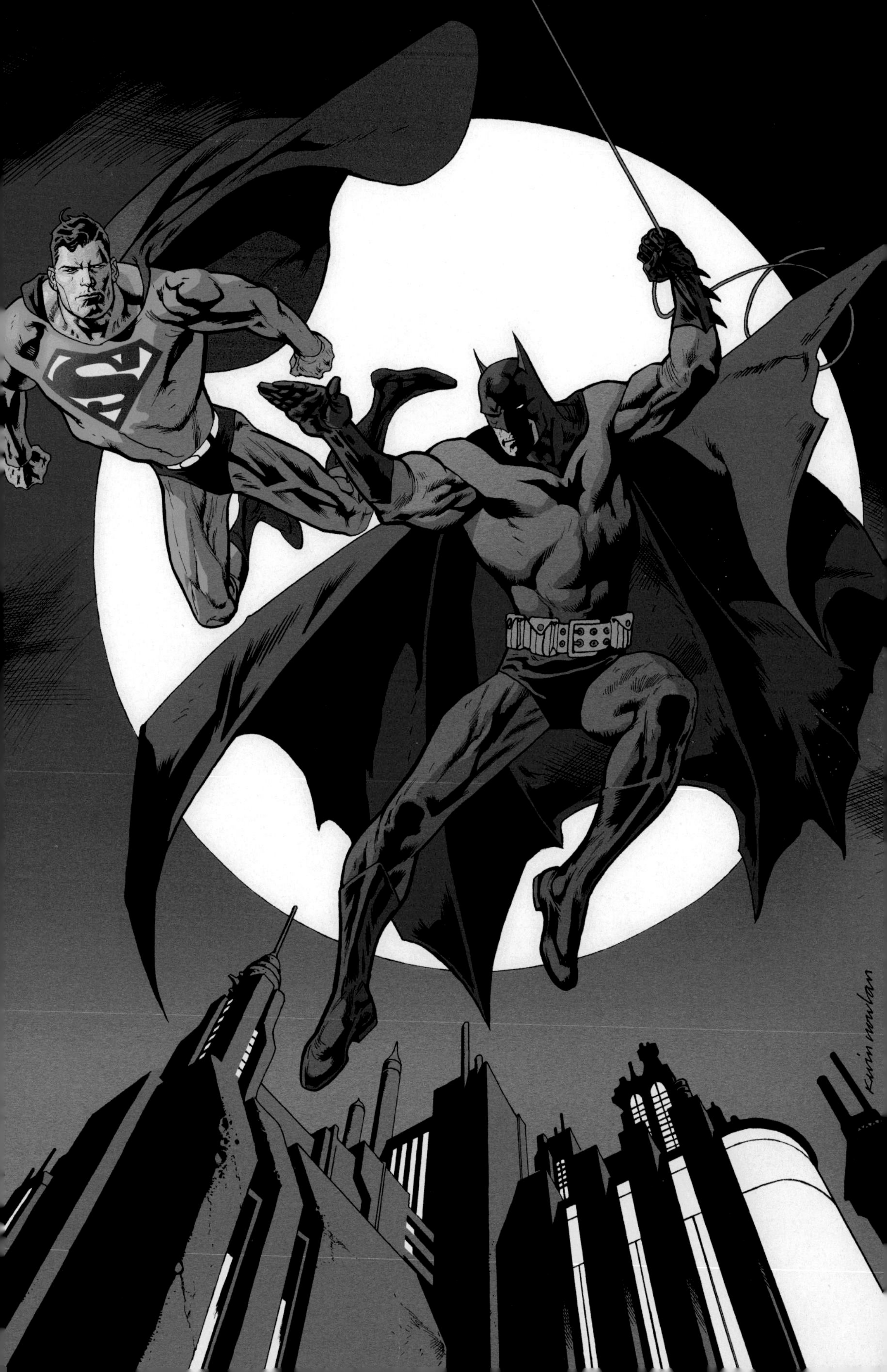

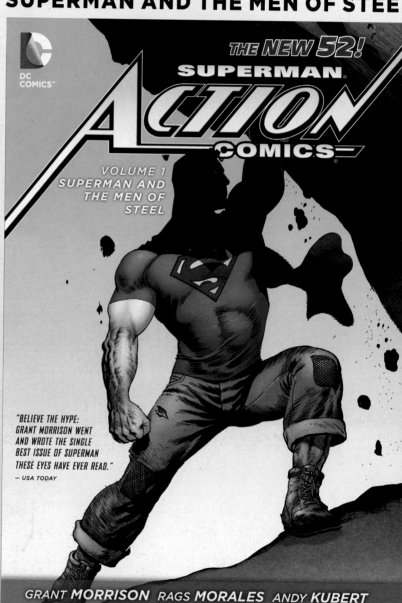

"Superman is still super."
—WALL STREET JOURNAL

"The SUPERMAN world is also one now where fans new and old, young and not-so-young, can come to a common ground to talk about the superhero that started it all."
—CRAVE ONLINE

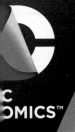

START AT THE BEGINNING!

SUPERMAN VOLUME 1: WHAT PRICE TOMORROW?

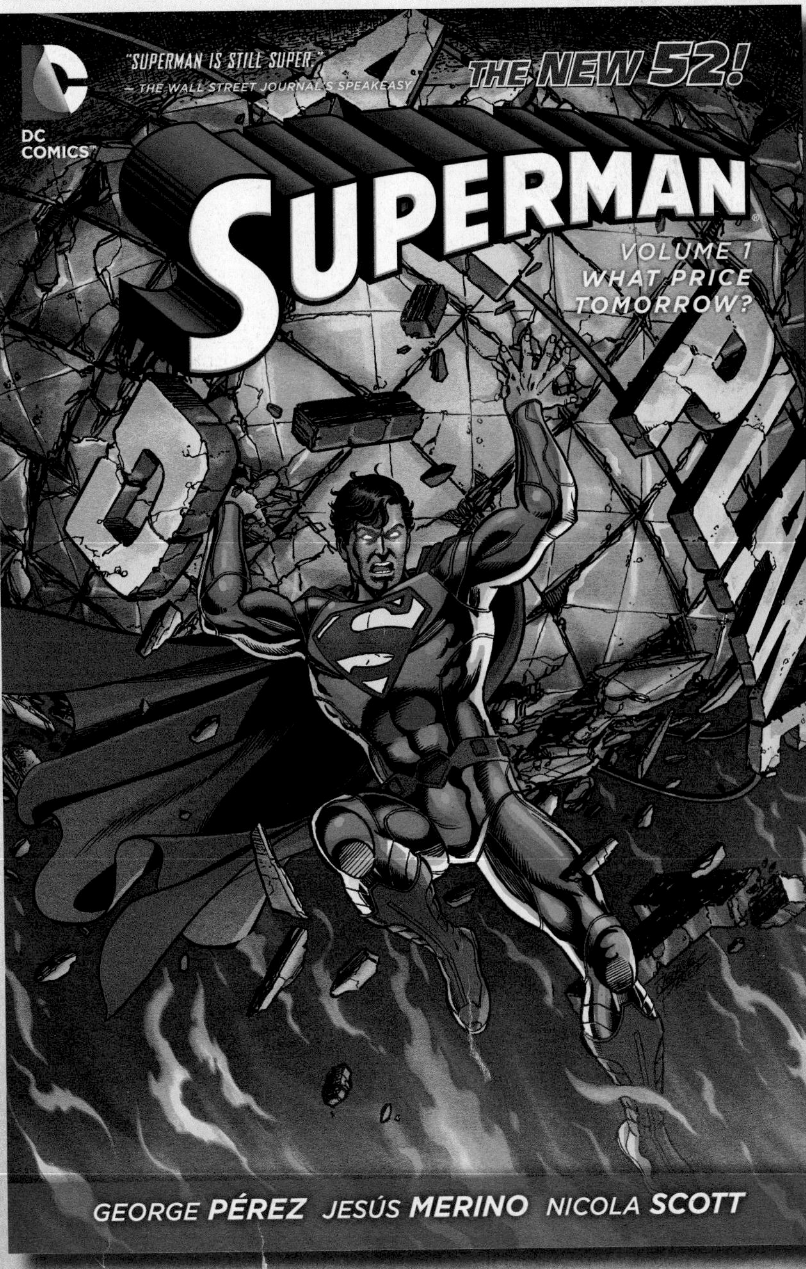

DC COMICS
"SUPERMAN IS STILL SUPER."
— THE WALL STREET JOURNAL'S SPEAKEASY
THE NEW 52!
SUPERMAN
VOLUME 1
WHAT PRICE
TOMORROW?
GEORGE PÉREZ JESÚS MERINO NICOLA SCOTT

SUPERMAN VOL. 2:
SECRETS & LIES

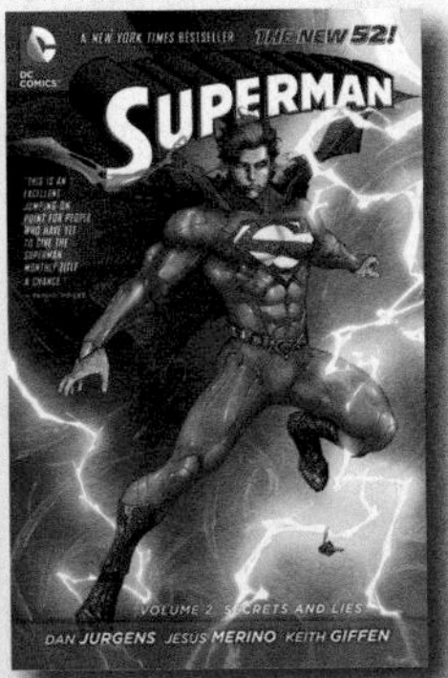

A NEW YORK TIMES BESTSELLER
THE NEW 52!
SUPERMAN
VOLUME 2 SECRETS AND LIES
DAN JURGENS JESUS MERINO KEITH GIFFEN

SUPERMAN VOL. 3:
FURY AT WORLD'S
END

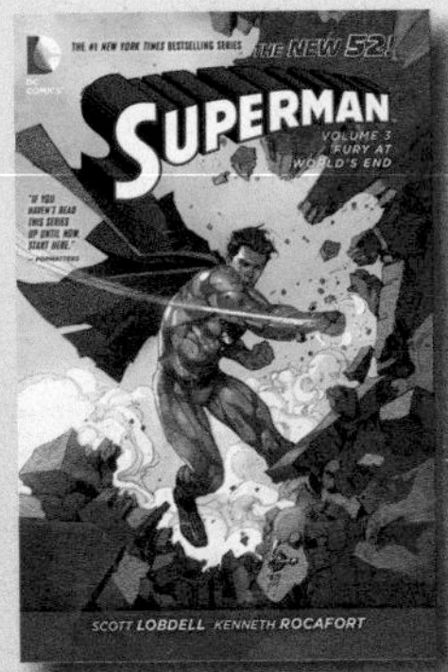

THE #1 NEW YORK TIMES BESTSELLING SERIES
THE NEW 52!
SUPERMAN
VOLUME 3
FURY AT
WORLD'S END
SCOTT LOBDELL KENNETH ROCAFORT

SUPERMAN:
H'EL ON EARTH

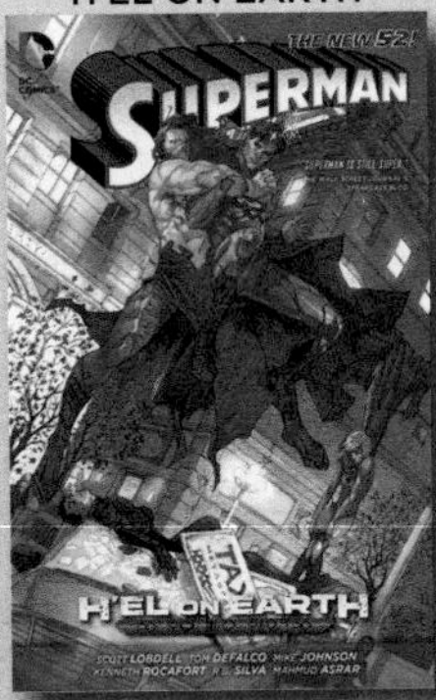

THE NEW 52!
SUPERMAN
H'EL ON EARTH

DC COMICS™

START AT THE BEGINNING!

JUSTICE LEAGUE
VOLUME 1: ORIGIN
GEOFF JOHNS and JIM LEE

JUSTICE LEAGUE
VOL. 2: THE VILLAIN'S
JOURNEY

JUSTICE LEAGUE
VOL. 3: THRONE OF
ATLANTIS

JUSTICE LEAGUE
OF AMERICA VOL. 1:
WORLD'S MOST
DANGEROUS

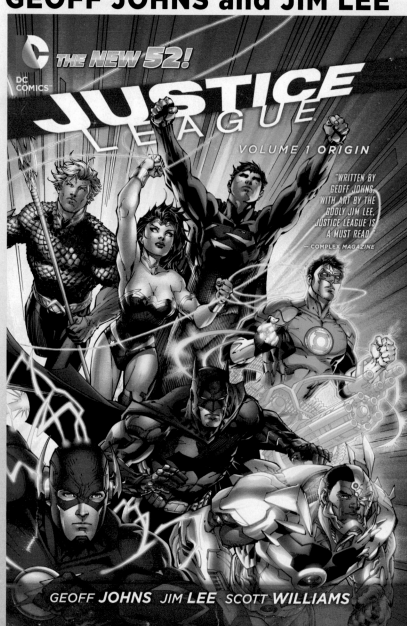